*Refine our truths.*

SOCIO-ECONOMIC R

GW00761062

# Social Justice Matters

## 2019 guide to a Fairer Irish society

Seán Healy, Colette Bennett, Ann Leahy, Eamon Murphy, Michelle Murphy and Brigid Reynolds

*1904 Elizabeth Magie — The landlords game. College students & ec. Professors. Everybody benefited from the creation of wealth. Building property benefited everyone in the game. To illustrate the benefits of a more egalitarian ec. System*

**Social Justice Ireland**

*If players wanted it test it single Tase would benefit everyone by equalizing, & opportunities & raising wages. Can test it it 2 players*

SOCIO-ECONOMIC REVIEW 2019

ISBN No. 978-1-907501-23-4


First Published February 2019



Published by
Social Justice Ireland
Arena House
Arena Road
Sandyford
Dublin D18 V8P6
Ireland


www.socialjustice.ie

Tel: 01- 2130724


e-mail: secretary@socialjustice.ie

government supporting communities

This work is partly supported by the Department of Rural and Community Development via the
Scheme to Support National Organisations and Pobal.

## TABLE OF CONTENTS

| | | |
|---|---|---:|
| 1. | A Development Model in Need of Revision | 7 |
| 2. | A Development Model and a Policy Framework for the 21$^{st}$ Century | 14 |
| 3. | Income and Income Distribution | 36 |
| 4. | Taxation | 76 |
| 5. | Work, Unemployment and Job Creation | 110 |
| 6. | Housing and Accommodation | 128 |
| 7. | Healthcare | 156 |
| 8. | Education and Educational Disadvantage | 184 |
| 9. | Other Public Services | 206 |
| 10. | People and Participation | 232 |
| 11. | Sustainability | 252 |
| 12. | Rural and Regional Development | 278 |
| 13. | The Global South | 302 |
| 14. | Values | 320 |

# 1.

# A DEVELOPMENT MODEL IN NEED OF REVISION

Irish society has been making a major mistake for several decades. It has believed the narrative that economic growth would lead to all the problems afflicting modern humanity being addressed efficiently and effectively. This narrative insisted that economic growth should therefore be prioritised over all other policies, as the wealth generated by this growth would 'trickle down' in a fair and just manner, leading to the relieving of poverty and the creation of a better world for all.

While economic growth has indeed allowed Ireland to improve living standards, invest in infrastructure and public services, and become one of the world's most prosperous countries (Legatum, 2018), the benefits of this improvement in living standards have been distributed in a grossly unequal fashion. This is true not only in Ireland but in other countries that have followed this same pathway of prioritising economic growth over all else.

Though Ireland is one of the richest countries in the world, with one of the fastest growing economies in Europe (Eurostat, 2018), more than 750,000 people live at risk of poverty, almost a quarter of a million of whom are children (CSO, 2018a). That is roughly one in six people, and one in five children. Ireland's current number of homeless people is not just at a record high but is a multiple of any high previously seen (Department of Housing, Planning and Local Government, 2018), and there has been no reduction despite seemingly endless rhetoric from government.

Our public services continue to lag behind the Western European norm: There are more than 500,000 households without quality broadband (Goodbody, 2018); Ireland's under-developed childcare infrastructure leads to reduced economic capacity and increased inequality in the workplace (ESRI, 2018); and Ireland is still lacking a universal healthcare system with a robust primary care network. Our performance in relation to our environmental and climate change targets is an embarrassment.

Many of the crises experienced in the aftermath of the financial crash of 2008 have receded somewhat: Unemployment has fallen dramatically from 16 per cent in early 2012 to 5.3 per cent at the end of 2018 (CSO, 2018b). Ireland's debt levels reached 120 per cent of GDP but are expected to be 101 per cent of GNI* in 2019 and will continue to fall (Department of Finance, 2018). Enforced deprivation stood at over 30 per cent in 2013 but has since fallen to 18.5 per cent (CSO, 2018a). Many of these indicators are still too high for Irish society to be satisfied, but progress deserves to be acknowledged.

However, it is clear that we live in an unequal society. Without social transfers, 43.8 per cent of Irish people would be living at risk of poverty (CSO, 2018a). This is a startling statistic and one that should be borne in mind when considering the importance of Ireland's welfare system. This kind of inequality is due in no small part to the model of development we have been following, and it is not just economic inequality that is the result. Significant political and social divisions have also emerged since the financial crisis – not just in Ireland, but in the United Kingdom, North America and on mainland Europe. At the heart of these divisions is a rejection by many people of how economic resources are distributed, how political decision-making excludes many, and how social progress is denied to large numbers of people.

The current model of development has brought prosperity to many and produced technological improvements that could not have been imagined even a couple of decades ago. However, it is increasingly clear that this model is no longer fit for purpose.

Since the 1950s, Ireland's development model has relied on attracting Foreign Direct Investment – mainly through providing tax incentives, grants and a well-educated labour force – in order to encourage economic development. This has worked to an extent. The inward investment helped to generate the economic resources which were used to improve living standards and these resources, along with transfers from the European Union for development purposes, brought Ireland into line with (eventually surpassing) many of our peer countries of the EU-15 in terms of GDP per capita.

However, while indicators such as per capita wealth and GDP rank Ireland among the world's most developed countries, Irish people do not experience the same high standards of living as our European neighbours. High quality public services are what underpin the living standards of the majority of people in most European countries, and Ireland is too often found lacking in this regard.

Many of the aforementioned problems – including poverty, sub-par public services, and environmental degradation – existed at the height of the so-called Celtic Tiger boom experienced by Ireland in the late 1990s and for much of the 2000s. Most are not new, and generally cannot be blamed on the financial crisis and the consequent shortage of resources. It seems they are systemic; a consequence of how successive governments sought to develop Irish society. The increased prevalence of homelessness and the lengthening of social housing waiting lists across the country only add to what was already a problematic social position.

The need to change Ireland's development model comes into greater focus when we realise that it may now be exacerbating the problem. For example, an announcement that a major transnational company proposes to create a substantial number of new jobs is greeted with delight, particularly when many of these will jobs will go to local people. A proportion of them, will, however, be filled by bringing people into Ireland from abroad because there are no Irish people available with the required skills. Providing for these immigrants from abroad then brings huge additional pressure on a situation which already has a housing shortage and inadequate health, education and public transport services.

Government periodically announces plans to deal with many of the 'headline' issues of concern to people, but little progress is made. The implementation of the National Broadband Plan is a case in point where the issue created heated debate but no solutions over many years. Minimal progress has been made on the implementation of the *SlainteCare* plan for the future of Irish healthcare. Homelessness now seems entrenched and insufficient progress is being made on reducing social housing waiting lists.

New technologies have improved our living standards and increased the convenience of modern life, but combined with the reorganisation of labour market practices and traditional views such as that 'a job is the best way out of poverty' and 'any job will do', they have led indirectly to increased instances of low paid employment, zero-hours and if-and-when contracts, increased temporary employment arrangements, reduced in-work benefits, and other precarious working practices (Collins, 2015; ICTU, 2017; Social Justice Ireland, 2017).

Numbers such as 109,000 working poor (5 per cent of all those employed) attest to the fact that a job is not always enough to be a poverty reliever – it needs to be a well-paid, secure job. EU directives and national legislation need to ensure the standard employment relationships meets the conditions required to produce such an outcome. Government should also move towards a situation where the National Minimum Wage is set at the level of the Living Wage[1].

Despite economic and social progress in the century since the formation of the state, Ireland has never delivered to its citizens public services and social infrastructure equivalent to the average among other countries in Western Europe. The only time at which Ireland achieved full employment was in the mid-2000s, the foundations on which it was built were wholly unsustainable.

There was a time when there was good reason for these deficiencies; Ireland was an underdeveloped nation without the economic capability to raise the necessary

---

[1] The current National Minimum Wage is €9.80 per hour. However, the Living Wage – the hourly rate which a single person working 39 hours per week needs to earn in order to achieve the minimum socially acceptable standard of living in Ireland is €11.90. See https://www.livingwage.ie/ for more information.

revenue. This has long-since changed, but there has not been a concomitant revision of the model for continued development or the goals for what our society can and should provide. There is no acceptable reason why Ireland shouldn't be capable of delivering public services and social infrastructure equivalent to those of the similarly developed economies of the EU-15. Indeed, Irish people expect these standards and have every right to expect a future where there is no poverty, where good health is the norm and where wellbeing, decent work, reduced inequality and sustainability are at the core of policy development.

As part of a new model for development, Ireland should reconceptualise the interaction of employment and taxation, welfare and work. The Irish economy of the future must recognise people's right to meaningful work and should operationalise this right even when sufficient jobs are not available for all those seeking employment. A Basic Income[2] system would go some distance to addressing the new world of work and should, therefore, be part of a new vision for Ireland for the 21st century. It would be particularly apt, given the ongoing technological progress referred to above which continues to make many skills and jobs obsolete. It would provide options for those who are experiencing precarious working practices. It would also help address some of the problems associated with Ireland's changing demographics, and the need for a fairer distribution of economic resources.

The global context for corporate taxation is also changing dramatically and Ireland must adjust accordingly. The activities of corporations often have big impacts on social, environmental and intergenerational justice. In their search for competitive advantage they often ignore the values and needs of local communities (Healy and Reynolds, 2011:171). A model for development and for society is required where corporations acknowledge that they benefit from Ireland's social and economic infrastructure – most obviously roads and telecommunications, and Ireland's highly educated labour force – and should therefore make a fair and proportionate contribution with the interests of society in mind, instead of engaging in aggressive tax planning to maximise their profits.

In 2015, the United Nations published its list of 17 Global Goals for Sustainable Development (United Nations, 2015a). Known as the SDGs, the list includes goals such as no poverty, zero hunger, responsible consumption, and good health and wellbeing. They are to be achieved in all parts of the world by 2030 and Ireland has signed up to achieve these goals by that date.

These goals call on all people particularly those in the developed world to rethink their lifestyle and consumption patterns. At a time when humanity is generating more financial and material wealth than at any time in history, when we are producing so much food that parts of the developed world is experiencing an

---

[2]   For further information on how a system of Basic Income could be implemented, see Costing a Basic Income for Ireland (Murphy & Ward, 2016) at https://www. socialjustice.ie/sites/default/files/attach/policy-issue-article/4642/chapter9.pdf

obesity crisis, when we have more technological innovations and advances than ever before, hundreds of millions of people go to bed hungry every night; millions of children are denied the basic right to an education; and human 'development' is on such an unsustainable path that it may threaten the very existence of our species within a century.

The most obvious example of where this model has gone wrong is in its environmental effects. The goal of ever-expanding GDP, the concomitant use of scarce resources of water, fuel and various minerals, and the creation of waste and environmental pollution, conflicts directly with the widely acknowledged need to reduce carbon emissions and preserve our environment. The Paris Agreement of 2015 (United Nations, 2015b) set a long-term goal of keeping the increase in global average temperature to well below 2 °C above pre-industrial level and aims to limit the increase to 1.5 °C, thereby substantially reducing the risks and effects of climate change. The need for such an agreement, not to mention the need for the aforementioned SDGs, is evidence enough of a defective development model, but the subsequent political wrangling as countries attempt to gain exemptions and prioritisation for their various special economic interests (including Ireland, which shamefully looked for exemptions from our climate action targets in order to pursue self-interested goals in our indigenous agriculture industry) has brought additional ignominy.

The need for the SDGs is an acknowledgement of the flaws in development models that prioritise economic growth without putting in place the structures necessary to ensure that benefits are spread evenly across countries and citizens, and that progress is sustainable and does not compromise the needs of future generations.

There is a need for a new model: one that acknowledges the need for a just society in which human rights are guaranteed, human dignity is respected, human development is facilitated, and the environment is protected.

*Social Justice Ireland* has developed such a model. It involves working to achieve five key outcomes simultaneously – (a) a vibrant economy; (b) decent services and infrastructure; (c) just taxation; (d) real participation and (e) sustainability. In Chapter 2, we will illustrate this model and describe the constituent parts in detail.

Ireland is dealing with many challenges. Brexit, our housing and health crises, our gradually growing and ageing population, the effects of climate change, and the challenges inherent in our environmental obligations have been with us for many years now. They will not be solved by continuing with 'business as usual'.

*Social Justice Ireland* believes that every person has seven core rights (Healy et al, 2015: 31) whose vindication should be part of any vision for Ireland. These core rights are the right to sufficient income to live life with dignity; the right to meaningful work; the right to appropriate accommodation; the right to relevant education; the right to essential healthcare; the right to real participation and the right to cultural respect. The achievement of each of these rights should be an overarching goal of any model for development and social progress.

Ireland faces many challenges, but there are solutions available. Ireland's high and persistent rates of poverty and deprivation (CSOb, 2018), and sub-par public services are unacceptable in a country that has the fastest growing economy in Europe and is one of the wealthiest in the world (Clark et al, 2018). In this book, *Social Justice Ireland* sets out a new model for development, more appropriate to the 21$^{st}$ century, which we believe Ireland should adopt in order to build a just society, and a policy framework that would see us get there in a coherent and integrated way. In Chapter 2, we explain this model, and look at where Ireland currently stands in 15 keys areas, before asking: where do we *want* to go, and what do we need to do to get there? In subsequent chapters we look at particular policy issues in greater detail.

# REFERENCES

Central Statistics Office (2018a) *Survey on Income and Living Conditions (SILC) 2017 Results*. Available at: https://www.cso.ie/en/releasesandpublications/ep/p-silc/surveyonincomeandlivingconditionssilc2017/introductionandsummary ofresults/

Central Statistics Office (2018b) *Monthly Unemployment*. Available at: https://www.cso.ie/en/releasesandpublications/er/mue/monthlyunemployment november2018/

Clark, C., Kavanagh, C. and Lenihan, N. (2018) *Sustainable Progress Index 2018*. Accessed on 01/03/2018 at https://www.socialjustice.ie/sites/default/files/file/SustainableProgressIndex/sustainableprogressindex2018.pdf

Collins, M. (2015) *Earnings and Low Pay in the Republic of Ireland: A Profile and Some Policy Issues*. Access on 08/03/2017 at http://www.nerinstitute.net/download/pdf/earnings_and_lowpay_in_roi_neri_wp29.pdf

Department of Housing, Planning and Local Government (2018) *Homelessness Report November 2018*. Available at: https://www.housing.gov.ie/sites/default/files/publications/files/homeless_report_-_november_2018_0.pdf

Department of Finance (2018) *Economic and Fiscal Outlook 2019*. Available at: http://www.budget.gov.ie/Budgets/2019/Documents/Budget_2019_Economic_and_Fiscal_Outlook_F.pdf

ESRI (2018) *High childcare costs linked to lower employment among mothers*. Available at: https://www.esri.ie/news/high-childcare-costs-linked-to-lower-employment-among-mothers/

Eurostat (2018) *Highest GDP Growth for Ireland in 2018*. Available at: https://ec.europa.eu/ireland/news/highest-gdp-growth-for-ireland-in-2018_en

Goodbody, W., (2018) *Explainer: The saga of the National Broadband Plan*. Available at: https://www.rte.ie/news/analysis-and-comment/2018/1127/1013745-broad-band-analysis/

Healy, S., Delaney, A., Leahy, A., Murphy, M., Reynolds, B., and Robinson, J. (2015) *Towards a Just Society*. Dublin: Social Justice Ireland

Healy, S., & Reynolds, B., (2011) 'Sharing Responsibility and Shaping the Future: Why and How? In Healy & Reynolds eds *Sharing Responsibility and Shaping the Future*. Dublin: Social Justice Ireland

ICTU (2017) *'Insecure and Uncertain': Precarious Work in the Republic of Ireland & Northern Ireland*. Accessed on 31/01/2018 at https://www.ictu.ie/download/pdf/precarious_work_final_dec_2017.pdf

Legatum (2018) *The Legatum Prosperity Index*. Available at: https://www.prosperity.com/rankings

Social Justice Ireland (2017) *Employment Monitor - Issue 5*. Available at: https://www.socialjustice.ie/content/publications/social-justice-ireland-employment-monitor-issue-5

United Nations (2015a) *Sustainable Development Goals*. Available at: http://www.un.org/sustainabledevelopment/sustainable-development-goals/

United Nations (2015b) Paris Agreement. Available at: https://unfccc.int/sites/default/files/english_paris_agreement.pdf

# 2.

# A DEVELOPMENT MODEL AND A POLICY FRAMEWORK FOR THE 21ST CENTURY

While much of the last decade has been very hard for most Irish people, the economic recovery of the past few years has been strong.

Most of Ireland's economic fundamentals have been on a positive trend for many years now. Consumer spending remains strong (Department of Finance, 2018a), unemployment continues to fall and there are more people at work in Ireland now than ever before (CSO, 2018a). The export growth of recent years is expected to continue, though at a slower pace (Department of Finance, 2018b). Indeed, Ireland's economy – regardless of fanciful GDP growth rates and so-called "leprechaun economics" – has been among the fastest growing in Europe for several years now[1] (Eurostat, 2018).

However, as noted in Chapter 1, measurements of Ireland's social wellbeing have been far less impressive. Roughly one in six in Ireland (more than 750,000 people) and one in five children (almost a quarter of a million) live at risk of poverty (CSO, 2018b). Public services remain stretched, with new record-highs of people waiting on trollies in Irish hospitals[2]. The number of homeless people in Ireland has risen dramatically in the last few years (Department of Housing, Planning and Local Government, 2018), and Irish people face a housing supply crisis, both in the public and private sectors, with rents now well beyond boom-time levels (Lyons, 2018).

Something is fundamentally wrong with the development path Ireland has been taking. Thanks to the current housing situation and several other factors, many Irish citizens are facing the prospect that their children's standard of living will not

---

[1] Ireland has the fastest growing economy in Europe when measured according to GDP. We note that there are numerous issues with Ireland's GDP figures and deal with these in more details later in this chapter.

[2] The number of patients counted as spending time waiting on hospital trollies broke records for several months in 2018, according to counts by industry union the Irish Nurse and Midwives Organisation. See https://inmo.ie/Home/Index/217/13181 as an example.

equal that of their own (Fahey, 2018). It is clear that Ireland's recovery has not been experienced by all equally.

*Ireland 2040*, the National Planning Framework (Department of Housing, Planning and Local Government, 2018a), has set out a plan for developing the infrastructure that will underpin the social and economic fabric of Ireland over the next quarter of a century. It is the first coherent attempt in well over a decade to develop a long-term integrated plan to deliver the social infrastructure and public services that Irish people, as citizens of a wealthy Western country, expect and deserve.

However, it does not provide sufficient detail about the standard of living that can be expected in 2040, the type of society being worked towards, or how government is going to deliver and fund those services that will deliver a decent standard of living for all.

*Social Justice Ireland* has a vision for an Irish society that we believe most Irish citizens would aspire to living in. This vision, and a model for its development and achievement, is outlined in this chapter and in subsequent chapters of this publication. However, it must be acknowledged that while this society is eminently deliverable, it will cost money. This requires an acknowledgement from Government and from people that Ireland's current model of revenue generation does not provide the resources necessary to deliver the public services and social infrastructure that Ireland needs in order to be compared favourably with our peer countries of the EU-15.

Decisions must be made about whether this cost is to be met by increasing taxation, by imposing or increasing charges, by increasing efficiency, or through the private sector. *Social Justice Ireland* is of the view that a broadening of the tax base will be required together with an increase in the total tax-take towards the European average. Most Western European Governments provide a far more comprehensive programme of public services and social infrastructure. Many are much closer to the ideal described herein than Ireland is. Therefore, if we wish to emulate these countries, we must secure a level of revenue similar to these countries.

To achieve the vision set out in this chapter, we have proposed a policy framework that identifies five key policy outcomes and sets out key areas for action.

- The first outcome we seek is a vibrant and sustainable economy. This is required to generate the resources needed to deliver the society we desire. This outcome requires fiscal and financial stability and sustainable economic growth. Adequate public investment is also required – something which will aid in the development of a more just economic model. (These issues are dealt with below and in Chapter 4).

- The second outcome we aim for is decent services and infrastructure, at a level equivalent to our European peer countries. This requires action aimed at strengthening social services and social infrastructure, delivery of adequate levels of quality employment, and a commitment to quantitative targets to reduce poverty and inequality. (Chapters 3, 4, 5, 6, 7, 8 and 9).

• The third outcome we propose in our framework is fair taxation, a key requirement of which requires an increase in the overall tax-take, moving us closer to the European average. Such an increase must be implemented equitably and in a way that reduces income inequality. It would also require that a fair share of corporate profits would be paid in tax. (These issues are dealt with in detail in Chapter 4).

• The fourth outcome we propose is good governance. This requires the promotion of deliberative democracy, as well as new criteria in policy evaluation and the continued development of a social dialogue process involving all sectors of society. (Chapter 10).

• Finally, the fifth outcome we seek is sustainability. This would require the development of policies focused on creating a sustainable future through the introduction of measures to promote climate justice, protect the environment, and generate balanced regional development. New economic and social indicators to measure progress are also required, alongside traditional national accounting measures such as GDP, GNP and GNI. (Chapters 11, 12 and 13).

**Table 2.1: A Policy Framework for a Just Ireland**

| Vibrant economy | Decent services and infrastructure | Just taxation | Good governance | Sustainability |
|---|---|---|---|---|
| Fiscal and financial stability and sustainable economic growth | Secure, well-funded public services and social infrastructure | A tax-take closer to the EU average | Deliberative democracy and PPNs | Increased environmental protection and climate justice |
| Adequate public investment | Reduced unemployment and underemployment | Increased equity in taxation and reduced income inequality | Social dialogue – all sectors in deliberative process | Balanced regional development |
| A more just economic structure | Seven social, economic and cultural rights to be achieved | A fair share of corporate profits for the State | Reformed policy and budgetary evaluation | New indicators of progress and Satellite National Accounts |

## i) *Fostering a vibrant economy*

One of the main expectations of citizens of a modern democracy is an economy that is not only well run but run in the interests of all society. Macroeconomic stability requires fiscal and financial stability, the support of a public investment programme of sufficient scale, and a more just structuring of Ireland's economy. All these measures are connected. An investment programme will contribute to economic growth, which would in turn lower Ireland's debt burden as a proportion of national income. If properly structured and well-targeted, it would also create the employment needed and produce the social infrastructure required to reduce inequality and deliver improved living standards in Ireland.

## a) *Fiscal and financial stability and sustainable economic growth*

Ireland's macroeconomic situation continues to improve with each release of national income figures from the Central Statistics Office (CSO, 2018c). Employment continues to rise at an impressive rate and long-term unemployment is falling (CSO, 2018a). However, there are several factors, both internal and external, that are capable of halting this progress.

Brexit is likely to have a net negative economic effect, even if it does present some sectoral opportunities. "Buoyancy" in our main export markets and historically low interest rates[3] have contributed significantly to Ireland's economic performance, which has been impressive even taking into account so-called "leprechaun economics". These are factors that are largely outside of Ireland's control, and it is well documented how reliant we are on exports for economic growth. Ireland is in an economically vulnerable position due to external factors such as Brexit, the EU's drive to change how corporate taxation is addressed across the Union, and the threats of conflict in global trade; as well as due to internal infrastructural factors that are limiting our economic capacity such as a shortage of housing[4] and the lack of a comprehensive rural broadband network.

If the lessons of the late-2000s have taught us nothing else, it is that our small open economy is prone to shocks that can cause large swathes of revenue to disappear very quickly. Ireland must broaden its tax base in order to mitigate against the effects of a future economic slowdown or crash. The best way to fortify Ireland's economy in preparation for potential future shocks is to increase public investment.

## b) *Adequate Public Investment*

Ireland has an infrastructure deficit in many areas as a result of low public investment over a number of years. *Budget 2019* documentation projects that Ireland's gross capital expenditure will be €8.4bn in 2019 (Department of Finance, 2018b). This is

---

[3]    It should be noted that these are now rising.

[4]    This shortage is evidenced by the 115,350 in need of sustainable social housing (see Housing Agency, 2018, and Housing Assistance Payment figures from June 2018), and the significant growth in rental costs and the price of house purchases in the last few years (Lyons, 2018).

a significant increase – both on the 2018 figure and on what was projected for 2019 in *Budget 2018*. These are positive trends that should continue.

*Ireland 2040* (Department of Housing, Planning and Local Government, 2018a) and the *National Development Plan* (Department of Housing, Planning and Local Government, 2018b) contain details of a significant investment package over the coming years. This is very welcome, but these documents lack definite timelines for achieving the kind of infrastructure development required.

Ireland's levels of public investment have historically been quite low. The effects of inadequate investment are most obvious in the current crisis in housing, as well as in our dilapidated water infrastructure, the lack of an adequate rural broadband network, and the insufficient flood defences in towns and communities across the country.

Governments never really cut infrastructure investment; they merely postpone it. Doing so over a prolonged period creates an infrastructural deficit that can hinder the delivery of public services and lower general living standards. In August 2017, the American Chamber of Commerce in Ireland published a report warning that Ireland's current housing crisis is so severe that it could damage Ireland's competitiveness (American Chamber of Commerce in Ireland, 2017). While there are certainly other, more socially worthy, reasons for investing in Ireland's productive social and economic infrastructure, there is perhaps no clearer or more obvious example of the need for large-scale government investment to maintain Ireland's medium-to-long-term economic potential, given the prevailing circumstances.

Well-targeted social investment would reduce unemployment, contribute to robust public finances, and help to secure wellbeing. It is difficult, if not impossible, to meet the macroeconomic goals of full employment or infrastructural maintenance and expansion, or the social goals of adequate housing, healthcare and education services, without adequate levels of investment. *Social Justice Ireland* continues to argue for a significant investment programme, starting with social housing.

c) *A More Just Economic Structure*
As noted already, many of the fundamentals of the Irish economy – headline employment numbers, consumption, exports – are on positive trajectories. However, they are in sharp contrast with other progress indicators that show high levels of poverty and deprivation, record levels of homelessness, a lack of affordable childcare, and an absence of effective broadband in rural areas that has major negative economic and social impacts.

Figures from the most recent Survey on Income and Living Conditions (SILC) indicate that one in six people in Ireland are living at risk of poverty, and one in five children are living in households at risk of poverty. Perhaps more shockingly, there are over 100,000 people in Ireland with a job who are living at risk of poverty, and almost a quarter of a million people who experience deprivation despite being employed. Without social transfers, 43.8 per cent of Irish people would be living at risk of poverty (CSO, 2018b).

Such numbers in a society with a thriving economy are unacceptable and are sure proof of major flaws in Ireland's development model, including a grossly unequal division of the benefits of economic growth. We have structured society in a way that makes homelessness and poverty inevitable. Reliance on the private sector to provide all of society's accommodation needs has created a situation where thousands are incapable of meeting their accommodation requirements via 'the market'.

Government should strive to create a new economic model based on fairness. Among other things, this would mean that people with a job have sufficient income to live life with dignity, that social welfare payments are set at an adequate level and are indexed, and that public services are funded sufficiently in order to close the gap between the living standards of the least well off in society and what is considered to be a minimum socially acceptable standard of living in a developed Western country. Government can also improve matters by setting an ambitious target of poverty eradication, particularly among children.

Much of the economic inequality experienced in Ireland, and indeed in other countries, has been caused by economic changes that were either inevitable or the downside of desirable developments; technological progress cannot be arrested, nor can the improving competitiveness of emerging economies of the Global South. But there has been a failure to ensure the gains from these trends are shared more widely and more fairly.

*Social Justice Ireland* has been saying for years that the economy cannot be treated in isolation. Policymakers must acknowledge that a thriving economy is not a goal in itself but a means to social development and wellbeing for all. Substantial evidence has emerged in recent years to support the view that economies and societies perform better across a number of different metrics, from better health to lower crime rates, where there is less inequality (Wilkinson & Pickett, 2009).

With this in mind, Government should move to implement a system of Basic Income[5] in Ireland. This would have the benefit of placing an income floor underneath every individual which can be relied upon regardless of changing circumstances, whilst also structuring Ireland's welfare system in a way that better meets the needs of the modern economy, increasing flexibility for individuals of working age and reducing inequality in society.

---

[5]   In February 2018, the Council of Europe voted in favour of a resolution to introduce a system of Basic Income. More at: http://basicincome.org/news/2018/02/europe-council-europe-adopts-resolution-basic-income/

Another aspect of a more just economic system would see an acknowledgement that creditors, as well as debtors, are responsible for their actions. This should result in a better deal for Ireland on our national debt. A significant portion of Ireland's national debt originated from bailouts of the Irish financial sector; liabilities guaranteed by the Irish State on the basis of inaccurate, possibly fraudulent, information. Part of Ireland's debt represents a direct subsidy from the Irish public to international bondholders and the European banking system, the total cost of which was €64bn. There has yet to be sufficient recognition of this by our European partners.

## ii) *Providing Decent Services and Infrastructure*
Despite the economic gains of the last three decades or so, Ireland continues to trail our Western European counterparts in terms of service delivery and infrastructure investment. As a result, a deficit has emerged between Ireland and our peer countries of the EU-15.

It should not need stating that this deficit cannot be closed without increasing our current levels of public investment. Gross capital expenditure was €9bn in 2008 and after years of severe cuts to this budget, it will be a projected €8.4bn in 2019 (Department of Finance, 2018b). This is almost €800m more than had been planned for 2019 in the previous budget, and a significant step in the right direction.

Government should continue to increase capital expenditure, particularly in light of the recent significant unexpected – and presumably temporary – windfalls in corporation tax which would be best used on once-off infrastructure projects. It is doubtful however that even this investment would be sufficient to eliminate Ireland's infrastructure deficits any time soon. Social housing in particular requires very substantial investment over a long timeframe to be on the scale required to address current and future demand. *Social Justice Ireland* suggests that other methods may be required to finance such initiatives such as through a major cost rental programme in housing that would pay for itself over time and would not be on the Exchequer balance sheet. More details of such an approach are set out in Chapter 6.

## a) *Secure well-funded public services and social infrastructure*
As part of a new model for development, government should ensure that future tax and spending policy should focus on building up Ireland's social infrastructure, prioritising areas such as social housing, primary care and mental health facilities, and childcare and early education facilities. These are areas in particular where Ireland is experiencing an infrastructure deficit. Without adequate social infrastructure and services, it is impossible to achieve the minimum standard of living to which all citizens, from children to older people, aspire.

As a means of reducing the budget deficit during Ireland's years of recession and subsequent bailout, a disproportionate focus was placed on spending reductions over tax increases. This led to the underfunding of the public services that most

Irish people rely on to underpin their standard of living and meant that the brunt of the negative impact was felt by the most vulnerable in society.

*Ireland 2040* and the *National Development Plan* are important initiatives, in particular because they are a welcome return to some element of long-term planning in this country. However, as much as they have been heralded by government and the media, these Plans feature a significant number of projects that have already been announced, as well as relatively little additional spending compared to that which would have taken place anyway had government's capital budget increased gradually over the period. There is certainly not sufficient capital spending included to close the deficit between Ireland and our European counterparts.

b) *Reduced Unemployment and Underemployment*
Ireland's rising employment numbers and falling unemployment rate are most welcome. Unemployment in Ireland stood at 5.3 per cent in November 2018, down from 6.4 per cent 12 months previously (CSO, 2018d). Considering that three years ago, unemployment stood at more than 9.5 per cent, this is a major achievement.

However, a focus on headline figures means that many underlying problems are missed. For example, underemployment remains a significant issue, with an estimated 111,500 people (approximately a quarter of all part-time employees) working part-time hours who would take full-time employment if they could find it (CSO, 2018a).

A report published in late 2017 by the Irish Congress of Trade Unions (ICTU, 2017) asserted that while employment is rising in the aftermath of the recession, so too is the instance of precarious employment, with nearly 160,000 people – or 8 per cent of the workforce in Ireland – having significant variations in their hours of work from week to week or month to month. Over half of those were in temporary employment because they could not find permanent work – a 179 per cent increase since 2008.

Supporting an adequate public investment programme is essential if Ireland is to have a vibrant economy that maximises good, well-paid employment and reduces underemployment. Concerns that the Irish economy may be 'overheating' are misplaced, with most of the supposed symptoms being related to other factors, particularly a supply crisis in housing. The current situation, particularly given the economic uncertainty abroad, calls for an increase in public expenditure, not a reduction.

c) *Ensuring Seven Social, Economic, and Cultural Rights are Achieved*
*Social Justice Ireland* believes strongly in the importance of developing a rights-based approach to social, economic, and cultural policy. Such an approach would go a long way towards addressing the growing inequality Ireland has been experiencing and should be at the heart of the development model for a just society.

*Social Justice Ireland* believes seven basic rights should be acknowledged and recognised. These are the rights to: sufficient income to live life with dignity; meaningful work; appropriate accommodation; relevant education; essential healthcare; cultural respect; and real participation in society (Healy et al, 2015). For these seven rights to be vindicated, greater public expenditure to fund a broader provision of services is required.

It is also important that all people and all nations recognise their duty to uphold the rights of others. As an example, the current refugee crisis, precipitated by the chaos in the Middle East, has created a situation of immense suffering for millions of people. Along with our European counterparts, Ireland has a part to play in assisting these refugees. There can be economic and social benefits to this too (Gagnon, 2014; OECD, 2014). But more importantly, Ireland should not allow some of the social trends of other countries to occur here. Resistance to the integration of people from a different culture may be guided by misunderstanding, or fear of the unknown. We must not allow fear to overwhelm our humanity.

iii) *Just Taxation*
If a country is setting social and economic goals, it is important that taxation policy supports these goals. Tax justice must be a key building block of any functioning model of development.

Ireland needs to have a real debate about the levels of services and infrastructure it wishes to have in the coming decades, and how these are to be financed. The current trajectory of government policy is for reductions in total revenue (of which tax revenue is by far the largest component) as a percentage of national income and a corresponding reduction in expenditure. It is simply not possible to provide the high-quality public services Irish people aspire to having while failing to collect adequate revenue to pay for them. Allowing total expenditure to fall as a proportion of national income will only result in a greater infrastructure deficit compared to our EU counterparts. The re-emergence of economic growth should be seen as an opportunity to increase expenditure on our depleted social infrastructure, not to reduce taxes.

A new development model is required; one that recognises that European-average levels of services and infrastructure cannot be delivered without European-average levels of taxation.

a) *A Tax-Take Closer to the EU average*
The Department of Finance's *Economic and Fiscal Outlook – Budget 2019* projects total revenue and expenditure each falling to 25 per cent of GDP or to 41.1 per cent of GNI* in 2019[6] (Department of Finance, 2018b). However, for reasons that have

---

[6] Though comparisons to Irish GDP are becoming increasingly meaningless, the figures with reference to GNI* also compare poorly to our European peers. (The numbers for the EU-15, the cohort of countries most similar to Ireland in terms of

been well documented[7], Ireland's GDP figures have in recent years offered a poor measure of the economic activity genuinely occurring in the country, and GNI* is not without its problems either.

*Social Justice Ireland* believes that Ireland should aim to collect an additional €2.5bn to €3bn per annum in taxation. This calculation is based on a more realistic estimation of Ireland's actual economic growth figures, as well as on per capita taxation numbers, population growth, and the estimated gap between Ireland's actual tax-take and the tax-take needed if Ireland is to provide a level of public services consistent with the expectations of a developed Western European democracy[8].

The need for a broader more stable tax base is a lesson painfully learned by Ireland during the recent economic crisis. The narrowness of the Irish tax base resulted in almost 25 per cent of tax revenues disappearing, plunging the exchequer and the country into a series of fiscal policy crises (cf. Chapter 4).

As a policy objective, Ireland should remain a low-tax economy, but not one incapable of adequately supporting the economic, social and infrastructural requirements necessary to support our society and complete our convergence with the rest of Europe. Ireland can never hope to address its long-term deficits in these two areas if we continue to collect substantially less income than that required by other European countries (cf. chapter 4 for a more detailed discussion of this issue).

b) *Increased equity in taxation and reduced income inequality*
Ireland should increase its total tax-take, but it must do so in a fair and equitable manner. *Social Justice Ireland* believes that the necessary extra revenue should be partly attained by increasing income taxes for those on the highest incomes, and partly by reforming the tax code and broadening the tax base. This will involve shifting taxation towards wealth and higher incomes, ensuring that those who benefit the most from Ireland's economic system contribute the most.

*Social Justice Ireland* advocates a minimum effective tax rate of 10 per cent[9] for corporation tax; a reform of tax reliefs and incentives, particularly those accruing to individuals with income in the higher band; and the introduction of a Financial Transactions Tax (FTT) in line with proposals outlined by the European Commission and accepted by leading member states.

---

development - and indeed the countries that most Irish people wish to emulate - were approximately 46.6 and 48.6 respectively in 2015).

[7] In the summer of 2016, it was estimated that Ireland's GDP had grown by more than 26 per cent in 2015. This measure, while technically correct based on the procedure for measuring GDP, was clearly an inaccurate reflection of Ireland's true economic growth in that year.

[8] This calculation is explained in further detail in Chapter 4.

[9] As an interim measure, *Social Justice Ireland* believes Government should introduce a 6 per cent minimum effective rate in *Budget 2020*.

Unless they are well-designed and limited, tax-based incentives can significantly erode the revenue base without achieving offsetting benefits from increased investment (International Monetary Fund, 2015). Pension-related tax incentives, in particular, are in need of revision, as in their current format they redistribute income towards the better off in society (Collins & Hughes, 2017).

Making income tax credits refundable would help make low-paid work more rewarding. Initiatives like an FTT and a Site Value Tax would perform the dual role of raising revenue for Government and encouraging the flow of capital towards productive social and economic enterprise. A well-structured taxation system would help reallocate capital to productive investment and away from speculative finance. Under such a system, any speculation that takes place would be taxed in such a way as to discourage such practices, whilst generating revenue for social infrastructure.

*Social Justice Ireland* also advocates the implementation of the recommendations of the Kenny Report, something which is long overdue. 2010 did see the introduction of a windfall tax which would have had a similar impact to that recommended in the report. *Social Justice Ireland* welcomed this initiative at the time and viewed its removal as part of *Budget 2015* as a retrograde step. Following a recovery in land values and the commercial property market in particular, and with shortages in land for housing, now is the perfect opportunity for the application of a windfall tax. This and the aforementioned policies would increase the fairness of the Irish taxation system, as well as broadening its base.

In general *Social Justice Ireland* favours shifting the burden of taxation away from employment and other productive pursuits, and onto rent-seeking activity, actions that cause environmental damage and other negative side-effects, or other market failures such as land hoarding. We believe there may be scope for reductions in income tax if these are done in a fair and just manner, and if the money can be replaced with revenue from other sources.

c) *A Fair Share of Corporate Profits for the State*
As noted in Chapter 1, it has long been a key part of Ireland's industrial strategy to attract Foreign Direct Investment. One of the ways this has been done is by using a low headline corporation tax rate. This has led to reputational damage due to the utilisation of the Irish tax regime by multinational corporations (MNCs) to avoid taxes on their profits. This is most apparent in the ruling of the European Commission in 2016 that Apple used Ireland to facilitate tax avoidance to the tune of approximately €13bn over the preceding decade.

A crucial medium-term priority must be the re-conceptualisation of the role of the Irish corporation tax regime. There has been a growing international focus on the way MNCs manage their tax affairs. The OECD's Base Erosion and Profits Shifting (BEPS) examination has established the manner and methods by which MNCs exploit international tax structures to minimise the tax they pay. Similarly, the European Commission has undertaken a series of investigations into the tax management and tax minimisation practices of a number of large MNCs operating within the EU, including Ireland.

Already, controversial loopholes have been closed but a serious discussion must take place about the role of corporation tax in Ireland's industrial strategy. *Social Justice Ireland* advocates that Ireland change its stance towards the corporation tax debate in Europe and take the lead in negotiating a Europe-wide minimum headline corporation tax rate of 17.5 per cent with a minimum effective rate of 10 per cent[10].

Aggressive tax planning by corporations relies on exploiting mismatches between the tax rules of individual countries. Many of these mismatches can be removed. Were a minimum effective rate in place in Ireland in 2018, corporate tax income would have been between €1bn and €2bn higher.

iv) *Delivering Good Governance*
It has been widely recognised that Ireland's governance was poor in certain areas prior to the economic crisis. This is particularly so in relation to financial regulation. Moreover, the economic crisis led Government to make rash decisions, particularly in relation to fiscal policy. These decisions were often made without any consultation, and many have since been recognised as very damaging, particularly in the case of the bank guarantee.

Reforming governance and widening participation must remain a key goal. There can be no return to the failed patterns of decision-making that led to the crisis. An increased recognition of the need to include all stakeholders in the decision-making process is needed.

a) *Deliberative Democracy*
For too long, too many decisions have been taken at an elite level, without explanation or justification, instead of following reasoned debate with citizen and civil society participation. Social dialogue involving all sectors of society is hugely beneficial. It helps highlight issues at an early stage which would allow them to be addressed promptly. More importantly, it ensures that the various sectors of society are involved in developing mutually acceptable solutions to problems that emerge which in turn would be most likely to ensure their support for such solutions when implemented by Government.

A commitment to deliberative democracy[11] is needed, where decisions about what kind of society and economy Ireland needs are founded upon reasoned, evidence-based and enlightened debate, and in which decisions taken by government are

---

[10] As already noted, *Social Justice Ireland* believes Government should introduce a 6 per cent minimum effective rate in *Budget 2020* as an interim measure.
[11] See Gutmann & Thompson (2004) and Healy and Reynolds (2011) for more on the concept of deliberative democracy.

justified and acceptable to the public. A deliberative decision-making process is one where all stakeholders are involved, but the power differentials are removed (Healy and Reynolds, 2011). In such a process, stakeholders are involved in the framing, implementing, and evaluating of policies and measures that impact on them. Public Participation Networks provide an opportunity for real engagement between local people and the local authorities across the country (for further information on this cf. Chapter 10).

b) *Social Dialogue*
Government held the first National Economic Dialogue (NED) in July 2015 and has reprised this format each year since. *Social Justice Ireland* welcomes this deliberative approach to policymaking but believes Government should make the following two changes: It should convene such a forum more regularly than once a year, and it should broaden its deliberations beyond the economy. A wide range of areas need to be addressed simultaneously if the economy and society are to thrive.

Such social dialogue, in various forms, is common across Europe's most successful economies and can play a key role in building a vibrant and sustainable society here in Ireland. Government will make the final decisions on all policy issues; that has always been the case. But it is important that any new policymaking approach adopted by Government is integrated and inclusive and engages all sectors of society.

At previous NEDs, *Social Justice Ireland* has posed four questions for discussion that we believe should be at the core of any discussion on a framework for Ireland's future:

- What services and infrastructure are required?
- How are these to be delivered?
- How are these services and infrastructure to be paid for?
- How can we maintain a vibrant and sustainable economy and society as we develop our services and infrastructure?

If Government wishes for all of society to take responsibility for producing a more viable social and economic development model, it must involve all of us in shaping it. When groups have been involved in shaping decisions they are far more likely to take responsibility for implementing these decisions, difficult and demanding though they may be.

c) *Reformed Policy and Budgetary Evaluation*
There were many instances of poor, or non-existent, policy evaluation during the past decade. *Social Justice Ireland* welcomes the steps taken by Government in recent years to increase their research and evaluation capacity. However, we believe

that Government should also take further steps to increase the transparency of budgetary and other important decisions, which are often opaque.

A 2015 report by the OECD on the Irish budgetary process stated bluntly that "the level of budget engagement by the Houses of the Oireachtas is the lowest observed in any OECD country". It rebuked government for a lack of engagement with parliament as a partner throughout the budget process and noted a lack of parliamentary input to medium-term fiscal planning. It also accused government of delaying and limiting legislative scrutiny of Budget Bills and meaningful debate (OECD, 2015). There have been some improvements since; an Oireachtas Committee has been established to address these issues and the Parliamentary Budget Office has also been established to provide independent and impartial information, analysis and advice to the Houses of the Oireachtas, but much more remains to be done.

For example, Government should publish its analysis of the distributional impact of budgetary measures and engage in public debate on that analysis. Previously, the Government published Poverty Impact Assessment Guidelines provided by the Office of Social Inclusion (2008) in the budgetary documentation using the ESRI's SWITCH tax-benefit model which captured the distributional impact of changes in most taxes and benefits, but this practice was discontinued from *Budget 2010*. Government should reintroduce this practice and also adopt gender equality and regional analyses and apply these to each budgetary measure. The Revised Estimates for 2019 contain initial steps towards addressing the nine equality grounds. But much remains to be done. In particular, there is a need to measure the socio-economic impact of each budget. This should be a statutory responsibility for Government.

v) *Creating a Sustainable Future*
Sustainable development is development which meets the needs of the present while not compromising the needs of the future. Financial and economic, environmental, and social sustainability are all key objectives and are all interlinked. To reflect this, Ireland needs new indicators measuring both wellbeing and sustainability in society, to be used alongside measures of national income like GDP, GNP and GNI. The use of such indicators would ensure that issues such as climate justice and balanced regional development, among other key indicators of wellbeing, are given the priority they deserve by policymakers.

A report last year from Professor Charles Clark of St John's University, New York, and Dr. Catherine Kavanagh and Niamh Lenihan of University College Cork (Clark et al, 2018), showed that while Ireland was ranked 2nd in the EU-15 in terms of economic growth, our environmental performance was below average. This points to policies that have prioritised economic growth above sustainability and this is an approach that cannot be allowed to continue.

a) *Increased Environmental Protection and Climate Justice*

Climate change remains the greatest long-term challenge facing Ireland today. The challenge of reducing Ireland's fossil fuel emissions should not be postponed in deference to the goal of economic growth and *Social Justice Ireland* was disappointed by the government's decision to forego the anticipated increase in Ireland's carbon tax in *Budget 2019*. Ireland should adopt ambitious statutory targets aimed at limiting fossil fuel emissions and introduce taxation measures necessary to compensate for the full costs of resource extraction and pollution. These should be accompanied by mitigation measures to protect the vulnerable and those whose livelihoods would be severely impacted.

Commitments made at the COP21 conference in Paris in 2015 (United Nations, 2015a) were based on the growing realisation that the resources of the planet and its environment are finite – a fact that had often been ignored in the past. Failure to tackle climate change now will have significant impacts into the future, including on food production, regional and global ecosystems, and on flood-prone regions.

According to the EPA (2018), Ireland's greenhouse gas emissions are likely to be 1 per cent below 2005 levels in 2020, compared to a target of 20 per cent below 2005 levels, and fossil fuels such as coal and peat are expected to continue to be significant contributors to emissions from power generation. Ireland's performance should be considered a national embarrassment.

b) *Balanced Regional Development*

A sustainable recovery requires balanced regional development. Government must move to correct the growing disparity in the standard of living and the distribution of population between rural and urban Ireland. The proportion of the population living in and around the capital city is already very high by international standards. This is projected to keep growing and Dublin already accounts for half of economic output in Ireland. Yet we are continuing to model our growth path, and design our public services, in a way that encourages rather than discourages such concentration. By continuing to locate a disproportionate amount of our best health, education, and cultural institutions in Dublin, we are driving a model of development that precludes the kind of regional balance required for Ireland to thrive.

The boom years saw an attempt to redress growing regional imbalances in socio-economic development through a National Spatial Strategy. This failed, partly because of Government's own initiatives such as the decentralisation programme for public servants which undermined the Strategy (Meredith and van Egeraat, 2013). Policy must ensure balanced regional development through the provision of public services and through capital spending projects. *Ireland 2040* and the *National Development Plan* must not go the same way as the National Spatial Strategy and must keep their commitments to not leaving rural Ireland behind, as this would result in a further unsustainable concentration of the population around our major cities, particularly Dublin.

c) *New Indicators of Progress and Satellite National Accounts*

As Nobel Laureate Joseph Stiglitz recently noted, 'GDP is not a good measure of wellbeing. What we measure affects what we do, and if we measure the wrong thing, we will do the wrong thing' (Stiglitz, 2019)[12]. Creating a sustainable Ireland requires the adoption of new indicators to measure progress. National Income figures are limited to measuring the monetary value of gross output, income and expenditure in an economy, and include many activities that are in fact detrimental to society and incompatible with the common good while omitting activities that are essential for society to survive.

*Social Justice Ireland* published *Sustainable Progress Index 2018* (Clark et al, 2018) last year, based on the Sustainable Development Goals (United Nations, 2015b). This Index moves beyond national income as a measure of societal advancement, encompassing environmental and social indicators of progress as well as economic ones. We suggest that such an Index be adopted by Government as a means to truly measure Ireland's progress.

## Conclusion

The model for society outlined in this chapter and the policy framework underpinning it are based on a very simple premise: that we understand where we are as a society; that we can see where we want to go; and that there is a logical pathway, outlined in this book, that will get us there.

Ireland has for too long been afflicted by a state of affairs whereby we understand the issues, we know what needs to be done to improve matters, yet we find ourselves failing to take the correct steps. It is time to change that.

It is time, too, to acknowledge that the model of development being pursued is broken, leading as it has to unacceptable levels of poverty and deprivation, inferior quality public services, environmental degradation, and an unsustainable future.

Contained herein is a comprehensive framework setting out the current situation and the issues we face, the goals that we wish to reach as a society, and the policy changes needed to attain them. Having set out our vision for Ireland and presented a policy framework for a just society and provided some details of the policy initiatives required under each of its five pillars, we now move on to look in much greater detail at key aspects of these five pillars.

We provide a fuller analysis of both the first pillar, **a vibrant economy**, and the associated **just taxation** system, in chapter 4 where we also set out a more detailed set of policy proposals.

---

[12]  See also Healy & Reynolds, 2009, and Healy & Reynolds, 2015, for further information on how to move beyond GDP as a measure of progress.

We address **decent social services and infrastructure** in chapters 3 – on income distribution; 4 – taxation; 5 - work, unemployment and job creation; 6 - housing and accommodation; 7 – healthcare; 8 – education; 9 - other public services. On each of these we provide an analysis and critique of the present situation, set out a vision for a fairer future and make a detailed set of policy proposals aimed at moving in that direction.

The fourth pillar, **good governance**, is addressed in chapter 10, where we again provide analysis and critique together with concrete policy proposals.

The fifth pillar, **sustainability**, is addressed in chapters 11 – sustainability; 12 - rural development; and 13 - the global south, following the same approach.

Chapter 14 provides further details on the values that underpin our approach, our focus and our proposals.

# REFERENCES

American Chamber of Commerce in Ireland (2017) *Growing Great Teams in Ireland: The Role of the Residential Rental Sector*. Accessed on 01/02/2018 at: http://www.amcham.ie/getattachment/887a1551-cc8f-4b2b-a3cb-312775e40f75/Growing-Great-Teams-in-Ireland-The-Role-of-the-Residential-Rental-Sector.pdf.aspx?ext=.pdf

Central Statistics Office (2018a) *Labour Force Survey Quarter 3 2018*. Available at: https://www.cso.ie/en/releasesandpublications/er/lfs/labourforcesurveyquarter32018/

Central Statistics Office (2018b) *Survey on Income and Living Conditions (SILC) 2017 Results*. Available at: https://www.cso.ie/en/releasesandpublications/ep/p-silc/surveyonincomeandlivingconditionssilc2017/introductionandsummaryofresults/

Central Statistics Office (2018c) *Quarterly National Accounts Quarter 3*. Available at: https://www.cso.ie/en/releasesandpublications/er/na/quarterlynationalaccountsquarter32018/

Central Statistics Office (2018d) *Monthly Unemployment*. Available at: https://www.cso.ie/en/releasesandpublications/er/mue/monthlyunemploymentnovember2018/

Clark, C., Kavanagh, C. and Lenihan, N. (2018) *Sustainable Progress Index 2018*. Available at: https://www.socialjustice.ie/sites/default/files/file/SustainableProgressIndex/sustainableprogressindex2018.pdf

Collins, Micheál, and Hughes, Gerard (2017) *Supporting pension contributions through the tax system: outcomes, costs and examining reform*. The Economic and Social Review, Vol. 8, No. 4, Winter (2017) Accessed on 01/02/2018 at http://www.esr.ie/article/view/824/174

Department of Finance (2018a) *Monthly Economic Bulletin December 2018*. Available at: https://www.finance.gov.ie/wp-content/uploads/2018/12/Monthly-Economic-December-2018.pdf

Department of Finance (2018b) *Economic and Fiscal Outlook 2019*. Available at: http://www.budget.gov.ie/Budgets/2019/Documents/Budget_2019_Economic_and_Fiscal_Outlook_F.pdf

Department of Housing, Planning and Local Government (2018a) *National Planning Framework*. Accessed 05/03/2018 at http://www.gov.ie/en/project-ireland-2040/

Department of Housing, Planning and Local Government (2018b) *National Development Plan 2018-2027*. Accessed 05/03/2018 at http://www.gov.ie/en/project-ireland-2040/

Department of Housing, Planning and Local Government (2018c) *Homelessness Report November 2018*. Available at: https://www.housing.gov.ie/sites/default/files/publications/files/homeless_report_-_november_2018_0.pdf

Environmental Protection Agency (2018) *Ireland's Provisional Greenhouse Gas Emissions Projections 2017-2035*. Available at: http://www.epa.ie/pubs/reports/air/airemissions/ghgprojections2017-2035/EPA_2018_GHG_Emissions_Projections_Summary_Report.pdf

Eurostat (2018) *Highest GDP Growth for Ireland in 2018*. Available at: https://ec.europa.eu/ireland/news/highest-gdp-growth-for-ireland-in-2018_en

Fahey, T., (2018) *Worse off than their parents? The rising generation of private renters*. In Healy & Reynolds eds. From Here to Where? Negotiating a Better and Fairer Future. Social Justice Ireland: Dublin

Gagnon, J. (2014) *Demographic Change and the Future of the Labour Force in the EU27, in other OECD Countries and Selected Large Emerging Economies*. OECD Publishing, Paris.

Gutmann, A. and Thompson, D. (2004) *Why deliberative Democracy?*. Princeton: Princeton University Press.

Healy, S., Delaney, A., Leahy, A., Murphy, M., Reynolds, B., & Robinson, J. (2015) *Towards a Just Society*. Dublin: Social Justice Ireland

Healy, S., & Reynolds, B. (2009) *Beyond GDP: What is prosperity and how should it be measured?* Social Justice Ireland: Dublin

Healy, S., & Reynolds, B. (2015) *Measuring Up? Ireland's progress: past, present and future*. Social Justice Ireland: Dublin

Housing Agency (2018) *Summary of Social Housing Assessments 2018*. Available at: https://www.housing.gov.ie/sites/default/files/publications/files/summary_of_social_housing_assessments_2018_-_key_findings.pdf

ICTU (2017) *'Insecure and Uncertain': Precarious Work in the Republic of Ireland & Northern Ireland*. Available at: https://www.ictu.ie/download/pdf/precarious_work_final_dec_2017.pdf

International Monetary Fund (2015) IMF Policy Paper: Fiscal Policy and Long-term Growth. Accessed on 13/03/2017 at https://www.imf.org/external/np/pp/eng/2015/042015.pdf

Lyons, R. (2018) *The Daft.ie Rental Price Report - An analysis of recent trends in the Irish rental market 2018 Q3*. Available at https://www.daft.ie/report/ronan-lyons-2018q3-rental

Meredith, D and Van Egeraat, D. (2013) 'Revisiting the National Spatial Strategy ten years on', *IPA Administration Journal*, 60 (3) pp.3-9. Dublin: IPA.

Organisation for Economic Co-operation and Development (2015) *Review of budget oversight by parliament: Ireland*. Accessed on 03/02/2016 at http://www.oecd.org/gov/budgeting/Ireland-Parliamentary-Budget-Review-Preliminary.pdf

Organisation for Economic Co-operation and Development (2014) *Migration Policy Debates*, accessed on 01/02/2016 at http://www.oecd.org/migration/OECD%20Migration%20Policy%20Debates%20Numero%202.pdf

Stiglitz, J., (2019) *Beyond GDP*. Available at: https://www.socialeurope.eu/beyond-gdp

United Nations (2015a) Paris Agreement. Available at: https://unfccc.int/sites/default/files/english_paris_agreement.pdf

United Nations (2015b) *Sustainable Development Goals*. Available at: http://www.un.org/sustainabledevelopment/sustainable-development-goals/

Wilkinson, R. and Pickett, K., (2009) *The Spirit Level: Why More Equal Societies Almost Always do Better*. London, UK: Penguin

## Chapter 3
Income and Income Distribution

**Core Policy Objective:**
To provide all with sufficient income to live life with dignity. This would require enough income to provide a minimum floor of social and economic resources in such a way as to ensure that no person in Ireland falls below the threshold of social provision necessary to enable him or her to participate in activities that are considered the norm for society generally.

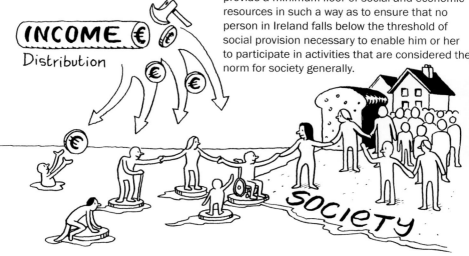

### Key Issues and Evidence

**15.7%** of the population at risk of **POVERTY**

**1 in 5 Children**

The **WORKING POOR**

109,000 people

5% of all people with a job are living in poverty

**INCOME INEQUALITY**

2014 2015 2016 2017 2018 2019?

Largely unchanged over the past decade or more in Ireland

**Policy Solutions**

Set a goal of eliminating poverty
in a single five year Dáil term

Benchmark
adequate levels
of social welfare
payments

Introduce a full
basic income
system over time

Introduce a cost of disability payment

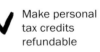

Make personal
tax credits
refundable

Introduce a Living Wage

Adequate
payments for
children

# 3.

# INCOME AND INCOME DISTRIBUTION

**CORE POLICY OBJECTIVE: INCOME AND INCOME DISTRIBUTION**

To provide all with sufficient income to live life with dignity. This would require enough income to provide a minimum floor of social and economic resources in such a way as to ensure that no person in Ireland falls below the threshold of social provision necessary to enable him or her to participate in activities that are considered the norm for society generally.

High rates of poverty and income inequality have been the norm in Irish society for some time. They are problems that require greater attention than they currently receive, but tackling these problems effectively is a multifaceted task. It requires action on many fronts, ranging from healthcare and education to accommodation and employment. However, the most important requirement in tackling poverty is the provision of sufficient income to enable people to live life with dignity. No anti-poverty strategy can possibly be successful without an effective approach to addressing low incomes.[1]

This chapter addresses the issue of income in three parts. The first (section 3.1) examines key evidence relating to the extent and nature of poverty and the income distribution in Ireland today. Subsequently section 3.2 considers the key policy reforms that we believe should be pursued. The chapter concludes (section 3.3) by summarising our key policy priorities in this area.

If the challenges addressed in this chapter are to be effectively addressed in the years ahead, *Social Justice Ireland* believes that the following key initiatives are required:[2]

• increase in social welfare payments.

---

[1] Annex 3, containing additional information relevant to this chapter, is available on the *Social Justice Ireland* website: http://www.socialjustice.ie/content/publications/type/socioeconomic-review-annex

[2] Further detail on these and related initiatives is provided throughout this chapter.

- equity of social welfare rates.

- adequate payments for children.

- refundable tax credits.

- decent rates of pay for low paid workers.

- a universal state pension.

- a cost of disability payment.

## 3.1 Key Evidence

### Poverty
While there is still considerable poverty in Ireland, there has been much progress on this issue over the past two decades. Driven by increases in social welfare payments, particularly payments to the unemployed, the elderly and people with disabilities, the rate of poverty significantly declined between 2001 and 2009. However, since reaching a record low level in 2009 it has increased and now stands at 15.7 per cent of the population according to the latest data, for 2017.[3]

Data on Ireland's income and poverty levels are provided by the annual *SILC* survey *(Survey on Income and Living Conditions)*. This survey replaced the *European Household Panel Survey* and the *Living in Ireland Survey* which had run throughout the 1990s. Since 2003 the *SILC / EU-SILC* survey has collected detailed information on income and living conditions from up to 120 households in Ireland each week; giving a total sample of between 4,000 and 6,000 households each year.

*Social Justice Ireland* welcomes this survey and in particular the accessibility of the data produced. Because this survey is conducted simultaneously across all of the EU states, the results are an important contribution to the ongoing discussion on relative income and poverty levels across the EU. It also provides the basis for informed analysis of the relative position of the citizens of member states. In particular, this analysis is informed by a set of agreed indicators of social exclusion which the EU Heads of Government adopted at Laeken in 2001. These indicators are calculated from the survey results and cover four dimensions of social exclusion: financial poverty, employment, health and education. They also form the basis of the EU Open Method of Co-ordination for social protection and social inclusion and the Europe 2020 poverty and social exclusion targets.

### What is poverty?
The National Anti-Poverty Strategy (NAPS) published by Government in 1997 adopted the following definition of poverty:

---

[3]  Irish household income data has been collected since 1973 and all surveys up to the period 2008-2010 recorded poverty levels above 15 per cent.

*People are living in poverty if their income and resources (material, cultural and social) are so inadequate as to preclude them from having a standard of living that is regarded as acceptable by Irish society generally. As a result of inadequate income and resources people may be excluded and marginalised from participating in activities that are considered the norm for other people in society.*

This definition was reiterated in the subsequent *National Action Plan for Social Inclusion 2007-2016 (NAPinclusion)*.

### Where is the poverty line?

How many people are poor? On what basis are they classified as poor? These and related questions are constantly asked when poverty is discussed or analysed.

In trying to measure the extent of poverty, the most common approach has been to identify a poverty line (or lines) based on people's disposable income (earned income after taxes and including all benefits). The European Commission and the UN, among others, use a poverty line located at 60 per cent of median income. The median disposable income is the income of the middle person in society's income distribution. This poverty line is the one adopted in the *SILC* survey. While the 60 per cent median income line has been adopted as the primary poverty line, alternatives set at 50 per cent and 70 per cent of median income are also used to clarify and lend robustness to assessments of poverty.

The most up-to-date data available on poverty in Ireland comes from the 2017 *SILC* survey, conducted by the CSO (published December 2018). In that year the CSO gathered data from a statistically representative sample of 5,029 households containing 12,612 individuals. The data gathered by the CSO is very detailed. It incorporates income from work, welfare, pensions, rental income, dividends, capital gains and other regular transfers. This data was subsequently verified anonymously using PPS numbers.

According to the CSO, the median disposable income per adult in Ireland during 2017 was €20,869 per annum or €399.94 per week. Consequently, the income poverty lines for a single adult derived from this are:

| | |
|---|---|
| 50 per cent line | €199.97 a week |
| 60 per cent line | €239.97 a week |
| 70 per cent line | €279.96 a week |

Updating the 60 per cent median income poverty line to 2019 levels, using published CSO data on the growth in average hourly earnings in 2018 (+2.1 per cent) and ESRI projections for 2019 (+2.9 per cent) produces a relative income poverty line of €252.11 for a single person. In 2019, any adult below this weekly income level will be counted as being at risk of poverty (CSO, 2018; McQuinn, O'Toole and Economides, 2018: ii).

Table 3.1 shows what income corresponds to this poverty line for a number of household types. The figure of €252.11 is an income per adult equivalent figure. It is the minimum weekly disposable income (after taxes and including all benefits) that one adult needs to be above the poverty line. For each additional adult in the household this minimum income figure is increased by €166.39 (66 per cent of the poverty line figure) and for each child in the household the minimum income figure is increased by €83.20 (33 per cent of the poverty line).[4] These adjustments reflect the fact that as households increase in size they require more income to meet the basic standard of living implied by the poverty line. In all cases a household below the corresponding weekly disposable income figure is classified as living at risk of poverty. For clarity, corresponding annual figures are also included.

**Table 3.1: The Minimum Weekly Disposable Income Required to Avoid Poverty in 2019, by Household Types**

| Household containing: | Weekly poverty line | Annual poverty line |
|---|---|---|
| 1 adult | €252.11 | €13,155 |
| 1 adult + 1 child | €335.31 | €17,496 |
| 1 adult + 2 children | €418.50 | €21,837 |
| 1 adult + 3 children | €501.70 | €26,179 |
| 2 adults | €418.50 | €21,837 |
| 2 adults + 1 child | €501.70 | €26,179 |
| 2 adults + 2 children | €584.90 | €30,520 |
| 2 adults + 3 children | €668.09 | €34,861 |
| 3 adults | €584.90 | €30,520 |

**Source:** *Social Justice Ireland* calculation based on CSO and ESRI data.

One immediate implication of this analysis is that most weekly social assistance rates paid to single people are €49 below the poverty line.

### How many have incomes below the poverty line?

Table 3.2 outlines the findings of various poverty studies since detailed national poverty assessments commenced in 1994. Using the EU poverty line set at 60 per cent of median income, the findings reveal that almost 16 out of every 100 people in Ireland were living in poverty in 2017. The table shows that the rates of poverty decreased significantly after 2001, reaching a record low in 2009. These decreases in poverty levels were welcome. They were directly related to the increases in social welfare payments delivered over the Budgets spanning these years.[5] However

---

[4]   For example, the poverty line for a household with 2 adults and 1 child would be calculated as €252.11 + €166.39 + €83.20 = €501.70.

[5]   See table 3.8 below for further analysis of this point.

poverty increased again in the period since then as the effect of budgetary changes to welfare and taxes, as well as wage movements and unemployment, drove more low income households into poverty. These increases were tempered over recent years by increases in core social welfare payments.

**Table 3.2: Percentage of Population Below Various Relative Income Poverty Lines, 1994-2017**

|          | 1994 | 1998 | 2001 | 2005 | 2009 | 2013 | 2016 | 2017 |
|----------|------|------|------|------|------|------|------|------|
| 50% line | 6.0  | 9.9  | 12.9 | 10.7 | 6.9  | 8.5  | 9.2  | 8.1  |
| 60% line | 15.6 | 19.8 | 21.9 | 18.3 | 14.1 | 16.2 | 16.2 | 15.7 |
| 70% line | 26.7 | 26.9 | 29.3 | 28.0 | 24.5 | 23.9 | 26.0 | 24.6 |

Source: CSO SILC reports (various years) and Whelan et al (2003:12).
Note: All poverty lines calculated as a percentage of median income.

Because it is sometimes easy to overlook the scale of Ireland's poverty problem, it is useful to translate these poverty percentages into numbers of people. Using the percentages for the 60 per cent median income poverty line and population statistics from CSO population estimates, we can calculate the numbers of people in Ireland who have been in poverty for a number of years between 1994 and 2017. These calculations are presented in table 3.3. The results give a better picture of just how significant this problem is.

**Table 3.3: The Numbers of People Below Relative Income Poverty Lines in Ireland, 1994-2017**

|      | % of persons in poverty | Population of Ireland | Numbers in poverty |
|------|-------------------------|-----------------------|--------------------|
| 1994 | 15.6 | 3,585,900 | 559,400 |
| 1998 | 19.8 | 3,703,100 | 733,214 |
| 2001 | 21.9 | 3,847,200 | 842,537 |
| 2004 | 19.4 | 4,045,200 | 784,769 |
| 2007 | 16.5 | 4,375,800 | 722,007 |
| 2009 | 14.1 | 4,533,400 | 639,209 |
| 2013 | 16.2 | 4,614,700 | 747,581 |
| 2017 | 15.7 | 4,857,000 | 762,549 |

Source: See Table 3.2 and CSO online database of population estimates.
Note: Population estimates are for April of each year.

The table's figures are telling. Looking over the past decade, despite a reduction in the headline poverty rate (from 16.5 per cent to 15.7 per cent) there are over 40,000 more people in poverty. Notably, over the period from 2004-2008, the period corresponding with consistent Budget increases in social welfare payments, almost 140,000 people left poverty. Despite this, the cumulative impact of the recession and subsequent recovery has been that the number in poverty has increased once again, rising by 123,000 since 2009.

The fact that there are more than 760,000 people in Ireland living life on a level of income that is this low remains a major concern. As shown in table 3.1 these levels of income are low and those below them clearly face difficulties in achieving what the NAPS described as *"a standard of living that is regarded as acceptable by Irish society generally"*.

The annex that accompanies this chapter (available online at: http://www. socialjustice.ie/content/publications/type/socioeconomic-review-annex) provides a more detailed profile of those groups in Ireland that are living in poverty.

### The incidence of poverty

Figures detailing the incidence of poverty reveal the proportion of all those in poverty that belong to particular groups in Irish society. Tables 3.4 and 3.5 report all those below the 60 per cent of median income poverty line, classifying them by their principal economic status (the main thing people do). The first table examines the population as a whole, including children, while the second table focuses exclusively on adults (using the ILO definition of an adult as a person aged 16 years and above).

Table 3.4 shows that in 2017, the largest group of the population who are poor, accounting for 23.9 per cent of the total, were children. The second largest group are students and children above 16 years who are still in school (18.3 per cent) while the third largest group are those at work (14.3 per cent). Of all those who are poor, 27.8 per cent were in the labour force and the remainder (72.2 per cent) were outside the labour market.[6]

Table 3.5 looks at adults only and provides a more informed assessment of the nature of poverty. This is an important perspective as children depend on adults for their upbringing and support. Irrespective of how policy interventions are structured, it is through adults that any attempts to reduce the number of children in poverty must be directed. The table shows that in 2017 almost one-fifth of Ireland's adults with an income below the poverty line were employed. Overall, 36.5 per cent of adults at risk of poverty in Ireland were associated with the labour market.

---

[6]   This does not include the ill and people with a disability, some of whom will be active in the labour force. The SILC data does not distinguish between those temporally unable to work due to illness and those permanently outside the labour market due to illness or disability.

**Table 3.4: Incidence of Persons Below 60% of Median Income by Principal Economic Status, 2003-2017**

|  | 2003 | 2006 | 2009 | 2012 | 2015 | 2017 |
|---|---|---|---|---|---|---|
| At work | 16.0 | 16.1 | 14.3 | 12.2 | 13.7 | 14.3 |
| Unemployed | 7.6 | 8.3 | 12.9 | 19.2 | 14.2 | 13.5 |
| Students/ school | 8.6 | 15.0 | 14.6 | 14.2 | 15.4 | 18.3 |
| On home duties | 22.5 | 18.4 | 18.0 | 15.5 | 14.8 | 13.1 |
| Retired | 9.0 | 5.8 | 4.7 | 5.9 | 7.3 | 5.9 |
| Ill/disabled | 9.1 | 8.0 | 6.4 | 7.3 | 8.4 | 9.0 |
| Children (under 16 years) | 25.4 | 26.6 | 27.6 | 23.8 | 24.3 | 23.9 |
| Others | 1.9 | 1.8 | 1.5 | 1.9 | 1.9 | 2.0 |
| **Total** | **100.0** | **100.0** | **100.0** | **100.0** | **100.0** | **100.0** |

Source: Collins (2006:141), CSO SILC Reports (various years).

The incidence of being at risk of poverty amongst those in employment is particularly alarming. Many people in this group do not benefit from Budget changes in welfare or income tax. They would be the main beneficiaries of any move to make tax credits refundable, a topic addressed in Chapter 4.

**Table 3.5: Incidence of Adults (16yrs+) Below 60% of Median Income by Principal Economic Status, 2003-2017**

|  | 2003 | 2006 | 2009 | 2012 | 2015 | 2017 |
|---|---|---|---|---|---|---|
| At work | 21.4 | 21.9 | 19.8 | 16.0 | 18.1 | 18.8 |
| Unemployed | 10.2 | 11.3 | 17.8 | 25.2 | 18.8 | 17.7 |
| Students/ school | 11.5 | 20.4 | 20.2 | 18.6 | 20.3 | 24.0 |
| On home duties | 30.1 | 25.1 | 24.9 | 20.3 | 19.6 | 17.2 |
| Retired | 12.0 | 7.9 | 6.5 | 7.7 | 9.6 | 7.8 |
| Ill/disabled | 12.2 | 10.9 | 8.8 | 9.6 | 11.1 | 11.8 |
| Others | 2.5 | 2.5 | 2.1 | 2.5 | 2.5 | 2.6 |
| **Total** | **100.0** | **100.0** | **100.0** | **100.0** | **100.0** | **100.0** |

Source: Calculated from Collins (2006:141) and CSO SILC Reports (various years).

**The Scale of Poverty - Numbers of People**
As the two tables in the last subsection deal only in percentages it is useful to transform these proportions into numbers of people. Table 3.3 revealed that just over 760,000 people were living below the 60 per cent of median income poverty line in 2017. Using this figure, table 3.6 presents the number of people in poverty in that year within various categories. Comparable figures are also presented for selected years over the last decade (2006, 2009 and 2012).

The data in table 3.6 is particularly useful in the context of framing anti-poverty policy. Groups such as the retired and the ill/disabled, although carrying a high risk of poverty, involve smaller numbers of people than groups such as adults who are employed (the working poor), people on home duties (i.e. working in the home, carers) and children/students. Among the primary drivers of the 2006-09 poverty reductions were increasing incomes among those who were on home duties, those who are classified as ill/disabled, the retired and children. Between 2006 and 2009 the numbers of workers in poverty declined while the numbers of unemployed people in poverty notably increased. This reflected the rise in unemployment in the labour market as a whole during those years. As the table shows, the increase in poverty between 2009 and 2016 can be principally explained by the increase in poverty among individuals largely dependent on the welfare system, in particular the unemployed, those who are retired and people who are ill or have a disability.

**Table 3.6: Poverty Levels Expressed in Numbers of People, 2006-2017**

|  | 2006 | 2009 | 2012 | 2017 |
|---|---|---|---|---|
| **Overall** | 719,593 | 639,209 | 776,335 | 762,549 |
| **Adults** | | | | |
| At work | 115,854 | 91,407 | 94,713 | 109,045 |
| Unemployed | 59,726 | 82,458 | 149,056 | 102,944 |
| Students/school | 107,939 | 93,325 | 110,240 | 139,546 |
| On home duties | 132,405 | 115,058 | 120,332 | 99,894 |
| Retired | 41,736 | 30,043 | 45,804 | 44,990 |
| Ill/disability | 57,567 | 40,909 | 56,672 | 68,629 |
| Other | 12,953 | 9,588 | 14,750 | 15,251 |
| **Children** | | | | |
| Children (under 16 yrs) | 191,412 | 176,422 | 184,768 | 182,249 |
| Children (under 18 yrs) | 250,418 | 223,084 | 232,124 | 231,052 |

**Source:** Calculated using CSO SILC Reports (various years) and data from table 3.3.

**Poverty and social welfare recipients**

*Social Justice Ireland* believes in the very important role that social welfare plays in addressing poverty. As part of the *SILC* results the CSO has provided an interesting insight into the role that social welfare payments play in tackling Ireland's poverty levels. It has calculated the levels of poverty before and after the payment of social welfare benefits.

Table 3.7 shows that without the social welfare system just over 4 in every 10 people in the Irish population (43.8 per cent) would have been living in poverty in 2017. Such an underlying poverty rate suggests a deeply unequal distribution of direct income – an issue we address further in the income distribution section of this chapter. In 2017, the actual poverty figure of 15.8 per cent reflects the fact that social welfare payments reduced poverty by 28.1 percentage points.

Looking at the impact of these payments on poverty over time, the increases in social welfare over the period 2005-2007 yielded noticeable reductions in poverty levels. The small increases in social welfare payments in 2001 are reflected in the smaller effects achieved in that year. Conversely, the larger increases, and therefore higher levels of social welfare payments, in subsequent years delivered greater reductions. This has occurred even as poverty levels before social welfare increased.

A report by Watson and Maitre (2013) examined these effects in greater detail and noted the effectiveness of social welfare payments, with child benefit and the growth in the value of social welfare payments, playing a key role in reducing poverty levels up until 2009. The CSO have also shown that in 2009 poverty among those aged 65 plus reduced from 88 per cent to 9.6 per cent once social welfare payments were included. The same study also found that social welfare payments (including child benefit) reduced poverty among those under 18 years of age from 47.3 per cent to 18.6 per cent – a 60 per cent reduction in poverty risk (CSO, 2010:47).[7]

These findings, combined with the social welfare impact data in table 3.7, underscore the importance of social transfer payments in addressing poverty; a point that needs to be borne in mind as Government forms policy and priorities in the years to come.

**Table 3.7: The Role of Social Welfare (SW) Payments in Addressing Poverty**

|                 | 2001   | 2004   | 2007   | 2010   | 2013   | 2017   |
|-----------------|--------|--------|--------|--------|--------|--------|
| Poverty pre SW  | 35.6   | 39.8   | 40.9   | 50.2   | 49.5   | 43.8   |
| Poverty post SW | 21.9   | 19.4   | 16.5   | 14.7   | 16.2   | 15.7   |
| **The role of SW** | **-13.7** | **-20.4** | **-24.4** | **-35.5** | **-33.3** | **-28.1** |

**Source:** CSO SILC Reports (various years) using national equivalence scale.

---

[7] This data has not been updated in subsequent SILC publications.

Analysis in the accompanying Annex to this chapter (see table A3.1 and the subsequent text) shows that many of the groups in Irish society which experienced increases in poverty levels over the last decade have been dependent on social welfare payments. These include pensioners, the unemployed, lone parents and those who are ill or have a disability. Table 3.8 presents the results of an analysis of five key welfare recipient groups performed by the ESRI using poverty data for five of the years between 1994 and 2001. These were the years that the Irish economy grew fastest and the core years of the 'Celtic Tiger' boom. Between 1994 and 2001 all categories experienced large growth in their poverty risk. For example, in 1994 only five out of every 100 old age pension recipients were in poverty. In 2001 this had increased ten-fold to almost 50 out of every 100. The experience of widow's pension recipients is similar.

**Table 3.8: Percentage of Persons in Receipt of Welfare Benefits/Assistance Who Were Below the 60 Per Cent Median Income Poverty Line, 1994-2001**

|  | 1994 | 1997 | 1998 | 2000 | 2001 |
|---|---|---|---|---|---|
| Old age pension | 5.3 | 19.2 | 30.7 | 42.9 | 49.0 |
| Unemployment benefit/ assistance | 23.9 | 30.6 | 44.8 | 40.5 | 43.1 |
| Illness/disability | 10.4 | 25.4 | 38.5 | 48.4 | 49.4 |
| Lone Parents allowance | 25.8 | 38.4 | 36.9 | 42.7 | 39.7 |
| Widow's pension | 5.5 | 38.0 | 49.4 | 42.4 | 42.1 |

**Source:** Whelan et al (2003: 31).

Table 3.8 highlights the importance of adequate social welfare payments to prevent people becoming at risk of poverty. Over the period covered by these studies, groups similar to *Social Justice Ireland* repeatedly pointed out that these payments had failed to rise in proportion to earnings and incomes elsewhere in society. The primary consequence of this was that recipients slipped further and further back and therefore more and more fell into poverty. In 2019, as talk of wage increases and income tax cuts continues, it is important that adequate levels of social welfare be maintained to ensure that the mistakes of the past are not repeated. We outline our proposals to achieve this later in the chapter.

### The poverty gap

As part of the 2001 Laeken indicators, the EU asked all member countries to begin measuring their relative "at risk of poverty gap". This indicator assesses how far below the poverty line the income of the median (middle) person in poverty is. The size of that difference is calculated as a percentage of the poverty line and therefore represents the gap between the income of the middle person in poverty and the poverty line. The higher the percentage figure, the greater the poverty gap and the further people are falling beneath the poverty line. As there is a considerable difference between being 2 per cent and 20 per cent below the poverty line this insight is significant.

**Table 3.9: The Poverty Gap, 2003-2017**

|                  | 2003 | 2006 | 2009 | 2012 | 2014 | 2017 |
|------------------|------|------|------|------|------|------|
| Poverty gap size | 21.5 | 17.5 | 16.2 | 20.1 | 18.9 | 17.5 |

**Source:** CSO SILC Reports (various years).

The *SILC* results for 2017 show that the poverty gap was 17.5 per cent, compared to 20.1 per cent in 2012 and 16.2 per cent in 2009. Over time, the gap had decreased from a figure of 21.5 per cent in 2003. The 2017 poverty gap figure implies that 50 per cent of those in poverty had an equivalised income below 82.5 per cent of the poverty line. Watson and Maitre (2013:39) compared the size of the market income poverty gap over the years 2004, 2007 and 2011. Adjusting for changes in prices, they found that in 2011 terms the gap was €261 for households below the poverty line, an increase from a figure of €214 in 2004. They also found that after social transfers, those remaining below the poverty line were further from that threshold in 2011 than in 2004.

As the depth of poverty is an important issue, we will monitor closely the movement of this indicator in future editions of the *SILC*. It is crucial that, as part of Ireland's approach to addressing poverty, this figure further declines in the future.

### Poverty and deprivation
Income alone does not tell the whole story concerning living standards and command over resources. As we have seen in the NAPS definition of poverty, it is necessary to look more broadly at exclusion from society because of a lack of resources. This requires looking at other areas where 'as a result of inadequate income and resources people may be excluded and marginalised from participating in activities that are considered the norm for other people in society' (NAPS, 1997). Although income is the principal indicator used to assess wellbeing and ability to participate in society, there are other measures. In particular, these measures assess the standards of living people achieve by assessing deprivation through use of different indicators.

### *Deprivation in the SILC survey*
Since 2007 the CSO has presented 11 measures of deprivation in the *SILC* survey, compared to just eight before that. While this increase was welcome, *Social Justice Ireland* and others have expressed serious reservations about the overall range of measures employed. We believe that a whole new approach to measuring deprivation should be developed. Continuing to collect information on a limited number of static indicators is problematic in itself and does not present a true picture of the dynamic nature of Irish society. However, given these reservations, the trends are informative and offer some insight into the changes in income over recent years on households and living standards across the state.

The results presented in table 3.10 shows that in 2017 the rates of deprivation recorded across the set of 11 items varied between 1.6 and 20 per cent of the Irish population. Overall 68 per cent of the population were not deprived of any item, while 13.5 per cent were deprived of one item, 6 per cent were without two items and almost 13 per cent were without three or more items. Among those living on an income below the poverty line, more than four in ten (42.8 per cent) experienced deprivation of 2 or more items.

**Table 3.10: Levels of Deprivation For Eleven Items Among the Population And Those in Poverty, 2017 (%)**

| Deprivation Item | Total Population | Those in Poverty |
|---|---|---|
| Without heating at some stage in the past year | 8.1 | 22.5 |
| Unable to afford a morning, afternoon or evening out in the last fortnight | 13.2 | 31.0 |
| Unable to afford two pairs of strong shoes | 3.3 | 7.8 |
| Unable to afford a roast once a week | 5.3 | 11.7 |
| Unable to afford a meal with meat, chicken or fish every second day | 1.7 | 4.6 |
| Unable to afford new (not second-hand) clothes | 8.0 | 21.0 |
| Unable to afford a warm waterproof coat | 1.6 | 3.2 |
| Unable to afford to keep the home adequately warm | 4.4 | 13.1 |
| Unable to replace any worn out furniture | 20.4 | 43.3 |
| Unable to afford to have family or friends for a drink or meal once a month | 13.9 | 28.6 |
| Unable to afford to buy presents for family or friends at least once a year | 4.2 | 14.4 |

Source: CSO (2018).
Note: Poverty as measured using the 60 per cent median income poverty line.

It is of interest that from 2007 to 2013, as the economic crisis took hold, the proportion of the population which experienced no deprivation fell from 75.6 per cent in 2007 to 55.1 per cent in 2013. Since then this figure has increased. Simultaneously, the proportion of the population experiencing deprivation of two or more items (the deprivation rate) more than doubled – see Chart 3.1. By 2017 just over 900,000 people (18.8 per cent of the population) were experiencing deprivation at this level. Most notable have been increases in the numbers: going without heating at some stage in the year; unable to afford a morning, afternoon or evening out in the last fortnight; unable to buy new (not second hand) clothes; and unable to afford to have family or friends for a drink or meal once a month.

**Chart 3.1: Deprivation Rate, 2005-2017**

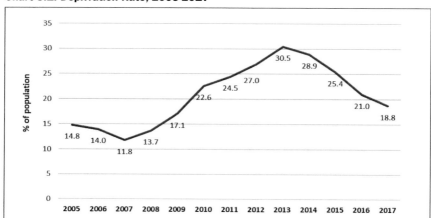

**Source:** CSO SILC Reports (various years).

*Deprivation and poverty combined: consistent poverty*
'Consistent poverty' combines deprivation and poverty into a single indicator. It does this by calculating the proportion of the population simultaneously experiencing poverty and registering as deprived of two or more of the items in table 3.10. As such, it captures a sub-group of those who are poor.

The *National Action Plan for Social Inclusion 2007-2016* (*NAPinclusion*) published in early 2007 set its overall poverty goal using this earlier consistent poverty measure. One of its aims was to reduce the number of people experiencing consistent poverty to between 2 per cent and 4 per cent of the total population by 2012, with a further aim of eliminating consistent poverty by 2016. A revision to this target was published as part of the Government's *National Reform Programme 2012 Update for Ireland* (2012). The revised poverty target was to reduce the numbers experiencing consistent poverty to 4 per cent by 2016 and to 2 per cent or less by 2020. *Social Justice Ireland* participated in the consultation process on the revision of this and other poverty targets. While we agree with the revised 2020 consistent poverty target (it is not possible to measure below this 2 per cent level using survey data) we proposed that this target should be accompanied by other targets focused on the overall population and vulnerable groups.[8] These proposals which remain relevant to considerations of any new National Action Plan are outlined at the end of this chapter.

---

8    See also Leahy et al (2012:61).

It should also be noted that, despite various Governments establishing and revising poverty targets on a number of occasions over the past decade, none of these have been achieved.

Using the combined poverty and deprivation measures, the 2017 *SILC* data indicates that 6.7 per cent of the population experience consistent poverty, an increase from 4.2 per cent in 2008 and 5.5 per cent in 2009 (CSO, 2018). In terms of the population, the 2017 figures suggest that approximately 325,000 people live in consistent poverty. The reality of the recent recession, the uneven nature of the subsequent recovery, and the limited sense of urgency to adequately address these issues, is pushing Ireland further away from these targets.

The Annex accompanying this chapter also examines the experience of people who are in food poverty, fuel poverty alongside an assessment of the research on minimum incomes standards in Ireland.

**Moving to Persistent Poverty**
*Social Justice Ireland* is committed to using the best and most up-to-date data in its ongoing socio-economic analysis of Ireland. We believe that to do so is crucial to the emergence of accurate evidence-based policy formation. It also assists in establishing appropriate and justifiable targeting of state resources.

As part of the EU structure of social indicators, Ireland agreed to produce an indicator of persistent poverty. This indicator measures the proportion of those living below the poverty line in the current year and for two of the three preceding years. It therefore identifies those who have experienced sustained exposure to poverty which is seen to harm their quality of life seriously and to increase levels of deprivation.

To date the Irish *SILC* survey has not produced any detailed results and breakdowns for this measure. We regret the unavailability of this data and note that there remain some sampling and technical issues impeding its annual publication. However, we note ongoing moves by the CSO to address this issue.

*Social Justice Ireland* believes that this data should be used as the primary basis for setting poverty targets and monitoring changes in poverty status. Existing measures of relative and consistent poverty should be maintained as secondary indicators. If there are impediments to the annual production of this indicator, they should be addressed and the SILC sample augmented if required. A measure of persistent poverty is long overdue and a crucial missing piece in society's knowledge of households and individuals on low income.

**Poverty: a European perspective**
It is helpful to compare Irish measures of poverty with those elsewhere in Europe. Eurostat, the European Statistics Agency, produces comparable 'at risk of poverty'

figures (proportions of the population living below the poverty line) for each EU member state. The data is calculated using the 60 per cent of median income poverty line in each country. Comparable EU-wide definitions of income and equivalence scale are used.[9] The latest data available for all member states is for the year 2017.

As table 3.11 shows, Irish people experience a below average risk of poverty when compared to all other EU member states. Eurostat's 2008 figures marked the first time Ireland's poverty levels fell below average EU levels. This phenomenon was driven, as outlined earlier in this review, by sustained increases in welfare payments in the years prior to 2008. Ireland's poverty levels have remained below average EU levels since then to 2017. In 2017, across the EU, the highest poverty levels were found in the recent accession countries and in some of the countries most impacted by the recent economic crisis - Romania, Bulgaria, Lithuania, Latvia, Spain, Estonia, Italy and Greece. The lowest levels were in Denmark, Slovakia, Finland and the Czech Republic.

**Table 3.11: The Risk of Poverty in the European Union, 2017**

| Country | Poverty Risk | Country | Poverty Risk |
|---|---|---|---|
| Romania | 23.6 | Belgium | 15.9 |
| Bulgaria | 23.4 | Sweden | 15.8 |
| Lithuania | 22.9 | Cyprus | 15.7 |
| Latvia | 22.1 | Poland | 15.0 |
| Spain | 21.6 | Austria | 14.4 |
| Estonia | 21.0 | Hungary | 13.4 |
| Italy | 20.3 | France | 13.3 |
| Greece | 20.2 | Slovenia | 13.3 |
| Croatia | 20.0 | Netherlands | 13.2 |
| Luxembourg | 18.7 | Denmark | 12.4 |
| Portugal | 18.3 | Slovakia | 12.4 |
| UK | 17.0 | Finland | 11.5 |
| Malta | 16.8 | Czech Rep | 9.1 |
| **IRELAND** | **16.6** | | |
| Germany | 16.1 | **EU-28 average** | **17.0** |

Source: Eurostat online database (ilc_li02).
Note: Data for Ireland is for 2016.

[9]   Differences in definitions of income and equivalence scales result in slight differences in the poverty rates reported for Ireland when compared to those reported earlier which have been calculated by the CSO using national definitions of income and the Irish equivalence scale.

The average risk of poverty in the EU-28 for 2017 was 17 per cent. Overall, while there have been some reductions in poverty in recent years across the EU, the data suggests that poverty remains a large and ongoing EU-wide problem. In 2017 the average EU-28 level implied that 85.3 million people live in poverty across the EU.

**Europe 2020 Strategy – Risk of Poverty or Social Exclusion**
As part of the Europe 2020 Strategy, European governments have adopted policies to target these poverty levels and are using as their main benchmark the proportion of the population at risk of poverty or social exclusion. One of the five headline targets for this strategy aims to lift at least 20 million people out of the risk or poverty or exclusion by 2020 (using 2008 as the baseline year).

The indicator has been defined by the European Council on the basis of three indicators: the aforementioned 'at risk of poverty' rate after social transfers; an index of material deprivation;[10] and the percentage of people living in households with very low work intensity.[11] It is calculated as the sum of persons relative to the national population who are at risk of poverty or severely materially deprived or living in households with very low work intensity, where a person is only counted once even if recorded in more than one indicator.[12]

**Table 3.12: People at Risk of Poverty or Social Exclusion in Ireland and the EU, 2008-2016**

|                      | 2008    | 2011    | 2014    | 2016    |
| -------------------- | ------- | ------- | ------- | ------- |
| Ireland % Population | 23.7    | 29.4    | 27.7    | 24.2    |
| Ireland 000s people  | 1,050   | 1,319   | 1,279   | 1,135   |
| EU % Population*     | 23.7    | 24.3    | 24.4    | 23.5    |
| EU 000s people*      | 116,070 | 120,858 | 122,026 | 118,040 |

**Source:** Eurostat online database.

**Note:** *EU data for 2008 is for the EU-27 and it is against this figure that the Europe 2020 target is set; all other EU data is for the EU-28 (including Croatia).

---

[10] Material deprivation covers indicators relating to economic strain and durables. Severely materially deprived persons have living conditions severely constrained by a lack of resources. They experience at least 4 out of 9 listed deprivations items (Eurostat 2012).
[11] People living in households with very low work intensity are those aged 0-59 living in households where the adults (aged 18-59) work less than 20% of their total work potential during the past year.
[12] See European Commission (2011) for a more detailed explanation of this indicator.

**Chart 3.2: Population at Risk of Poverty or Social Exclusion, Ireland 2016**

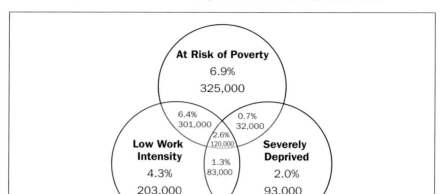

**Source:** Compiled from Eurostat online database (ilc_pees01).

Table 3.12 summarises the latest data on this indicator for Europe and chart 3.2 summarises the latest Irish data (which is for 2016). While *Social Justice Ireland* regrets that the Europe 2020 process shifted its indicator focus away from an exclusive concentration on the 'at risk of poverty' rate, we welcome the added attention at a European level to issues regarding poverty, deprivation and joblessness.

Since 2011 *Social Justice Ireland* has published an annual report analysing how Ireland is performing vis a vis the Europe 2020 goals.[13] What is clear is that the austerity measures and broader policy initiatives which have been pursued in many EU countries will result in the erosion of social services and lead to the further exclusion of people who already find themselves on the margins of society. This is in direct contradiction to the inclusive growth focus of the Europe 2020 Strategy. It is reflected in the figures in table 3.12 which show almost no progress since 2008. On the basis of EU-28 figures, the 2020 target is going to be very challenging to achieve.

### Income Distribution
As previously outlined, despite some improvements poverty remains a significant problem. The purpose of economic development should be to improve the living standards of all of the population. A further loss of social cohesion will mean that large numbers of people continue to experience deprivation and the gap between that cohort and the better-off will widen. This has implications for all of society,

---

[13]    See Leahy et al, 2012, Social Justice Ireland, 2015 & 2017.

not just those who are poor, a reality that has begun to receive welcome attention recently.

Analysis of the annual income and expenditure accounts yields information on trends in the distribution of national income. However, the limitations of this accounting system need to be acknowledged. Measures of income are far from perfect gauges of a society. They ignore many relevant non-market features, such as volunteerism, caring and environmental protection. Many environmental factors, such as the depletion of natural resources, are registered as income but not seen as a cost. Pollution is not registered as a cost but cleaning up after pollution is seen as income. Increased spending on prisons and security, which are a response to crime, are seen as increasing national income but not registered as reducing human well-being.

The point is that national accounts fail to include items that cannot easily be assigned a monetary value. But progress cannot be measured by economic growth alone. Many other factors are required, as we highlight elsewhere in this review.[14] However, when judging economic performance and making judgements about how well Ireland is really doing, it is important to look at the distribution of national income as well as its absolute amount.[15]

**Ireland's income distribution: latest data**
The most recent data on Ireland's income distribution, from the 2017 SILC survey, is summarised in chart 3.3. It examines the income distribution by household deciles starting with the 10 per cent of households with the lowest income (the bottom decile) up to the 10 per cent of households with the highest income (the top decile).

The data presented is equivalised meaning that it has been adjusted to reflect the number of adults and children in a household and to make it possible to compare across different household sizes and compositions. It measures disposable income which captures the amount of money available to spend after receipt of any employment/pension income, payment of all income taxes and receipt of any welfare entitlements.

In 2017, the top 10 per cent of the population received almost one quarter of the total income while the bottom decile received just 3.3 per cent. Collectively, the poorest 60 per cent of households received a very similar share (37.5 per cent) to the top 20 per cent (39.8 per cent). Overall the share of the top 10 per cent is more than 7 times the share of the bottom 10 per cent.

An NERI study by Collins provided a detailed insight into the nature of the underlying market or direct income distribution - that linked to earnings of all

---

[14] We return to critique National Income statistics in chapter 11. There, we also propose some alternatives.
[15] We examine the issue of the world's income and wealth distribution in chapter 13.

types. His research showed that the distribution of market income is concentrated on incomes of less than €50,000 per annum – representing 80 per cent of all earners. Some 15 per cent of all those with a market income, about 290,000 people, receive less than €5,000 (the average direct income for this group is €2,000 and most receive less than €1,000).

A further 50 per cent of those with a market income receive between €5,000 and €35,000. The top 10 per cent of earners have an income of more than €65,000 while the top 5 per cent have an income of more than €85,000; this group approximates to the top 100,000 earners in the state.

A conclusion of the study is that "the shape of that [earnings] distribution, and the prevalence of low income earners within it, points towards a need for greater consideration to be given to the underlying nature and distribution of market earnings" (Collins, 2017).

**Chart 3.3: Ireland's Income Distribution by 10% (decile) Group, 2017**

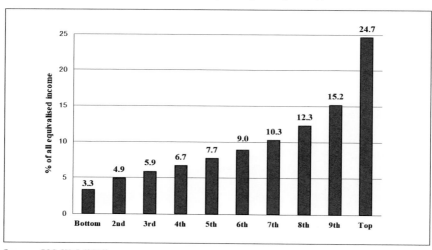

Source: CSO SILC (2018).

Income distribution data for the last few decades suggested that the overall structure of that distribution has been largely unchanged. One overall inequality measure, the Gini coefficient, ranges from 0 (no inequality) to 100 (maximum inequality) and has stood at approximately 30-32 for Ireland for some time. In 2017 it stood at 31.5.

Chart 3.4 compares the change in income between 2008 and 2017. 2008 represented the year when average incomes in Ireland peaked before the economic crash and 2017 is the year when average incomes recovered to exceed the 2008 peak. In between, incomes fell for all (2008-2011), but the impact of the recession and subsequent recovery (2012-current) has been felt in different ways by different people/households.

Over that period, the changes to the income shares received by deciles has been small; between + and -0.5 per cent. However, it is only the top three deciles that have recorded an increase in income share over the decade. The decline in the share of the bottom two deciles highlights the reality that if we wish to address and close these income divides, future Government policy must prioritise those at the bottom of the income distribution. Otherwise, these divides will persist for further generations and perhaps widen. A further examination of income distribution over the period 1987-2017 is provided in the annex.

**Chart 3.4: Change in Decile Shares of Equivalised Disposable Income, 2008-2017**

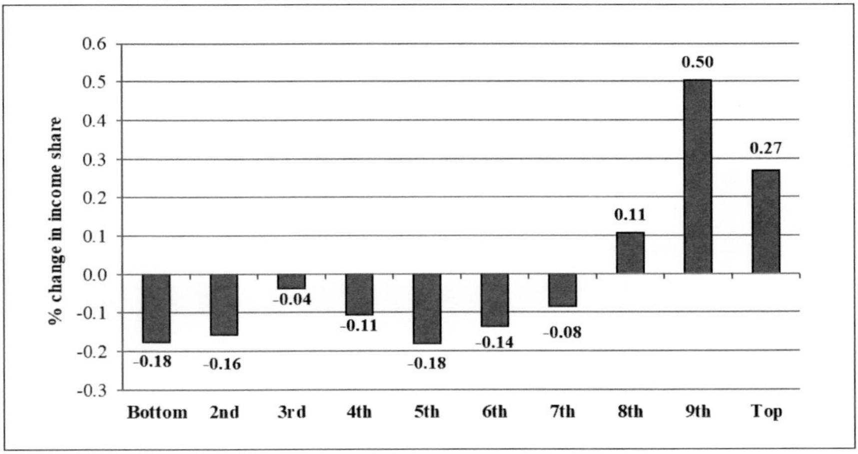

**Source:** Calculated from CSO SILC Reports (various years).

### Income distribution: a European perspective

Another of the indicators adopted by the EU at Laeken assesses the income distribution of member states by comparing the ratio of equivalised disposable income received by the bottom quintile (20 per cent) to that of the top quintile. This indicator reveals how far away from each other the shares of these two groups are – the higher the ratio, the greater the income difference. Table 3.13 presents the most up-to-date results of this indicator for the 28 EU states. The data indicate that the Irish figure increased to 4.4 from a ratio of 4.2 in 2009, reflecting the already noted shifts in the income distribution since then. Ireland now has a ratio below the EU average but, given recent economic and budgetary policy, it seems likely that this divide will widen in the years ahead. Overall, the greatest differences in the shares of those at the top and bottom of income distribution are found in many of the newer and poorer member states. However, some EU-15 members, including the Spain, Greece, Italy and Portugal also record large differences.

**Table 3.13: Ratio of Disposable Income Received by Bottom Quintile to That of the Top Quintile in the EU-28, 2017**

| Country | Ratio | Country | Ratio |
|---|---|---|---|
| Bulgaria | 8.2 | **IRELAND** | **4.4** |
| Lithuania | 7.3 | France | 4.4 |
| Spain | 6.6 | Hungary | 4.3 |
| Romania | 6.5 | Austria | 4.3 |
| Latvia | 6.3 | Sweden | 4.3 |
| Greece | 6.1 | Malta | 4.2 |
| Italy | 5.9 | Denmark | 4.1 |
| Portugal | 5.7 | Netherlands | 4.0 |
| Estonia | 5.4 | Belgium | 3.8 |
| UK | 5.4 | Slovakia | 3.5 |
| Croatia | 5.0 | Finland | 3.5 |
| Luxembourg | 5.0 | Czech Rep | 3.4 |
| Cyprus | 4.6 | Slovenia | 3.4 |
| Poland | 4.6 | | |
| Germany | 4.5 | **EU-28 average** | **5.1** |

**Source:** Eurostat online database (ilc_di11).
**Note:** Data for Ireland is for 2016.

A further measure of income inequality is the Gini coefficient, which ranges from 0 to 100 and summarises the degree of inequality across the entire income distribution (rather than just at the top and bottom).[16] The higher the Gini coefficient score the greater the degree of income inequality in a society. As table 3.14 shows, over time income inequality has been reasonably static in the EU as a whole, although within the EU there are notable differences. Countries such as Ireland cluster around the average EU score and differ from other high-income EU member states which record lower levels of inequality. As the table shows, the degree of inequality is at a notably lower scale in countries like Finland, Sweden and the Netherlands. For Ireland, the key point is that despite the aforementioned role of the social transfer system, the underlying degree of direct income inequality (see earlier) dictates that our income distribution remains much more unequal than in many of the EU countries we wish to emulate in terms of economic and social development.

---

[16] See Collins and Kavanagh (2006: 159-160) who provide a more detailed explanation of this measure.

**Table 3.14: Gini Coefficient Measure of Income Inequality for Selected EU States, 2005-2017**

|  | 2005 | 2008 | 2011 | 2013 | 2016 | 2017 |
|---|---|---|---|---|---|---|
| EU-27/28 | 30.6 | 31.0 | 30.8 | 30.5 | 30.8 | 30.7 |
| IRELAND | 31.9 | 29.9 | 29.8 | 30.7 | 29.5 | n/a |
| UK | 34.6 | 33.9 | 33.0 | 30.2 | 31.5 | 33.1 |
| France | 27.7 | 29.8 | 30.8 | 30.1 | 29.3 | 29.3 |
| Germany | 26.1 | 30.2 | 29.0 | 29.7 | 29.5 | 29.1 |
| Sweden | 23.4 | 25.1 | 26.0 | 26.0 | 27.6 | 28.0 |
| Finland | 26.0 | 26.3 | 25.8 | 25.4 | 25.4 | 25.3 |
| Netherlands | 26.9 | 27.6 | 25.8 | 25.1 | 26.9 | 27.1 |

**Source:** Eurostat online database (ilc_di12).

**Notes:** The Gini coefficient ranges from 0-100 with a higher score indicating a higher level of inequality. EU data for 2005-2009 is for the EU-27, 2010 onwards data are for the EU-28 (including Croatia). The 2017 Eurostat measures for Ireland is not available.

**Income Distribution and Recent Budgets**

Budget 2019 marked the third Budget of the current Government. It was a Budget that *Social Justice Ireland* described as failing *'to make any notable impact on Ireland's entrenched inequalities and failing to tackle any of the major challenges the country currently faces'*. In this subsection, we first review the distributive impact of Budget 2019 before presenting the results of our analysis of the cumulative impact changes to income taxation and welfare since 2017.

*Impact of Budget 2019*

When assessing the change in people's incomes following any Budget, it is important that tax changes be included as well as changes to basic social welfare payments. In our calculations, we have not included any changes to other welfare allowances and secondary benefits as these payments do not flow to all households. Similarly, we have not included changes to other taxes (including indirect taxes and property taxes) as these are also experienced differently by households. Wage increases, including those for the statutory minimum wage, are also excluded as the nature and value of these changes will differ across earners. Chart 3.5 sets out the direct implications of the Budget tax and welfare announcements on various household groupings in 2019.

Single people who are unemployed will benefit from the weekly increase from March and the Christmas bonus which equates to €5.10 a week (€265 a year). Those on €25,000 a year will see an increase of €0.51 a week (€27 a year) in their take-home pay while those on €50,000 will be €4.58 a week (€239 a year) better off and those on €75,000 a year will be €5.54 a week (€289 a year) better-off.

Couples with one income on €25,000 a year will be €0.51 a week (€27 a year) better-off while those on €50,000 will be €4.58 a week (€239 a year) better off. Couples with two incomes on €25,000 a year will not be better off in 2019 versus 2018 while those on €50,000 will be €0.87 a week (€45 a year) better-off in 2019 compared to 2018.

**Chart 3.5: Impact of Income Tax and Welfare Payment Changes from Budget 2019**

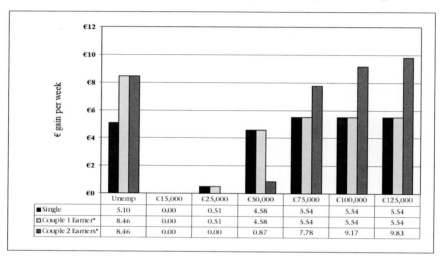

| | Unemp | €15,000 | €25,000 | €50,000 | €75,000 | €100,000 | €125,000 |
|---|---|---|---|---|---|---|---|
| ■ Single | 5.10 | 0.00 | 0.51 | 4.58 | 5.54 | 5.54 | 5.54 |
| ▢ Couple 1 Earner* | 8.46 | 0.00 | 0.51 | 4.58 | 5.54 | 5.54 | 5.54 |
| ■ Couple 2 Earners* | 8.46 | 0.00 | 0.00 | 0.87 | 7.78 | 9.17 | 9.83 |

**Source:** Social Justice Ireland (2018:6).
**Notes:** * Except in case of the unemployed where there is no earner. Unemployed aged 26 years and over. All other earners have PAYE income. Increase is annual average increase. Couple with 2 earners are assumed to have a 65%/35% income division.

### *Impact of Tax and Benefit Changes on Families, 2017-2019*

Over the past few years *Social Justice Ireland* has developed its ability to track the distributive impact of annual Budget's on households across Irish society. Our analysis tracks changes from year to year (pre and post a Budget) and across a number of recent years (the lifetime of a Government etc).[17]

Following Budget 2019, we assess the cumulative impact of changes to taxation and welfare over the three Budgets of the current Government (Budgets 2017, 2018 and 2019). As different policy priorities can be articulated for each Budget, it is useful to being together the cumulative effect of policy changes on various household types.

---

[17] A document on our website entitled *'Tracking the Distributive Effects of Budget 2019'* provides a more detailed overview of the approach taken by *Social Justice Ireland* to generate these results.

Social Justice Matters 2019

The households we examine are spread across all areas of society and capture those with a job, families with children, those unemployed and pensioner households. Within those households that have income from a job, we include workers on the minimum wage, on the living wage, workers on average earnings and multiples of this benchmark, and families with incomes ranging from €25,000 to €200,000.

In the case of working households, the analysis is focused on PAYE earners only and therefore does not capture the changes in recent Budgets that were targeted at the self-employed.

At the outset it is important to stress that our analysis does not take account of other budgetary changes, most particularly to indirect taxes (VAT and excises), other charges (such as prescription charges) and property taxes. Similarly, it does not capture the impact of changes to the provision of public services. As the impact of these measures differs between households it is impossible to quantify precise household impacts and include them here. However, as we have demonstrated in previous publications, these changes impact greatest upon those living on the lowest incomes in Irish society.

**Chart 3.6: Cumulative Impact on Households with Jobs, 2017-2019**

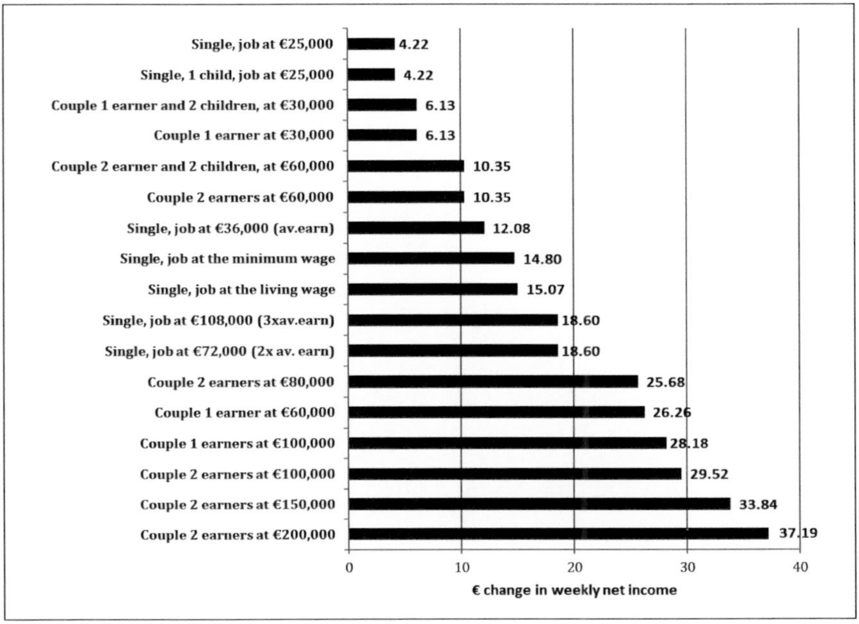

| Household | € change in weekly net income |
|---|---|
| Single, job at €25,000 | 4.22 |
| Single, 1 child, job at €25,000 | 4.22 |
| Couple 1 earner and 2 children, at €30,000 | 6.13 |
| Couple 1 earner at €30,000 | 6.13 |
| Couple 2 earner and 2 children, at €60,000 | 10.35 |
| Couple 2 earners at €60,000 | 10.35 |
| Single, job at €36,000 (av.earn) | 12.08 |
| Single, job at the minimum wage | 14.80 |
| Single, job at the living wage | 15.07 |
| Single, job at €108,000 (3xav.earn) | 18.60 |
| Single, job at €72,000 (2x av. earn) | 18.60 |
| Couple 2 earners at €80,000 | 25.68 |
| Couple 1 earner at €60,000 | 26.26 |
| Couple 1 earners at €100,000 | 28.18 |
| Couple 2 earners at €100,000 | 29.52 |
| Couple 2 earners at €150,000 | 33.84 |
| Couple 2 earners at €200,000 | 37.19 |

**Source:** *Social Justice Ireland* Income Distribution Model.

## Chart 3.7: Cumulative Impact on Welfare Dependent Households, 2017-2019

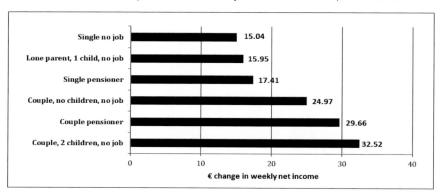

Source: *Social Justice Ireland* Income Distribution Model.

Over the years examined (2017-2019) all household types recorded increases in their disposable income (after taxes and welfare payments). Among households with jobs (see chart 3.6), the net income gains experienced range from €4.22 per week (for a single worker on €25,000) to almost nine times as much, €37.19 per week, for a couple with two earners and an income of €200,000. Overall, across these households the main gains have flowed to those on the highest incomes.

Among households dependent on welfare, the gains have ranged from €15.04 per week (to single unemployed individuals) to €32.52 per week to unemployed couples with two children - see chart 3.7.

Our analysis points towards the choices and priorities the current Government has made. Overall these choices have given least to single welfare dependent households and those on the lowest earnings. These outcomes that will be reflected in future income distribution data and are likely to lead to further increases in Ireland recorded levels of income inequality.

### Ireland's Wealth Distribution
While data on income and poverty levels has improved dramatically over the past 15 years, a persistent gap has been our knowledge of levels of wealth in Irish society. Data on wealth is important, as it provides a further insight into the distribution of resources and an insight into some of the underlying structural components of inequality.

A welcome development in early 2015 was the publication by the CSO of the first Household Finance and Consumption Survey (HFCS). The HFCS is part of a European initiative to improve countries knowledge of the socio-economic and financial situations of households across the EU. For the first time, its results offer robust information on the types and levels of wealth that households in Ireland possess. The data was collected for 2013 across 5,545 households.

The result of the survey showed that the level of household net wealth in Ireland amounts to €364 billion. The CSO's net wealth measure includes the value of all assets (housing, land, investments, valuables, savings and private pensions) and removes any borrowings (mortgages, loans, credit card debt etc) to give the most informative picture of households' wealth. On average the results imply that Irish households have a net wealth of approximately €220,000 each. However, as table 3.15 shows, averages are very misleading for wealth data, as they are skewed upwards by high wealth households. Looking closer at the data, the CSO illustrates that the bottom 50 per cent of households have a net wealth of less than €105,000.

Chart 3.8 presents the distribution of net wealth across the income distribution – the CSO has only presented data for quintiles (20 per cent groups). The HFCS results show that those in the top 20 per cent of the income distribution possess 39.7 per cent of all the wealth – this is the same share as those in the bottom 60 per cent of the income distribution. Across the various household types that the CSO examined, those with the lowest wealth were single parents, the unemployed and those under 35 years.

**Chart 3.8: Distribution of Net Wealth by Gross Income Quintile, 2013**

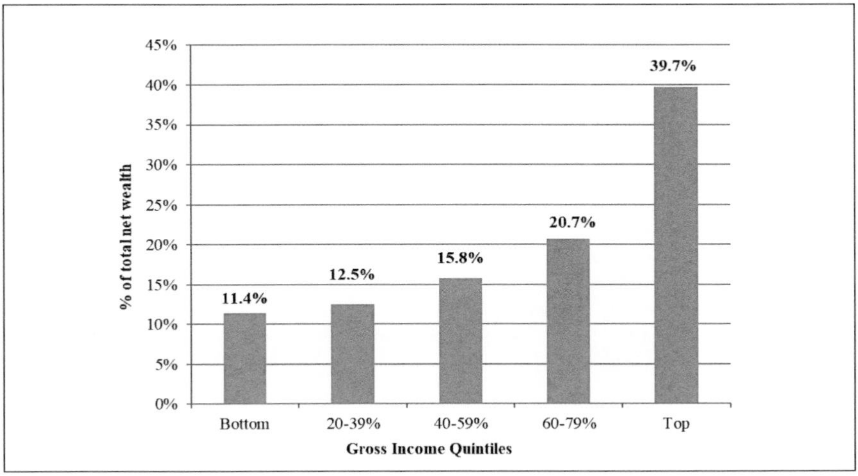

Source: CSO HFCS (2014: 40).

A study by TASC (Staunton, 2015) provided a further insight into this data, in particular giving details on the distribution of wealth across households given their wealth status. Chart 3.9 presents these results. It shows the dramatic concentration of wealth at the top of the distribution. Overall, the bottom 30 per cent of the distribution have either no wealth or are in negative wealth (more debts than assets). At the top, the top 10 per cent hold 54 per cent of all the wealth in Ireland. Within the top decile the TASC study found further divides with the top 5 per cent possessing 38 per cent of the wealth and within this, the top one per cent holding almost 15 per cent.

**Chart 3.9: Distribution of Net Wealth by Net Wealth Decile, 2013**

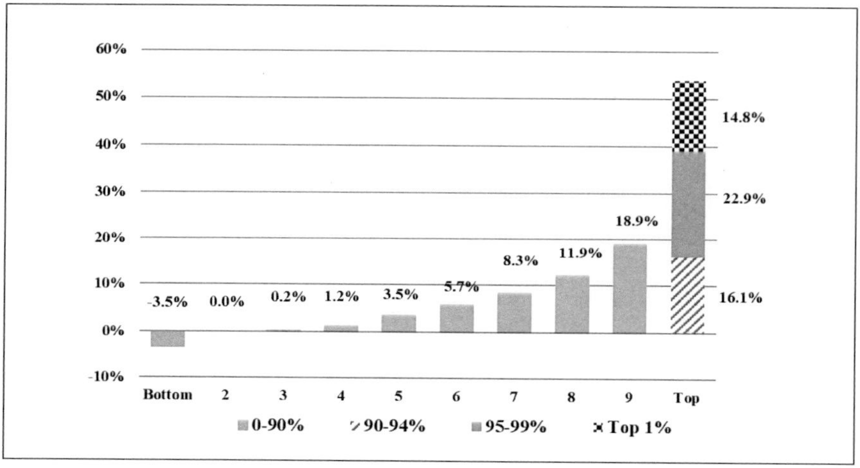

Source: Staunton (2015: 9).

The TASC report also provided details on the levels of wealth by household type and its distribution across the age groups. Table 3.15 summarises these findings. Across society as a whole, wealth increases with age. However, reflecting the data in Chart 3.9, there are large differences between and within household types.

**Table 3.15: Net Wealth in Ireland by Household Type and Age Group, 2013**

| Household Type € | | | Age Group % | |
|---|---|---|---|---|
| | Mean | Median | Under 35 yrs | 4% |
| Single adult | €153,400 | €80,500 | 35-44 yrs | 13% |
| Couple | €255,200 | €144,800 | 45-54 yrs | 25% |
| Couples with children | €144,000 | €33,100 | 55-64yrs | 26% |
| Single Parent | €30,600 | €1,400 | 65+ | 33% |
| All | €218,700 | €102,600 | Total | 100% |

Source: Staunton (2015: 19, 26).

The composition and distribution of wealth points towards policy issues to be considered, concerning inheritance taxes (capital acquisitions tax), gift taxes and capital gains taxes – some of which are addressed in the next chapter. The arrival of this new data also allows, for the first time, an opportunity for informed consideration of policy options around wealth, as well as income inequality. As further analysis of this data, and new editions emerge, *Social Justice Ireland* looks forward to contributing to that debate.

## 3.2 Key Policies and Reforms

*Paying a Living Wage*
During the past few years *Social Justice Ireland* and a number of other organisations came together to form a technical group which researched and developed a Living Wage for Ireland. In July 2014 the group launched a website (www.livingwage.ie) and a technical paper outlining how the concept is calculated. The latest update to the figure was published in July 2018 and reported a Living Wage rate of €11.90 per hour.

**What is a Living Wage?**
The establishment of a Living Wage Rate for Ireland adds to a growing international set of similar figures which reflect a belief across societies that individuals working full-time should be able to earn enough income to enjoy a decent standard of living. The Living Wage is a wage which makes possible a minimum acceptable standard of living. Its calculation is evidence based and built on budget standards research which is grounded in social consensus. The figure is:

- based on the concept that work should provide an adequate income to enable individuals to afford a socially acceptable standard of living;

- the average gross salary which will enable full time employed adults (without dependents) across Ireland to afford a socially acceptable standard of living;

- a living wage which provides for needs not wants;

- an evidence based rate of pay which is grounded in social consensus and is derived from Consensual Budget Standards research which establishes the cost of a Minimum Essential Standard of Living in Ireland;

- unlike the National Minimum Wage which is not based on the cost of living.

In principle, a living wage is intended to establish an hourly wage rate that should provide employees with sufficient income to achieve an agreed acceptable minimum standard of living. In that sense it is an income floor; representing a figure which allows employees to afford the essentials of life. Earnings below the living wage suggest employees are forced to do without certain essentials so they can make ends meet.

### How is the Living Wage Calculated?

The Living Wage for Ireland is calculated on the basis of the Minimum Essential Standard of Living research in Ireland, conducted by the Vincentian Partnership for Social Justice (VPSJ). This research establishes a consensus on what members of the public believe is a minimum standard that no individual or household should live below.

The Living Wage Technical Group decided to focus the calculation of a Living Wage for the Republic of Ireland on a single-adult household. In its examination of the methodological options for calculating a robust annual measure, the group concluded that a focus on a single-adult household was the most practical approach. However, in recognition of the fact that households with children experience additional costs which are relevant to any consideration of such households standards of living, the group has also published estimates of a Family Living Income each year.[18]

The calculations established a Living Wage for the country as a whole, with costs examined in four regions: Dublin, other Cities, Towns with a population above 5,000, and the rest of Ireland. The expenditure required varied across these regions and reflecting this so too did the annual gross income required to meet this expenditure. To produce a single national rate, the results of the gross income calculation for the four regions were averaged; with each regional rate being weighted in proportion to the population in the labour force in that region. The weighted annual gross income is then divided by the number of weeks in the year (52.14) and the number of working hours in the week (39) to give an hourly wage. Where necessary, this figure is rounded up or down to the nearest five cent.[19] The Technical Group plans to update this number on an annual basis.

### The Merits of a Living Wage

*Social Justice Ireland* believes that concepts such as the Living Wage have an important role to play in addressing the persistent income inequality and poverty levels outlined earlier in this chapter. As shown in tables 3.4 to 3.6, there are many adults living in poverty despite having a job – the working poor. Improvements in the low pay rates received by many employees offers an important method by which levels of poverty and exclusion can be reduced. Paying low paid employees a Living Wage offers the prospect of significantly benefiting the living standards of these employees and we hope to see this new benchmark adopted across many sectors of society in the years to come.

---

[18]  See Living Wage Technical Group (2018:4).

[19]  A more detailed account of the methodology used to calculate the Living Wage has been published by the Living Wage Technical Group and is available at www. livingwage.ie

## Maintaining an Adequate Level of Social Welfare

Budget 2019 delivered a welcome increase to the minimum social welfare payment. From March 2019 onwards it increased by €5 per week (to €203) complementing similar increases in Budgets 2017 and 2018. The Budget 2017 increase was the first increase to these payments since 2011.

As outlined earlier, a lesson from past experiences of economic recovery and growth is that the weakest in our society get left behind unless welfare increases keep track with increases elsewhere in the economy. Benchmarking minimum rates of social welfare payments to movements in average earnings is therefore an important policy priority.

Just over a decade ago Budget 2007 benchmarked the minimum social welfare rate at 30 per cent of Gross Average Industrial Earnings (GAIE). This was a key achievement and one that we correctly predicted would lead to reductions in poverty rates, complementing those already achieved and detailed earlier.[20] Since then the CSO discontinued its *Industrial Earnings and Hours Worked* dataset and replaced it with a more comprehensive set of income statistics for a broader set of Irish employment sectors. A subsequent report for *Social Justice Ireland* found that 30 per cent of GAIE is equivalent to 27.5 per cent of the new average earnings data being collected by the CSO (Collins, 2011). A figure of 27.5 per cent of average earnings is therefore the appropriate benchmark for minimum social welfare payments and reflects a continuation of the previous benchmark using the current CSO earnings dataset.

Table 3.16 applies this benchmark using CSO data for 2017. The data is updated using ESRI projections for wage growth in 2018 (2.6 per cent) and 2019 (2.9 per cent). In 2019 the updated value of 27.5 per cent of average weekly earnings equals €210.13 implying a shortfall of €7 between the minimum social welfare rates being paid from March 2019 (€203) and this threshold.

Given the importance of this benchmark to the living standards of many in Irish society, and its relevance to anti-poverty commitments, the current deficit highlights a need for Budget 2020 to further increase minimum social welfare rates to ensure that they are equivalent to 27.5 per cent of average weekly earnings. We will develop this proposal further in our pre-Budget submission, *Budget Choices*, in mid-2019.

---

[20] Annex 3 outlines how this significant development occurred.

**Table 3.16: Benchmarking Social Welfare Payments for 2019 (€)**

| Year | Average Weekly Earnings | 27.5% of Average Weekly Earnings |
|------|-------------------------|----------------------------------|
| 2017* | 723.76 | 199.03 |
| 2018** | 742.58 | 204.21 |
| 2019** | 764.12 | 210.13 |

Notes: * actual data from CSO average earnings.
       ** simulated value based on CSO data and ESRI QEC wage growth projections.

### Individualising social welfare payments

The issue of individualising payments so that all recipients receive their own social welfare payments has been on the policy agenda in Ireland and across the EU for several years. *Social Justice Ireland* welcomed the report of the Working Group, *Examining the Treatment of Married, Cohabiting and One-Parent Families under the Tax and Social Welfare Codes*, which addressed some of these individualisation issues.

At present the welfare system provides a basic payment for a claimant, whether that be, for example, for a pension, a disability payment or a jobseeker's payment. It then adds an additional payment of about two-thirds of the basic payment for the second person. For example, following Budget 2019, a couple on the lowest social welfare rate receives a payment of €337.40 per week. This amount is approximately 1.66 times the payment for a single person (€203). Were these two people living separately they would receive €203 each; giving a total of €406. Thus by living as a household unit such a couple receive a lower income than they would were they to live apart.

*Social Justice Ireland* believes that this system is unfair and inequitable. We also believe that the system as currently structured is not compatible with the Equal Status Acts. People, more often than not, women, are disadvantaged by living as part of a household unit because they receive a lower income. We believe that where a couple is in receipt of welfare payments, the payment to the second person should be increased to equal that of the first. Such a change would remove the current inequity and bring the current social welfare system in line with the terms of the Equal Status Acts (2000-2015). An effective way of doing this would be to introduce a basic income system (see next subsection) which is far more appropriate for the world of the 21st century.

### Introducing a Basic Income

Over the past two decades major progress has been achieved in building the case for the introduction of a basic income in Ireland. This includes the publication of a *Green Paper on Basic Income* by the Government in September 2002 and the publication of a book by Clark entitled *The Basic Income Guarantee* (2002). A major international conference on basic income was held in Dublin during Summer 2008 at which more than 70 papers from 30 countries were presented. More recently,

*Social Justice Ireland* hosted a conference and published a book on basic income (*Basic Income: Radical Utopia or Practical Solution?*), new European and Irish Basic Income networks have emerged and the concept of a Basic Income has moved to become one commonly discussed and considered in public policy contexts.[21] Recent results from the European Social Survey suggest that 58 per cent of the Irish population are in favour of the introduction of a Basic Income.

## The case for a basic income

*Social Justice Ireland* has consistently argued that the present tax and social welfare systems should be integrated and reformed to make them more appropriate to the changing world of the 21st century. To this end we have sought the introduction of a basic income system. This proposal is especially relevant at the present moment of economic upheaval.

A basic income is an income that is unconditionally granted to every person on an individual basis, without any means test or work requirement. In a basic income system every person receives a weekly tax-free payment from the Exchequer while all other personal income is taxed, usually at a single rate. The basic-income payment would replace income from social welfare for a person who is unemployed and replace tax credits for a person who is employed.

Basic income is a form of minimum income guarantee that avoids many of the negative side-effects inherent in social welfare payments. A basic income differs from other forms of income support in that:

• It is paid to individuals rather than households;

• It is paid irrespective of any income from other sources;

• It is paid without conditions; it does not require the performance of any work or the willingness to accept a job if offered one; and

• It is always tax free.

There is real danger that the plight of large numbers of people excluded from the benefits of the modern economy will be ignored. Images of rising tides lifting all boats are often offered as government's policy makers and commentators assure society that prosperity for all is just around the corner. Likewise, the claim is often made that a job is the best poverty fighter and consequently priority must be given to securing a paid job for everyone. These images and claims are no substitute for concrete policies to ensure that all members of society are included. Twenty-first century society needs a radical approach to ensure the inclusion of all people in the benefits of present economic growth and development. Basic income is such an approach.

---

[21]  These networks are the European Citizens' Initiative for Unconditional Basic Income and Basic Income Ireland.

As we are proposing it, a basic income system would replace most social welfare payments and income tax credits. It could be set at a level that would guarantee an income above the poverty line for everyone. It would not be means tested. There would be no 'signing on' and no restrictions or conditions. In practice, a basic income recognises the right of every person to a share of the resources of society.

The basic income system ensures that looking for a paid job and earning an income, or increasing one's income while in employment, is always worth pursuing, because for every euro earned the person will retain a large part. It thus removes poverty traps and unemployment traps in the present system. Furthermore, women and men would receive equal payments in a basic income system. Consequently, the basic income system promotes gender equality because it treats every person equally.

It is a system that is altogether more secure, rewarding, simple and transparent than the present tax and welfare systems. It is far more employment friendly than the present system. It also respects other forms of work besides paid employment. This is crucial in a world where these benefits need to be recognised and respected. It is also very important in a world where paid employment cannot be permanently guaranteed for everyone seeking it. There is growing pressure and need in Irish society to ensure recognition and monetary reward for unpaid work. Basic income is a transparent, efficient and affordable mechanism for ensuring such recognition and reward.

Basic income also lifts people out of poverty and the dependency mode of survival. In doing this, it restores self-esteem and broadens horizons. Poor people, however, are not the only ones who should welcome a basic income system. Employers, for example, should welcome it because its introduction would mean they would not be in competition with the social welfare system. Since employees would not lose their basic income when taking a job, there would always be an incentive to take up employment. Healy and Reynolds (2016: 22-26) address, and refute, a number of other objections raised against the basic income proposal.

### Costing a basic income

During 2016 Murphy and Ward presented an estimate for the cost of a basic income for Ireland. Using administrative data from the Census, social protection system and taxation system, the paper estimated a cost where payments were structured as follows: children = €31.05 per week; adults of working age = €150.00 per week; older people aged 66-79 = €230.30 per week; and older people aged 80+ = €240.30 per week). The paper estimated a total cost of €31.3 billion per annum for a basic income and outlined a requirement to collect a total of €41.3 billion in revenue (tax and social insurance) to fund a basic income plus the retention of other existing targeted welfare supports. It is proposed that the revenue should be raised via a flat 40 per cent personal income tax and a increase in employers PRSI contributions, from 10.75 per cent to 13.5 per cent. It is important to remember that no individual would have an effective tax rate of 40 per cent in this system as they would always receive their full basic income and it would always be tax-free. For example, a single earner on €60,000 would face a net tax rate (after receiving their basic income payment) of 27 per cent (Murphy and Ward, 2016: 132).

Overall the paper offers an affordable and sustainable structure for implementing a basic income system in Ireland.

### Arguing for a basic income

For many decades, the European social model has been offering its citizens a future that it has obviously failed to deliver. Despite strong rhetoric to the contrary, economic issues, targets and outcomes are constantly prioritised over social issues. As a result, poverty, unemployment and social exclusion have been growing. It is time to recognise that current policy approaches are not working and that an alternative is required.

A Basic Income system has the capacity to be the cornerstone of a new paradigm that would be simple and clear, that would support people, families and communities, that would have the capacity to adapt to rapid technological change in a fair manner, that would enable all people to develop their creativity and could do all of this in a sustainable manner.

The introduction of a Basic Income system would be a radical step towards a desirable future where nobody would be excluded. It would also provide a practical solution to several of the major challenges faced by our societies today if they wish to ensure that every man, woman and child has sufficient income to live life with dignity, has access to meaningful work and can genuinely participate in shaping the world around them and the decisions that impact on them.

The following are ten reasons to introduce a basic income:

- It is work and employment friendly.
- It eliminates poverty traps and unemployment traps.
- It promotes equity and ensures that everyone receives at least the poverty threshold level of income.
- It spreads the burden of taxation more equitably.
- It treats men and women equally.
- It is simple and transparent.
- It is efficient in labour-market terms.
- It rewards types of work in the social economy that the market economy often ignores, e.g. home duties, caring, etc.
- It facilitates further education and training in the labour force.
- It faces up to the changes in the global economy.

## 3.3 Key Policy Priorities

*Social Justice Ireland* believes that the following policy positions should be adopted in responding to the poverty, inequality and income distribution challenges highlighted throughout this chapter.

- If poverty rates are to fall in the years ahead, *Social Justice Ireland* believes that the following are required:

    - increase in social welfare payments.
    - equity of social welfare rates.
    - adequate payments for children.
    - refundable tax credits.
    - decent rates of pay for low paid workers.
    - a universal state pension.
    - a cost of disability payment.

*Social Justice Ireland* believes that in the period ahead Government and policy-makers generally should:

- Acknowledge that Ireland has an on-going poverty problem.

- Adopt targets aimed at reducing poverty among particular vulnerable groups such as children, lone parents, jobless households and those in social rented housing.

- Examine and support viable, alternative policy options aimed at giving priority to protecting vulnerable sectors of society.

- Carry out in-depth social impact assessments prior to implementing proposed policy initiatives that impact on the income and public services that many low income households depend on. This should include the poverty-proofing of all public policy initiatives.

- Provide substantial new measures to address long-term unemployment. This should include programmes aimed at re-training and re-skilling those at highest risk.

- Recognise the problem of the 'working poor'. Make tax credits refundable to address the situation of households in poverty which are headed by a person with a job.

- Support the widespread adoption of the Living Wage so that low paid workers receive an adequate income and can afford a minimum, but decent, standard of living.

- Introduce a cost of disability allowance to address the poverty and social exclusion of people with a disability.

- Recognise the reality of poverty among migrants and adopt policies to assist this group. In addressing this issue also replace direct provision with a fairer system that ensures adequate allowances are paid to asylum seekers.

- Accept that persistent poverty should be used as the primary indicator of poverty measurement and assist the CSO in allocating sufficient resources to collect this data.

- Move towards introducing a basic income system. No other approach has the capacity to ensure all members of society have sufficient income to live life with dignity.

# REFERENCES

Central Statistics Office (2015) *Household Finance and Consumption Survey, 2013,* Dublin: Stationery Office.

Central Statistics Office (2018) *Survey on Income and Living Conditions 2017,* Dublin: Stationery Office.

Central Statistics Office (various) *Survey on Income and Living Conditions Results.* Dublin: Stationery Office.

Clark C.M.A. (2002) *The Basic Income Guarantee: ensuring progress and prosperity in the 21st century.* Dublin: Liffey Press and CORI Justice Commission.

Collins, M.L. (2006) "Poverty: Measurement, Trends and Future Directions", in Healy, S., B. Reynolds and M.L. Collins, *Social Policy in Ireland: Principles, Practice and Problems.* Dublin: Liffey Press.

Collins, M.L. (2011) *Establishing a Benchmark for Ireland's Social Welfare Payments.* Paper for Social Justice Ireland. Dublin: Social Justice Ireland.

Collins, M.L. (2017) 'Earnings and Low Pay in the Republic of Ireland'. *Journal of the Statistical and Social Inquiry Society of Ireland, Vol. XLV pp. 146-176.*

Collins, M.L. and Kavanagh, C. (2006) "The Changing Patterns of Income Distribution and Inequality in Ireland, 1973-2004", in Healy, S., B. Reynolds and M.L. Collins, *Social Policy in Ireland: Principles, Practice and Problems.* Dublin: Liffey Press.

Department of An Taoiseach (2002) *Basic Income, A Green Paper.* Dublin: Stationery Office.

Department of Finance (2018) *Budget 2019.* Dublin: Stationery Office.

European Commission (2011) *The Social Dimension of the Europe 2020 Strategy A report of the Social Protection Committee.* Luxembourg: Publications Office of the European Union.

Eurostat (2012) *Europe 2020 Strategy – towards a smarter, greener and more inclusive EU economy?* Luxembourg: Eurostat.

Government of Ireland (1997) *National Anti-Poverty Strategy: Sharing in Progress.* Dublin: Stationery Office.

Government of Ireland (2007) *National Action Plan for Social Inclusion 2007-2016.* Dublin: Stationery Office.

Government of Ireland (2012) *Ireland's National Reform Programme 2012 – Update.* Dublin: Stationery Office.

Healy, S. and B. Reynolds (2016) 'Basic Income: Radical Utopia or Practical Solution?' in Social Justice Ireland, *Basic Income: Radical Utopia or Practical Solution?* Dublin: Social Justice Ireland.

Leahy, A., M. Murphy, S. Mallon and Healy, S. (2012) *Ireland and the Europe 2020 Strategy – Employment, Education and Poverty.* Dublin: Social Justice Ireland.

Living Wage Technical Group (2018) *Technical Paper.* Dublin, Living Wage Technical Group.

McQuinn, K., C. O'Toole and P. Economides (2018) *Quarterly Economic Commentary Winter 2018.* Dublin: ESRI.

Murphy, E. and S. Ward (2016) 'Costing a Basic Income for Ireland' in Social Justice Ireland, *Basic Income: Radical Utopia or Practical Solution?* Dublin: Social Justice Ireland.

Social Justice Ireland (2015) *Ireland and the Europe 2020 Strategy: Employment, Education and Poverty.* Dublin: Social Justice Ireland.

Social Justice Ireland (2016) *Basic Income: Radical Utopia or Practical Solution?* Dublin: Social Justice Ireland.

Social Justice Ireland (2018) *Analysis and Critique of Budget 2019.* Dublin: Social Justice Ireland.

Social Justice Ireland (2017) *Europe: The Excluded Suffer while Europe Stagnates.* Dublin: Social Justice Ireland.

Social Justice Ireland (2019) *Tracking the Distributive Effects of Budget 2019.* Dublin: Social Justice Ireland.

Staunton, C. (2015) The Distribution of Wealth in Ireland. Dublin: TASC.

Watson, D, and Maître, B. (2013). 'Social Transfers and Poverty Alleviation in Ireland: An Analysis of the CSO Survey on Income and Living Conditions 2004 – 2011', *Social Inclusion Report No. 4.* Dublin: Department of Social Protection/ESRI.

Whelan, C.T., R. Layte, B. Maitre, B. Gannon, B. Nolan, W. Watson, and Williams, J. (2003) 'Monitoring Poverty Trends in Ireland: Results from the 2001 Living in Ireland Survey', *Policy Research Series No. 51.* Dublin: ESRI.

**Online databases**

CSO online database, web address: http://www.cso.ie/en/databases/
Eurostat online database, web address: http://ec.europa.eu/eurostat

# Chapter 4
## Taxation

**Core Policy Objective:**
To collect sufficient taxes to ensure full participation in society for all, through a fair tax system in which those who have more pay more, while those who have less pay less.

SOCIETY

**Key Issues/Evidence**

Ireland needs to broaden its tax base and increase its overall tax take.

Decisions to raise or reduce overall taxation revenue should be linked to demands on resources now and into the future including:

**funding local government**

**repairing and modernising our water infrastructure**

**paying for the health and pension needs of an ageing population**

**paying EU contributions and funding any pollution reducing environmental initiatives**

Suggestions that higher levels of taxation will damage Ireland's competitiveness relative to other countries is not supported by international studies of competitiveness.

**Policy Solutions**

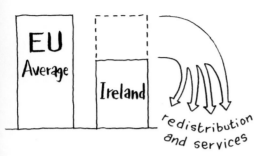

Move towards increasing the total tax-take so that sufficient revenue is collected to provide redistribution and public services at European-average levels.

Adopt policies which further shift the burden of taxation from income tax to eco-taxes on the consumption of fuel and fertilisers, waste taxes and a site value tax.

Make tax credits refundable to address the 'working poor' issue.

Ensure that corporations based in Ireland pay a minimum effective corporate tax rate of 6 per cent

# 4.

# TAXATION

> **CORE POLICY OBJECTIVE: TAXATION**
> To collect sufficient taxes to ensure full participation in society for all, through a fair tax system in which those who have more pay more, while those who have less pay less.

The experience of the last decade has highlighted the centrality of taxation in budget deliberations and to policy development at both macro and micro level. Taxation plays a key role in shaping Irish society through funding public services, supporting economic activity and redistributing resources to enhance the fairness of society. Consequently, it is crucial that clarity exist with regard to both the objectives and instruments aimed at achieving these goals. To ensure the creation of a fairer and more equitable tax system, policy development in this area should adhere to our core policy objective outlined above. In that regard, *Social Justice Ireland* is committed to increasing the level of detailed analysis and debate addressing this area.[1]

This chapter addresses the issue of taxation in three parts. The first (section 4.1) examines key evidence relating to Ireland's present taxation position and outlines the anticipated future taxation needs of the country. Subsequently section 4.2 considers the key policy reforms that we believe should be pursued including approaches to reforming and broadening the tax base and proposals for building a fairer tax system. The chapter concludes (section 4.3) by summarising our key policy priorities in this area.

If the challenges and needed reforms we address in chapter are to be effectively addressed, *Social Justice Ireland* believes that Government's key policy priorities in this area should be to:

- increase the overall tax-take;
- adopt policies to broaden the tax base; and
- develop a fairer taxation system.[2]

---

[1]    We present our analysis in this chapter and in the accompanying Annex 4.
[2]    Much greater detail on each of these and related areas is provided later in this chapter.

# 4.1 Key Evidence

### Assessing the Adequacy of Ireland's Total Tax-Take

The need for a wider tax base is a lesson painfully learnt by Ireland during the recent economic crisis. A disastrous combination of a naïve housing policy, a failed regulatory system, and foolish fiscal policy and economic planning caused a collapse in exchequer revenues. It is only through a strategic and determined effort to reform Ireland's taxation system that these mistakes can avoided in the future. The narrowness of the Irish tax base resulted in almost 25 per cent of tax revenues disappearing, plunging the exchequer and the country into a series of fiscal policy crises. As shown in Table 4.1, tax revenues collapsed from over €63bn in 2007 to a low of €47.4bn in 2010; it has since increased exceeding 2007 levels in 2016 and reaching just over €68.5bn in 2017.

**Table 4.1: The Changing Nature of Ireland's Tax Revenue (€m)**

|  | 2007 | 2008 | 2010 | 2014 | 2017 |
|---|---|---|---|---|---|
| Direct Taxes | 26,087 | 22,964 | 19,569 | 24,889 | 30,799 |
| Indirect Taxes | 25,854 | 22,557 | 18,076 | 21,213 | 24,680 |
| Capital Taxes | 432 | 368 | 245 | 359 | 448 |
| Social Contributions | 10,697 | 10,984 | 9,485 | 10,983 | 12,641 |
| **Total Taxation** | **63,071** | **56,873** | **47,376** | **57,443** | **68,568** |
|  |  |  |  |  |  |
| % GDP | 32.0% | 30.3% | 28.2% | 29.4% | 23.3% |
| % GNP | 37.3% | 35.3% | 34.0% | 35.1% | 29.4% |
| % GNI | 37.0% | 35.0% | 33.7% | 34.8% | 29.3% |

**Source:** CSO online database (GFA03 and N1703).
**Note:** Total taxation expressed as a percentage of published CSO national income figures at current prices.

### *Future taxation needs*

Government decisions to raise or reduce overall taxation revenue needs to be linked to the demands on its resources. These demands depend on what Government is required to address or decides to pursue. The effects of the recent economic crisis, and the way it was handled, carry significant implications for our future taxation needs. The rapid increase in our national debt, driven by the need to borrow both to replace disappearing taxation revenues and to fund emergency 'investments' in the failing commercial banks, has increased the on-going annual costs associated with servicing the national debt.

Ireland's national debt increased from a level of 24 per cent of GDP in 2007 - low by international standards - to peak at 119.9 per cent of GDP in 2012. Documents from the Department of Finance, to accompany Budget 2019, project that the national debt will decrease to 61.4 per cent of GDP in 2019 and to 55 per cent by 2021. The large revision in GDP for 2015 has had a significant effect on this indicator (Department of Finance, 2018a: 29). Despite favourable lending rates and payback terms, there remains a recurring cost to service this debt – costs which have to be financed by current taxation revenues. The estimated debt servicing cost for 2019 is €5.3bn (Department of Finance, 2018a: 56). Furthermore, the erosion of the National Pension Reserve Fund (NPRF) through using it to fund various bank rescues has transferred the liability for future public sector pensions onto future exchequer expenditure. Although there will be some return from a number of the rescued banks, it is likely to be small relative to the total of funds committed and therefore will require additional taxation resources.

These new future taxation needs are in addition to those that already exist for funding local government, repairing and modernising our water infrastructure, paying for the health and pension needs of an ageing population, paying EU contributions and funding any pollution reducing environmental initiatives that are required by European and International agreements. Collectively, they mean that Ireland's overall level of taxation will have to rise significantly in the years to come – a reality Irish society and the political system need to begin to seriously address.

As an organisation that has highlighted the obvious implications of these long-terms trends for some time, *Social Justice Ireland* welcomes the development over the past few years where the Government has published a section of the April *Stability Programme Update* (SPU) focused on the long-term sustainability of public finances.

Research by Bennett et al (2003), the OECD (2008) and the ESRI (2010) have all provided some insight into future exchequer demands associated with healthcare and pensions in Ireland in the decades to come. The Department of Finance has used the European Commission *2018 Ageing Report* as the basis for its assumptions from 2016-2070 which are summarised in table 4.3. Over the period the report anticipates an increase in the elderly population (65 years +) from approximately 630,000 people in 2016 to 1.2m in 2040 and to a peak of 1.49m in 2060. Over the same period, the proportion of those of working age will decline as a percentage of the population and the old-age dependency ratio will increase from almost five people of working age for every elderly person today to less than three for every elderly person from 2040 onwards (Department of Finance, 2018b: 42). While these increases imply a range of necessary policy initiatives in the decades to come, there is an inevitability that an overall higher level of taxation will have to be collected.

**Table 4.2: Projected Age-Related Expenditure, as % GDP 2016-2070**

| Expenditure areas | 2016 | 2020 | 2030 | 2040 | 2050 | 2060 | 2070 |
|---|---|---|---|---|---|---|---|
| Gross Public Pensions | 5.0 | 5.1 | 5.8 | 6.7 | 7.4 | 7.2 | 6.6 |
| *of which:* | | | | | | | |
| *Social protection pensions* | *3.8* | *3.8* | *4.3* | *5.2* | *6.1* | *6.3* | *6.0* |
| *Public service pensions* | *1.2* | *1.3* | *1.5* | *1.5* | *1.4* | *0.9* | *0.6* |
| Health care | 4.1 | 4.3 | 4.6 | 4.9 | 5.1 | 5.2 | 5.1 |
| Long-term care | 1.3 | 1.4 | 1.7 | 2.1 | 2.7 | 3.1 | 3.3 |
| Education | 3.6 | 3.5 | 3.6 | 3.2 | 3.4 | 3.5 | 3.3 |
| Other age-related (JA etc.) | 1.1 | 0.8 | 0.9 | 0.9 | 0.9 | 0.9 | 0.9 |
| Total age-related spending | 15.2 | 15.0 | 16.6 | 17.8 | 19.4 | 20.0 | 19.3 |

**Source:** Department of Finance (2018b: 42)

### How much should Ireland collect in taxation?

As detailed in Chapter 2, *Social Justice Ireland* believes that, over the next few years, policy should focus on increasing Ireland's tax-take. Previous benchmarks, set relative to the overall proportion of national income collected in taxation, have become redundant following recent revisions to Ireland's GDP and GNP levels as a result of the tax-minimising operations of a small number of large multinational firms.[3] Consequently, an alternative benchmark is required.

We propose a new tax take target set on a per-capita basis; an approach which minimises some of the distortionary effects that have emerged in recent years. Our target is calculated using CSO population data, ESRI population projections, and CSO and Department of Finance data on recent and future nominal overall taxation levels. The target is as follows:

> *Ireland's overall level of taxation should reach a level equivalent to €15,000 per capita in 2017 terms. This target should increase each year in line with growth in GNI\*.*

Table 4.3 compares our target to the Budget 2019 expectations of the Department of Finance. We also calculate the overall tax gap for the economy; the difference between the level of taxation that is proposed to be collected and that which would be collected if the *Social Justice Ireland* target was achieved. In 2019 the overall tax

---

[3]   For many years *Social Justice Ireland* proposed that the overall level of taxation should reach 34.9 per cent of GDP.

gap is €3.5 billion and the average gap over the period 2018-2020 will be €3.2 billion per annum.

**Table 4.3:Ireland's Tax Gap, 2018-2020**

|  | 2018 | 2019 | 2020 |
|---|---|---|---|
| **Tax-take € per capita** |  |  |  |
| Budget 2019 projection | €15,366 | €15,959 | €16,617 |
| *Social Justice Ireland* target | €15,885 | €16,505 | €17,049 |
| Difference | €519 | €545 | €432 |
| **Overall Tax-take €m** |  |  |  |
| Budget 2019 projection | €73,641m | €77,515m | €81,354m |
| *Social Justice Ireland* target | €77,153m | €80,804m | €84,138m |
| **Tax Gap** | **€3,513m** | **€3,289m** | **€2,784m** |

**Notes:** Calculated from Department of Finance (2018a: 54), CSO population data and ESRI population projections (Morgenroth, 2018:48). GNI* is assumed to move in line with GNP – as per Department of Finance (2017:49). The Tax Gap is calculated as the difference between the Department of Finance projected tax take and that which would be collected if total tax receipts were equal to the *Social Justice Ireland* target.

Increasing the overall tax take to this level would require a number of changes to the tax base and the current structure of the Irish taxation system, reforms which we address in the next section of this chapter. Increasing the overall taxation revenue to meet this new target would represent a small overall increase in taxation levels and one which is unlikely to have any significant negative impact on the economy.

Chart 4.1 compares the target to the situation in other comparable high-income EU states (the EU-15) using the latest Eurostat data which is for 2017. In that year Ireland's per capita tax figure was €14,422. The *Social Justice Ireland* tax target of €15,000 per capita does not alter Ireland's relative position or alter its status as among the lowest taxed economies in Europe. As a policy objective, Ireland can remain a low-tax economy, but it should not be incapable of adequately supporting the economic, social and infrastructural requirements necessary to support our society and complete our convergence with the rest of Europe.

**Chart 4.1: Per-Capita Tax Take in EU-15 States, 2017**

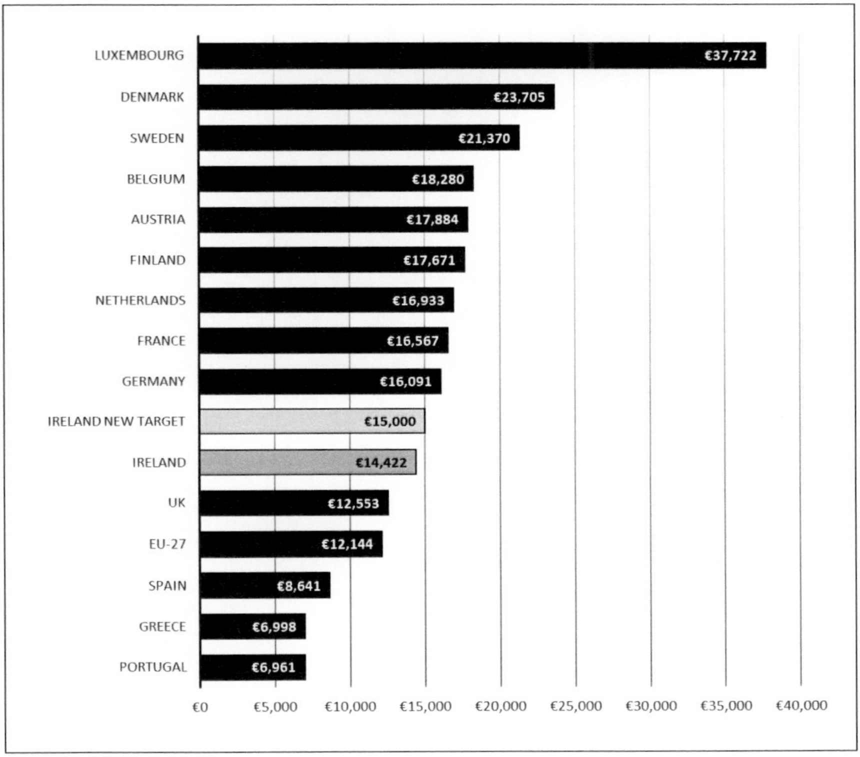

|  |  |
|---|---|
| LUXEMBOURG | €37,722 |
| DENMARK | €23,705 |
| SWEDEN | €21,370 |
| BELGIUM | €18,280 |
| AUSTRIA | €17,884 |
| FINLAND | €17,671 |
| NETHERLANDS | €16,933 |
| FRANCE | €16,567 |
| GERMANY | €16,091 |
| IRELAND NEW TARGET | €15,000 |
| IRELAND | €14,422 |
| UK | €12,553 |
| EU-27 | €12,144 |
| SPAIN | €8,641 |
| GREECE | €6,998 |
| PORTUGAL | €6,961 |

**Source:** Calculated from Eurostat online database and see notes to Table 4.3.

### Is a higher tax-take problematic?

Suggesting that any country's tax-take should increase often produces negative responses. People think first of their incomes and increases in income tax, rather than more broadly of reforms to the tax base. Furthermore, proposals that taxation should increase are often rejected with suggestions that they would undermine economic growth. However, a review of the performance of a number of economies over recent years sheds a different light on this issue and shows limited or no relationship between overall taxation levels and economic growth.

### Taxation and competitiveness

Another argument made against increases in Ireland's overall taxation levels is that it will undermine competitiveness. However, the suggestion that higher levels of taxation would damage our position relative to other countries is not supported by international studies of competitiveness.

Annually the World Economic Forum publishes a *Global Competitiveness Report* ranking the most competitive economies across the world.[4] Table 4.4 outlines the top fifteen economies in this index for 2018 as well as the ranking for Ireland (which comes 23rd). It also presents the difference between the size of the tax-take in these, the most competitive economies in the world, and Ireland, for 2017.[5]

**Table 4.4: Differences in Taxation Levels Between the World's 15 Most Competitive Economies and Ireland**

| Competitiveness Rank | Country | Taxation level versus Ireland |
|:---:|:---:|:---:|
| 1 | United States | +4.3 |
| 2 | Singapore | *not available* |
| 3 | Germany | +14.7 |
| 4 | Switzerland | +5.7 |
| 5 | Japan | +7.8 |
| 6 | Netherlands | +16.0 |
| 7 | Hong Kong SAR | *not available* |
| 8 | United Kingdom | +10.5 |
| 9 | Sweden | +21.2 |
| 10 | Denmark | +23.2 |
| 11 | Finland | +20.5 |
| 12 | Canada | +9.4 |
| 13 | Taiwan, China | *not available* |
| 14 | Australia | +5.0 |
| 15 | South Korea | +4.1 |
| 23 | **IRELAND** | - |

**Source:** World Economic Forum (2018).
**Notes:** a) Taxation data from OECD (2019) for the year 2017 except for Japan and Australia where the taxation data is for 2016.
b) For some non-OECD countries comparable data is *not available*.
c) The OECD's estimate for Ireland in 2017 = 22.8 per cent of GDP.

---

[4] Competitiveness is measured across 12 pillars including: institutions, infrastructure, macroeconomic environment, health and primary education, higher education and training, goods markets efficiency, labour market efficiency, financial market development, technological readiness, market size, business sophistication and innovation. See WEF (2018) for further details on how these are measured.
[5] This analysis updates that first produced by Collins (2004: 15-18).

None of the top fifteen countries, for which there is data available, report a lower taxation level than Ireland; although this effect is exaggerated by the aforementioned revisions to Ireland national income statistics. However, even accounting for this, compared to Ireland almost all other leading competitive economies collect a notably greater proportion of national income in taxation. Over time Ireland's position on this index has varied, most recently rising from 31st to 23rd, although in previous years Ireland had been in 22nd position. When Ireland has slipped back the reasons stated for Ireland's loss of competitiveness included decreases in economic growth and fiscal stability, poor performances by public institutions and a decline in the technological competitiveness of the economy (WEF, 2003: xv; 2008:193; 2011: 25-26; 210-211). Interestingly, a major factor in that decline is related to underinvestment in state funded areas: education; research; infrastructure; and broadband connectivity. Each of these areas is dependent on taxation revenue and they have been highlighted by the report, and by domestic bodies such as the National Competitiveness Council, as necessary areas of investment to achieve enhanced competitiveness. As such, lower taxes do not feature as a significant priority; rather the focus is on increased and targeted efficient government spending.

A similar point was expressed by the Nobel Prize winning economist Professor Joseph Stiglitz while visiting Ireland in June 2004. Commenting on Ireland's long-term development prospects, he stated that "all the evidence is that the low tax, low service strategy for attracting investment is short-sighted" and that "far more important in terms of attracting good businesses is the quality of education, infrastructure and services." Professor Stiglitz added that "low tax was not the critical factor in the Republic's economic development and it is now becoming an impediment".[6]

## 4.2 Key Policies and Reforms

### Reforming and broadening the tax base
*Social Justice Ireland* believes that there is merit in developing a tax package which places less emphasis on taxing people and organisations on what they earn by their own useful work and enterprise, or on the value they add or on what they contribute to the common good. Rather, the tax that people and organisations should be required to pay should be based more on the value they subtract by their use of common resources. Whatever changes are made should also be guided by the need to build a fairer taxation system; one which adheres to our already stated core policy objective.

There are a number of approaches available to Government in reforming the tax base. Recent Budgets have made some progress in addressing some of these issues while the 2009 Commission on Taxation Report highlighted many areas

---

[6]  In an interview with John McManus, Irish Times, June 2nd 2004.

that require further reform. A short review of the areas we consider a priority are presented below across the following subsections:

- Tax Expenditures / Tax Reliefs
- Minimum Effective Tax Rates for Higher Earners
- Corporation Taxes
- Site Value Tax
- Second Homes
- Empty Houses and Underdeveloped Land
- Taxing Windfall Gains
- Financial Transactions Tax
- Carbon Taxes

### Tax Expenditures / Tax Reliefs

A significant outcome from the Commission on Taxation is contained in part eight of its Report which details all the tax breaks (or "tax expenditures" as they are referred to officially). Subsequently, two members of the Commission produced a detailed report for the Trinity College Policy Institute which offered further insight into this issue (Collins and Walsh, 2010). Since then, the annual reporting of the costs of tax expenditures has improved considerably with much more detail than in the past being published annually by the Revenue Commissioners.

The most recent comprehensive tax expenditure data published by the Revenue Commissioners covers the tax year 2016. In total it provides data for 120 tax breaks ranging from those associated with tax credits for earners (Personal, PAYE, Couple, Single Parent etc.) to reliefs on capital investment and films. Thirty-one per cent of tax breaks did not report any cost data either on account of delays, non-collection or discontinuation. These include the tax breaks for some pension reliefs which are only available for earlier years. Overall, the tax breaks with available data involve revenue forgone of €32bn.

Some progress has been made in addressing and reforming these tax breaks since 2009, and we welcome this progress. However, despite this, recent Budgets and Finance Bills have introduced new tax breaks targeted at high earning multinational executives and research and development schemes, and extended tax breaks for film production and the refurbishment of older buildings in urban areas. For the most part, there has been no, or limited, accompanying documentation evaluating the cost, distributive impacts or appropriateness of these proposals.

Both the Commission on Taxation (2009:230) and Collins and Walsh (2010:20-21) have highlighted and detailed the need for new methods for evaluation/introducing tax reliefs. We strongly welcomed these proposals, which were similar to those made by the directors of *Social Justice Ireland* to the Commission in written and oral submissions. The proposals focused on prior evaluation of the costs and benefits of any proposed expenditure, the need to collect detailed information on each expenditure, the introduction of time limits for expenditures, the creation of an annual tax expenditures report as part of the Budget process and the regular scrutiny of this area by an Oireachtas committee. Recently there has been some progress in this direction with a report for the Department of Finance, accompanying Budget 2015, proposing a new process for considering and evaluating tax breaks. Documentation accompanying Budgets 2016-2019 also included an annual tax expenditure report. We welcome this development and believe it is important to further develop this work, to deepen the proposed analysis and to further improve the ability of the Oireachtas to regularly review all of the tax expenditures in the Irish taxation system.

*Social Justice Ireland* believes that reforming the tax break system would make the tax system fairer. It would also provide substantial additional resources which would contribute to raising the overall tax-take towards the modest and realistic target we outlined earlier.[7]

### Minimum Effective Tax Rates for Higher Earners

The suggestion that it is the better-off who principally gain from the provision of tax exemption schemes is reflected in a series of reports published by the Revenue Commissioners entitled *Effective Tax Rates for High Earning Individuals* and *Analysis of High Income Individuals' Restriction*. These reports provided details of the Revenue's assessment of top earners in Ireland and the rates of effective taxation they incur.[8] The reports led to the introduction of a minimum 20 per cent effective tax rate as part of the 2006 and 2007 Finance Acts for all those with incomes in excess of €500,000. Subsequently, Budgets have revised up the minimum effective rate and revised down the income threshold from where it applies – reforms we have welcomed as necessary and long-overdue. Most recently, the 2010 Finance Bill introduced a requirement that all earners above €400,000 pay a minimum effective rate of tax of 30 per cent. It also reduced from €250,000 to €125,000 the income threshold where restrictions on the use of tax expenditures to decrease income tax liabilities commence.

The latest Revenue Commissioners analysis of the operation of these new rules is for the tax year 2016 (Revenue Commissioners, 2018). Table 4.5 gives the findings of that analysis for the 149 individuals subject to the restriction with income in excess of €400,000. The report also includes information on the distribution of effective income tax rates among the 372 earners subject to the restriction and with incomes between €125,000 and €400,000.

---

[7]  See section later in this chapter on the standard rating of tax expenditures.
[8]  The effective taxation rate is calculated as the percentage of the individual's total pre-tax income that is liable to income tax and that is paid in taxation.

**Table 4.5: The Distribution of Effective Income Tax Rates Among Those Earning in Excess of €125,000 in 2016 (% of total)**

| Effective Tax Rate | Individuals with incomes of €400,000+ | Individuals with incomes of €125,000 - €400,000 |
|---|---|---|
| < 15% | - | -* |
| 15% < 20% | - | 11.29% |
| 20% < 25% | - | 15.86% |
| 25% < 30% | -* | 25.00% |
| 30% < 35% | -* | 24.46% |
| 35%< 40% | 38.26% | 17.74% |
| 40%< 45% | 48.32% | 2.96% |
| 45%< 50% | 7.38% | - |
| > 50% | -* | - |
| **Total Cases** | **149** | **372** |

Source: Revenue Commissioners (2018).
Note: Effective rates are for income taxation and USC only. They do not include PRSI. * indicates that there are less than 10 individuals in this category and as such the Revenue Commissioners do not release details of this breakdown.

*Social Justice Ireland* welcomed the introduction of this scheme which marked a major improvement in the fairness of the tax system. The published data indicate that is seems to be working well; however, there are still surprisingly low effective income taxation rates being reported.

The report states that the average effective tax rate faced by earners above €400,000 in 2016 was 40.9 per cent, equivalent to the amount of income tax and USC paid by a single PAYE worker with a gross income of €175,000 in that year. Similarly, the average income tax and USC effective tax rate faced by people earning between €125,000 - €400,000 in 2016 (28.61 per cent) was equivalent to the amount of income tax paid by a single PAYE worker with a gross income of approximately €64,000 in that year. The contrast in these income levels for the same overall rate of income taxation brings into question the fairness of the taxation system as a whole. Such an outcome may be better than in the past, but it still has some way to go to reflect a situation where a fair contribution is being paid.

*Social Justice Ireland* believes that it is important that Government continues to raise the minimum effective tax rate so that it is in line with that faced by PAYE earners on equivalent high-income levels. Following Budget 2019 a single individual on an income of €125,000 gross will pay an income tax and USC effective tax rate of 37.2 per cent (down from 39.3 per cent in 2014); a figure which suggests that the minimum threshold for high earners has potential to adjust upwards over the next few years. We also believe that Government should reform the High Income

Individuals' Restriction so that all tax expenditures are included within it. The restriction currently does not apply to all tax breaks individuals avail of, including pension contributions. This should change in Budget 2020.

## Corporation Taxes

Over the past few years there has been a growing international focus on the way multi-national corporations (MNCs) manage their tax affairs. The OECD's Base Erosion and Profits Shifting (BEPS) examination has established the manner and methods by which MNCs exploit international tax structures to minimise the tax they pay.[9] Similarly, the European Commission has undertaken a series of investigations into the tax management and tax minimisation practices of a number of large MNCs operating within the EU, including Ireland. The European Parliament's Special Committee on Tax Rulings has also completed a review of the EU tax system and highlighted its problems and failures (TAXE, 2015).[10]

Given the timeliness and comprehensiveness of this work, it is important that it leads to the emergence of a transparent international corporate finance and corporate taxation system where multinational firms pay a reasonable and credible effective corporate tax rate.

A chapter within the 2016 Report of the Comptroller and Auditor General (C&AG, September 2017) provided a welcome new insight into corporation tax receipts in Ireland. The report is the first comprehensive examination of this area for some time, even though corporation taxes comprise around 15 per cent of annual tax revenue. Looking at tax receipts for 2016 it found that there were 44,000 corporate taxpayers but that receipts were dominated by "a small number of taxpayers, mainly multi-national enterprises (MNEs)" (2017:289). Noting the fiscal risk associated with this, the report indicated that 37 per cent of the 2016 corporation tax was paid by the top 10 taxpayers and 70 per cent by the top 100 taxpaying companies. Four sectors accounted for 84 per cent of the €7.35 billion in revenue collected in 2016 and these were: financial and insurance activities (28%); manufacturing including pharmaceutical manufacturing (25%); information and communications (17%); and wholesale and retail trade (14%). The report noted that the three largest of these are sectors "dominated by MNEs" (2017:291).

Despite a low headline rate (12.5%), to date there has been limited data on the effective rate of corporate taxation in Ireland. A report from the Department of Finance in 2014 explored the issue and the C&AG (2017) provides a more detailed assessment. Using the approach used by the Revenue Commissioners to calculate the effective tax rate, tax due as a proportion of taxable income, they found an overall effective corporation tax rate of 9.8 per cent in 2016. The effective rate varied between sectors and the C&AG findings are summarised in chart 4.2. The C&AG

---

9   See www.oecd.org/ctp/beps.htm
10   See www.europarl.europa.eu/committees/en/taxe/home.html

findings for the effective rate among the top 100 corporate taxpayers, who account for 70 per cent of tax revenue, is summarised in Table 4.6.

**Chart 4.2: Effective Corporation Tax Rates by Sector in Ireland, 2016**

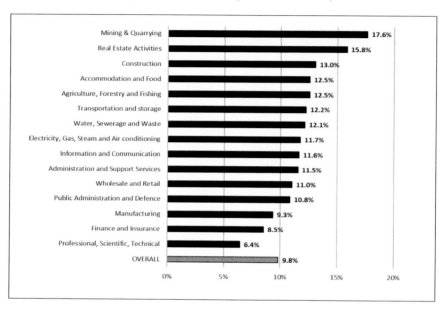

**Source:** C&AG (2017: 296)

**Note:** Effective tax rates can exceed the statutory rate of 12.5% where there is income beyond trading profits such as passive income which is charged at 25%.

**Table 4.6: Effective Corporate Tax Rates of the Top 100 Taxpayers, 2016**

| Effective Rate | Number of Companies |
|---|---|
| 0% or less | 8 |
| Between 0% and 1% | 5 |
| Between 1% and 5% | 1 |
| Between 5% and 10% | 7 |
| Between 10% and 12% | 14 |
| More than 12% | 65 |
| **Total** | **100** |

**Source:** C&AG (2017: 299)

Overall the C&AG report points towards a concentration of corporation tax among a small group of multi-national firms and highlights that it is a small number of these firms who are aggressively minimising their tax liabilities.

*Social Justice Ireland* believes that an EU-wide agreement on a minimum effective rate of corporation tax should be negotiated and this could evolve from the ongoing discussions around a Common Consolidated Corporate Tax Base (CCCTB). We believe that the minimum rate should be set well below the 2018 EU-28 average headline rate of 21.9 per cent but above the existing low Irish level.[11] A headline rate of 17.5 per cent and a minimum effective rate of 10 per cent seem appropriate. This reform would simultaneously maintain Ireland's low corporate tax position and provide additional revenues to the exchequer. Based on the C&AG report the impact of such a reform would be confined to a small number of firms yet it is likely to raise overall corporate tax revenues. Rather than introducing this change overnight, agreement may need to be reached at EU level to phase it in over three to five years. Reflecting this, we proposed prior to Budget 2019 that the effective rate be adjusted to a minimum of 6 per cent – an opportunity regrettably missed.

*Social Justice Ireland* believes that the issue of corporate tax contributions is principally one of fairness. Profitable firms with substantial income should make a contribution to society rather than pursue various schemes and methods to avoid such contributions.

### Site Value Tax
Taxes on wealth are minimal in Ireland. Revenue is negligible from capital acquisitions tax (CAT) because it has a very high threshold in respect of bequests and gifts within families and the rates of tax on transfers of family farms and firms are very generous (see tax revenue tables at the start of this chapter). Budget 2019 further extended the Group A (parent to child) CAT threshold and the likely future revenue from this area remains limited given the tax's current structure.[12] The requirement, as part of the EU/IMF/ECB bailout agreement, to introduce a recurring property tax led Government in Budget 2012 to introduce an unfairly structured flat €100 per annum household charge and a value-based Local Property Tax in Budget 2013. While we welcome the overdue need to extend the tax base to include a recurring revenue source from property, we believe that a Site Value Tax, also known as a Land Rent Tax, would be a more appropriate and fairer approach.

In previous editions of this publication we have reviewed this proposal in greater detail.[13] There has also been a number of research papers published on this issue over the past decade.[14] Overall, they point towards a recurring site value tax that is

---

[11]   Data from Eurostat (2018: 34).
[12]   Budget 2017 previously extended the Group B and C thresholds further reducing the revenue yield of this tax source.
[13]   See for example the 2013 edition of the Socio-Economic Review pages 132-134.
[14]   These include O'Siochru (2004:23-57), Dunne (2004:93-122), Chambers of Commerce of Ireland (2004), Collins and Larragy (2011), and O'Siochru (2012).

fairer and more efficient than other alternatives. *Social Justice Ireland* believes that the introduction of a site value tax would be a better alternative than the current value based local property tax. A site value tax would lead to more efficient land use within the structure of social, environmental and economic goals embodied in planning and other legislation.

### Second Homes, Empty Houses and Underdeveloped Land
A feature of the housing boom of the last decade was the rapid increase in ownership of holiday homes and second homes. For the most part these homes remain empty for at least nine months of the year. It is a paradox that many were built at the same time as the rapid increases in housing waiting lists (see chapter 6).

Results from Census 2016 identified that the number of vacant houses on Census night was 259,562 (April 2016) implying that 12.8 per cent of the national housing stock was vacant. 61,204 of these units were classified as holiday homes meaning that almost 200,000 were empty homes that could act as the main accommodation for an individual or family. Given that there is always some 'natural' turnover in the housing market, the true 'empty' figure is somewhat lower but still very significant.

What is often overlooked when the second home issue is being discussed is that the infrastructure to support these houses is substantially subsidised by the taxpayer. Roads, water, sewage and electricity infrastructure are just part of this subsidy which goes, by definition, to those who are already better off as they can afford these second homes in the first place. *Social Justice Ireland* supports the views of the Bergin et al (ESRI, 2003) and the Indecon report (2005:183-186; 189-190) on this issue. We believe that people purchasing second houses should have to pay these full infrastructural costs, much of which is currently borne by society through the Exchequer and local authorities. There is something perverse in the fact that the taxpayer subsidies the owners of these unoccupied houses while many people do not have basic adequate accommodation.

The introduction of the Non-Principal Private Residence (NPPR) charge in 2009 was a welcome step forward. However, notwithstanding subsequent increases, the charge was very low relative to the previous and on-going benefits that are derived from these properties. It stood at €200 in 2013 and was abolished under the 2014 Local Government Reform Act. While second homes are liable for the local property tax, as are all homes, *Social Justice Ireland* believes that second homes should be required to make a further annual contribution in respect of the additional benefits these investment properties receive. We believe that Government should re-introduce this charge and that it should be further increased and retained as a separate substantial second homes payment. An annual charge of €500 would seem reasonable and would provide additional revenue to local government of approximately €170m per annum.

In the context of a shortage of housing stock (see chapter 6), building new units is not the entire solution. There remains a large number of empty units across the country, something reflected in the aforementioned 2016 Census data. *Social Justice Ireland* believes that policy should be designed to reduce the number of these units and penalise those who own units and leave them vacant for more than a six month period. We propose that Government should introduce a levy on empty houses of €200 per month with the revenue from this charge collected and retained by local authorities.

Local authorities should also be charged with collecting a new site value tax on underdeveloped land, such as abandoned urban centre sites and land-banks of zoned land on the edges of urban areas. This tax, hinted at but not introduced in Budget 2018, should be levied at a rate of €2,000 per hectare (or part thereof) per annum. Income from both measures should reduce the central fund allocation to local authorities.

### Taxing Windfall Gains

The vast profits made by property speculators on the rezoning of land by local authorities was a particularly undesirable feature of the recent economic boom. For some time, *Social Justice Ireland* has called for a substantial tax to be imposed on the profits earned from such decisions. Re-zonings are made by elected representatives supposedly in the interest of society generally. It therefore seems appropriate that a sizeable proportion of the windfall gains they generate should be made available to local authorities and used to address the ongoing housing problems they face (see chapter 6). In this regard, *Social Justice Ireland* welcomed the decision to put such a tax in place in 2010 and strongly condemned its removal as part of Budget 2015. Its removal has been one of the most retrograde policy initiatives in recent years.

A windfall tax level of 80 per cent is appropriate and, as Table 4.7 illustrates, this still leaves speculators and land owners with substantial profits from these rezoning decisions. The profit from this process should be used to fund local authorities. In announcing his Budget 2016 decision, the Minister for Finance noted that the tax was not currently raising any revenue and so justified its abolition on this basis. However, as the property market recovers and as the population continues to grow in years to come, there will be many beneficiaries of vast unearned speculative windfalls.

*Social Justice Ireland* believes that this tax should be re-introduced. Taxes are not just about revenue, they are also about fairness.

**Table 4.7: Illustrative Examples of the Operation of an 80% Windfall Gain Tax on Rezoned Land**

| Agricultural Land Value | Rezoned Value | Profit | Tax @ 80% | Post-Tax Profit | Profit as % Original Value |
|---|---|---|---|---|---|
| €50,000 | €400,000 | €350,000 | €280,000 | €70,000 | 140% |
| €100,000 | €800,000 | €700,000 | €560,000 | €140,000 | 140% |
| €200,000 | €1,600,000 | €1,400,000 | €1,120,000 | €280,000 | 140% |
| €500,000 | €4,000,000 | €3,500,000 | €2,800,000 | €700,000 | 140% |
| €1,000,000 | €8,000,000 | €7,000,000 | €5,600,000 | €1,400,000 | 140% |

**Note:** Calculations assume an eight-fold increase on the agricultural land value upon rezoning.

### Financial Transactions Tax

As the international economic chaos of the past few years has shown, the world is now increasingly linked via millions of legitimate, speculative and opportunistic financial transactions. Similarly, global currency trading increased sharply throughout recent decades. It is estimated that a very high proportion of all financial transactions traded are speculative which are completely free of taxation.

Occasional insights are provided by surveys, the most comprehensive of which is provided by the Bank for International Settlements (BIS) *Triennial Central Bank Survey of Foreign Exchange and Derivatives Market Activity*. The most recent of these was conducted in April 2016 and published in late 2016. The data covered 52 countries and the activities of almost 1,300 banks and other dealers.

Relating to foreign exchange transactions, the key findings from the report were:

- In April 2016 the average daily turnover in global foreign exchange markets was US$5.1 trillion; a marginal decline on to that recorded in 2013 but an increase of more than 300 per cent since 2001.

- The major components of these activities were: $1,652bn in spot transactions each day, $700bn in outright forwards, $2,378bn in foreign exchange swaps, $82bn in currency swaps, and $254bn in foreign exchange options and other products.

- 64.5 per cent of trades were cross-border and 35.5 per cent local (within countries).

- The vast majority of trades involved four currencies on one side of trades: US Dollar (88% of all foreign exchange trades), Euro (31%), Japanese Yen (22%) and Pound Sterling (13%).

- Most of this activity occurred in the UK (37% of all foreign exchange trades) and the US (19%). EU member states, excluding the UK, accounted for 11% of all foreign exchange trades ($697bn per day).

Relating to interest rate derivative transactions, the key findings from the report were:

- In April 2016 the average daily turnover in global interest rate derivative markets was US$2.7 trillion; this has increased by more almost 450% since 2001.
- The major components of these activities were: $653bn in forward rate agreements, $1,859bn in interest rate swap transactions, and $166bn in Over the Counter (OTC) options and other products.
- Half of transactions were conducted in US$, one-quarter in Euro and 9% in Sterling. Most transactions originated in US (41%) and UK (39%).

The Irish Central Bank contributed to the BIS report providing specific data for activities based in Ireland. They found that in April 2016:

- The estimated daily foreign exchange turnover for Ireland was US$2.2bn.
- The estimated daily turnover in interest rate derivative markets in Ireland was US$1.1bn.
- The importance of Ireland in both these sectors declined between 2013 and 2016 as a result of trading decreasing and growth in other trading locations.

Transactions in these markets represent a mixture of legitimate, speculative and opportunistic financial transactions. Estimates continue to highlight that a very large proportion of these activities are speculative, implying that large and growing amounts of these transactions make no real or worthwhile contribution to economies and societies beyond increasing risk and instability. Taken together, the daily value of international trading in foreign exchange and interest rate derivatives markets is more than 25 times the annual GDP of Ireland, almost three times that of the UK, and between 40-50% of annual GDP in the EU-28 and US. On an annualised basis, Irish based trading in foreign exchange markets is equivalent to 263% of GDP while trading in interest rate derivatives are equivalent to 132% of the annual value of GDP.

*Social Justice Ireland* regrets that to date Government has not committed to supporting recent European moves to introduce a Financial Transactions Tax (FTT) or Tobin Tax. The Tobin tax, first proposed by the Nobel Prize winner James Tobin, is a progressive tax, designed to target only those profiting from speculation. It is levied at a very small rate on all transactions but given the scale of these transactions globally, it has the ability to raise significant funds. In September 2011 the EU Commission proposed an FTT and its proposal has evolved since then through a series of revisions and updates.

The EU initially proposed a tax rate of 0.1% (one tenth of one percent) on the trading of bonds and shares and 0.01% (one hundredth of one percent) on the value of derivative agreements. The rates proposed were minimums as countries could set higher rates if they wished. The proposal was also comprehensively designed such that it captured all trades involving any EU registered entity, and all trades involving any EU issued securities. The initial proposal anticipated an annual EU-wide FTT income of between €30bn-€50bn per annum.

The subsequent development of the FTT proposal has seen slow progress at EU level. While between 9 and 11 member states have signalled a willingness to implement the proposal, the precise nature of the tax and breath of the tax base has remained under discussion. Ireland is one of the EU member states that has not, as yet, signalled an intention to implement the tax. However, it has not impeded its development under the enhanced cooperation mechanism.

EU debates are currently focused on the FTT tax base with proposals to narrow it to shares only competing with alternative views focused on retaining a wide base across shares, bonds and derivatives. There is also a considerable financial lobby working to encourage a dilution of the initial broad EU FTT proposal. The scale of this initiative is understandable, given that the tax would most likely reduce the commissions and profits associates with the speculative transactions these financial firms engage in.

However, policy makers need to be reminded that the core argument for these taxes is that they are in the broader interest as they dampen irrelevant and unnecessary financial speculation and thereby underpin the stability of European states. For societies an FTT is a win-win; less needless financial speculation and more state revenue.

Over the past few years a group has emerged in Ireland to support the adoption of the FTT.[15] In our opinion, the tax offers the dual benefit of dampening needless and often reckless financial speculation and generating significant funds. A report from the Nevin Economic Research Institute estimated the likely revenue yield from the FTT's adoption by Ireland. Taking account of the need for Government to abolish stamp duty on shares, the report estimated a net revenue yield of between €320m and €350m per annum (Collins, 2016).

We believe that the revenue generated by this tax should be used for national economic and social development and international development co-operation purposes, in particular assisting Ireland and other developed countries to fund overseas aid and reach the UN ODA target (see chapter 13). According to the United Nations, the amount of annual income raised from a Tobin tax would be enough to guarantee to every citizen of the world basic access to water, food, shelter, health

---

[15] *Social Justice Ireland* is a member of this group, see www.robinhoodtax.ie

and education. Therefore, this tax has the potential to wipe out the worst forms of material poverty throughout the world.

*Social Justice Ireland* believes that the time has come for Ireland to support the introduction of a Financial Transactions Tax.

## Carbon Taxes

Budget 2010 announced the long-overdue introduction of a carbon tax. This had been promised in Budget 2003 and committed to in the *National Climate Change Strategy* (2007). The tax has been structured along the lines of the proposal from the Commission on Taxation (2009: 325-372) and is linked to the price of carbon credits which was set at an initial rate of €15 per tonne of $CO_2$ and subsequently increased in Budget 2012 to €20 per tonne. Budget 2013 extended the tax to cover solid fuels on a phased basis from May 2013 with the full tax applying from May 2014. Products are taxed based on the level of the emissions they create.

While *Social Justice Ireland* welcomed the introduction of this tax, we regret the lack of accompanying measures to protect those most affected by it, in particular low-income households and rural dwellers. *Social Justice Ireland* believes that as the tax increases the Government should be more specific in defining how it will assist these households. Furthermore, we are concerned that the effectiveness of the tax is being undermined as there is limited focus on the original intention of encouraging behavioural change and greater emphasis on simply raising revenue.

## Building a Fairer Taxation System

The need for fairness in the tax system was clearly recognised in the first report of the Commission on Taxation almost four decades ago. It stated:

> "...in our recommendations the spirit of equity is the first and most important consideration. Departures from equity must be clearly justified by reference to the needs of economic development or to avoid imposing unreasonable compliance costs on individuals or high administrative costs on the Revenue Commissioners." (1982:29)

The need for fairness is just as obvious today and *Social Justice Ireland* believes that this should be a central objective of the current reform of the taxation system. Below we outline a series of reforms that would greatly enhance the fairness of Ireland's taxation system. This subsection is structured in five parts:

- Standard rating discretionary tax expenditures
- Favouring fair changes to income taxes
- Introducing Refundable Tax Credits
- Reforming individualisation
- Making the taxation system simpler

**Table 4.8: Comparing Gains Under 7 Possible Income Tax Reforms (€ per annum)**

| Gross Income | €15,000 | €25,000 | €50,000 | €75,000 | €100,000 | €125,000 |
|---|---|---|---|---|---|---|
| **Decrease in the top tax rate from 40% to 39% (full year cost €340m)** | | | | | | |
| Single earner | 0 | 0 | 147.00 | 397.00 | 647.00 | 897.00 |
| Couple 1 earner | 0 | 0 | 57.00 | 307.00 | 557.00 | 807.00 |
| Couple 2 earners | 0 | 0 | 0 | 44.00 | 294.00 | 544.00 |
| **Decrease in the standard tax rate from 20% to 19.5% (full year cost €334m)** | | | | | | |
| Single earner | 0 | 125.00 | 176.50 | 176.50 | 176.50 | 176.50 |
| Couple 1 earner | 0 | 50.00 | 221.50 | 221.50 | 221.50 | 221.50 |
| Couple 2 earners | 0 | 0 | 250.00 | 353.00 | 353.00 | 353.00 |
| **Increase in the personal tax credit of €125 (full year cost €317 million)** | | | | | | |
| Single earner | 0 | 125 | 125 | 125 | 125 | 125 |
| Couple 1 earner | 0 | 50 | 250 | 250 | 250 | 250 |
| Couple 2 earners | 0 | 0 | 250 | 250 | 250 | 250 |
| **Increase in the standard rate band of €1,500 (full year cost €305 million)** | | | | | | |
| Single earner | 0 | 0 | 300 | 300 | 300 | 300 |
| Couple 1 earner | 0 | 0 | 300 | 300 | 300 | 300 |
| Couple 2 earners | 0 | 0 | 0 | 600 | 600 | 600 |
| **Abolish 0.5% USC rate and a 1% point decrease in the 2% rate (full year cost €328m)** | | | | | | |
| Single earner | 89.94 | 138.68 | 138.68 | 138.68 | 138.68 | 138.68 |
| Couple 1 earner | 89.94 | 138.68 | 138.68 | 138.68 | 138.68 | 138.68 |
| Couple 2 earners | 0 | 102.44 | 253.62 | 277.36 | 277.36 | 277.36 |
| **A 0.75% point decrease in the 4.5% USC rate (full year cost €299m)** | | | | | | |
| Single earner | 0 | 38.45 | 225.95 | 376.28 | 376.28 | 376.28 |
| Couple 1 earner | 0 | 38.45 | 225.95 | 376.28 | 376.28 | 376.28 |
| Couple 2 earners | 0 | 0 | 94.69 | 264.39 | 451.89 | 555.35 |
| **A 2% point decrease in the 8% USC rate (full year cost €342m)** | | | | | | |
| Single earner | 0 | 0 | 0 | 99.12 | 599.12 | 1,099.12 |
| Couple 1 earner | 0 | 0 | 0 | 99.12 | 599.12 | 1,099.12 |
| Couple 2 earners | 0 | 0 | 0 | 0 | 0 | 224.12 |

**Note:** All workers are assumed to be PAYE workers. For couples with 2 earners the income is assumed to be split 65%/35%. Cost estimates are based on the latest available Revenue Commissioners taxation ready reckoner and are applied to the structure of the 2019 income taxation system. The increase in the personal tax credit assumes a commensurate increase in the couple, widowed parents and the single person child carer credit. USC calculations assume earners pay the standard rate of USC.

## Standard rating discretionary tax expenditures

Making all discretionary tax reliefs/expenditures only available at the standard 20 per cent rate would represent a crucial step towards achieving a fairer tax system. If there is a legitimate case for making a tax relief/expenditure available, then it should be made available in the same way to all. It is inequitable that people on higher incomes should be able to claim certain tax reliefs at their top marginal tax rates while people with less income are restricted to claim benefit for the same relief at the lower standard rate of 20 per cent. The standard rating of tax expenditures, otherwise known as reliefs, offers the potential to simultaneously make the tax system fairer and fund the necessary developments they are designed to stimulate without any significant macroeconomic implications.[16]

Recent Budgets have made substantial progress towards achieving this objective and we welcome these developments. However, there remains considerable potential to introduce further reform. Notably, Collins (2013:17) reported that in 2009 (the latest Revenue data available) there were €2.3bn of tax breaks made available at the marginal rate and that if these were standardised the estimated saving was just over €1bn.

## Favouring fair changes to income taxes

Reducing taxes is not a priority for *Social Justice Ireland* either in the forthcoming Budget 2020 or any future plans for taxation policy reform. We believe that any available money should be used to improve Ireland's social services and infrastructure, reduce poverty and social exclusion and increase the number of jobs – policy priorities detailed throughout this publication. However, discussion and policy considerations often focus on income taxation reductions, and as a consequence, we have published a series of documents over the past few years that have examined, from the perspectives of fairness, various reform choices. The most recent document is entitled *Fairness in Changing Income Taxes* (Social Justice Ireland, 2019).[17] As a minimum, the analysis highlights the distributive impact taxation policy choices can have and the potential policy has to pursue both fair and unfair outcomes.

Table 4.8 presents a comparison of the reforms to tax rates, tax credits, tax bands and the USC as examined in the document. In all cases the policy examined would carry a full year cost of between 1.3 per cent and 1.5 per cent of the total income taxation yield (€299m-€342m).[18] The reforms examined are for the 2019 income taxation system and are:

• a decrease in the top tax rate from 40% to 39% (full year cost €340m)

• a decrease in the standard rate of tax from 20% to 19.5% (full year cost €334m)

---

[16] See O'Toole and Cahill (2006:215) who also reach this conclusion.

[17] The document is available on our website.

[18] The cost estimates are based on the most recent taxation ready reckoner available from the Revenue Commissioners (post-Budget 2019).

- an increase in the personal tax credit of €125 with commensurate increases in couple, widowed parents and the single person child carer credit (full year cost €317m)

- an increase in the standard rate band (20% tax band) of €1,500 (full year cost €305m)

- the abolition of the 0.5% USC rate - that applies to income below €12,012 **and** a 1% point decrease in the 2% USC rate – that applies to income between €12,012 and €19,874 (full year cost €328m)

- a 0.75% point decrease in the 4.5% USC rate – that applies to income between €19,874 and €70,044 (full year cost €299m)

- a 2% point decrease in the 8% USC rate – that applies to income above €70,044 (full year cost €342m)

Although all of the income taxation options have similar costs (1.3 per cent-1.5 per cent of the income taxation yield), they each carry different effects on the income distribution. Overall, two of the changes would produce fairer outcomes:

- increasing the personal tax credit; and
- reducing the 0.5% and 2% USC rates.

Five of the changes would produce unfair outcomes:

- reducing the top tax rate to 39%;
- reducing the standard tax rate to 19%;
- increasing the standard rate band;
- reducing the 4.5% USC rate; and
- reducing the 8% USC rate.

Each of the two fair options would provide beneficiaries with an improvement in their annual income of around €90-€140. Each of the five unfair options would skew benefits towards those with higher incomes.

### Introducing refundable tax credits
The move from tax allowances to tax credits was completed in Budget 2001. This was a very welcome change because it put in place a system that had been advocated for a long time by a range of groups. One problem persists, however. If a low-income worker does not earn enough to use up his or her full tax credit then he or she will not benefit from any income tax reductions introduced by Government in its annual budget. As we have demonstrated earlier in this publication (see Chapter 3) this has been the case for a large number of low income workers following recent Budgets.

Making tax credits refundable would be a simple solution to this problem. It would mean that the part of the tax credit that an employee did not benefit from would be "refunded" to him/her by the state.

The major advantage of making tax credits refundable lies in addressing the disincentives currently associated with low-paid employment. The main beneficiaries of refundable tax credits would be low-paid employees (full-time and part-time). Chart 4.3 displays the impacts of the introduction of this policy across various gross income levels. It shows that all of the benefits from introducing this policy would go directly to those on the lowest incomes.

**Chart 4.3: How Much Better Off Would People Be If Tax Credits Were Made Refundable?**

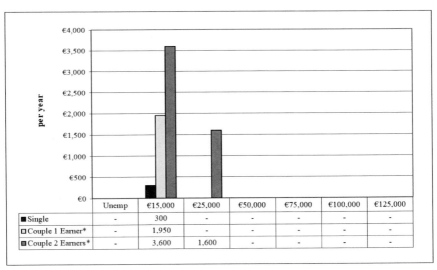

| | Unemp | €15,000 | €25,000 | €50,000 | €75,000 | €100,000 | €125,000 |
|---|---|---|---|---|---|---|---|
| ■ Single | - | 300 | - | - | - | - | - |
| ◻ Couple 1 Earner* | - | 1,950 | - | - | - | - | - |
| ▨ Couple 2 Earners* | - | 3,600 | 1,600 | - | - | - | - |

**Note:** * Except where unemployed as there is no earner.

With regard to administering this reform, the central idea recognises that most people with regular incomes and jobs would not receive a cash refund of their tax credit because their incomes are too high. They would simply benefit from the tax credit as a reduction in their tax bill. Therefore, as chart 4.3 shows, no change is proposed for these people and they would continue to pay tax via their employers, based on their net liability after deduction of tax credits by their employers on behalf of the Revenue Commissioners. For other people on low or irregular incomes, the refundable tax credit could be paid via a refund by the Revenue Commissioners at the end of the tax year. Following the introduction of refundable tax credits, all subsequent increases in the level of the tax credit would be of equal value to all employees.

To illustrate the benefits of this approach, charts 4.4 and 4.5 compare the effects of a €100 increase in the personal tax credit before and after the introduction of refundable tax credits. Chart 4.4 shows the effect as the system is currently structured – an increase of €100 in credits, but these are not refundable. It shows that the gains are allocated equally to all categories of earners above €50,000. However, there is no benefit for those workers whose earnings are not in the income tax net.

Chart 4.5 shows how the benefits of a €100 a year increase in personal tax credits would be distributed under a system of refundable tax credits. This simulation demonstrates the equity attached to using the tax-credit instrument to distribute budgetary taxation changes. The benefit to all categories of income earners (single/couple, one-earner/couple, dual-earners) is the same. Consequently, in relative terms, those earners at the bottom of the distribution do best.

**Chart 4.4: How Much Better Off Would People Be if Tax Credits Were Increased by €100 Per Person?**

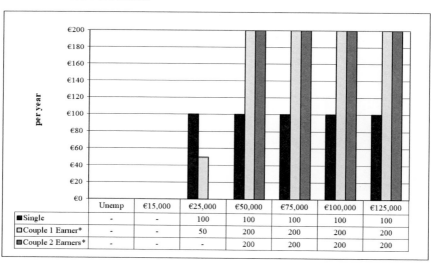

| | Unemp | €15,000 | €25,000 | €50,000 | €75,000 | €100,000 | €125,000 |
|---|---|---|---|---|---|---|---|
| ■Single | - | - | 100 | 100 | 100 | 100 | 100 |
| □Couple 1 Earner* | - | - | 50 | 200 | 200 | 200 | 200 |
| ■Couple 2 Earners* | - | - | - | 200 | 200 | 200 | 200 |

Note: * Except where unemployed, as there is no earner.

**Chart 4.5: How Much Better Off Would People Be if Tax Credits Were Increased by €100 Per Person and This was Refundable?**

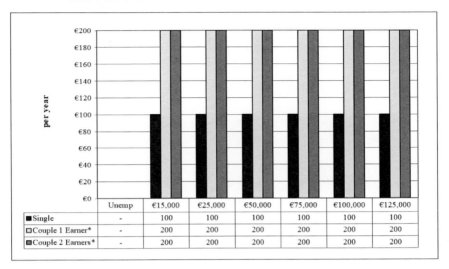

| | Unemp | €15,000 | €25,000 | €50,000 | €75,000 | €100,000 | €125,000 |
|---|---|---|---|---|---|---|---|
| ■ Single | - | 100 | 100 | 100 | 100 | 100 | 100 |
| □ Couple 1 Earner* | - | 200 | 200 | 200 | 200 | 200 | 200 |
| ▨ Couple 2 Earners* | - | 200 | 200 | 200 | 200 | 200 | 200 |

**Note:** * Except where unemployed, as there is no earner.

Overall the merits of adopting this approach are: that every beneficiary of tax credits would receive the full value of the tax credit; that the system would improve the net income of the workers whose incomes are lowest, at modest cost; and that there would be no additional administrative burden placed on employers.

During 2010 *Social Justice Ireland* published a detailed study on the subject of refundable tax credits. Entitled *'Building a Fairer Tax System: The Working Poor and the Cost of Refundable Tax Credits'*, the study identified that the proposed system would benefit 113,000 low-income individuals in an efficient and cost-effective manner.[19] When children and other adults in the household are taken into account the total number of beneficiaries would be 240,000. The cost of making this change would be €140m. The *Social Justice Ireland* proposal to make tax credits refundable would make Ireland's tax system fairer, address part of the working poor problem, and improve the living standards of a substantial number of people in Ireland. The following is a summary of that proposal:

*Making tax credits refundable: the benefits*
- Would address the problem identified already in a straightforward and cost-effective manner;

- No administrative cost to the employer;

---

[19]  The study is available from our website: www.socialjustice.ie

- Would incentivise employment over welfare as it would widen the gap between pay and welfare rates;
- Would be more appropriate for a 21st century system of tax and welfare.

*Details of Social Justice Ireland proposal*
- Unused portion of the Personal and PAYE tax credit (and only these) would be refunded;
- Eligibility criteria in the relevant year;
- Individuals must have unused personal and/or PAYE tax credits (by definition);
- Individuals must have been in paid employment;
- Individuals must be at least 23 years of age;
- Individuals must have earned a minimum annual income from employment of €4,000;
- Individuals must have accrued a minimum of 40 PRSI weeks;
- Individuals must not have earned an annual total income greater than €15,600;
- Married couples must not have earned a combined annual total income greater than €31,200;
- Payments would be made at the end of the tax year.

*Cost of implementing the proposal*
- The total cost of refunding unused tax credits to individuals satisfying all of the criteria mentioned in this proposal is estimated at €140.1m.

*Major findings*
- Almost 113,300 low income individuals would receive a refund and would see their disposable income increase as a result of the proposal.
- The majority of the refunds are valued at under €2,400 per annum, or €46 per week, with the most common value being individuals receiving a refund of between €800 to €1,000 per annum, or €15 to €19 per week.
- Considering that the individuals receiving these payments have incomes of less than €15,600 (or €299 per week), such payments are significant to them.
- Almost 40 per cent of refunds flow to people in low-income working poor households who live below the poverty line.
- A total of 91,056 men, women and children below the poverty threshold benefit either directly through a payment to themselves or indirectly through a payment to their household from a refundable tax credit.

- Of the 91,056 individuals living below the poverty line that benefit from refunds, most (over 71 per cent) receive refunds of more than €10 per week with 32 per cent receiving in excess of €20 per week.

- A total of 148,863 men, women and children above the poverty line benefit from refundable tax credits either directly through a payment to themselves or indirectly (through a payment to their household. Most of these beneficiaries have income less than €120 per week above the poverty line.

- Overall, some 240,000 individuals (91,056 + 148,863) living in low-income households would experience an increase in income as a result of the introduction of refundable tax credits, either directly through a refund to themselves or indirectly through a payment to their household.

Once adopted, a system of refundable tax credits as proposed in our study would result in all future changes in tax credits being experienced equally by all employees in Irish society. Such a reform would mark a significant step in the direction of building a fairer taxation system and represent a fairer way for Irish society to allocate its resources.

### Reforming individualisation

*Social Justice Ireland* supports individualisation of the tax system. However, the process of individualisation followed to date has been deeply flawed and unfair. The cost to the exchequer of this transition has been in excess of €0.75bn, and almost all of this money went to the richest 30 per cent of the population. A significantly fairer process would have been to introduce a basic income system that would have treated all people fairly and ensured that a windfall of this nature did not accrue to the best off in this society (see Chapter 3).

Given the current form of individualisation, couples with one partner losing his/her job end up even worse off than they would have been had the current form of individualisation not been introduced. Before individualisation was introduced, the standard-rate income-tax band was €35,553 for all couples. Above that, they would start paying the higher rate of tax. Now, the standard-rate income-tax band for single-income couples is €44,300 while the band for dual-income couples covers a maximum of a further €25,550 (up to €70,600). If one spouse (of a couple previously earning two salaries) leaves a job voluntarily or through redundancy, the couple loses the value of the second tax band.

### Making the taxation system simpler

Ireland's tax system is not simple. Bristow (2004) argued that "some features of it, notably VAT, are among the most complex in the world". The reasons given to justify this complexity vary but they are focused principally around the need to reward particular kinds of behaviour which are seen as desirable by legislators. This, in effect, is discrimination either in favour of one kind of activity or against another. There are many arguments against the present complexity and in favour of a simpler system.

Discriminatory tax concessions in favour of particular positions are often very inequitable, contributing far less to equity than might appear to be the case. In many circumstances they also fail to produce the economic or social outcomes which were being sought and sometimes they even generate very undesirable effects. At other times they may be a complete waste of money, since the outcomes they seek would have occurred without the introduction of a tax incentive. Having a complex system has other down-sides. It can, for example, have high compliance costs both for taxpayers and for the Revenue Commissioners.

For the most part, society at large gains little or nothing from the discrimination contained in the tax system. Mortgage interest relief, for example, and the absence of any residential or land-rent tax contributed to the rise in house prices up to 2007. Complexity makes taxes easier to evade, invites consultants to devise avoidance schemes and greatly increases the cost of collection. It is also inequitable because those who can afford professional advice are in a far better position to take advantage of that complexity than those who cannot. A simpler taxation system would better serve Irish society and all individuals within it, irrespective of means.

## 4.3 Key Policy Priorities

*Social Justice Ireland* believes that if the challenges and needed reforms we have highlighted throughout this chapter are to be effectively addressed, Government's key policy priorities in this area should be to:

- increase the overall tax-take;
- adopt policies to broaden the tax base; and
- develop a fairer taxation system.

Policy priorities under each of these headings are listed below.

*Increase the overall tax-take*
- Move towards increasing the total tax-take so that sufficient revenue is collected to provide redistribution and public services at average-European levels.

*Broaden the tax base*
- Continue to reform the area of tax expenditures and further enhance procedures within the Department of Finance and the Revenue Commissioners to monitor on an on-going basis the cost and benefits of all current and new tax expenditures;
- Continue to increase the minimum effective tax rates on very high earners (those with incomes in excess of €125,000) so that these rates are consistent with the levels faced by PAYE workers;

- Move to negotiate an EU wide agreement on minimum corporate taxation rates (a rate of 17.5 per cent would seem fair in this situation);

- Adopt policies to ensure that corporations based in Ireland pay a minimum effective corporate tax rate of 10 per cent. As an interim measure introduce a 6 per cent rate in the next Budget;

- Impose charges so that those who construct or purchase second homes pay the full infrastructural costs of these dwellings;

- Restore the 80 per cent windfall tax on the profits generated from all land re-zonings;

- Join with other EU member states to adopt a financial transactions tax (FTT);

- Adopt policies which further shift the burden of taxation from income tax to eco-taxes on the consumption of fuel and fertilisers, waste taxes and a land rent tax. In doing this, government should minimise any negative impact on people with low incomes.

*Develop a fairer taxation system*
- Apply only the standard rate of tax to all discretionary tax expenditures;

- Make tax credits refundable;

- Accept that where reductions in income taxes are being implemented, they should favour fair options which do not skew the benefits towards higher earners;

- Ensure that individualisation in the income tax system is done in a fair and equitable manner;

- Integrate the taxation and social welfare systems;

- Begin to monitor and report tax levels (personal and corporate) in terms of effective tax rates;

- Develop policies which allow taxation on wealth to be increased;

- Ensure that the distribution of all changes in indirect taxes discriminate positively in favour of those with lower incomes;

- Adopt policies to simplify the taxation system;

- Poverty-proof all budget tax packages to ensure that tax changes do not further widen the gap between those with low income and the better off.

# REFERENCES

Bank for International Settlements (2016) *Triennial Central Bank Survey of Foreign Exchange and Derivatives Market Activity*. Basel: BIS.

Bennett M., D. Fadden, D. Harney, P. O'Malley, C. Regan and L. Sloyan (2003) *Population Ageing in Ireland and its Impact on Pension and Healthcare Costs - Report of Society of Actuaries Working Party on Population Studies*. Dublin: Society of Actuaries in Ireland.

Bergin, A., J. Cullen, D. Duffy, J. Fitzgerald, I. Kearney and D. McCoy (2003) *Medium-Term Review: 2003-2010*. Dublin: ESRI.

Bristow, J. (2004) *Taxation in Ireland: an economist's perspective*. Dublin: Institute of Public Administration.

Chambers of Commerce of Ireland (2004) *Local Authority Funding – Government in Denial,* Dublin: Chambers of Commerce Ireland.

Collins, M.L. (2004) "Taxation in Ireland: an overview" in B. Reynolds, and S. Healy (eds.) *A Fairer Tax System for a Fairer Ireland*. Dublin: CORI Justice Commission.

Collins, M.L. (2013) 'Income Taxes and Income Tax Options – a context for Budget 2014' *NERI Working Paper*, 2013/05. Dublin: NERI.

Collins, M.L. (2016) 'Estimating the Revenue Yield from a Financial Transactions Tax for the Republic of Ireland' *NERI Working Paper, 2016/34*. Dublin: NERI.

Collins, M.L. and A. Larragy (2011) 'A Site Value Tax for Ireland: approach, design and implementation' *Trinity Economics Papers Working Paper 1911*. Dublin: Trinity College Dublin.

Collins, M.L. and Walsh, M. (2010) *Ireland's Tax Expenditure System: International Comparisons and a Reform Agenda – Studies in Public Policy No. 24*. Dublin: Policy Institute, Trinity College Dublin.

Commission on Taxation (1982) *Commission on Taxation First Report*. Dublin: Stationery Office.

Commission on Taxation (2009) *Commission on Taxation Report 2009*. Dublin: Stationery Office.

Comptroller and Auditor General (2017) *Reports on the Accounts of the Public Service 2016*. Dublin, C&AG.

Department of Finance (2018a) *Budget 2019*. Dublin: Stationery Office.

Department of Finance (2018b) *Stability Programme Update*. Dublin: Stationery Office.

Department of Finance (2017) *Budget 2018*. Dublin: Stationery Office.

Department of Finance (various*) Budget Documentation – various years*. Dublin: Stationery Office.

Dunne, T. (2004) "Land Values as a Source of Local Government Finance" in B. Reynolds, and S. Healy (eds.) *A Fairer Tax System for a Fairer Ireland*. Dublin: CORI Justice Commission.

European Commission (2018) *The 2018 Ageing Report: Economic and budgetary projections for the EU Member States (2016-2070)*. Brussels, European Commission.

Eurostat (2018) *Taxation Trends in the European Union*. Luxembourg: Eurostat.

Government of Ireland (2007) *National Climate Change Strategy*. Dublin: Stationery Office.

Indecon (2005), *Indecon Review of Local Government Funding – Report commissioned by the Minister for Environment, Heritage and Local Government.* Dublin, Stationery Office.

Morgenroth, E. (2018) *Prospects for Irish Regions and Counties.* Dublin: ESRI.

O'Siochru, E. (2004) "Land Value Tax: unfinished business" in B. Reynolds, and S. Healy eds. *A Fairer Tax System for a Fairer Ireland.* Dublin: CORI Justice Commission.

O'Siochru, E. (Ed.). (2012) *The Fair Tax.* Dublin: Smart Taxes Network.

O'Toole, F. and N. Cahill (2006) "Taxation Policy and Reform", in Healy, S., B. Reynolds and M.L. Collins eds., *Social Policy in Ireland: Principles, Practice and Problems.* Dublin: Liffey Press.

OECD (2008) *Economic Survey of Ireland.* Paris: OECD.

OECD (2018) *Revenue Statistics.* Paris: OECD.

Revenue Commissioners (various) *Analysis of High Income Individuals' Restriction.* Dublin: Stationery Office.

Revenue Commissioners (various) *Effective Tax Rates for High Earning Individuals.* Dublin: Stationery Office.

Revenue Commissioners (2018) Ready Reckoner - *Post-Budget 2019.* Dublin: Stationery Office.

Social Justice Ireland (2010) *Building a Fairer Taxation System: The Working Poor and the Cost of Refundable Tax Credits.* Dublin: Social Justice Ireland.

Social Justice Ireland (2018) *Analysis and Critique of Budget 2019.* Dublin: Social Justice Ireland.

Social Justice Ireland (2019) *Fairness in Changing Income Tax.* Dublin: Social Justice Ireland.

World Economic Forum (2003). *Global Competitiveness Report 2003-04.* www.weforum.org.

World Economic Forum (2008) *Global Competitiveness Report 2008-09.* www.weforum.org.

World Economic Forum (2011) *Global Competitiveness Report 2011-12.* www.weforum.org.

World Economic Forum (2018) *Global Competitiveness Report 2018.* www.weforum.org.


**Online databases**
CSO online database, web address: http://www.cso.ie/en/databases/
Eurostat online database, web address: http://ec.europa.eu/eurostat

# Chapter 5
## Work, Unemployment and Job Creation

**Core Policy Objective:**
To ensure that all people have access to meaningful work

**Key Issues/Evidence**

The increased numbers of people in employment is very welcome but the working poor issue persists.

The growth in the number of individuals with less work hours than ideal, as well as those with persistent uncertainties concerning the number and times of hours required for work, is a major labour market challenge.

Participation rate in the labour force:

**Persons with a disability**

**Population in general**

**4.1%**
of the population provided some care for sick or disabled family members or friends on an unpaid basis.

60% of carers are female.

The priority given to paid employment over other forms of work is an assumption that must be challenged.

**Voluntary work**

**Work in the home**

**Community Work**

## Policy Solutions

Recognise that the term "work" is not synonymous with the concept of "paid employment". Everybody has a right to work, i.e. to contribute to his or her own development and that of the community and the wider society. This, however, should not be confined to job creation.

Policy should seek at all times to ensure that new jobs have reasonable pay rates, and adequately resource the labour inspectorate.

As part of the process of addressing the working poor issue, reform the taxation system to make tax credits refundable.

Reduce the impediments faced by people with a disability in achieving employment.

Give greater recognition to the work carried out by carers in Ireland and introduce policy reforms to reduce the financial and emotional pressures on carers.

Resource the up-skilling of those who are unemployed and at risk of becoming unemployed through integrating training and labour market programmes.

# 5.

# WORK, UNEMPLOYMENT AND JOB CREATION

> **CORE POLICY OBJECTIVE: WORK, UNEMPLOYMENT AND JOB CREATION**
>
> To ensure that all people have access to meaningful work

The scale and severity of the 2008-2010 economic collapse saw Ireland revert to the phenomenon of widespread unemployment. Despite the attention given to the banking and fiscal collapse, the transition from near full-employment to high unemployment was the most telling characteristic of that recession. It carried implications for individuals, families, social cohesion and the exchequer's finances which were serious and the effects continue to be felt. CSO data and economic forecasts for the remainder of 2019 indicate that unemployment will reach an annual rate of between 5.3 and 5 per cent of the labour force in 2019, having been 4.7 per cent before the recession in 2007. This represents a very welcome improvement from the peak unemployment rate of 16.0% at the beginning of 2012.

This chapter addresses the topic of Work, Unemployment and Job Creation in three parts. The first (section 5.1) reviews current and historic trends in Ireland's labour market. Subsequently section 5.2 considers the key policy reforms that arise for various sectors of the working-age population and outlines a series of proposals for responding to current labour market challenges around employment, unemployment and participation. Despite progress on the headline numbers, *Social Justice Ireland* considers that the policy response in a number of areas has been weak. The section concludes with some thoughts on the narrowness of how we consider and measure the concept of 'work'. The chapter concludes (section 5.3) by summarising our key policy priorities in this area.[1]

---

[1] The analysis complements information on the measurement of the labour market and long-term trends in employment and unemployment detailed in Annex 5 which is available online at: http://www.socialjustice.ie/

If the challenges we address in this chapter are to be effectively addressed, *Social Justice Ireland* believes that Government should[2]:

- Launch a major investment programme focused on prioritising initiatives that strengthen social infrastructure, including a comprehensive school building programme and a much larger social housing programme;

- Resource the up-skilling of those who are unemployed and at risk of becoming unemployed through integrating training and labour market programmes;

- Adopt policies to address the worrying issue of youth unemployment. In particular, these should include education and literacy initiatives as well as retraining schemes;

- Recognise the challenge of long-term unemployment and of precarious employment and adopt targeted policies to address these;

- Recognise that the term "work" is not synonymous with the concept of "paid employment". Everybody has a right to work, i.e. to contribute to his or her own development and that of the community and the wider society. This, however, should not be confined to job creation. Work and a job are not the same thing.

## 5.1 Key Evidence

### Recent Trends in Employment and Unemployment

The nature and scale of the recent transformation in Ireland's labour market is highlighted by the data in Table 5.1. Over the 12 years from 2007 to 2018 the labour force has grown by 45,000 individuals, but participation and employment rates dropped, full-time employment fell by 1.2 per cent, representing 22,500 jobs, while part-time employment increased by almost 10 per cent. In 2018 the number of underemployed people, defined as those employed part-time but wishing to work additional hours, stood at 111,500 people equivalent to 4.6 per cent of the labour force. Over this period unemployment increased by just over 24,000 people, bringing the unemployment rate up from 5.1 per cent to 6.0 per cent; although the 2018 figure represents a dramatic improvement on the levels experienced during the height of the economic crisis around 2010-2012.

This transformation in the labour market has significantly altered the nature of employment in Ireland when compared to the pre-recession picture in 2007. Overall, employment grew by almost 1 per cent (21,000 jobs) between 2007-2018 and Table 5.2 traces the impact of this change across various sectors, groups and regions. Within the CSO's broadly defined employment sectors three of the four decreased in size over the period: construction employment has seen the biggest fall of 38 per cent (90,600 jobs); industrial employment fell by 12 per cent (40,400 jobs); and agricultural employment experienced a 7 per cent decrease (8,300 jobs).

---

[2]  Much greater detail on these and related initiatives is provided later in this chapter.

In contrast, employment in the services sector grew substantially with 10 per cent more employment in this sector in 2018 compared to 2007 (157,700 jobs). The services sector now accounts for 76 per cent of all employees. Compared to 2012, employment has been growing in all sectors bar agriculture, representing a welcome recovery that took a long time to emerge.

**Table 5.1: Ireland's Labour Force Data, 2007 – 2018**

|  | 2007 | 2012 | 2018 | Change 07-18 |
|---|---|---|---|---|
| Labour Force | 2,371,900 | 2,241,400 | 2,417,000 | +45,100 |
| LFPR% | 67.4 | 62.1 | 62.6 | -4.8 |
| Employment% | 72.5 | 60.2 | 69.1 | -3.4 |
| Employment | 2,252,200 | 1,887,000 | 2,273,200 | +21,000 |
| *Full-time* | *1,835,400* | *1,424,600* | *1,812,900* | *-22,500* |
| *Part-time* | *416,800* | *462,400* | *460,300* | *+43,500* |
| *Underemployed* | *n/a* | *150,400* | *111,500* | *n/a* |
| Unemployed% | 5.1 | 15.9 | 6.0 | +0.9 |
| Unemployed | 119,700 | 354,300 | 143,800 | +24,100 |
| LT Unemployed% | 1.4% | 9.1% | 2.1% | +0.7% |
| LT Unemployed | 33,300 | 203,800 | 50,200 | +16,900 |
| Potential Additional LF | n/a | n/a | 118,600 | n/a |

Source:  CSO, LFS on-line database.
Notes:  All data is for Quarter 3 of the reference year.
LFPR = ILO labour force participation rate and measures the percentage of the adult population who are in the labour market.
Employment% is for those aged 15-64 years.
Underemployment measures part-time workers who indicate that they wish to work additional hours which are not currently available.
n/a = comparable data is not available.
LT = Long Term (12 months or more). LF = Labour Force.

Overall, job losses have had a greater impact on males than females with male employment down 3.9 per cent since 2007 (50,300 jobs) while female employment has surpassed its 2007 level (+71,200). Over the period the number of employees grew by 3.2 per cent while the number of self-employed decreased by 8.6 per cent.

**Table 5.2: Employment in Ireland, 2007 – 2018**

|  | 2007 | 2012 | 2018 | Change 07-18 |
|---|---|---|---|---|
| Employment | 2,252,200 | 1,887,000 | 2,273,200 | +21,000 |
| **Sector** | | | | |
| Agriculture | 113,200 | 110,100 | 104,900 | - 8,300 |
| Industry | 325,000 | 232,800 | 284,600 | - 40,400 |
| Construction | 237,100 | 82,800 | 146,500 | - 90,600 |
| Services | 1,571,000 | 1,458,300 | 1,728,700 | +157,700 |
| **Gender** | | | | |
| Male | 1,281,800 | 1,010,500 | 1,231,500 | - 50,300 |
| Female | 970,400 | 876,600 | 1,041,600 | +71,200 |
| **Employment Status** | | | | |
| Employees* | 1,883,300 | 1,577,100 | 1,942,700 | +59,400 |
| Self Employed | 348,400 | 290,800 | 318,500 | - 29,900 |
| Assisting relative | 20,500 | 19,200 | 12,000 | - 8,500 |
| **Region** | | | | |
| Border | n/a | 145,300 | 178,300 | n/a |
| West | n/a | 182,000 | 208,700 | n/a |
| Mid-West | n/a | 189,100 | 215,300 | n/a |
| South-East | n/a | 157,500 | 186,500 | n/a |
| South-West | n/a | 285,500 | 333,900 | n/a |
| Dublin | n/a | 552,000 | 696,200 | n/a |
| Mid-East | n/a | 276,300 | 327,100 | n/a |
| Midland | n/a | 99,500 | 127,200 | n/a |

**Source:** CSO, LFS on-line database.
**Notes:** * Numbers recorded as employed include those on various active labour market policy schemes. Regional data only available from 2012. See also notes to Table 5.1.

The consequence of the crisis period job losses was a sharp increase in unemployment and emigration which has only recently began to dissipate. Dealing with unemployment, Table 5.3 shows how it has changed between 2007 and 2018, a period when the numbers unemployed increased by 20.1 per cent. As the table shows, male unemployment increased by 8,800 and female unemployment by 15,300. Most of the unemployed are seeking to return to a full-time job with just over 22 per cent of those unemployed in 2018 indicating that they were seeking part-time employment. The impact of the unemployment crisis was felt right across the age groups with younger age groups seeing their numbers unemployed fall since 2012.

**Table 5.3: Unemployment in Ireland, 2007 - 2018**

|  | 2007 | 2012 | 2018 | Change 07-18 |
|---|---|---|---|---|
| Unemployment | 119,700 | 354,300 | 143,800 | +24,100 |
| **Gender** | | | | |
| Male | 67,600 | 219,600 | 76,400 | +8,800 |
| Female | 52,100 | 134,700 | 67,400 | +15,300 |
| **Employment sought** | | | | |
| Seeking FT work | 97,900 | 305,300 | 106,700 | +8,800 |
| Seeking PT work | 18,400 | 35,500 | 32,100 | +13,700 |
| **Age group** | | | | |
| 15-24 years | 45,100 | 95,100 | 45,900 | +800 |
| 25-44 years | 54,200 | 171,600 | 59,200 | +5,000 |
| 45-65 years | 20,100 | 87,000 | 37,400 | +17,300 |
| **Region** | | | | |
| Border | n/a | 27,700 | 9,500 | n/a |
| West | n/a | 35,500 | 14,500 | n/a |
| Mid-West | n/a | 48,600 | 16,500 | n/a |
| South-East | n/a | 31,200 | 17,400 | n/a |
| South-West | n/a | 46,700 | 17,300 | n/a |
| Dublin | n/a | 84,900 | 38,900 | n/a |
| Mid-East | n/a | 53,600 | 20,100 | n/a |
| Midland | n/a | 26,300 | 9,700 | n/a |
| **Duration** | | | | |
| Unemp. less than 1 yr | 85,200 | 147,000 | 89,200 | +4,000 |
| Unemp. more than 1 yr | 33,300 | 203,800 | 50,200 | +16,900 |
| LT Unemp. as % Unemp | 27.8% | 57.5% | 34.9% | |

**Source:** CSO, LFS on-line database
**Note:** See also notes to Table 5.1.

The rapid growth in the number and rates of long-term unemployment are also highlighted in Table 5.3 and in chart 5.1. The number of long-term unemployed was 33,300 in 2007 and has increased since, exceeding 200,000 in 2012 before falling again to just over 50,000 in 2018. For the first time on record, in late 2010 the Labour Force Survey (LFS) data indicated that long-term unemployment accounted for more than 50 per cent of the unemployed. It took from then until late 2017 for this number to consistently drop below that threshold, reaching 34.9 per cent of the unemployed in the third quarter of 2018. As Chart 5.1 shows, the transition to these high levels was rapid. The experience of the 1980s showed the dangers and long-lasting implications of an unemployment crisis characterised by high long-term unemployment rates. It remains a policy challenge that Ireland's level of long-term unemployment remains high and that it is a policy area which receives limited attention.

Addressing a crisis such as this is a major challenge and we outline our suggestions for targeted policy action later in the chapter. However, it is clear that reskilling many of the unemployed, in particular those with low education levels, will be a key component of the response. Using data for the third quarter of 2018, 48 per cent of the unemployed had no more than second level education with 21 per cent not having completed more than lower secondary (equivalent to the junior certificate). As employment recovers and as unemployment continues to decline, *Social Justice Ireland* believes that major emphasis should be placed on those who are trapped in long term unemployment – particularly those with the lowest education levels.

**Chart 5.1: Long-Term Unemployment in Ireland, 2007-2018**

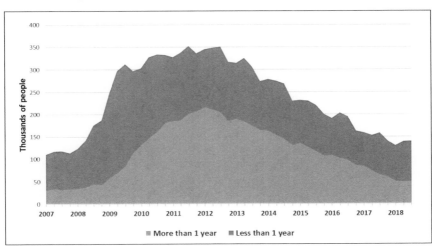

**Source:** CSO, LFS on-line database
**Note:** Long term unemployment is defined as those unemployed for more than one year

Previous experiences, in Ireland and elsewhere, have shown that many of those under 25 and many of those over 55 find it challenging to return to employment after a period of unemployment. This highlights the danger of the aforementioned increases in long-term unemployment and suggests a major commitment to retraining and re-skilling will be required.

*The Live Register*
Complementing these trends, data on the number of people signing on for social protection payments or social insurance credits is also informative of labour market trends. While the live register is not an accurate measure of unemployment, it is a rich dataset and offers a useful barometer of the nature and pace of change in employment and unemployment. Increases suggest a combination of more people unemployed, more people on reduced employment weeks and consequently reductions in the availability of employment hours to the labour force. Conversely, reductions signal signs of improvements in job opportunities and/or longer working weeks. Table 5.4 shows that the number of people signing on the live register increased rapidly since the onset of the economic crisis in 2007. The numbers peaked in July 2011 and by December 2018 the numbers signing-on the live register had increased by almost 41,000 compared to twelve years earlier.

**Table 5.4: Numbers on the Live Register, Jan. 2007 – Dec. 2018**

| Year | Month | Males | Females | Total |
|------|-------|-------|---------|-------|
| 2007 | January | 95,824 | 62,928 | 158,752 |
| 2008 | January | 116,160 | 65,289 | 181,449 |
| 2009 | January | 220,412 | 105,860 | 326,272 |
| 2010 | January | 291,648 | 145,288 | 436,936 |
| 2011 | January | 292,003 | 150,674 | 442,677 |
| 2011 | July (peak) | 297,770 | 172,514 | 470,284 |
| 2012 | January | 283,548 | 155,337 | 438,885 |
| 2013 | January | 273,247 | 155,465 | 428,712 |
| 2014 | January | 248,533 | 150,711 | 399,244 |
| 2015 | January | 218,527 | 139,849 | 358,376 |
| 2016 | January | 191,631 | 129,882 | 321,513 |
| 2017 | January | 161,365 | 115,527 | 276,892 |
| 2018 | January | 136,735 | 100,651 | 237,386 |
| 2018 | December | · 112,414 | 87,255 | 199,669 |

**Source:** CSO, LFS on-line database.
**Note:** Unadjusted Live Register data.

## 5.2 Key Policies and Reforms

### Tackling Youth Unemployment

While the increase in unemployment over the last 12 years was spread across all ages and sectors (see Table 5.3), Chart 5.2 highlights the very rapid increase in the numbers unemployed under 25 years-of-age. The numbers in this group more than doubled between 2007 and 2009, peaking at almost 105,000 in Quarter 2 2009. Since then decreases have occurred, reaching 45,900 in 2018.

**Chart 5.2: Youth Unemployment by Gender 2007-2018**

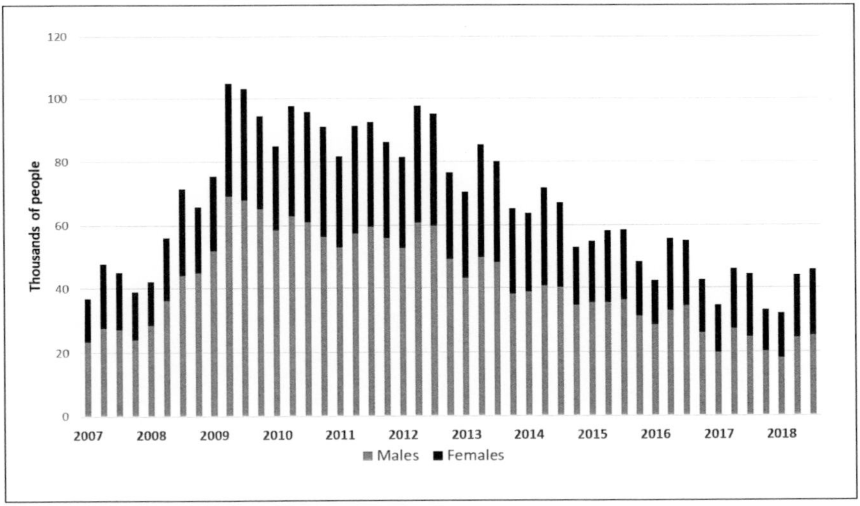

Source: CSO, QNHS on-line database.

As youth unemployment represents almost one-third of the total population that are unemployed, there is merit in giving it particular attention. Experiences of unemployment, and in particular long-term unemployment, alongside an inability to access any work, training or education, tends to leave a 'scarring effect' on young people. It increases the challenges associated with getting them active in the labour market at any stage in the future.

In the short-term it makes sense for Government to invest in the 'youth unemployed' and *Social Justice Ireland* considers this to be a central priority. At a European level, this issue has been receiving welcome attention over the past few years, driven by high levels of youth unemployment in other crisis countries.

## Upskilling and Retaining the Unemployed

The live register data offers a useful insight into the skills and experience of those signing on. Table 5.5 presents a breakdown of the December 2018 live register number by people's last occupation, and also examines the differences between those over and under 25 years. The figures highlight the need for targeted reskilling of people who hold skills in sectors of the economy that are unlikely to return to the employment levels of the early part of the last decade. As such they frame challenges for upskilling and retraining of many unemployed and underemployed individuals.

**Table 5.5: Persons on Live Register by Last Occupation – December 2018**

| Occupational group | Overall | Under 25 yrs | Over 25 yrs |
|---|---|---|---|
| Managers and administrators | 10,339 | 189 | 10,150 |
| Professional | 12,399 | 496 | 11,903 |
| Associate prof. and technical | 6,848 | 426 | 6,422 |
| Clerical and secretarial | 22,405 | 1,026 | 21,379 |
| Craft and related | 33,712 | 2,660 | 31,052 |
| Personal and protective service | 27,060 | 2,651 | 24,409 |
| Sales | 19,470 | 2,992 | 16,478 |
| Plant and machine operatives | 30,931 | 3,094 | 27,837 |
| Other occupation | 24,461 | 3,212 | 21,249 |
| No occupation | 12,044 | 3,175 | 8,869 |
| **Total** | **199,669** | **19,921** | **179,748** |

Source: CSO Live Register on-line database.

## Addressing Under-employment and Precarious Employment

The figures in Table 5.1 also point towards the growth of various forms of precarious employment over recent years. The number of people employed is higher now than it ever has been. Because of the population increase, however, since 2007 employment has fallen by just under 1 per cent; but this figure masks a bigger decline in full-time employment (1.2 per cent) and a growth in part-time employment (+10.4 per cent). Within those part-time employed it is worth focusing on those who are underemployed, that is working part-time but at less hours than they are willing to work. By the third quarter of 2018 the numbers underemployed stood at 111,500 people, 4.6 per cent of the total labour force and about one-quarter of all part-time employees.

These figures suggest the emergence of a greater number of workers in precarious employment situations. The growth in the number of individuals with less work hours than ideal, as well as those with persistent uncertainties concerning the number and times of hours required for work, is a major labour market challenge. Aside from the impact this has on the well-being of individuals and their families, it also impacts on their financial situation and adds to the working-poor challenges we outlined in Chapter 3. There are also impacts on the state, given that the Working Family Payment (formerly known as Family Income Supplement (FIS)) and the structure of jobseeker payments tend to lead to Government subsidising these families' incomes, and indirectly subsidising some employers who create persistent precarious employment patterns for their workers.

Given the current strength of the labour market, *Social Justice Ireland* believes that now is the time to adopt substantial measures to address and eliminate these problems. Our commitment to the development and adoption of a Living Wage (see Section 3.2) reflects this. Also in that context, the establishment of the Low Pay Commission is a welcome development. It is important that this group provides credible solutions to these labour market challenges and that such proposals are implemented.

### Boosting Labour Force Participation

Increasing labour force participation, in particular among women, represents a further policy challenge for labour market policy. As Table 5.6 illustrates, the proportion of individuals who are actively participating in the labour market has declined since 2007 despite the overall growth in employment.

Policy responses to this challenge need to be broad-based, and include initiatives addressing childcare provision and affordability, retraining, family-friendly employment strategies and enhanced employment quality. It is important that we remember these participation rates, and the challenges they imply, as we review the aforementioned recovery in employment and decreases in unemployment.

**Table 5.6: Labour Force Participation Rates by Gender, 2007-2018**

|  | 2007 | 2012 | 2018 | Change 07-18 |
|---|---|---|---|---|
| Both sexes | 67.4 | 62.1 | 62.6 | -4.8 |
| Males | 77.1 | 69.4 | 69.0 | -8.1 |
| Females | 57.7 | 55.0 | 56.4 | -1.3 |
| **Gender Gap\*** | **19.4** | **14.4** | **12.6** | |

**Source:** CSO, LFS on-line database.
**Note:** * the gender gap is the difference in percentage points between male and female participation levels.

**Work and People with Disabilities**

Results from Census 2016 provide the most recent insight into the scale and nature of disability in Ireland. In a report published in November 2017, the CSO reported that a total of 643,131 people had a disability in Ireland; equivalent to 13.5 per cent of the population. The most common disability was a difficulty with pain, breathing or other chronic illness which was experienced by 46.1 per cent of all people with a disability. This was followed by a difficulty with basic physical activities, experienced by 40.9 per cent. The report found that both these disabilities were strongly age-related. It also showed that 1.2 per cent of the population were blind or had a sight related disability (54,810 people); 1.4 per cent of the population suffered from an intellectual disability (66,611 people); 2.2 per cent of the population were deaf or had a hearing related disability (103,676 people); 2.6 per cent of the population had a psychological or emotional condition (123,515 people); 3.3 per cent of the population had a difficulty with learning, remembering or concentrating (156,968 people); 5.5 per cent of the population had a difficulty with basic physical activities (262,818 people); and 6.2 per cent of the population had a disability connected with pain, breathing or another chronic illness or condition (296,783 people).[3]

The Census 2016 data also revealed that there was 176,445 persons with a disability in the labour force representing a participation rate of 30.2 per cent, less than half that for the population in general. These findings reflect earlier results from Census 2011, the 2006 National Disability Survey (CSO, 2008 and 2010) and a QNHS special module on disability (CSO, 2004).

A 2017 ESRI report examined the employment transitions of people with a disability and found that among those of working age most (82 per cent) had worked at some stage in their life but that 35 per cent had been without work for more than four years (Watson et al, 2017). It also found that were Government policy to facilitate the employment of people with a disability who want to work, some 35,600 additional people with a disability would join the active workforce; a figure equivalent to 1.5 per cent of the 2017 labour force (Watson et al, 2017:56).

This low rate of employment among people with a disability is of concern. Apart from restricting their participation in society it also ties them into state-dependent low-income situations. Therefore, it is not surprising that Ireland's poverty figures reveal that people who are ill or have a disability are part of a group at high risk of poverty (see Chapter 3).

*Social Justice Ireland* believes that further efforts should be made to reduce the impediments faced by people with a disability to obtain employment. In particular, consideration should be given to reforming the current situation in which many such people face losing their benefits, in particular their medical card, when they take up employment. This situation ignores the additional costs faced by people

---

[3] Note, some individuals will experience more than one disability and feature in more than one of these categories.

with a disability in pursuing their day-to-day lives. For many people with disabilities the opportunity to take up employment is denied to them and they are trapped in unemployment, poverty, or both.

Some progress was made in Budget 2005 to increase supports intended to help people with disabilities access employment. However, sufficient progress has not been made and recent Budgets have begun to reduce these services. New policies, including that outlined above, need to be adopted if this issue is to be addressed successfully. It is even more relevant today, given the growing employment challenges of the past few years.

### Asylum Seekers and Work
During February 2018 the Supreme Court formally declared the absolute ban preventing asylum seekers taking up work as unconstitutional. The declaration followed an initial decision in May 2017 with the court giving the Government time to adopt new legislation and procedures to accommodate the decision. In effect, the Government failed to do so, and the Supreme Court removed the ban.

*Social Justice Ireland* welcomed this long overdue recognition; we have called for policy reform in this area for some time. However, we are concerned by Government attempts to limit these rights and restrict the opportunities of Asylum Seekers. At the root of these problems are issues regarding the effectiveness of the current system of processing asylum applications. Along with others, we have consistently advocated that where Government fails to meet its own stated objective of processing asylum applications in six months, the right to work should be automatically granted to asylum seekers. That right should extend to all types and areas of work. Detaining people for an unnecessarily prolonged period in such an excluded state is completely unacceptable. Recognising and facilitating asylum seekers' right to work would assist in alleviating poverty and social exclusion among one of Ireland's most vulnerable groups.[4]

### Acknowledging the Work of Carers
The work of Ireland's carers receives minimal recognition despite the essential role their work plays in society. Results from the 2016 Census offered an insight into the scale of these commitments, which save the state large costs that it would otherwise have to bear.

Census 2016 found that 4.1 per cent of the population provided some care for sick or disabled family members or friends on an unpaid basis. This figure equates to 195,263 people. The dominant caring role played by women was highlighted by the fact that 118,151 (60.5 per cent) of these care providers were female.[5] When

---

[4]   We examine this issue in further detail in chapter 10.

[5]   A CSO QNHS special module on carers (CSO, 2010) and a 2008 ESRI study entitled '*Gender Inequalities in Time Use*' found similar trends (McGinnity and Russell, 2008:36, 70).

assessed by length of time, the census found that a total of 6,608,515 hours of care were provided by carers each week, representing an average of 38.3 hours of unpaid help and assistance each. Two thirds of this volume of care was provided by female carers. Using the minimum wage as a simple (if unrealistically low) benchmark to establish the benefit which carers provide each year suggests that Ireland's carers provide care valued at more than €3.14bn per annum.[6]

*Social Justice Ireland* welcomed the long overdue publication of a *National Carers Strategy* in July 2012 (Department of Health, 2012). The document included a 'roadmap for implementation' involving a suite of actions and associated timelines, and identifies the Government Department responsible for their implementation. However, these actions were confined to those that could be achieved on a cost neutral basis. Various progress reports of the strategy have been published to date and point towards some progress on the actions set out. However, these are, as a group, limited given the unwillingness of Government to allocate sufficient resources to supporting those in this sector.

*Social Justice Ireland* believes that further policy reforms should be introduced to reduce the financial and emotional pressures on carers. In particular, these should focus on addressing the poverty experienced by many carers and their families alongside increasing the provision of respite care for carers and for those for whom they care. In this context, the 24 hour responsibilities of carers contrast with the improvements over recent years in employment legislation setting limits on working-hours of people in paid employment.

### Recognising All Work
A major question raised by the current labour-market situation concerns assumptions underpinning culture and policymaking in this area. The priority given to paid employment over other forms of work is one such assumption. Most people recognise that a person can be working very hard outside a conventionally accepted "job". Much of the work carried out in the community and in the voluntary sector comes under this heading. So too does much of the work done in the home. *Social Justice Ireland*'s support for the introduction of a basic income system comes, in part, because it believes that all work should be recognised and supported (see Chapter 3).

The need to recognise voluntary work has been acknowledged in the Government White Paper, *Supporting Voluntary Activity* (Department of Social, Community and Family Affairs, 2000). The report was prepared to mark the UN International Year of the Volunteer 2001 by Government and representatives of numerous voluntary organisations in Ireland. The report made a series of recommendations to assist in the future development and recognition of voluntary activity throughout Ireland. A 2005 report presented to the Joint Oireachtas Committee on Arts, Sport, Tourism, Community, Rural and Gaeltacht Affairs also provided an insight into this issue. It

---

[6]   Calculation based on 2016 minimum wage of €9.15 per hour.

established that the cost to the state of replacing the 475,000 volunteers working for charitable organisations would be at least €205 million and could be as high as €485 million per year.

*Social Justice Ireland* believes that government should recognise, in a more formal way, all forms of work. We believe that everyone has a right to work, to contribute to his or her own development and that of the community and wider society. We also believe that policymaking in this area should not be exclusively focused on job creation. Policy should recognise that *work* and a *job* are not always the same thing.

## 5.3 Key Policy Priorities

*Social Justice Ireland* believes that if the challenges and needed reforms we have highlighted throughout this chapter are to be effectively addressed, Government's key policy priorities in this area should be to:

- Launch a major investment programme focused on prioritising initiatives that strengthen social infrastructure, including a comprehensive school building programme and a much larger social housing programme;

- Resource the up-skilling of those who are unemployed and at risk of becoming unemployed through integrating training and labour market programmes;

- Adopt policies to address the worrying issue of youth unemployment. In particular, these should include education and literacy initiatives as well as retraining schemes;

- Recognise the challenge of long-term unemployment and of precarious employment and adopt targeted policies to address these;

- Recognise that the term "work" is not synonymous with the concept of "paid employment". Everybody has a right to work, i.e. to contribute to his or her own development and that of the community and the wider society. This, however, should not be confined to job creation. Work and a job are not the same thing.

*Social Justice Ireland* believes that in the period ahead Government and policymakers generally should:

- Expand funded programmes supporting the community to meet the growing pressures throughout our society;

- Establish a new programme targeting those who are very long-term unemployed (i.e. 5+ years);

- Ensure that at all times policy seeks to ensure that new jobs have reasonable pay rates, and adequate resource are provided for the labour inspectorate;

- Adopt policies to address the working poor issue including a reform the taxation system to make the two main income tax credits refundable;

- Develop employment-friendly income tax policies which ensure that no unemployment traps exist. Policies should also ease the transition from unemployment to employment;

- Adopt policies to address the obstacles facing women when they return to the labour force. These should focus on care initiatives, employment flexibility and the provision of information and training;

- Reduce the impediments faced by people with a disability in achieving employment. In particular, address the current situation in which many face losing their benefits, including the medical card, when they take up employment;

- Facilitate the right to work of all asylum seekers and resource the improvement of the current system of processing asylum applications;

- Give greater recognition to the work carried out by carers in Ireland and introduce policy reforms to reduce the financial and emotional pressures on carers. In particular, these should focus on addressing the poverty experienced by many carers and their families, as well as on increasing the provision of respite opportunities to carers and to those for whom they care.

- Request the CSO to conduct an annual survey to discover the value of all unpaid work in the country (including community and voluntary work and work in the home). Publish the results of this survey as soon as they become available;

- Recognise that the term "work" is not synonymous with the concept of "paid employment". Everybody has a right to work, i.e. to contribute to his or her own development and that of the community and the wider society. This, however, should not be confined to job creation. *Work* and a *job* are not the same thing.

# REFERENCES

Central Statistics Office (2004) *Quarterly National Household Survey: Special Module on Disability Quarter 1 2004*. Dublin: Stationery Office.

Central Statistics Office (2008) *National Disability Survey 2006 – First Results*. Dublin: Stationery Office.

Central Statistics Office (2010) *National Disability Survey 2006 – Volume Two*. Dublin: Stationery Office.

Central Statistics Office (2010) *Quarterly National Household Survey: Special Module on Carers Quarter 3 2009*. Dublin: Stationery Office.

Central Statistics Office (2012) *Census 2011 Profile 8: Our Bill of Health – Health, Disability and Carers in Ireland*. Dublin: Stationery Office.

Central Statistics Office (2019) *Seasonally Adjusted Monthly Unemployment Rate (%) by Sex, Age Group and Month*. Available at: https://www.cso.ie/px/pxeirestat/Database/eirestat/Monthly%20Unemployment/Monthly%20Unemployment_statbank.asp?SP=Monthly%20Unemployment&Planguage=0

Department of Finance (various*) Budget Documentation – various years*. Dublin: Stationery Office.

Department of Health (2012) *National Carers Strategy*. Department of Health.

Department of Social, Community and Family Affairs (2000) *Supporting Voluntary Activity*. Dublin: Stationery Office.

Joint Oireachtas Committee on Arts, Sport, Tourism, Community, Rural and Gaeltacht Affairs (2005) *Volunteers and Volunteering in Ireland*. Dublin: Stationery Office.

McGinnity, F. and Russell, H. (2008) *Gender Inequalities in Time Use*. Dublin: ESRI.

Watson, D., M. Lawless and B. Maitre (2017) *Employment Transitions among People with Disabilities in Ireland: an analysis of the Quarterly National Household Survey 2010-2015*. Dublin: ESRI.


***Online database***
CSO online database, web address: http://www.cso.ie/en/databases/

# Chapter 6
## Housing and Accommodation

**Core Policy Objective:**
To ensure that adequate and
appropriate accommodation is
available for all people and to develop
an equitable system for allocating
resources within the housing sector.

### Key Issues/Evidence

**115,000+**
households in need of
long-term social housing

**11,000+**
homeless people
including
almost
**4,000**
Children

**72,000**
families
in mortgage
arrears

**340,000**
private
tenancies

**173,400**
landlords

Lack of
construction of
social housing

**Policy Solutions**

Strengthen Mortgage to Rent for people in late stage mortgage arrears

Construction of more social housing

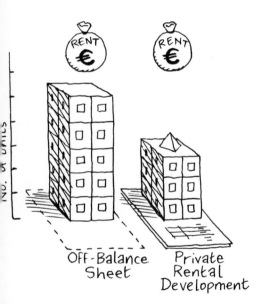

Develop cost rental (where the rent is set based on the cost of providing the accommodation) to scale, using off-balance sheet financing

Increased protections for private tenants

Legislation to limit time in Family Hubs

# 6.

# HOUSING AND ACCOMMODATION

---

**CORE POLICY OBJECTIVE: HOUSING & ACCOMMODATION**

To ensure that adequate and appropriate accommodation is available for all people and to develop an equitable system for allocating resources within the housing sector.

**The provision of adequate, and appropriate accommodation is a key element of** *Social Justice Ireland's* **Social Charter framework as outlined in Chapter 2. To achieve this objective in the years ahead,** *Social Justice Ireland* believes that the Government must:

- Build more social housing and allow local authorities and Approved Housing Bodies pool resources to finance this increased supply in a sustainable way.

- Develop a system of affordable rent through the cost rental model, financed 'off-balance-sheet' to allow for supply to scale up without adding to the general government debt.

- Increase the provision of Housing First accommodation for families in emergency accommodation and limit the length of time families can spend in Family Hubs.

- Develop a spectrum of housing supports for people with disabilities.

- Review the Mortgage to Rent scheme for those in late stage mortgage arrears.

- Introduce sanctions for local authorities who do not utilise funding available to provide safe, sustainable Traveller accommodation.

# Key Evidence

## *6.1 Current Housing Supply*

*Construction*

Census 2016 puts the current housing stock at 2,003,645 in 2016, of which just under 1.7 million are occupied and over 180,000 are vacant units, excluding holiday homes (CSO, 2017(a)). New figures released by the CSO last year showed that housing construction between 2011 and 2017 had been continuously overestimated through the use of ESB Connections data as a substitute for an actual dwelling completions count. The CSO is now collating this data, with the latest results set out in Chart 6.1. From 2011 to 2014, two thirds of all new dwelling completions comprised of single units, while less than a quarter comprised of scheme developments. Between 2015 and the third quarter of 2018, this trend has reversed with one third of all new dwellings comprising of single units compared to over half attributed to schemes. As might be expected, these trends are also evident when considering the urban / rural development. Between 2011 and 2013, more dwellings were completed in rural areas (60 per cent) than urban areas (40 per cent), reversing between 2014 and Q3 2018 (to 40 per cent rural, 60 per cent urban).

While the number of new dwelling completions being delivered is still below what is required to keep pace with demographic changes and accounting for obsolescence, the upward overall trend, and that of scheme developments, is a positive sign. However, dwelling completions are not of themselves enough to address our current housing crisis. This increase needs to be reflected in the provision of social and affordable housing and long term private rental solutions, discussed later in this Chapter.

**Chart 6.1: New Dwelling Completions 2011 to 2018**

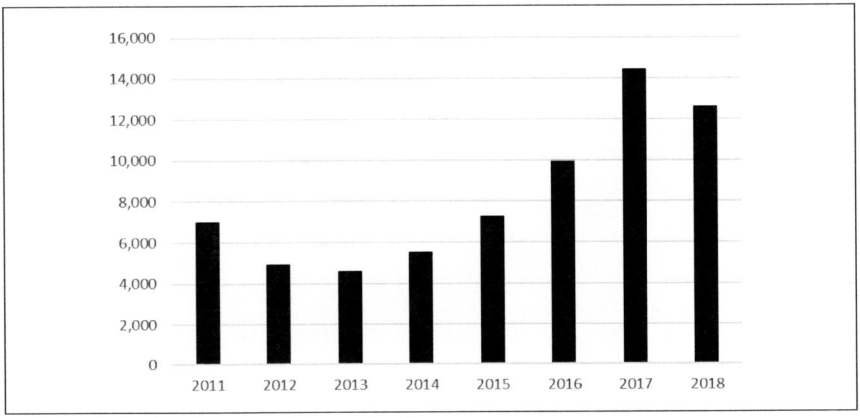

**Source:** CSO, Table 1 New dwelling completions classified by type 2011 to Q3 2018
**Note:** Data for 2018 is for the first three quarters.

*Vacant Homes*

According to the most recent figures there were 183,312 (excluding holiday homes) vacant properties on Census night 2016 (CSO, 2017(a)). Of these, 140,120 were houses and 43,192 were apartments. While this figure represents a decrease in vacancy rates per population size in all counties when compared to Census 2011, when the preliminary figures for each county are compared to the county breakdown of the Social Housing Needs Assessment 2018 (Housing Agency, 2018) there remains more vacant properties than households in need (Chart 6.2) in every county, assuming the figures produced in the Summary of Housing Needs Assessment 2018 are correct, which we discuss later in this Chapter.

In early 2017, the Government introduced the Repair and Leasing Scheme for owners of vacant properties to access funding of up to €40,000 to repair their properties which would then be leased to the local authority for use as social housing for a term of between five and 20 years. The latest data available from the Department shows that up to Q1 of 2018, 942 applications had been made to the scheme. Of these, less than half (445) were deemed suitable, with only 52 leases signed (5.5 per cent of the total applications received) and 15 properties (1.5 per cent of total applications) coming into operation.

In July 2018, the Government launched its Vacant Housing Reuse Strategy 2018-2021, aimed at bringing existing vacant properties back into use. The Department of Housing, Planning and Local Government is establishing an Empty Homes unit to coordinate across central and local government, and each local government was requested to develop a Vacant Homes Action Plan to identify vacant homes within their areas. While *Social Justice Ireland* welcomed its publication at the time, and its intention to review bringing many of the 183,000 houses under the control of the local authority or Approved Housing Bodies to provide social homes, we were disappointed to note the timeframes involved, which looked to bring the first homes into use in late 2019 or 2020.

Data released by the Department also show just 605 local authority 'voids' were put back into use in the first three quarters of 2018. In its 2017 Local Authority Performance Indicators Report, NOAC noted the number of vacant local authority properties in 2017 as 3,631 (NOAC, 2018), meaning just 17 per cent were returned to use in 2018.

**Chart 6.2: Vacant units 2016 v Social Housing Waiting Lists 2018, by County**

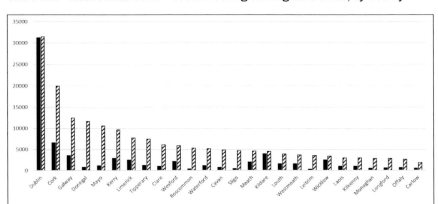

**Source:** Census 2016, www.cso.ie and Housing Agency, Summary of Social Housing Assessments 2018

*Social Housing Rented Stock*
The latest data released by the Department show 141,504 homes were let by local authorities in 2016. In their report *The Future of Council Housing, An analysis of the financial sustainability of local authority provided social housing*, published in July 2018, Prof. Michelle Norris and Dr. Aideen Hayden examined the existing structures for the provision of social housing to low income households (Norris and Hayden, 2018). They examined Government housing policies since the 1980s, which saw a move away from construction of social housing to a more cost-effective outsourcing to the private market and the subsidisation of private landlords through Rent Supplement, the Rent Accommodation Scheme and Housing Assistance Payment (HAP). With increasing private rents, many private properties have been taken out of the reach of low-income tenants, particularly in urban centres. Lack of low-cost accommodation on the market and the reduction in new local authority construction means that Government, and local authorities particularly, need to overhaul the provision of housing to those on low incomes.

The report ends with a comprehensive suite of recommendations, from minor scale reforms such as ring-fencing rents paid to local authorities to spend on council housing (a recommendation made by *Social Justice Ireland* in previous editions of our socio-economic review) and undertaking a valuation of local authority housing stock and recording these valuations in local authority accounts; to medium scale reforms such as the suspension of the tenant purchase scheme for council housing given the shortage of available council housing.

The conclusion of the report on the sustainability of financing council housing centres on a 'radical restructuring of arrangements for funding social housing' and the introduction of a cost rental model (Norris and Hayden, 2018). *Social Justice Ireland* have been advocating for the introduction of a cost rental model of affordable rental (in addition to the need to scale up social housing provision), which we will discuss later in this Chapter.

*Social Housing Output*
As noted by Norris and Hayden, the last three decades have seen 'a significant reduction in the traditional role of council housing as the primary source of accommodation for low-income renters. Their report attributes this reduction to the contraction of capital funding for council housing, which fell by 94 per cent between 2008 and 2013 (Norris and Hayden, 2018:38). The expansion and contraction of capital spending on housing by central government demonstrates just how volatile this basic necessity for low-income families is, and how responsive to economic shocks. Chart 6.3 shows the pro-cyclical nature of central government capital expenditure allocations to the Department of Housing, Planning and Local Government since 1994. Expenditure increased steadily from 1994 to 2000, before declining sharply. A further period of increase between 2004 and 2008 was followed by another, more severe decline in the years 2009 to 2015. Since then, gross capital expenditure allocation has increased again, however the volatile nature of this expenditure pattern calls into question the sustainability of any long-term capital projects.

**Chart 6.3: Gross Capital Expenditure on Housing, 1994 to 2018, €,000**

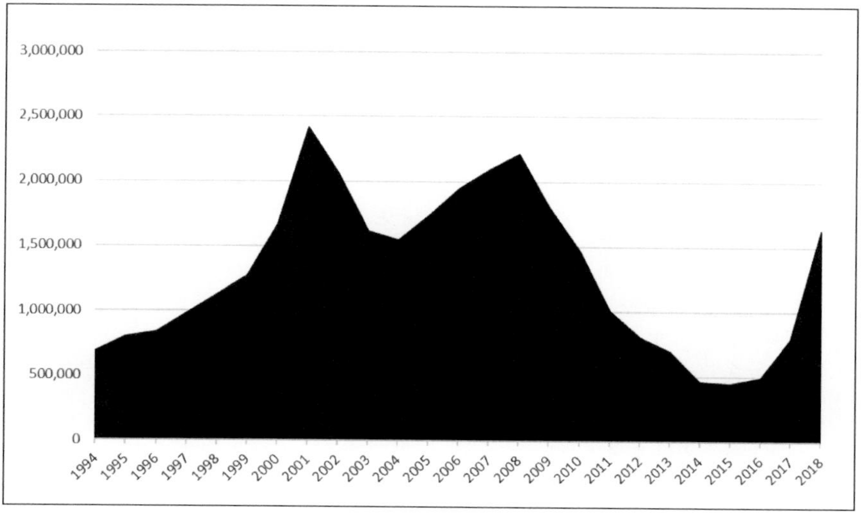

**Source:** Department of Public Expenditure and Reform, Databank

The role of local authorities in building long-term social housing was diminishing even before the crash in 2008, however, as Government looked to Approved Housing Bodies, seen until recently as 'off-balance sheet' providers of social housing. While capital spending increased in the years to 2008, neither this, nor the subsequent increase since 2015, is reflected in the proportion of Social Housing Output attributed to local authority 'builds', which currently stands at just over 4 per cent (Chart 6.4).

**Chart 6.4: Local Authority 'builds' as a % of all 'Social Housing Output', 2004 to 2018**

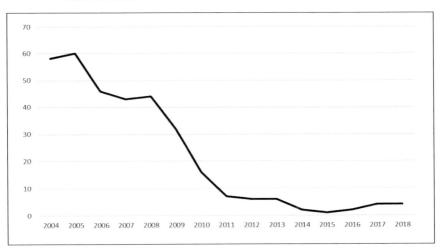

Source: Department of Housing, Planning and Local Government, Housing Statistics, Overview of Social Housing Activity various years
Notes: Local Authority 'builds' include Turnkey, Traditional, Rapid and Regenerations, data from 2004 to 2015 also includes some units acquired under Part V of the Planning and Development Acts for rental purposes
Data for 2018 refers to the first three quarters of 2018

As stated earlier, recent Government policy has seen a shift away from the construction of social housing to an over-reliance on the private rented sector to provide social housing 'solutions'. This is evident from both the increase and change in nature of the current expenditure on housing in recent years. According to a report prepared by the Irish Government Economic and Evaluation Service (IGEES) for the Department of Public Expenditure and Reform (IGEES, 2018), from 2006 to 2017 Rent Supplement was the main area of current housing expenditure. While the proportion attributed to the Rental Accommodation Scheme (RAS) was growing steadily during this period, the introduction of the Housing Assistance Payment (HAP) in 2014 has had the greatest impact on the distribution of current housing expenditure (2018:24).

Ostensibly, the introduction of HAP was to provide a longer-term supplementary payment for the growing number of private tenants in receipt of Rent Supplement for longer than its intended duration. Since 2014, the importance of HAP as a means of providing 'social housing supports' increased dramatically. Commencing in September 2014, HAP accounted for 11 per cent of all 'Social Housing Output' that year. In the first three quarters of 2018, this increased to over 73 per cent (Chart 6.5).

HAP is a payment made by the local authority directly to the landlord in respect of a household assessed as needing long-term social housing. The tenancy is between the landlord and the tenant, and notwithstanding the introduction of anti-discrimination laws in favour of tenants in receipt of HAP, choosing to accept, and retain, HAP tenants in a time of double-digit rent inflation remains at the discretion of the landlord.

**Chart 6.5: HAP as a % of all 'Social Housing Output', 2014 to 2018**

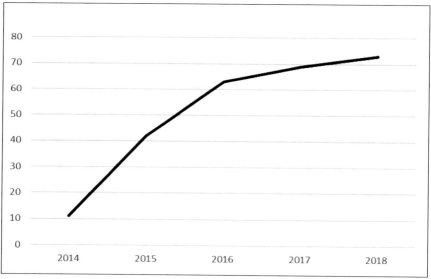

Source: Department of Housing, Planning and Local Government, Housing Statistics, Overview of Social Housing Activity various years
Note: Data for 2014 refers to the period September to December 2014; data for 2018 refers to the first three quarters of 2018

The decline in local authority construction, discretionary nature of HAP tenancies, increase in the cost of private rents and the promotion by Government of policies which seek to rely on the private rented sector for the provision of social housing places low-income households in precarious living situations. This is not a long-term solution, but a short-term fix that will have repercussions for generations.

## 6.2 Current Housing Need

*Summary of Social Housing Assessments 2018*

According to the Social Housing Needs Assessments 2018, published in September 2018, there were 71,858 *households* on the waiting list for social housing, presenting as a decrease of 16 per cent on the previous year (Housing Agency, 2018). However, the truth is that the housing crisis is worsening as Government continues to look to the private sector for solutions.

In 2011, the number of households assessed as having a social housing need was 98,318 – the highest number since 1993 (when it was 28,200) (Housing Agency, 2011). A change in the way need was calculated, and a removal of duplicates, saw this number reduce in 2013 to 89,872. The introduction of HAP, and the transfer of households in long-term receipt of Rent Supplement to this payment further reduced these numbers. Households in receipt of HAP are deemed to have their social housing need met and are not counted in the Summary of Social Housing Assessments, the official figure used to determine need. This means that households who would, pre-2014, have been given Rent Supplement and included in the social housing waiting list data, are no longer included. It also means that, notwithstanding the fact that the actual circumstances of the 8,989 households that were transferred from Rent Supplement to HAP between 2016 and Q2 of 2018 (disaggregated data not available for previous years) may not have changed, they have been removed from the list.

The number of households in receipt of HAP up to Q2 of 2018 was 43,492. When this number is added to the number of households on the housing list, the number of households in need of long-term, sustainable social housing in 2018 was 115,350, 4,425 more households than during the same period in the previous year[1].

There has also been some debate surrounding the methodology used by local authorities in collecting information about those still on the housing waiting list, namely an 'opt in' letter requesting information on housing status which, if not returned, resulted in automatic removal from the list. While discretion was given to local authorities to make further contacts by telephone and text message, this method of data collection adversely affects those with low literacy skills and those with reduced capacity to engage in this manner, whether through stress or other socio-economic factors. It therefore risks excluding the most vulnerable households and could be a contributory factor to the rising rate of family homelessness, discussed later in this Chapter.

Another factor may be that while those in receipt of Rent Supplement are counted, and account for 34.8 per cent of households on the social housing waiting list, those in receipt of the HAP, living in local authority rented accommodation, accommodation under the Rental Accommodation Scheme, accommodation

---

[1]    Data up to end Q2 used for both years

provided under the Social Housing Capital Expenditure Programmes or any households on the transfer list are not counted as in need of social housing assistance. Almost 10,000 households have been transferred from Rent Supplement to HAP since 2016. Rent Supplement transfers accounted for 20 per cent of the total number of HAP tenancies in the first two quarters of 2018. We have previously discussed the precariousness of these tenancies. While they continue to be omitted from official statistics on housing need, policy in this area will continue to focus on short-term fixes, rather than long-term solutions.

*Social Housing Needs Assessments – The People*
Of the 71,858 households on the waiting list, the highest percentage is in Dublin (43 per cent), followed by Cork (9 per cent), Kildare (5.5 per cent) and Galway (five per cent). The age profile of households on the waiting list has changed little in the last two years, with the highest proportion being those aged between 30-39 years old (32.2 per cent), followed by those aged between 40-49 years old (23.6 per cent) and those aged between 50-59 years old (13.9 per cent). This is unsurprising, given the length of time households are waiting for social housing, with 51.6 per cent (up 1.6 percentage points on the previous year) waiting four years or more, and 26.7 per cent, or 19,185 households, waiting more than seven years, compared to 24.2 per cent in 2017, 21.2 per cent in 2016 and only 9 per cent in 2013.

There has been a slight decrease in the proportion of families on the social housing waiting list, at 52.7 per cent in 2018 (37,838 households) compared to 55 per cent in 2017. Single person households increased from 44.5 per cent in 2017 to 46.7 per cent in 2018. The remaining 0.6[2] per cent is multi-adult households. 4.8 per cent (3,465 households) cited 'overcrowding' as the main need for social housing in 2018 compared to 4.1 per cent the previous year. Census 2016 reported a 28 per cent increase in overcrowding (from 73,997 permanent households to 95,013) in the intercensal period from 2011 to 2016, accounting for close to 10 per cent of the population (CSO, 2017(a)).

The majority of households on the social housing waiting list (61.7 per cent) are entirely dependent on social welfare income, demonstrating its inadequacy as a living income. 59.1 per cent of households on the social housing waiting list in 2018 are living in private rented accommodation, compared to 64.6 per cent the previous year. This decrease, coupled with the corresponding increase in the proportion of households living with parents (19.1 per cent, compared to 17.4 per cent in 2017), family or friends (7.6 per cent, compared to 6.5 per cent in 2017) or emergency accommodation (6.6 per cent, compared to 5.1 per cent in 2017) shows just how unsuitable the private rented sector is at providing sustainable housing for low income households.

Those households who cited their tenure status as 'owner occupier' increased from 1.3 per cent (1,119 households) in 2017 to 1.7 per cent (1,216 households) in 2018.

---

[2]   This is an anomaly in the Housing Agency document, most likely due to rounding off

With the persistent level of late stage mortgage arrears, the increase of mortgage sales to private investment funds, and the corresponding reduction in borrower protections, more households are looking to secure social housing, adding even greater pressure to a flagging social housing sector.

*Mortgage Arrears*
Up to September 2018, there were 64,510 home mortgages in arrears, with 45,178 of these in arrears of more than 90 days (Central Bank of Ireland, 2018). This represents a decrease on the previous year of 11 per cent of both all mortgage accounts in arrears and those in arrears of more than 90 days.

113,871 home mortgages are in restructured arrangements (a decrease of 4 per cent on Q3 of 2017), with 33.2 per cent having had their arrears capitalised (that is, where the arrears are added to the outstanding balance of the mortgage and repayments recalculated based on this higher amount), 25.9 per cent on reduced payments, 17 per cent classified as 'Other' (which can include reduced repayment arrangements or temporary arrangements) and 24 per cent on 'split mortgages'. Households with 'split mortgages' are most precarious where it is unlikely that they will experience a change in financial circumstances over the term of the loan and will therefore be dependent on realising the equity at the end of the warehoused period in order to pay the amount due. These families will then be faced with the prospect of selling their family home when they are at or close to retirement age.

By the end of Q3 of 2018, 1,702 residential properties were in possession of Central Bank lenders, including 1,657 'PDHs' or primary dwelling houses, that is, where the mortgage was taken out in respect of a family home. Of the 161 family homes repossessed during this quarter, 42 per cent were on foot of a court order, with the remaining 58 per cent being voluntarily surrendered or abandoned.

*Mortgage Arrears – Non-bank Entities*
Non-bank entities held 69,579 family home mortgages, 11,531 of which are held by unregulated loan owners. This represents an increase of 42 per cent on all family home mortgages held by non-bank entities on the same period in 2017, with the majority of this increase attributed to the additional 31,462 mortgages held by retail credit firms. Of the 69,579 family home mortgages, 21 per cent are in arrears, with 17 per cent in arrears of more than 90 days.

The mortgages held by unregulated loan owners are more likely to be in severe arrears situations. 50 per cent of home mortgages held by unregulated loan owners are in arrears of more than 90 days, with 41 per cent in arrears more than 720 days. This compares with 10 per cent and 5 per cent respectively for those home mortgages held by retail credit firms and 8.8 per cent and 6.2 per cent respectively for banks. Due to the nature of such funds, whose motives are profit-driven, repossessions are likely to be more prevalent among this cohort, resulting in greater need for social housing.

There has been much commentary recently about the sale of mortgage loans by banks to non-bank entities as part of a strategy to reduce the number of non-performing loans (NPLs) to within EU parameters. Consumer advocates have expressed concerned about the lack of consumer protections for borrowers, particularly those whose loans were performing, while those in favour of this strategy cite the high level of NPLs acting as a barrier to accessing better credit terms, thereby contributing to Ireland's high mortgage rates. Data extracted from the Central Bank's quarterly statistical report on mortgage arrears show that while the number of PDH mortgages held by non-bank entities has risen by 89 per cent since 2016, the number in arrears has remained relatively static (Chart 6.6).

**Chart 6.6:  PDH Mortgages held and Mortgage Arrears, Non-Bank Entities, 2016 to 2018**

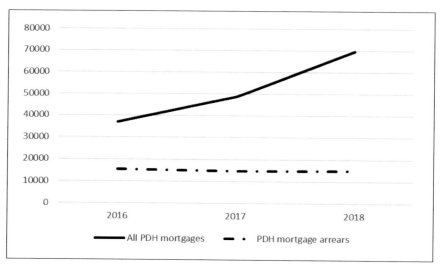

**Source:** Central Bank of Ireland, Residential Mortgage Arrears and Repossession Statistics, various years
**Note:** Data for end Q3 each year.

*Mortgage Arrears – Local Authorities*
Of the 15,420 local authority mortgages, 44 per cent were in arrears as at Q3 2018, representing 6,770 low-income households, 3,298 of which are in arrears of more than 90 days (Department of Housing, Planning and Local Government, 2018(a)). This represents a reduction of 558 mortgages in arrears and 655 mortgages in arrears of more than 90 days when compared to the same period in 2017. During this period there were also 687 fewer mortgages recorded in total.

The latest local authority repossession figures show 11 forced and 26 voluntary repossessions took place in 2017, a reduction of 50 per cent and 42 per cent respectively on the previous year (Department of Housing, Planning and Local Government, 2018(b)). The only option for these families is adequate social housing, which this and previous Governments have failed to provide. This social housing could be provided by the expansion of a Local Authority Mortgage to Rent Scheme, piloted in 2013 and rolled out in subsequent years. There were 90 Local Authority Mortgage to Rent transactions completed in 2017, three more that the previous year but 22 less than 2016.

*Population Expansion*
The latest Census data (CSO, 2017(b)) shows a population increase between 2011 and 2016 of 3.8 per cent, or 173,613 people (when migration is accounted for), bringing the total population of the State to over 4.7 billion people. The natural increase in population (births minus deaths) was 196,100, a reduction of 30,000 on the previous intercensal period which is largely attributed to a fall in births (22,800 decrease on figures produced in Census 2011). 80 per cent of the net increase of 173,613 in population (138,899) was experienced in urban areas, with Dublin and surrounding counties and parts of Munster experiencing the largest percentage increases in population.

In addition to increased population, Census 2016 also noted an increase in household formation (i.e. the number of new households is growing) of 2.9 per cent compared to an increase in population of 3.7 per cent and has resulted in an increase in average household size for the first time since 1996. This means that in areas such as Fingal where the rate of population growth (8.1 per cent) was almost twice that of household formation (4.4 per cent – based on preliminary figures), further investment in construction is urgently needed to accommodate a young and expanding community.

A preliminary update of Housing Supply Requirements 2016 to 2020 prepared by Future Analytics for the Housing Agency in February 2017 (Future Analytics, 2017) indicated that the 445 urban settlements which were home to 500 people or more in 2011 are predicted to experience a growth of 8.6 per cent to 2020; an increase of 262,000 people. Of these 445 urban settlements, 248 will experience a supply deficit in the five years up to and including 2020 at the current rate of supply. Two-thirds of those likely to experience a deficit are currently home to 1,000 people or more. This update further identifies a minimum housing supply requirement of 81,118 homes nationally, with 79,215 of these needed in the largest population centres. The average annual minimum home provision requirement is therefore 16,224 nationally, with 15,843 in the largest population centres (Future Analytics, 2017:1). Dublin County is predicted to need the highest housing supply nationally, with 35,242 homes required each year, which is hardly surprising given the number of households on the social housing waiting list and the number of homeless persons in the county.

In an article on household formation, the ESRI (Duffy et al, 2014) projected annual growth in household formation of up to 33,000 to 2030. While the figures may vary to an extent, it is a reasonable extrapolation to predict a net demand requirement of somewhere between 16,000 and 33,000. This is further supported by a NERI Working Paper (Healy and Goldrick-Kelly, 2017:51) which cites demand of 25,000 to 35,000 once population expansion and an obsolescence rate of 0.5 per cent per annum is accounted for.

*Homelessness*

Ireland's homelessness crisis continues to worsen. In November 2018, there were 9,968 homeless people listed in Ireland. The number of homeless adults increased by 126 per cent since 2014 (from 2,720 to 6,157), with the number of homeless children increasing by 329 per cent (from 887 to 3,811), and homeless families increasing by 336 per cent (from 396 to 1,728) in the same period (Chart 6.7 and Table 6.1).

**Chart 6.7: Homelessness, 2014 to 2018**

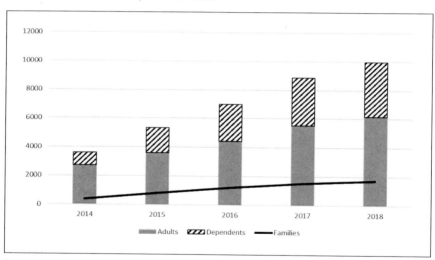

**Source:** Department of Housing, Planning and Local Government Homelessness Statistics, various years
**Note:** Data refers to November each year

Although still in double-digits, the rate of increase in homelessness across all groups was lowest in the period 2017 to 2018 (Table 6.1), however this could, at least in part, be attributed to the directive circulated by the Department of Housing, Planning and Local Government last year to exclude certain families previously included in the homelessness data by the local authorities. These families are temporarily housed in local authority owned accommodation, rather than hotels or B&Bs, as a cost saving measure for the local authorities; however while their need for permanent housing is the same as the 1,728 families included in the official homeless figures, their status for the purpose of data collection, and subsequent policy development, has changed.

**Table 6.1: Rate of Increase in Homelessness, Year on Year, 2014 to 2018**

|  | 2014-15 | 2015-16 | 2016-17 | 2017-18 | 2014-18 |
|---|---|---|---|---|---|
| Adults | 32.9 | 22.7 | 24.5 | 11.5 | 126.4 |
| Dependents | 92.7 | 49.2 | 30.8 | 14.3 | 329.7 |
| Families | 105.3 | 48.2 | 27.0 | 12.9 | 336.4 |

**Source:** Department of Housing, Planning and Local Government Homelessness Statistics, various years
**Note:** Data refers to November each year

The most recent rough sleeper count, taken in Winter (November) 2018 (Dublin Region Homeless Executive, 2018(a)), confirmed 156 persons sleeping rough on the night of the count, a decrease of 15 per cent on the previous Winter and over 70 per cent more than Winter 2015. After taking this number into account, the total number of people in need of emergency services in November 2018 (that is, 10,124) increased by 42 per cent since November 2016, and that is without considering the number of hidden homeless – those staying with friends and family or living in squats.

In the breakdown of Specific Accommodation Requirements contained in the Summary of Social Housing Assessments (Housing Agency, 2018), the number of households reporting 'Household member(s) is homeless' increased from 4,765 (5.6 per cent of the total) in 2017 to 5,329 (7.4 per cent of the total in 2018), an increase of 12 per cent overall. Even with the significant decrease in official numbers in need of social housing, the homelessness crisis is undeniable and must be addressed.

*Security of tenure in the Private Rental Market*
The latest Daft Rental Report (Lyons, 2018) indicates that rents are continuing to rise across the country and year-on-year rent inflation rising slightly from 11.2 per cent up to Q3 of 2017 to 11.3 per cent up to Q3 of 2018. This brings the national average rent to €1,334 per month. This continued increase places access to adequate private rent out of the reach of many low-income families. Rents in nine areas in Dublin have doubled since 2011 and South Dublin, which saw the smallest increase, experienced an increase of 84 per cent in the same period. Rent inflation was highest in cities outside of Dublin, with an average increase of 15.8 per cent. According to the report, there were 3,214 properties available to rent nationally on the 1st November 2018, representing a decrease of 4.5 per cent on the previous year. According to Census 2016, an increasing proportion of young occupiers are renting. Many of these may never buy their own homes, and so Government must develop policies to secure long term tenancies, increase tenant protections and enhance the

capacity of the Residential Tenancies Board to inspect rental properties and enforce regulations where landlords are found to be in breach.

In his press release following the announcement of Budget 2019, Minister Eoghan Murphy committed an increase of 67 per cent in the allocation to the Residential Tenancies Board and local authorities to increase inspections of rented properties. He further promised to introduce legislation in October 2018 to strengthen tenant protections by doubling the notice periods for the service of notices to quit after six months and to strengthen rent caps to student accommodation. The Residential Tenancies (Amendment)(No.2) Bill 2018 was initiated in the Dáil on the 21st December 2018. Given that the three Bills intended to strengthen tenant rights initiated in May 2018 have not yet made it past the third stage (of 11), while the increase in mortgage interest tax relief for landlords is effective from January 2019, there seems a disproportionate lack of urgency to protect tenants. The latest registration statistics released by the Residential Tenancies Board[3] indicate 339,117 tenancies are currently registered, with 173,472 landlords and 708,825 occupants. This is a significant proportion of the population in need of greater security of tenure.

*Accommodation for Persons with Disabilities*
In the breakdown of Accommodation Requirements in the Summary of Social Housing Needs Assessments, 4,037 reported a household member as having an enduring physical, sensory, mental health or intellectual disability, a decrease of seven per cent on the previous year, but still higher than 2013. A breakdown of the Main Need for Social Housing Support (Housing Agency, 2018) (Table 6.2) shows a slight decrease across all health factors, with the exception of 'Unsuitable accommodation due to exceptional medical or compassionate grounds' which decreased by 32 per cent on the previous year.

The National Housing Strategy for People with a Disability 2011-2016 (Department of the Environment, Community and Local Government, 2011) was established to 'facilitate access, for people with disabilities, to the appropriate range of housing and related support services, delivered in an integrated and sustainable manner, which promotes equality of opportunity, individual choice and independent living' (2011:7) through the achievement of nine strategic aims. This Strategy was affirmed and extended to 2020 under the Government's 'Rebuilding Ireland' programme. According to the 'Fourth Report on Implementation: January 2017 to December 2017' (Department of Housing, Planning and Local Government, 2018), 2,400 people were still resident in congregated settlements, with a total of 140 people completing their transition to community living. €20 million was allocated to the HSE to purchase and refurbish suitable properties for people currently still resident in these settlements. That equates to €8,333 in respect of each of the remaining residents. Funding of €3.9 million was approved to provide 41 homes for people moving from congregated settings and their carers. The report references other housing 'solutions' available generally, such as accommodation through Approved

---

[3]    *https://onestopshop.rtb.ie/images/uploads/Registration/Reg_Q3_2018.pdf*

Housing Bodies and the availability of HAP, however this data is not disaggregated for people living with disabilities. In 2017, 3,449 Home Adaptation Grants were paid in respect of people living with disabilities, an increase of 27 per cent on the previous year. In addition, 3,558 grants were paid in respect of older people and 2,073 grants for mobility aids. However, anecdotal evidence from groups and organisations working with people living with disabilities describe the difficulty accessing these grants, particularly due to the lack of availability of Occupational Therapists to sign-off on the applications. With some 112,904 people living with a disability reported as living alone in Census 2016 (CSO, 2017) (accounting for 28 per cent of all persons reported as living alone), it is likely that the need for these grants is far higher than the approval rate.

**Table 6.2: Main need for Social Housing Support**

| Main need for Social Housing Support | 2017 | 2018 | Change | Change (%) |
|---|---|---|---|---|
| Dependent on Rent Supplement | 35,204 | 25,023 | -10,181 | -28.9 |
| Unsuitable accommodation due to particular household circumstances | 21,130 | 18,920 | -2,210 | -10.5 |
| Reasonable requirement for separate accommodation | 11,914 | 11,108 | -806 | -6.8 |
| Homeless, living in an institution, emergency accommodation or hostel | 4,977 | 5,663 | 686 | 13.8 |
| Over-crowded accommodation | 3,544 | 3,465 | -79 | -2.2 |
| Unfit accommodation | 948 | 648 | -300 | 31.6 |
| Household member has a physical disability | 2,084 | 1,696 | -388 | -18.6 |
| Unsuitable accommodation due to exceptional medical or compassionate grounds | 1,564 | 1,063 | -501 | -32.0 |
| Household member has a mental health disability | 1,691 | 1,522 | -169 | -10.0 |
| Household member has an intellectual disability | 1,571 | 1,474 | -97 | -6.2 |
| Unsustainable mortgage | 746 | 873 | 127 | 17.0 |
| Household member has a sensory disability | 381 | 361 | -20 | -5.2 |
| Household member has another form of disability | 45 | 42 | -3 | -6.7 |
| Total | 85,799 | 71,858 | -13,941 | -16.2 |

**Source:** Summary of Social Housing Needs Assessments 2018, Housing Agency September 2018, p.18

According to Census 2016 (CSO, 2017(c)) 19.3 per cent (112,904) of persons with a disability were living alone, accounting for over a quarter (28 per cent) of all persons living alone on Census night, almost 55 per cent of whom were over 65 years old. Both the number of persons with a disability, and the rate of living alone among those persons has increased since 2011. A further 44,531 persons with a disability lived in communal establishments, a reduction of 421 (0.9 per cent) on 2011, with the majority (69.6 per cent) being older people in nursing homes. 3,465 persons with a disability were reported as living with religious institutions, shelters and refuges on Census night 2016.

Lack of availability of grants for home modifications coupled with low income, lower levels of educational attainment (13.7 per cent had completed no more than primary education (CSO, 2017(c)), compared to 4.2 per cent of the general population) and a prevalence of poverty means that those with a disability are unlikely to be able to afford adequate accommodation to support independent or assisted living.

*Social Justice Ireland* believes that ensuring that people with a disability can live independently where possible should be a key policy priority. Providing the resources for this, including suitable housing and housing-related supports, must be one of the foundations of such a policy.

*Traveller Accommodation*
According to statistics compiled by the Department of Housing, Planning and Local Government, the number of families in all accommodation increased by almost one third (32 per cent) between 2008 and 2017. The highest rate of increase, at 223 per cent (from 345 to 1,115 families), was in shared accommodation, followed by accommodation provided by Approved Housing Bodies with the assistance of the local authority (116 per cent, from 119 to 317 families), private rented accommodation (57 per cent, from 1,516 to 2,387 families), and those accommodated from their own resources (55 per cent, from 513 to 795 families). During this period, the number of families accommodated on local authority halting sites has decreased by 5 per cent and those accommodated in private houses provided by the local authority has decreased by 2 per cent. In 2017, the highest proportion of families were housed in local authority accommodation (3,701 families) and private rented accommodation (2,387 families) (Chart 6.8).

In their report undertaken on behalf of the Housing Agency, RSM PACEC ltd, identified overcrowding as a particular issue of concern (RSM, 2017). For families living in caravans and mobile homes, these homes are not intended for use as permanent dwellings, or to accommodate multiple families. The recent harsh weather events had a devastating effect on many low-income households, but particularly on Traveller families living in this type of accommodation. A recent Oireachtas Spotlight report also highlighted the issue of overcrowding in Traveller accommodation (Visser, 2018). This report cites Traveller organisations as stating that the current housing crisis is exacerbating overcrowding difficulties experienced by Traveller families. Families who have left private accommodation have, they state, 'relocated' to "sites that are already overcrowded, unsafe and uninhabitable" and reference increasing instances of safety and social behavioural problems as a result. Traveller families are also reported to experience greater levels of homelessness.

**Chart 6.8: Traveller Families in All Categories of Accommodation, 2008 to 2017**

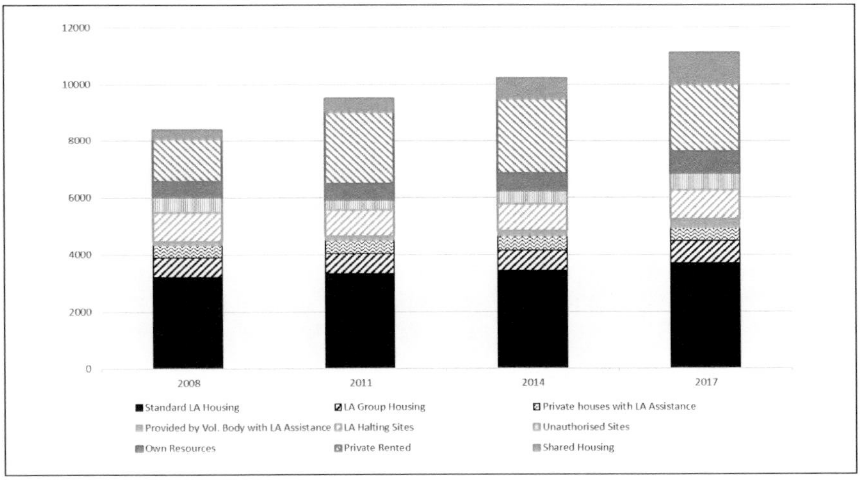

Source: Department of Housing, Planning and Local Government, Annual Estimate of
Accommodation of Traveller Families, various years

On the supply side, key challenges facing local authorities in implementing their Traveller Accommodation Programmes (TAPs) were reported as planning issues (the most pervasive planning challenges reported by local authorities and Traveller representatives were objections raised by settled communities and Elected Representatives which tend to delay the planning process); lack of effective assessment of need processes; and lack of effective monitoring and reporting processes. It is these reasons that are used to explain why less than one fifth of funding allocated by central government was drawn down, notwithstanding an increase in funding from €9 million in 2017 to €12 million in 2018. The Spotlight report referred to earlier identifies an 'implementation gap' "in that it appears to have resulted in housing outcomes which contradict the policy intention" (Visser, 2018:23). This would support the suggestion in the RSM report that some politicians are "involved in LTACCs [Local Traveller Accommodation Consultative Committee] for the purposes of opposing Traveller accommodation" (RSM, 2017:33). In November 2018, representatives from the Expert Review Group on Traveller Accommodation appeared before the Joint Oireachtas Committee on Housing where they gave evidence that over the past decade 67 per cent of the funding allocated for Traveller accommodation was drawn down, with nine local authorities spending nothing in 2018. When asked about sanctions for local authorities who refuse to utilise funding for Traveller accommodation, the Expert Group advised that this would be something it would consider.

The reported conditions experienced by Traveller families, that of increased overcrowding, greater risk of homelessness, and associated health difficulties warrants that this issue be treated as an emergency and that local authorities be compelled to utilise the increased funding available to ensure that Traveller families and their children are supported to live with dignity.

**Key Policy Reforms**
*Social Justice Ireland* previously welcomed the introduction of the Government's Rebuilding Ireland Action Plan for Housing and Homelessness (DHPCLG, 2016) – the 'Action Plan'. However, the substantive targets set out in this seemingly ambitious plan have consistently been missed, Government policy has doubled-down on its reliance on the private sector and, in the midst of a worsening crisis has excluded homeless families from official statistics. Rebuilding Ireland has failed. An overhaul of housing policy is needed that moves away from the commodity model to on which considers the purpose of housing as a means to provide homes. To this end, *Social Justice Ireland* has a series of policy recommendations which we strongly urge Government to adopt.

*Construction of Social Housing*
Reliance on the private rented sector, a sector entirely based on investments for return, to provide long-term accommodation for low income families is a clear policy failure. The introduction of HAP saw Government provide a subsidy for landlords which guaranteed them an income in leaner times while delivering no reciprocal protections for tenants in times of rent inflation. The difficulties accessing these tenancies, and their precariousness, means that low income families live in constant threat of eviction and homelessness. Government needs now to invest in capital projects to provide social housing and associated infrastructure. The change in classification of Tier 3 Approved Housing Bodies (AHBs), to inside the general government sector, means that local authorities and AHBs could pool their full property portfolios for the purpose of accessing low cost credit. This may initially see    The European Investment Bank has committed to funding social housing projects in Ireland, with two cost rental projects already in the pipeline in Dublin and Cork in partnership with private companies. A pool of approximately 180,000 rented properties between local authorities and AHBs would likely attract lower lending rates, so that differential rents, which traditionally do not cover costs associated with the provision of housing, could service more of the loan.

The ring-fencing by local authorities of rents received, any sale proceeds from tenant-purchase schemes should also be considered. Rather than forming part of the general local authority budget, money received should be dedicated to the maintenance and development of local authority housing. In their report last year,

Norris and Hayden (2018) recommended that local authorities freeze any tenant purchase schemes to maintain local authority housing stock and redesign the schemes so that former tenants can only sell their home back to the local authority. In the context of a national emergency, these are all areas which should be explored and implemented.

*Cost Rental*
While the rate of rent inflation in Dublin is slowing, it is still accelerating across the rest of the country and remains in double-digits. In Budget 2019, the Government prioritised private landlords over the protection of tenants by reintroducing full tax relief on property-related loans. This was packaged as a support to landlords, particularly accidental landlords, struggling to make ends meet on their rental property. In reality, this move will disproportionately benefit institutional landlords new to the market. Accidental landlords are likely to be making interest and capital payments on their mortgage, which if taken out pre-2008 will have a significant capital element. Institutional landlords capable of accessing long-term interest only loans will therefore benefit to a far greater extent from an interest relief of 100 per cent. This relief will make it more attractive for existing landlords to evict tenants for the purpose of carrying out renovations which, if financed on an interest-only basis, could be recouped through the tax system. These landlords would then be able to put these properties back on the market at higher rents. Even where these properties are in Rent Pressure Zones, the lack of enforcement of these regulations means that tenants are paying above the 4 per cent increase envisaged.

Rent affordability is not only a problem for tenants, but groups such as the American Chamber of Commerce and IBEC have also expressed concern about the effect of the rental crisis on Ireland's competitiveness. A report published by Mercer in June 2018 (Mercer, 2018) found that Dublin had the most expensive cost of living in the eurozone. This is clearly unsustainable from a social and economic perspective. In June 2018, *Social Justice Ireland* made a submission to the Department of Housing, Planning and Local Government with an off-balance sheet model of cost rental as an affordable rental system. This model would see investment by both Government and private finance (the European Investment Bank funding could be part-utilised here), where Government would have a non-controlling stake in the delivery of affordable rented properties, the costs of which are fully recouped through the rent. Any subsidies available to other developers and tenants would apply here, so that tenants could avail of HAP or Rent Supplement, however as the nature of cost rent is to decrease over time with amortisation, this would present a significant saving to the State, which is currently at the mercy of a dysfunctional market.

*Homes not Hubs*
As seen earlier in this Chapter, the homelessness crisis is showing no sign of abating. Child and family homelessness have risen by over 300 per cent from November 2014 to November 2018 and with private rent inflation, persistent mortgage arrears and lack of construction of social housing, it is likely that this crisis will continue to deepen. *Social Justice Ireland* welcomed the publication of the Housing First

National Implementation Plan 2018-2021 (Dublin Regional Homeless Executive, 2018(b)) in September 2018. The thinking behind Housing First is that immediate permanent housing would be provided to homeless people, followed by the full suite of 'wraparound' housing and health supports. So far, a total of 250 tenancies have been created or managed and 161 were active as of August 2018 (Dublin Regional Homeless Executive, 2018(b):18). The reported retention rate for Housing First tenancies is 85 per cent, meaning that the vast majority of homeless individuals housed in this way stay out of homelessness. Of the 250 tenancies created during the 5-year period covered by the introduction to the Implementation Plan, only 44 came from the private rented sector. The rest were secured through local authorities, AHBs and dedicated homeless service providers. This, coupled with the retention rate, shows that low income and vulnerable families fare better where tenancies are secured outside of the private sector. The Implementation Plan has identified 737 adults who would benefit most from Housing First interventions, of these 173 are sleeping rough and 564 have been accessing emergency accommodation on a long-term basis. While Housing First is aimed in the first instance at people with particular needs, the 564 people in emergency accommodation represent just 6 per cent of all people counted as homeless in November 2018. Targets have been set across local authorities to deliver on this plan within the timeframe, however without greater ambition to see greater numbers coming through the system, the number of families accessing emergency accommodation long-term will rise.

In Budget 2019, the Government committed to the expansion of family hubs for homeless families. The Family Hub programme, while a welcome departure from hotel, B&B and hostel accommodation, is not a permanent solution for families experiencing homelessness. The Irish Human Rights and Equality Commission, in their report on the provision of emergency accommodation to homeless families, expressed concern at the potential varied experiences of families housed within these hubs throughout the country and that these Family Hubs could normalise family homelessness causing families to be institutionalised (IHREC, 2017:9) and recommended an amendment to section 10 of the Housing Act 1988 to limit the amount of time a family may spend there. The Scottish Government allows for a maximum period of two weeks for families and vulnerable people accommodated in family hubs, a measure which should be introduced here and supported by the Housing First model.

*Spectrum of Housing for People with Disabilities*
A report from IHREC and the ESRI (Banks et al, 2018) found that people with disabilities were more than twice as likely to report discrimination in accessing housing and over 1.6 times more likely to live in poor conditions and socially disadvantaged areas. While Equality legislation exists to prevent such discrimination, it is clearly not having the intended impact. *Social Justice Ireland* urges Government to review this legislation in light of increasing reports of discriminatory practices by private landlords.

People living with disabilities have a range of needs, from the very minimal to the very complex in care. The first step is the winding down of congregated settings, which needs to accelerate to minimise the harmful effect on people currently accommodated there. The next step is then the provision of alternatives accommodation which takes account of a person's, and their carer's, needs. Housing design for people living with disabilities should incorporate a life-cycle approach to ensure that those with deteriorating conditions can continue to live a life with dignity and in their own home for as long as possible. This approach would see the adoption of Universal Design principles in the development of housing responses.

*Mortgage to Rent*
Mortgage to Rent is a mechanism for allowing overburdened mortgage holders to stay in their home as a tenant of the local authority / Approved Housing Body. Until recently, this was underutilised by lenders and housing bodies alike, due to issues with funding, difficulties managing properties in remote areas and lack of clarity about the status of any residual debt owed on the mortgage after the house had been sold. In 2018, private equity firms and investment vehicles entered the market to broaden the availability of this scheme. While at first glance this appears to be good news, it is imperative that all providers of Mortgage to Rent are held to the same standards of governance and accountability, and that security of tenure is guaranteed to the tenant should the investment vehicle wish to leave the market. A review of the Mortgage to Rent scheme, with particular focus on those households in late stage mortgage arrears, should be undertaken with the aim of both providing stability for the families concerned and clearing down those loans from bank balance sheets.

*Traveller Accommodation*
The primary issue relating to the lack of suitable Traveller accommodation is not that funding is not being made available, as is the case in other areas of housing policy, but that this funding is not being utilised by the local authorities tasked with providing this accommodation. Stakeholder reviews have been undertaken to identify the type of accommodation most suitable and preferable for Travellers, however it is the 'implementation gap' identified in the Oireachtas Spotlight report referred to earlier in this Chapter (Visser, 2018) that is creating the barrier. As with other areas of housing policy, realistic targets should be developed for local authorities to provide Traveller families with safe, suitable accommodation. Discrimination and bias among elected representatives must be challenged and sanctions imposed on local authorities who do not access funding to meet developed targets.

**Key Policy Priorities**
*Social Justice Ireland* believes that the following policy positions should be adopted in addressing Ireland's housing and homelessness crisis:

- Build more social housing and allow local authorities and Approved Housing Bodies pool resources to finance this increased supply in a sustainable way.

- Develop a system of affordable rent through the cost rental model, financed 'off-balance-sheet' to allow for supply to scale up without adding to the general government debt.

- Increase the provision of Housing First accommodation for families in emergency accommodation and limit the length of time families can spend in Family Hubs.

- Develop a spectrum of housing supports for people with disabilities.

- Review the Mortgage to Rent scheme for those in late stage mortgage arrears.

- Introduce sanctions for local authorities who do not utilise funding available to provide safe, sustainable Traveller accommodation.

# REFERENCES

Banks, J., Grotti, R., Fahey, E., and Watson, D. (2018): *Disability and Discrimination in Ireland: Evidence from the QNHS Equality Modules, 2004, 2010, 2014*

Central Bank of Ireland (Central Bank) (2017): *Residential Mortgage Arrears and Repossession Statistics: Q.3 2017*

Central Statistics Office (CSO) (2018): *New Dwelling Completions Q3 2018c*

Central Statistics Office (CSO) (2017(a)): *Census of Population 2016 – Profile 1 Housing in Ireland,*

Central Statistics Office (CSO) (2017(b)): *Census 2016 – Summary Results Part 1,* 06 April 2017

Central Statistics Office (CSO) (2017 (c)): *Census 2016 – Summary Results Part 2,* 15 June 2017

Central Statistics Office (CSO) (2017(d)): *Census of Population 2016 – Profile 8 Irish Travellers, Ethnicity and Religion*

Department of Housing, Planning and Local Government (DHPLG) (2018(a)): *Current Housing Expenditure Programmes, Housing Assistance Payment*

Department of Housing, Planning and Local Government (DHPLG) (2018(b)): *Construction Activity – starts*

Department of Housing, Planning and Local Government (DHPLG) (2018(c)): *Local authority loan arrears - DGI overall loan arrears by quarter Q3 2018*

Department of Housing, Planning and Local Government (DHPLG)(2018(d)): *Local authority loan arrears – Local authority repossessions*

Department of Housing, Planning and Local Government (DHPLG) (2018 (e)): *Housing Adaptation Grants by year*

Department of Housing, Planning and Local Government (DHPLG) (2018(f): *Fourth Report on Implementation of the National Disability Strategy*

Department of Housing, Planning, Community and Local Government (DHCPLG) (2016): *Rebuilding Ireland, Action Plan for Housing and Homelessness*

Department of Environment, Community and Local Government (DECLG) (2011): *National Housing Strategy for People with a Disability,* October 2011

Dublin Regional Homeless Executive (2018(a)): *Winter Count on Rough Sleeping,* November 2018

Dublin Regional Homeless Executive (2018(b)): *Housing First Implementation Plan 2018-2021*

Duffy, David; Byrne, David; Fitzgerald, John (2014): *ESRI Special Article, Alternative Scenarios for New Household Formation in Ireland*

Future Analytics (2017): *Housing Supply Requirements in Ireland's Urban Settlements 2016-2020, A Preliminary Update,* February 2017

Healy, Tom and Goldrick-Kelly, Paul (2017): *Ireland's Housing Emergency – Time for a Game Changer,* NERI Working Paper Series WP 2017/No 41, March 2017

Housing Agency (2018): *Summary of Social Housing Assessments 2018,* September 2018

Housing Agency (2017): *Summary of Social Housing Assessments 2017*, December 2017

Housing Agency (2011): *Summary of Social Housing Assessments 2011*

Irish Government Economic and Evaluation Service (IGEES) (2018): *Social Impact Assessment Series: Social Housing Supports*

Irish Human Rights and Equality Commission (IHREC) (2017): *The provision of emergency accommodation to families experiencing homelessness*, July 2017

Lyons (2018): *The Daft.ie Rental Price Report, An analysis of recent trends in the Irish rental market, 2018 Q3*

Mercer (2018): *Cost of Living City Ranking*

National Oversight and Audit Commission (NOAC) (2018): *Performance Indicators in Local Authorities 2017*

Norris, M. and Hayden, A. (2018): *Future of Council Housing: An Analysis of the financial sustainability of local authority provided social housing*

RSM PACEC Ltd (RSM) (2017): *Research Report, Review of Funding for Traveller-Specific Accommodation and the Implementation of Traveller Accommodation Programmes*

Visser (2018): *Spotlight: Traveller Accommodation*, Oireachtas Library & Research Service

Chapter seven

# Chapter 7
## Healthcare

**Core Policy Objective:**
To provide an adequate healthcare service focused on enabling people to attain the World Health Organisation's definition of health as a state of complete physical, mental and social wellbeing and not merely the absence of disease or infirmity.

## Key Issues/Evidence

Health = a state of complete physical, mental and social wellbeing and must be seen as so.

Access to healthcare is an issue for many – Ireland doesn't offer universal coverage of primary care.

Ireland has one of the worst waiting list times in Europe.

Our population is growing and it is ageing which means we need a different approach to healthcare – one we can access in our communities, close to home

**Policy Solutions**

We must invest now to change how we deliver healthcare to ensure we can cope with changing demands over the coming decades as we age.

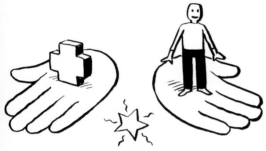

We must increase the availability and quality of Primary Care and Social Care services

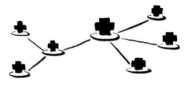

Roll out the required primary care networks across the country.

Create a statutory entitlement to Home Care Services to allow people to remain living in their own homes rather than entering residential nursing care.

Properly resource and develop mental health services.

# 7.

# HEALTHCARE

## CORE POLICY OBJECTIVE: HEALTHCARE

To provide an adequate healthcare service focused on enabling people to attain the World Health Organisation's definition of health as a *state of complete physical, mental and social wellbeing and not merely the absence of disease or infirmity.*

Healthcare services are fundamental to wellbeing - important in themselves and important to economic success in a range of ways, including improving work participation and productivity. Securing healthcare services and infrastructure is one of the key policy areas that must be addressed urgently as part of the Policy Framework for a Just Ireland set out in Chapter 2 under the heading of 'Decent Services and Infrastructure'. This is one of five priority areas identified by *Social Justice Ireland* which must be addressed in order to realise the vision for Ireland articulated there.

People should be assured of the required treatment and care in their times of illness or vulnerability. The standard of care is dependent to a great degree on the resources made available, which in turn are dependent on the expectations of society. The obligation to provide healthcare as a social right rests on all people. In a democratic society this obligation is transferred through the taxation and insurance systems to government and other bodies that assume or contract this responsibility. These are very important issues in Ireland today, where people attach importance to the health service.

This Chapter outlines some of the major considerations *Social Justice Ireland* believes Government should bring to bear on decision-making about the future of our health service.

In summary, if healthcare is to meet the standard set out here in the years ahead, *Social Justice Ireland* believes that Government needs to shift to a model that prioritises primary and social care that would:

- Increase the availability and quality of Primary Care and Social Care services.

- Ensure medical card-coverage for all people who are vulnerable.

- Create a statutory entitlement to a Home Care Package.

- Create additional respite care and long-stay care facilities for older people and people with disabilities, and provide capital investment to build additional community nursing facilities. Implement all aspects of the dementia strategy.

- Institute long-term planning and investment in the sector, acknowledging the impending demographic changes in Ireland, to ensure that we can cope with these changes.

## Key Evidence

### Changing Demographics

Ireland's population is growing and its composition is changing – it is getting older. These changes will have a profound impact on our healthcare needs and on how we should organise it. Taking overall population growth first, **Chart 7.1** shows how Ireland's population of all ages is projected to grow from approximately 4.7 million to 5.3million (+12.8 per cent) 2017 to 2037 (Department of Health 2017). Since 2008, the population has increased by 6.9 per cent with the most significant growth seen in the older population (Department of Health 2017).

Although Ireland's population is young in comparison to other European countries, it is ageing. In fact Ireland's rate of ageing continues to be considerably higher than the average for EU countries (Department of Health 2017). Ageing is particularly marked amongst those aged 85+. Some important facts about population ageing (Department of Health 2017):

- There were approximately 639,000 people aged 65 and over in 2017 and there will be 1,115,000 by 2037 (almost a 75 per cent increase).

- There were 69,000 people aged 85 or over in 2017, and there will be some 159,000 by 2037 (about 130 per cent increase).

- The old age dependency ratio (the ratio of those aged 65 years and over to those aged 15-64) was 21.1 in 2017, and it is projected to rise to 33.9 by 2037.

**Chart 7. 1: Ireland Population Projections 2017-2037**

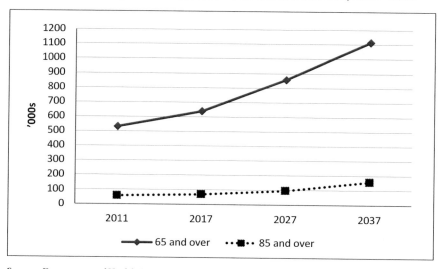

**Source:** Department of Health (2017).

**Chart 7. 2: Ireland Population Projections - Over 65s and Over 85s, 2011 - 2037**

**Source:** Department of Health (2015a; 2017).

Ageing populations are associated with increased longevity, a success story that is to be welcomed. But significant increases, particularly in the numbers of those who are over 85, will result in an increase in numbers living with long-term illness or disability and this must be planned for using an appropriate model of healthcare. Statistics from the 2016 Census (CSO, 2017b) demonstrate a strong link between disability and increased age: in 2016, over 220,000 people aged 65+ had a disability, representing 35 per cent of that age group and also 35 per cent of the overall disabled population.

One clear implication is additional demand for healthcare services and facilities. The ESRI projected that demand for health and social care will increase across all sectors in the years to 2030 (Wren *et al.* 2017). Home care packages are projected to show the greatest increase in demand - of 66 per cent, reflecting a high level of unmet demand. At 40 to 54 per cent, even greater percentage increases in demand are projected for long-term and intermediate care places. Demand for public hospital services could increase by up to 37 per cent in the case of inpatient bed days (Wren *et al.* 2017).

### Access and Waiting Times

One of the most obvious concerns about the Irish Healthcare system is to do with access. Ireland's health system ranked 21st out of 35 countries in 2016 (Health Consumer Powerhouse, 2017), but on the issue of accessibility, Ireland ranked among the three *worst* countries. That report notes that even if the (then) Irish waiting-list target of 18 months were reached, it would still be the worst waiting time situation in Europe. Irish hospitals are working near full capacity. The occupancy rate for acute care beds is among the highest in OECD countries, and while having a high utilisation rate of hospital beds can be a sign of hospital efficiency it can also mean that too many patients are treated at the secondary care level (OECD 2016). (See Chart 7.3, below).

Our complex two-tier system for access to public hospital care means that private patients have speedier access to both diagnostics and treatment, while those in the public system can spend lengthy periods waiting for a first appointment with a specialist and for treatment. National Treatment Purchase Fund figures suggest that 72,000 people were waiting for treatment as an in-patient or day case at the end of October 2018, a situation that had worsened since December 2014 (when it was just above 63,000) (National Treatment Purchase Fund 2018). See **Table 7.1**. Furthermore, those waiting 18 months or more show a tenfold increase in the same period. When we look at those waiting for outpatient appointments, the overall figures are even more alarming – over 516,000 people were waiting in October 2018 and this was a very large increase over the figure for the end of 2014 (when it had been nearly 386,000). Those waiting for 18+ months numbered 86,633, a figure that was over four times larger than that for December 2014. See Table 7.1.

**Table 7. 1: Waiting Lists for Outpatient and Inpatient/Day Case, 2014, 2016, 2018**

|  | Dec 2014 | Oct 2016 | Oct 2018 |
|---|---|---|---|
| **Outpatients** | | | |
| Total waiting | 385,781 | 438,931 | 516,363 |
| Waiting 18+ months | 20,474 | 26,796 | 86,633 |
| **Inpatient/Day Case** | | | |
| Total waiting | 63,105 | 79,621 | 72,001 |
| Waiting 18+ months | 566 | 4,949 | 5,625 |

**Source:** National Treatment Purchase Fund (2018).

## Healthcare Expenditure

Ireland's total expenditure on health was 7.8 per cent of GDP in 2015 (the latest year for which comparable data are available from the Central Statistics Office), the fifteenth highest rate in the EU (CSO 2018a). However, when expenditure on health in Ireland is calculated as a percentage of GNI* (that is, modified gross national income[1]), Ireland had the highest rate (11.8 per cent) of expenditure in the EU in 2015. Over the time period 2006 to 2015 current public expenditure on health care per person (at constant 2015 prices), increased by 11 per cent, from €2,668 to €2,964 (CSO 2018a). See Table 7.2.

Notwithstanding the fact that so many people have health insurance (around 45 per cent of the population), private health insurance, at 9 per cent of current public revenue, contributes relatively little to Ireland's overall spending on healthcare (Burke *et al* 2016). In assessing how efficient EU health systems are, the Health Consumer Powerhouse (2017) reports Ireland scored badly which is explained as being caused by 'inefficient, unequal semi-private funding' (Health Consumer Powerhouse, 2017).

Another issue is that healthcare costs tend to be higher in countries that have larger populations of older people, and Ireland currently has a relatively low proportion of older people (though it is growing, as already discussed). Those over 65 in Ireland make up just under 14 per cent of the population (2018) (Eurostat online database proj_15ndbims ), and while the old age dependency ratio[2] is 21.1, it is projected to reach 33.9 by 2037 (Department of Health, 2017, table 1.5). However, while increasing, is still the lowest ratio in EU, where the EU-28 average ratio is 30.5 (Eurostat online proj_15ndbims). See Table 7.3.

---

[1]   Modified GNI is an indicator recommended by the Economic Statistics Review Group designed to exclude globalisation effects that are disproportionally impacting the measurement of the size of the Irish economy.

[2]   The old age dependency Ratio refers to the number of persons aged 65 years and over as a percentage of those aged 15-64 years.

**Table 7. 2: EU Total Expenditure on Health as a Percentage of GDP, 2013-2015**

| Country | | | % GDP | PPS$ per capita |
|---|---|---|---|---|
| | 2013 | 2014 | 2015 | 2015 |
| Ireland (% of GNI*) | 13.1 | 12.5 | 11.8 | 3,489 |
| Germany | 11.0 | 11.1 | 11.2 | 4,113 |
| Sweden | 11.1 | 11.1 | 11.0 | 3,835 |
| France | 10.9 | 11.1 | 11.0 | 3,505 |
| Netherlands | 10.9 | 10.9 | 10.6 | 3,857 |
| Belgium | 10.4 | 10.4 | 10.5 | 3,546 |
| Denmark | 10.2 | 10.3 | 10.3 | 3,623 |
| Austria | 10.2 | 10.3 | 10.3 | 3,765 |
| United Kingdom | 9.9 | 9.8 | 9.9 | 2,910 |
| Finland | 9.5 | 9.5 | 9.5 | 3,000 |
| Spain | 9.0 | 9.1 | 9.2 | 2,320 |
| Italy | 9.0 | 9.0 | 9.0 | 2,459 |
| Portugal | 9.1 | 9.0 | 9.0 | 1,959 |
| Greece | 8.3 | 7.9 | 8.4 | 1,639 |
| Bulgaria | 7.9 | 8.5 | 8.2 | 1,224 |
| Ireland (% of GDP) | 10.4 | 9.9 | 7.8 | 3,489 |
| Croatia | 7.3 | 7.5 | 7.4 | 1,245 |
| Czech Republic | 7.8 | 7.7 | 7.2 | 1,992 |
| Hungary | 7.3 | 7.1 | 7.2 | 1,532 |
| Slovakia | 7.5 | 6.9 | 6.9 | 1,619 |
| Cyprus | 6.9 | 6.8 | 6.8 | 1,590 |
| Estonia | 6.0 | 6.2 | 6.5 | 1,458 |
| Lithuania | 6.1 | 6.2 | 6.5 | 1,483 |
| Poland | 6.4 | 6.3 | 6.3 | 1,396 |
| Luxembourg | 6.6 | 6.3 | 6.1 | 4,131 |
| Latvia | 5.4 | 5.5 | 5.7 | 1,090 |
| Romania | 5.2 | 5.0 | 5.0 | 865 |
| Slovenia | : | 8.5 : | | : |

**Source:** CSO (2018a)

**Table 7. 3: EU and Ireland, some Population Comparisons, 2018**

| 2018 | Ireland | EU-28 |
|---|---|---|
| Median age | 37.5 | 43.1 |
| Proportion aged 65+ | 13.9 | 19.8 |
| Proportion aged 85+ | 3.2 | 5.6 |
| Old age dependency ratio | 21.7 | 30.5 |

**Source:** Eurostat Online Database proj_15ndbims (2018).

Even though Ireland spends more per capita on Health than the OECD average, the number of beds per 1,000 population is less than three-quarters that of the OECD average, and our hospital bed occupancy rate is 94.7 per cent, almost 20 percentage points higher than the OECD 27 average (OECD 2017), which, as already noted, may signal over-reliance on the hospital or acute care sector. See **Chart 7.3.**

**Chart 7. 3: Occupancy Rate of Curative (acute) Care Beds, 2000 and 2015 (or nearest year)**

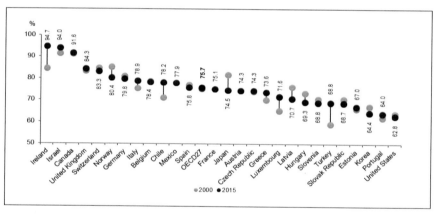

**Source:** OECD (2017).

Significant decreases in Ireland's health spending occurred over the austerity years at the same time as demands on health services increased. The 2019 allocation was approximately €17 bn (current and capital) (Department of Public Expenditure and Reform, 2018) and it has been widely discussed as the highest ever health budget in the State. When Budget 2019 was announced, *Social Justice Ireland* welcomed several proposed changes and initiatives, but (not for the first time) also suggested that the figures presented lacked transparency. In the last decade, health annual overspending has increased from €70million (2008) to almost €700 million in 2018. The 2019 National Service Plan from the HSE, published in December, suggests that when all the cost pressures are set out against the additional funding, it could end up with a €50 million *shortfall*. All of this suggests an unsustainable approach and suggests the need for a comprehensive reform of health policy. Part of these budgetary problems are due to the model of healthcare used in Ireland, including an over-emphasis on hospitals and acute care rather than primary and social care being more central, something we return to below. However, reform will not happen without prior investment.

**Key Policies and Reforms**
In the rest of this Chapter, we focus mainly on healthcare policies and how they address specific groups and issues, but we first make some preliminary points and outline some of the context for the analysis and discussion that follows. We first note that health is not just about healthcare – it is also about poverty and even life-expectancy is related to socio-economic status. The second issue is to do with the model of healthcare in Ireland, which as we noted already, is problematic.

**Poverty, Health and Life-Expectancy**
In the rest of this Chapter, we focus on healthcare policies, but wish to note first that health is not just about healthcare. The link between poverty and ill-health is well established by international and national research. A World Health Organization Commission that reported in 2008 on the social determinants of health found that health is influenced by factors like poverty, food security, social exclusion and discrimination, poor housing, unhealthy early childhood conditions, poor educational status, and low occupational status. In Ireland, studies from the Irish Public Health Alliance (IPHA) detail striking differences in life expectancy and premature death between people in different socio-economic groups. Analysis of Census 2016 data confirms the relationship between social class and health. While 96 per cent of professional workers enjoyed good or very good health, this proportion fell across social groups to just over 83 per cent for unskilled workers. Meanwhile, the proportion of those with bad or very bad health increased with lower social class, with 2.6 per cent indicating bad or very bad health for unskilled workers compared with only 0.5 per cent of professional workers (Central Statistics Office 2017a).

A range of studies provide evidence that is of great concern relative to inequality and health in Ireland. The most recent Healthy Ireland survey (Healthy Ireland, 2018) highlights some telling facts relative to health and social class, including how those in more deprived areas:

•   are less likely to rate their health as good or very good,

•   are  more likely to have a long-term health problem; and

•   are more likely to smoke and binge drink

Similarly, the *Growing Up in Ireland* study, which tracked a large cohort of Irish children from birth, highlights a widening health and social gap by the time children are just 5 years old. Children from the highest social class (professional/managerial) are more likely than those from the lowest socio-economic group to be considered very healthy and have no problems (Growing Up in Ireland, 2013). Children's wellbeing is still largely shaped by parental circumstances and social position, resulting in persistent inequalities despite improvements in health, education and other areas in Ireland over time (Economic and Social Research Institute 2016).

Life expectancy is another area where there are differences between socio-economic groups. At the national level in Ireland shows a rise over the past ten years (Department of Health 2017). Life expectancy for males has continued to rise since 2009 and the gap between male and female life expectancy has continued to narrow, with the male life expectancy now 3.7 years lower than female life expectancy. In 2016 life expectancy at birth for males was 79.9 (slightly above the EU average), for females it was 83.6 years (at the EU-28 average) (Eurostat online database demo_mlexpec). These improvements are largely due to lower mortality and better survival from conditions such as heart disease and cancer affecting older age groups (Department of Health 2016a).

However, life expectancy at birth for both men and women in Ireland is lower in the most deprived geographical areas than in the most affluent (CSO, 2010). For example, life expectancy at birth of men living in the most deprived areas was 73.7 years (in 2006-07) compared with 78 years for those living in the most affluent areas. For women, the corresponding figures were 80 and 82.7 years (CSO, 2010).

The above shows how poverty directly affects life-expectancy and the incidence of ill-health; it also limits access to affordable healthcare and reduces the opportunity for those living in poverty to adopt healthy lifestyles. In summary, poor people get sick more often and die younger than those in the higher socio-economic groups. The Department of Health (2017: 1) acknowledges that Ireland faces significant challenges in this area and that inequalities in health are amongst the issues that if not addressed now, 'will lead to an unhealthy and costly future'.

**Healthcare Model**
Problems with the Irish healthcare system are often apparent through difficulties of access though that is not the whole story. There are barriers in access to primary care, delays in Emergency Department admissions, and waiting times for access to hospital care in the public system. International experts note that Ireland is the only EU health system that does not offer universal coverage of primary care and that, despite increased investment during the previous decade, when the financial crisis occurred in 2008 Ireland still had poorly developed primary and community care services (WHO & European Observatory on Health Systems and Policies, 2014). Accessing our complex system depends on whether one has a medical card, a GP visit card, private health insurance, private resources to spend on health services,

where one lives and what type of services one is trying to access; it is also those who are poorest, sickest and those with disabilities who find it hardest to pay charges, to negotiate access, and who must wait longer for care (Burke 2016). Those who are poor and sick without medical cards fare worst in terms of coverage and access (Burke 2016). In 2017, 32.3 per cent of households where at least one person had a medical examination or treatment in the last 12 months reported that the costs were a financial burden (CSO, 2018b). For households with children where the corresponding rate was higher (35.3 per cent).

As well as waiting times to access treatment (see above), problems with overcrowding in emergency departments are a regular feature of the Irish system. During 2018, a new record of 714 patients waited for admission to hospital on one day in March (Cullen, 2018). In this situation many outpatient appointments and even serious surgery are cancelled and so the effects are felt throughout the system. A national survey of patients found that 70 per cent (5,910) waited for more than six hours before being admitted to a ward, and 241 people (3 per cent) said that they waited 48 hours or more (Health Information and Quality Authority, HSE and Department of Health 2017). We highlight these figures, conscious that behind each is unnecessary human suffering for many patients, often older patients, left waiting on trolleys or chairs for hours or days before they are admitted to hospital, to say nothing about the risk to patient safety created in cramped conditions.

One of the things that contributes to this situation is inability to discharge many patents, often older people, due to problems accessing support in the community and step-down facilities, nursing homes and other forms of support. It was estimated, for example, that increasing availability of rehabilitation beds would potentially free up 12 per cent of delayed discharge beds (HSE, 2017a). Thus, community services are not fully meeting growing demands associated with changing demographics reflected in the inappropriate levels of admission to, and delayed discharges from, acute hospitals. With increases in the population, especially amongst older people, the acute hospital system, which is already under some considerable pressure, will be unable to operate effectively unless there is a greater shift towards primary and community services as a principal means of meeting patient needs. This is particularly so in the areas of home support and continuing care, and other supports enabling older people to live in the community for as long as possible.

Between 2009 and 2014, the predominant influence on health policy choices was austerity leading to continuous cuts to staff and budgets alongside an increasing demand for care (Burke *et al* 2016). Research paints a picture of a fractured and uneven system of access (Burke *et al* 2016). The Department of Health (2018a) acknowledges that there is wide consensus that the current health service is not fit for purpose and needs to evolve considerably in the coming years, noting that there is an over-reliance on hospitals and that community-based services are fragmented and there is a lack of integration within and across different services.

The 2017 publication of Sláintecare by the Oireachtas Committee on the Future of Healthcare is welcome. Sláintecare makes proposals for a ten year strategy for health care and health policy in Ireland. *Social Justice Ireland* welcomed, in particular, its recognition that Ireland's health system should be built on the solid foundations of primary care and social care.   However, the required capital allocation of €500 million per year for the first six years to support the infrastructure to implement Sláintecare has not been made available in any Budget since the programme received cross-party support. In order to deliver the modern, responsive, integrated public health system that the report envisages it is vital that the necessary investment is made available.

One would have to conclude that overall the thrust of recent policy is disjointed, lacks coherence and until recently involved levels of expenditure reduction within a short space of time not compatible with a well-managed system. *Social Justice Ireland* is seriously concerned that the ageing of the population is not being properly planned for given that it will result in a steady increase in older people and people with disabilities accessing services. Courageous political leadership is needed to implement a significant change in the healthcare model – and this requires an open debate about the choices involved and the intended benefits of a universal system that focuses on primary and community care.

Thus, an open and transparent debate on the funding of healthcare services and on the optimal delivery model is also needed. This debate must acknowledge the enormous financial expenditure on healthcare and the issues we raise above about healthcare expenditure, including the fact that, in international comparison, Ireland's per capita expenditure on healthcare is relatively high, despite a relatively young population.  Since the formation of the HSE in 2005, healthcare has consistently accounted for approximately a quarter of all voted expenditure (Department of Expenditure & Reform, 2017).

Clearly significant efficiencies are possible within healthcare system – not least due to improvements in technologies. Experts in the area of health economics conclude that good versions of universal healthcare are affordable where services are provided efficiently (Normand, 2015). Obtaining value for money is essential, but efficiencies must be delivered without compromising the quality of the service and without disproportionately disadvantaging poorer people. As well as a debate on the overall budget for healthcare, there should be transparency on the allocation to each of the services. Approximately 59 per cent of the budget is allocated to Primary, Community and Continuing Care, which includes the medical card services schemes (Department of Health, 2017, figure 6.2). *Social Justice Ireland* recommends an increase in this percentage and greater clarity about the budget lines. Ireland must decide what services are required, how these should be funded and prioritized (geographically and in other respects). Reform will require investment *before* savings can be made. Not undertaking the required prior investment will mean that recurring problems illustrated above and in the rest of this Chapter will continue and will be exacerbated as our population ages.

Community-based health and social services require a model of care that:

- is accessible and acceptable to the communities they serve;
- is responsive to the particular needs and requirements of local communities;
- is supportive of local communities in their efforts to build social cohesion;
- accepts primary care as an integrated component of the model of care, affording it priority over acute services as the place where health and social care options are accessed by the community; and
- recognizes the need for adequate resources across the full continuum of care, including primary care, social care, and specialist acute hospital services, to fully meet the needs of our growing and ageing population.

There are several key areas requiring action if the basic model of care that is to underpin the health services is not to be undermined. There areas include:

- Older people's services
- Primary care, primary care teams and primary care networks
- Children and family services
- Disability,
- Obesity, and
- Mental health

We now address each of these in turn.

### Older People's Services
Support for people to remain in their own homes is a key and appropriate policy objective and coincides with the wishes of most older people. A well-developed, co-ordinated and integrated approach to the management of older people's needs reduces referrals to long-term residential care (Department of Health 2015b). However, formal home care funded by the State in Ireland is considered low by comparison with other countries (McGee *et al* 2005; Murphy, Whelan and Normand, 2015). For example, one study found that only 7 per cent of those aged 65+ used domestic help in Ireland, compared to 17 per cent in Northern Ireland (McGee *et al,* 2005).

The ostensible Government policy commitment was not evidenced by the significant decrease in the provision of Home Help hours[3] following 2008 at a time of population ageing. As **Table 7.4** shows, the numbers of people receiving

---

[3]   HSE reports make it clear that older people are the main beneficiaries of Home Help services and Home Care Packages.

home help and the hours allocated reduced from 2008 and especially from 2010. Notwithstanding increases in recent years, there were still fewer people in receipt of Home Help support in 2017 than there had been in 2008 – by more than 8,000 people (or -15 per cent), and there still were some 2.25 million fewer hours delivered (approximately -18 per cent). Following 2008, the number of people in receipt of Home Care Packages (HCPs) grew but the funding for this scheme was largely static for many years and the average value of each package fell (Department of Health 2015b). There was a welcome increase in numbers availing of HCPs in 2017.

**Table 7. 4: Support to Older People in the Community, 2008-2017**

|  | 2008 | 2009 | 2010 | 2012 | 2013 | 2015 | 2016 | 2017 |
|---|---|---|---|---|---|---|---|---|
| **Home Help** | | | | | | | | |
| People in Receipt | 55,366 | 53,791 | 54,000 | 45,706 | 46,454 | 47,915 | 46,948 | 47,000 |
| Hours Delivered | 12.64m | 11.97m | 11.68m | 9.8m | 9.73m | 10.4m | 10.54m | 10.39m |
| **Home Care Packages** | | | | | | | | |
| People in receipt | 8,990 | 8,959 | 9,941 | 11,023 | 11,873 | 15,272 | 16,354* | 19,807 |
| **NHSS (Fair Deal) funded places** | | | | | | | | |
|  | | | | 22,065 | 23,007 | 23,073 | 23,142 | 22,949 |
| % of 65+ population | | | | 4.02 | 4.06 | 3.96 | 3.7 | 3.5 |

Source: HSE Annual Report and Financial Statements (2010 – 2017). * +180 intensive home care packages.

Over 60 per cent of the older people's budget goes towards long-term residential care while only approximately 4 per cent of the over 65 population live in residential care settings (Department of Health, 2015b). The numbers supported by the NHSS (Fair Deal) scheme in 2017 were approximately 23,000 or around 3.5 per cent of those aged 65+ (see Table 7.4).

A consultation process was commenced to consider establishing a statutory homecare scheme. A statutory basis for home care packages has been called for by *Social Justice Ireland* and moves in this direction are welcome. However, supporting people to live at home requires an integrated approach that ensures access to a range of supports in the home as well as transitional facilities. To achieve this, deficits in infrastructure need to be addressed urgently with an emphasis on replacement and/or refurbishment of facilities. If this is not done, the inappropriate admission of older people to acute care facilities will continue with consequent negative effects on acute services and unnecessary stress on people and their families. A related issue is the shortage of short-stay community beds intended to enable people to return to their own homes after a period of intervention and support (including step-up, step-down, convalescence, assessment and review, respite and rehabilitation services).

The National Clinical Programme for Older People (2012) recommendations have not been implemented requiring that hospitals have a dedicated specialist geriatric ward and a multi-disciplinary team and access to structured rehabilitation (O'Neill, 2015). Thus the fundamental right of an older person to receive an adequate period of rehabilitation before a decision with regard to long-term care is made is not upheld.

Planning and investment is required to meet the challenges presented by demographic change, and also to address the infrastructural deficits created by underinvestment within the past decade. Health-promotion measures and action to facilitate the full participation of people with disabilities – including older disabled people - in social life are also required, as well as a comprehensive approach to care services that would include integrated services across the areas of GP care, public health nursing, home care supports, acute hospital care, rehabilitation, short-term and long-term care.

*Social Justice Ireland* believes that on the capital side, an investment in the order of a total of €500 million over five years, (€100 million each year), is required to meet growing need. This would enable some 12 to 15 community nursing facilities with about 50 beds each to be replaced or refurbished each year. In addition to supporting the needs of older people, this proposal would also stimulate economic activity and increase employment in many local communities during the construction periods.

*Social Justice Ireland* also believes that on the revenue side funding in excess of €100m is required at a minimum to bring core community services for HCPs, Home Help, and residential care supports through the Fair Deal scheme to more sustainable levels. This funding will assist in stabilising the current system and allow for a progressive development towards an integrated model of service over a period of years based on an appropriate allocation for demographic growth each year.

### Primary Care

Countries with a strong primary care sector have better health outcomes, greater equity, lower mortality rates and lower overall costs of healthcare (Department of Health 2016b). The development of primary care teams (PCTs) and primary care networks across the country was intended to have a substantial impact on reducing problems within healthcare provision, and to shift from over-reliance on acute hospital services to a more community based model of service delivery. The Primary Care Team is intended to be a team of health professionals that includes GPs and Practice Nurses, community nurses (i.e. public health nurses and community RGNs), physiotherapists, occupational therapists and home-care staff.

It was envisaged that 530 Primary Care Teams supported by 134 Health and Social Care Networks would cover the country by 2011. At end 2014, there were 85 Primary Care Centres in operation, and a further 37 locations were planned to be delivered by 2016/2017 and some funding had been secured from the European Investment Bank (Department of Health, 2015c). According to the Department of Health, at the end of 2017, 110 Primary Care Centres were operational with a further 18 expected to become operational during 2018 (Department of Health, 2018b).

The work done on existing centres and networks is welcome but much more is needed to ensure that they are properly operational, staffed and integrated within the entire system. Without this they are unlikely to command the confidence and trust of local communities. *Social Justice Ireland* has called for the roll out of 96 primary care networks (average population 50,000) intended, amongst other things, to support primary care teams. Greater transparency about their planning and roll-out is also needed. An important first step to address these concerns would be the publication of a comprehensive plan for their implementation. This plan should clearly outline how the Primary Care Teams and networks will link with mental health and social care services and how collectively these community services will be integrated with acute hospital services as well as other important services at local government, education and wider community level.

*Social Justice Ireland* believes that an investment of €250 million over a five-year period is needed to support the infrastructural development of the PCTs and networks.

**Children and Family Services**
In 2013, Ireland had the highest percentage of children in the European Union, representing over a quarter of our population (25.6 per cent) compared to the EU-28 average of 18.8 per cent (HSE 2017a). It is estimated that the Primary Care Division of the HSE would have delivered primary care services to 1,240,633 children in 2017, an increase from 2016 (HSE 2017a). The HSE estimated considerable levels of unmet need for children in primary care, including, for example, 11,237 children waiting for occupational therapy assessment (at end 2015) (HSE 2017a).

There is a need to focus on health and social care provision for children and families in tandem with the development of primary care networks and a universal approach to access to healthcare. In 2016 the United Nations Committee on the Rights of the Child voiced concerns about children's health in Ireland, including concern about the state of health of children in single-parent families, children in poverty and Traveller and Roma children (UN Committee on the Rights of the Child, 2016). The Committee also raised concerns about children's mental health services, including children being admitted to adult psychiatric wards, long waiting lists for access to mental health support, and insufficient out-of-hours services for children and adolescents with mental health needs, particularly eating disorders. The report also expressed concern about the high number of suicides among adolescents. It also stated that Ireland should adopt all-inclusive legislation that addresses the health needs of children.

*Social Justice Ireland* welcomed the extension of free GP care for under-sixes, and the proposed extension to children aged under 12. Another welcome initiative is the implementation of an automatic entitlement to a medical card for all children in receipt of Domiciliary Care Allowance.

According to the Children's Rights Alliance (2018), by November 2017, 362,380 children under the age of six (approximately 92 per cent of the eligible population) were registered for free GP care. This is welcome, but it is not clear why any children are not registered for the service. There are concerns that children from vulnerable groups (including Traveller, Roma, migrant and undocumented children) may experience barriers in accessing their entitlement to free GP care. Unfortunately, the roll-out of GP care to the under 12s, announced as part of Budget 2016, appears to have stalled (Children's Rights Alliance, 2018).

Many community and voluntary services are being provided in facilities badly in need of refurbishment or rebuilding. Despite poor infrastructure, these services are the heart of local communities, providing vital services that are locally 'owned'. There is a great need to support such activity and, in particular, to meet its infrastructural requirements.

*A Vision for Change* (revised as per Census 2011 data) recommended the establishment of 129 specialist Child and Adolescent Mental Health (or CAMHs) teams. But there have been problems with implementation and many gaps remain in both the primary care and in the specialised Child and Adolescent Mental Health Services (CAMHS) systems. For example, at the end of 2016, 53.1 per cent of the clinical staffing levels recommended in *A Vision for Change* were in place in the CAMHs teams nationally (HSE, 2017b). At a primary care level, there were 6,811 children under the age of 17 waiting for a community-based psychology appointment at the end of July 2017; a third had been waiting over a year, and children aged five to 17 make up 80 per cent of people waiting for an appointment nationwide (Children's Rights Alliance 2018). Currently, a young person who needs to access out-of-hours mental health treatment can generally do so only through hospital emergency departments. A fundamental issue is lack of age-appropriate in-patient beds for children and young people who need hospital care. For the country as a whole there are only 72 public in-patient beds for young people under the age of 18 (Children's Rights Alliance 2018). While a report of the Taskforce on Youth Mental Health was published in 2017, with many important recommendations, it needs to be implemented fully.

*Social Justice Ireland* believes that a total of €250 million is required over a five-year period to address the infrastructural deficit in Children and Family Services. This amounts to €27 million per area for each of the nine Children Services Committee areas, and a national investment of €7 million in Residential and Special Care.

As well as the issue of child protection, other current key issues include waiting times for treatment (see above), policy on early childhood care and education, child poverty, youth homelessness, addressing disability issues among young people and the issue of young carers.

## Disability

The latest Census suggests that 13.5 per cent of the population, or 643,121 people, experience disability (Central Statistics Office 2017a). This represented an increase of 47,796 persons (8 per cent) on the 2011 figure of 595,335. Disability policy remains largely as set out in the National Disability Strategy from 2004 and its Implementation Plan published in 2013. There are many areas within the disability sector in need of further development and core funding, and an ambitious implementation process needs to be pursued.[4]

People with disabilities were cumulatively affected by a range of decisions introduced as part of successive austerity Budgets. These included cuts to social welfare payments, changes in medical card eligibility, increased prescription charges, and cuts to supports such as respite, home support hours and housing adaptation grants. The cumulative effect of changes makes it more difficult for some people to continue to live in their communities.

Many disabled people depend on social welfare payments. As discussed in **Chapter 3**, people with disabilities are one of the groups in Irish society at greatest risk of poverty. They experience higher everyday costs of living because of disability; one study suggests that the estimated long-term cost of disability is about one third of an average weekly income (cited in Watson and Nolan, 2011).

A range of policy documents over recent years have proposed major changes in the way that disability services are delivered. Amongst them, *The Value for Money (VFM) & Policy Review of Disability Services in Ireland 2012* recommends radical transformation. A recent study suggests that almost 1,500 younger people with disabilities are currently residing in nursing homes in Ireland, in part because community supports are not sufficient (Pierce, Kilcullen and Duffy 2018). Recent HSE Service plans suggest that there has been some progress setting up the structures and processes necessary to implement the type of change-programme envisaged. However, *Social Justice Ireland* is concerned that the pace of change is too slow and that additional targeted resources will need to be provided to ensure that a comprehensive and lasting system-wide change initiative is delivered to the benefit of service users and local communities. *Social Justice Ireland* called for a dedicated reform fund to support the transition to a new model of service, given the scale of infrastructural development required to move away from communal settings towards a community based, person-centred model of service. It is to be welcomed that capital funding was announced, as well as the establishment of a

---

[4]    Other disability related issues are addressed throughout this review.

service reform fund (between Atlantic Philanthropies, the Department of Health, the HSE and Genio (HSE, 2015b).

A Taskforce on Personalised Budgets has recommended that the Department of Health and the HSE should establish demonstration projects to test the delivery of personalised budgets with a view to identifying the best approach to the wider roll-out of these payment models following the initial demonstration phase. As mentioned, a consultation process is also to take place in relation to establishing a statutory homecare scheme. How these two processes are to be linked to ensure that people with disabilities of all ages receive high quality, appropriate support at home needs to be clarified.

*Social Justice Ireland* welcomed steps taken to improve services and funding for disability in Budget 2019, including a Government commitment to undertake a cost of disability study. In December 2018, some further positive measures have been announced. Notably, the medical card earnings disregard for persons in receipt of Disability Allowance is to be significantly increased, from €120 to €427 per week, intended to provide that more people will retain access to a Medical card while they work. As we have long argued, if people with a disability are to be equal participants in society, the extra costs generated by their disability should not be borne by them alone and progress on these issues is long overdue.

Disabled people need to be supported, not only by the health service, but by the Department of the Environment through Local Authorities with regard to housing need, through the Department of Social Protection in terms of income supports, as well as by the Department of Education through education and training.

## Obesity and Chronic Illness
Obesity and food poverty impact on people's diets and there is a clear relationship between poor diet and disease. Ireland is experiencing high levels of both; 7 per cent of children, rising to 36 per cent of older people, are obese and food poverty affects almost one in eight citizens (Irish Hearth Foundation and *Social Justice Ireland* 2015). People from lower socio-economic backgrounds experience a greater degree of overweight and obesity, and without change, a significant impact on quality of life, life expectancy and healthcare costs in Ireland is predicted (Layte & McCrory, 2011).

*Social Justice Ireland* called for a Sugar Sweetened Drinks Tax and welcomed its introduction in Budget 2018. We have also called for an investment financed by the Sugar Sweetened Drinks tax should to develop effective obesity prevention programmes and meet the targets in the Obesity Policy and Action Plan 2016-2025.

## Mental Health
There is an urgent need to address the area of mental health. This arises not least in light of a World Health Report (2001) showing that mental health and behavioural

disorders are common, affecting 20–25 per cent of people at some time during their life. As well as having a major impact on individuals, they have large direct and indirect consequences. For example, in 2000, mental and neurological disorders accounted for 12 per cent of the total disability-adjusted life years (DALYs) lost due to all diseases and injuries. By 2020, it is projected that the burden of these disorders will have increased to 15 per cent (World Health Organization 2001). This has serious implications for services in all countries in coming years. In Ireland, the Pfizer Health Index suggested that about a quarter of Irish adults have reasonably direct experience of mental health issues, and almost 3 in 10 had experienced an incident of depression within their family circle or close peer group (Pfizer, 2013).

The policy blue-print, *A Vision for Change – Report of the Expert Group on Mental Health Policy* (2006), offered many worthwhile pathways to adequately address mental health issues in Irish society. Unfortunately, as noted already the pace of implementation has been extremely slow. Between 2008 and 2012, there was almost no increase in the transfer of either budget or staff from hospitals to the community resulting in the under-provision of community services and the overmedication and increased hospitalisation of people with mental health problems (Eurofound, 2014). Readmission rates were also found to have increased.

Funding has been allocated in recent budgets for mental health services. *Social Justice Ireland* welcomed these, including a considerable allocation announced in Budget 2019. However, progress in implementation has continued to be slow related partly to recruitment difficulties. According to the HSE, at the end of 2016, for example, staffing levels in General Adult Community Mental Health were still at approximately 74.8 per cent of the clinical staffing levels recommended in *A Vision for Change* (HSE, 2017b). The mental health services are going through a significant change process at a time when demands on services are growing in line with population increases. It is vital that ongoing reductions in inpatient beds are matched by adequate and effective alternative provision in the community.

*Areas of concern in mental health:* There is a need for effective outreach and follow-up programmes for people who have been in-patients in institutions upon their discharge into the wider community. These should provide:

• sheltered housing (high, medium and low supported housing);

• monitoring of medication;

• retraining and rehabilitation; and

• assistance with integration into community.

In the development of mental health teams there should be a particular focus on people with an intellectual disability and other vulnerable groups, including children, homeless people, prisoners, Travellers, asylum seekers, refugees and other minority groups. People in these and related categories have a right to a specialist service to provide for their often complex needs. A great deal remains to be done before this right could be acknowledged as having been recognised and honoured in the healthcare system.

The connection between disadvantage and ill health when the social determinants of health (such as housing, income, childcare support, education and so on) are not met is well documented. This is also true in respect of mental health issues.

Research and development in all areas of mental health are needed to ensure a quality service is delivered. Providing good mental health services is a necessary investment in the future wellbeing of the country. Public awareness-raising should continue, to ensure a clearer understanding of mental illness so that the rights of those with mental illness are recognised.

### Older people and Mental Health
Mental health issues affect all groups in society and people of all ages. Dementia is not the only mental health issue to affect older people. It is not an inevitable part of ageing nor is it solely a disease of older age, but older people with dementia are a particularly vulnerable group. It is estimated that 47,000 people in Ireland have dementia and that number is projected to rise with population ageing and could be as high as 132,000 people by 2041 (Pierce, Cahill & O'Shea, 2014). However, in Psychiatry of Old Age Service teams, only 54.8 per cent of the clinical staffing level recommended in *a Vision for Change* was in place by the end of 2016 (HSE 2017b).

A co-ordinated service needs to be provided to meet this demand. The uncoordinated and fragmented provision of specialist care units for people with dementia represents an example of a lack of planning and coherence. It is generally agreed that the needs of people with dementia are unmet within long-term care and that many symptoms are caused, not by dementia itself, but from the quality of care people with dementia receive in inappropriate settings (Cahill *et al,* 2015). As a consequence, specialist care units are required offering care in relatively small household-type settings with specially trained staff and meaningful activities provided. However, where they exist in Ireland, they account for only 11 per cent of the long-term care facilities (54 units), and accommodate only 7 per cent of long-term care residents despite the fact that more than 60 per cent of residents living in long-term care facilities are estimated to have dementia (Cahill *et al,* 2015). A high proportion of specialist units that do exist care for people in groups larger than the recommended small-group living arrangements, and there are significant inequities regarding access to them and their geographic location (over 50 per cent were in only four counties).

A National Dementia Strategy was published in 2014 and funding has been promised for three priority areas– intensive home care supports, GP education, and training and dementia awareness. This is welcome and implementation is required. However, the strategy's publication is only a first step and there are many other areas that also require investment, including day centres, respite services and other supports for carers, quality long-term care (at home and in care settings) and specialist care units, as well as evaluation and monitoring of all services.

### Suicide – a Mental Health Issue

Suicide is the ultimate, and most deadly, manifestation of mental health issues. Over time Ireland's suicide rate rose significantly from 6.4 suicides per 100,000 people in 1980 to a peak of 13.9 in 1998 (National Office of Suicide Prevention, 2011). A downward trend from 2003 stopped in 2007, something attributed by the National Office of Suicide Prevention in part to the change in the economy. The increase observed between 2007 and 2012 can be wholly attributed to an increase in the male rate of suicide. More recent years have seen a levelling-off and reductions in the numbers of suicides

Statistics from the National Suicide Research Foundation (2017), which are still provisional, suggest that there were 399 recorded suicides in 2016 (a rate of 8.5 per 100,000 people), of which 318 were males and 81 were females. The majority of people who die by suicide are male. For the age-group 15-19, Ireland had the 7th highest rate of suicide across 33 countries for which data was recorded by Eurostat in 2015 (7.02 per 100,000) (National Office of Suicide Prevention, 2018).

The sustained high level of suicides in Ireland is a significant healthcare and societal problem. Of course, the statistics only tell one part of the story. Behind each of these statistics are families and communities devastated by these tragedies. Likewise, behind each of the figures is a personal story which leads to people taking their own lives. *Social Justice Ireland* believes that further attention and resources need to be devoted to researching and addressing Ireland's suicide problem.

### Key Policy Priorities on Healthcare

A number of the factors highlighted throughout this review will have implications for the future of our healthcare system, notably the projected increases in population and the ageing of our population. An ESRI report concludes that two decades of rapid population growth, a decade of cutbacks in public provision of care and a consequent build-up of unmet need and demand for care, will require additional expenditure, capital investment and expanded staffing and will have major implications for capacity planning, workforce planning and training (Wren *et al.*, 2017).

As already mentioned, *Social Justice Ireland* welcomed the recognition of Sláintecare that Ireland's health system should be built on foundations of primary care and social care. *Social Justice Ireland* believes that access to healthcare based on need, not income, should remain an important aim for Ireland's healthcare system. Furthermore, investment in a reconfigured model of healthcare is overdue, one that emphasises primary and social care. In the context of our past mistakes, it is important that Ireland begins to plan for this additional demand and begins to train staff and construct the needed facilities. It is also necessary for leadership that communicates the need to invest in reform now so that the necessary services are in place to enable us to afterwards shift to a different model of care that emphasises primary care more.

The following is a summary of key policy priorities and actions that *Social Justice Ireland* recommends:

- Ensure that announced budgetary allocations are valid, realistic and transparent and that they take existing commitments into account.

- Increase the availability and quality of Primary Care and Social Care services.

- Ensure medical card-coverage for all people who are vulnerable.

- Act effectively to end the current hospital waiting list crisis.

- Create a statutory entitlement to Home Care Services. This will require increased funding, but may save the State money long-term, as HCPs allow people to remain living in their own homes, rather than entering residential nursing care.

- Create additional respite care and long-stay care facilities for older people and people with disabilities, and provide capital investment to build additional community nursing facilities. Implement all aspects of the dementia strategy.

- Increase educational campaigns promoting health, targeting particularly people who are economically disadvantaged, acknowledging that a preventative approach saves money in the long-run.

- Properly resource and develop mental health services, and facilitate campaigns giving greater attention to the issue of suicide.

- Institute long-term planning and investment in the sector, acknowledging the impending demographic changes in Ireland, to ensure that we can cope with these changes.

- Adopt a target to reduce the body mass index (BMI) of the population by 5 per cent by 2021.

- Work towards full universal healthcare for all. Ensure new system structures are fit for purpose, and publish detailed evidence of how new decisions taken will meet healthcare goals.

- Focus on obtaining better value for money in the health budget but without unfairly affecting lower income people or those with long-term illness or disability.

- Enhance the process of planning and investment so that the healthcare system can cope with the increase and diversity in population and the ageing of the population projected for the next few decades.

- Ensure that structural and systematic reform of the health system reflects key principles aimed at achieving high performance, person-centred quality of care and value for money in the health service.

# REFERENCES

Burke, S. (2016). 'Opening Statement: Oireachtas Committee on the Future of Healthcare Inequality and Access to Healthcare, Dr. Sara Burke, Research Fellow, Centre for Health Policy and Management, TCD' 6 October.

Burke, S, Normand, C., Barry, S., and Thomas, S. (2016) 'From Universal health insurance to universal healthcare? The shifting health policy landscape in Ireland since the economic crisis.' *Health Policy.* 120. 235-340

Cahill, S., O'Nolan, C., O'Caheny, D., Bobersky, A. (2015) *An Irish National Survey of Dementia in Long-term Residential Care.* Dementia Services Information and Development Centre

Central Statistics Office (2010). *Mortality Differentials in Ireland.* 22 December. Dublin, Stationery Office

Central Statistics Office (2017a). *Census of Population 2016 – Profile 9 Health, Disability and Carers.* [online]

https://www.cso.ie/en/releasesandpublications/ep/p-cp9hdc/p8hdc/p9d/

Released: 2 Nov 2017. Accessed 11 December 2018

Central Statistics Office. (2017b). *"Census 2016 Summary Results, Parts 1 and 2."* Dublin: Stationery Office.

Central Statistics Office (2018a). *Measuring Ireland's Progress 2016.* [Online] https://www.cso.ie/en/releasesandpublications/ep/p-mip/mip2016/ Published

1 May 2018

Central Statistics Office (2018b). *Survey on Income and Living Conditions (SILC) 2017.* Health Module. https://www.cso.ie/en/releasesandpublications/ep/p-silc/surveyonincomeandlivingconditionssilc2017/healthmodule/Published

17 Dec 2018

Children's Rights Alliance (2018) *Report Card 2018.* Dublin: Children's Rights Alliance. Dublin: Children's Rights Alliance

Cullen, P. (2018). 'Possibility of over 1,000 people on trolleys is truly terrifying. Analysis: Woefully inadequate winter plan and extra funding are coming late in the day'. *Irish Times.* Dec 7

Department of Expenditure & Reform (2017). *Spending Review 2017: Tracking Trends in Public Spending.* July. Dublin: Department Expenditure and Reform

Department of Health (2015a). *Health in Ireland: Key Trends, 2015.* Dublin: Department of Health

Department of Health (2015b). *Review of the Nursing Homes Support Scheme, A Fair Deal.* Dublin: Department of Health

Department of Health (2015c). *Annual Report 2014* Dublin: Department of Health

Department of Health (2016a). *Health in Ireland: Key Trends, 2016.* Dublin: Department of Health

Department of Health (2016b). *Better Health, Improving Healthcare.* Dublin: Healthy Ireland, Department of Health

Department of Health (2017). *Health in Ireland: Key Trends, 2017.* Dublin: Department of Health

Department of Health (2018a). *Health Service Capacity Review 018 Executive Report Review of Health Demand and Capacity Requirements In Ireland to 2031 – Findings And Recommendations.* Dublin: Department of Health.

Department of Health (2018b). *Annual Report 2017.* Dublin: Department of Health.

Department of Public Expenditure and Reform (2018). *Budget 2019 Expenditure Report.* Dublin: Government Publications

Economic and Social Research Institute (ESRI) (2016). *Cherishing All the Children Equally? Ireland 100 Years on From the Rising.* Cork: ESRI/Oak Tree Press

Eurofound (2014). *Access to Healthcare in times of crisis.* European Foundation for the Improvement of Living and Working Conditions. Publications Office of the European Union: Luxembourg

Eurostat online database proj_15ndbims. *Baseline projections: demographic balances and indicators [proj_15ndbims].* http://appsso.eurostat.ec.europa.eu/nui/show.do, Last update: 24.2.2017. Accessed: 10.12.2018

Eurostat online database demo_mlexpec. *Life expectancy by age and sex. http://appsso. eurostat.ec.europa.eu/nui/show.do?dataset=demo_mlexpec&lang=en Last update: 10.9.2018. Accessed 15.12.2018*

Growing Up in Ireland (2013) *Growing Up in Ireland - Key Findings: Infant Cohort (at 5 years) No. 3 Well-being, play and diet among five-year-olds* Dublin: ESRI, TCD, The Department of Children and Youth Affairs

Health Consumer Powerhouse (2017). *Euro Health Consumer Index 2016.* Health Consumer Powerhouse.

Health Information and Quality Authority, HSE and Department of Health (2017). *The National Patient Experience Survey*

Healthy Ireland (2018). *Healthy Ireland Survey 2018. Summary of Findings.* Ipsos/MRBI Dublin: Government Stationery Office

Health Service Executive (2015a). *Planning for Health: Trends and Priorities to Inform Health Service Planning 2016.*

Health Service Executive (2015b). *National Service Plan 2016.* November 2015.

Health Service Executive (2017a). *Planning for Health: Trends and Priorities to Inform Health Service Planning 2017.*

Health Service Executive (2017b). *HSE Mental Health Division: Delivering Specialist Mental Health Services, 2016.* August.

Health Service Executive (2018). *National Service Plan 2019.* Dece,ber

Irish Heart Foundation and Social Justice Ireland (2015). *Reducing Obesity and Future Health Costs: A Proposal for health related taxes.* Dublin: Irish Heart Foundation and Social Justice Ireland

Layte, R., McCrory, C.(2011) *Growing Up in Ireland: Overweight and Obesity Amongst Nine Year Olds.* Dublin: Department of Children and Youth Affairs

McGee, Hannah., Anne. O'Hanlon, M. Barker, R. Garavan, R. Conroy, R. Layte, E. Shelley, F. Horgan, V. Crawford, R. Stout and D. O'Neill. (2005). "One Island - Two Systems: A Comparison of Health Status and Health and Social Service Use by Community-Dwelling Older People in the Republic of Ireland and Northern Ireland." Dublin: Institute of Public Health in Ireland.

Murphy, Catriona, M., Brendan Whelan, J. and Charles. Normand. (2015). "Formal Home-Care Utilisation by Older Adults in Ireland: Evidence from the Irish Longitudinal Study on Ageing (Tilda)." *Health & Social Care in the Community* 23(4):408-18.

National Office for Suicide Prevention (2011). *Annual Report 2010.* Dublin.

National Office for Suicide Prevention (2018). *Annual Report, 2017.* Dublin: HSE

National Suicide Research Foundation (2017). *Statistics: Suicides in Republic of Ireland, 2001-2016.* [Online] www.nsrf.ie. [Accessed 15 December 2018]

National Treatment Purchase Fund (2018*). National Waiting List Data Inpatient / Day Case Waiting List/Outpatient Waiting List* [Online] http://www.ntpf.ie/home/inpatient.htm [accessed 10 December 2018]

OECD (2016). *Health Policy in Ireland. February.* [online] www.oecd.org.health [accessed 11.12.2018]

OECD (2017). *Health at a Glance 2017: OECD Indicators* [online] https://dx.doi.org/10.1787/health_glance-2017-graph158-en [accessed 11.12.2018]

O'Neill (2015) 'Second Opinion: Step-down care for older patients is often a backwards step.' *Irish Times.* 12 January

Pierce, M. Kilcullen, S. and Duffy, M. 2018. *The Situation of Younger People with Disabilities living in Nursing Homes in Ireland – Phase 1.* Dublin: Disability Federation of Ireland and DCU.

Pierce, M., Cahill, S., & O' Shea, E. (2014). *Prevalence and Projections of dementia in Ireland, 2011.* Genio: Mullingar.

Pfizer (2013) *The 2013 Pfizer Health Index.* Ireland: Pfizer Healthcare Ireland

U.N. Committee on the Rights of the Child (2016). *Concluding Observations on the Combined Third and Fourth Periodic Reports of Ireland. 29 January*

Watson, D., & Nolan, B. (2011). *A Social Portrait of People with Disabilities in Ireland.* Dublin: Department of Social Protection

Wren, M.A., Keegan, C, Walsh, B., Bergin, A., Eighan, J., Brick, A., Connolly, S. Watson, D. and Banks, J. 2017. *Healthcare in Ireland, 2015-2030.* First Report from the Hippocrates Model. Dublin: Economic and Social Research Institute

World Health Organization (WHO). (2001) *The World Health Report: New Understanding, New Hope*

World Health Organisation and European Observatory on Health Systems and Policies (2014). *Health System responses to pressures in Ireland: Policy Options in an International Context.* 16 November. Copenhagen: WHO Regional Office for Europe

# Chapter 8
## Education and Educational Disadvantage

**Core Policy Objective:**
To provide relevant education for all people throughout their lives, so that they can participate fully and meaningfully in developing themselves, their community and the wider society.

### Key Issues/Evidence

Despite progress still a large achievement gap between pupils from lower socio-economic background and their more affluent peers.

The achievement of pupils in schools with concentrations of pupils from disadvantaged backgrounds is well below that of other schools despite improvements since 2007.

2007

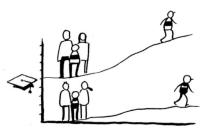

The children of parents with low levels of education have significantly lower proficiency than those whose parents have higher levels of education.

The longer a person stays in education the more likely they are to be in employment. The risk of unemployment increases considerably the lower the level of education.

Ireland still has a low take up of lifelong learning compared to rest of EU.

Ireland performs poorly on digital skills.

**20% NO** Digital Skills | **50% Low or Basic** Digital Skills

# Policy Solutions

Deliver a long-term sustainable, appropriately funded education strategy takes a whole-person, life-cycle approach to learning

Make the improvement of educational outcomes for pupils from disadvantaged backgrounds and disadvantaged communities a policy priority

Commit to increasing investment in Early Childhood Care and Education by 0.1 per cent of GDP annually to meet the OECD average by 2025

Commit to reach the lifelong learning target set out in the National Skills Strategy and ensure sufficient resources are made available

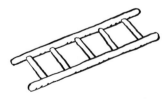

Develop an integrated skills development, vocation training, apprenticeship and reskilling strategy as part of the lifelong learning strategy and the Human Capital Initiative

Develop a framework to deliver sustainable funding revenues for higher education over the next five years with a roadmap to 2028

# 8.

# EDUCATION AND EDUCATIONAL DISADVANTAGE

**CORE POLICY OBJECTIVE: EDUCATION**

**To provide relevant education for all people throughout their lives, so that they can participate fully and meaningfully in developing themselves, their community and the wider society.**

The impact of education, particularly to improve the lives of the most disadvantaged, cannot be overstated. It is a Constitutionally-protected right for all and contributes to the well-being of our citizens. Investment in education at all levels and throughout the life cycle can deliver a more equal society and prepare citizens to participate in a democracy.

Access to appropriate education and skills development from early years to adulthood is one of the key public services that enables participation in society, public life and the labour market.

The focus of our education system must be to ensure people are engaged and active citizens and have the necessary critical and creative skills to navigate an ever-changing employment environment, can to adapt to transitions as they occur and participate fully in society. This is especially important for children and young people today, who upon leaving formal education will be entering a very different employment landscape to their parents.

To achieve this core policy objective in the years ahead, *Social Justice Ireland* believes that policy should:

• Deliver a long-term sustainable, appropriately funded education strategy that takes a whole-person, life-cycle approach to learning;

• Make the improvement of educational outcomes for pupils from disadvantaged backgrounds and disadvantaged communities a policy priority;

- Commit to increasing investment in Early Childhood Care and Education by 0.1 per cent of GDP annually to meet the OECD average by 2025;

- Commit to reach the lifelong learning target set out in the National Skills Strategy and ensure sufficient resources are made available;

- Develop an integrated skills development, vocation training, apprenticeship and reskilling strategy as part of the lifelong learning strategy and the Human Capital Initiative;

- Develop a framework to deliver sustainable funding revenues for higher education over the next five years with a roadmap to 2028.

## 8.1 Key Evidence

### Education in Ireland – the numbers

According to the Department of Education and Skills (DES) there were just over 1,104,509 full-time students in the formal Irish education system for the academic year 2017/2018. At primary level there are 563,459 students, at second level there are 357,408 students and 183,642 students are at third level.

The Department uses the Central Statistics Office (CSO) population projections to plan for future education needs, timing and spatial distribution. Based on the Department's own projections enrolments at primary level will peak at 559,822 students in 2020, and enrolments at second level will peak at in 401,754, at 2025 (DES, 2018a). At third level the number of students is expected to increase annually between 2018 and 2030, peaking at 222,514 fulltime enrolments (DES, 2018b).[1]

### Expenditure on Education

Expenditure on education in Ireland is not keeping pace with the increased number of students. Between 2010 and 2015 expenditure per student decreased by 15 per cent in primary to post-primary non-tertiary education and by 21 per cent in tertiary education while the number of students increased by 9 per cent and 13 per cent respectively (OECD, 2018:4). Increased funding capital and current expenditure on education announced in the most recent Budget, while welcome, is insufficient to both meet current and future demands and address the shortfall of funding between 2010 and 2015.

The Government's commitment to the provision of quality education throughout the life-cycle is evidenced by how we compare to our European counterparts in terms of expenditure. Chart 8.1 shows that while Ireland has the highest proportion of people aged 0 to 24 in the European Union, our expenditure on Education ranks 10th as a percentage of total general government expenditure. It is clear that a significant increase in funding is required if Ireland is to have a high quality

---

[1]  Projection based on scenario S1 (baseline) total enrolments.

education system that provides relevant education and training throughout the lifecycle. We return to the issue of funding later in the Chapter.

**Chart 8.1:** EU-28 % Population Aged 0-24, Education Expenditure as % of Total General Government Expenditure, 2016

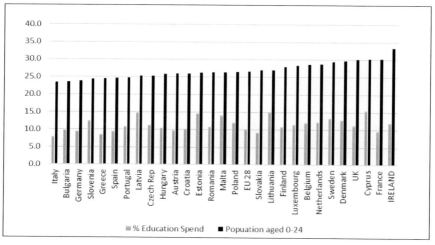

Source: Eurostat (2018).

## Early Childhood Care and Education

The most striking feature of investment in education in Ireland relative to other OECD countries is its under-investment in early childhood education.

Early childhood education and care has a profound and long-lasting impact on individual lives and on societies. It means that later learning is more effective and more likely to continue throughout life, lessening the risk of early school-leaving, increasing the equity of educational outcomes, and reducing costs for society in terms of lost talent and of public spending on social, health and even justice systems (European Commission 2011).

In consecutive studies, Ireland has spent just 0.1 per cent of GDP on pre-primary education compared to an OECD average which increased from 0.5 to 0.8 per cent (OECD, 2017(b):5, 2012: 339). The introduction of the Early Childhood Care and Education (ECCE) Scheme in 2010 represented a positive first step in addressing this[2]. ECCE, also known as the 'free pre-school' package, is designed

[2]  The ECCE scheme provides every child with three hours of pre-school care for thirty-eight weeks in each year free of charge from the age of three years until they start primary school.

as an educational measure to better integrate the educational experience of young children. It is not to be confused with providing families with quality and affordable childcare. The issue of childcare is discussed in Chapter 9.

Early childhood is the stage where education can most effectively influence the development of children and help reverse disadvantage (European Commission, 2011). Pupils who had access to quality early childhood education perform better on PISA testing than those who did not attend pre-primary education, even allowing for differences in their socio-economic backgrounds (OECD, 2016:233).

Ireland does not have a well-developed system of public provision of early education and we have one of the highest rates of all OECD countries of children attending pre-primary education in private, non-government dependent, institutions (OECD, 2018). A review of Early Years Education published by the Department of Education and Skills (2018) found that while almost all services provide warm and welcoming environments and strong evidence of positive relations was found between the staff, the children and their families, there remained many challenges. Among those raised in the review are:

(i)     the ability to provide rich outdoor learning opportunities for children which is vitally important to development

(ii)    the need to ensure all families and children are fully represented

(iii)   the need to provide ongoing training and professional development for staff, and

(iv)    the need to improve working conditions for staff in the sector.

A well-resourced and integrated policy is required to address the issues raised in the review and to deliver high quality early years learning provision for children and their families. 'First 5: A Whole of Government Strategy for Babies, Young Children and their Families' contains welcome high-level policy commitments and strategic actions. In order to deliver on the commitment of all children having access to safe, high-quality, developmentally appropriate early childhood education, long-term planning and sufficient resourcing are vital to embed quality and deliver on this commitment.

**Primary Level**
There are 563,459 pupils in primary level education in Ireland with numbers projected to peak in 2020. Ireland has a pupil teacher ratio (PTR) at primary level of 15.3 and an average class size of 25. As smaller class sizes make the biggest difference to the youngest classes Government policy must ensure that the PTR in the youngest classes in primary school is at a level which allows teachers to provide early interventions without disruption. This is vital to ensure the best educational outcomes for all children and a smooth transition from early years settings to the formal education system. *Social Justice Ireland* therefore welcomes the intention in

the *Action Plan for Education 2018* to improve the information transfer between pre-primary and primary level to support early interventions where necessary.

In 2016, 50 countries participated in at least one element of PIRLS, an assessment of reading skills among students in fourth class or equivalent, which for the first time included an assessment of reading in an online environment. Ireland performed extremely well, ranking fourth of the fifty countries who participated in reading skills, and third in reading skills in an online environment. Ireland's performance on PIRLS 2016 represented a significant improvement on PIRLS 2011 (Eivers and Delaney, 2018:4).

The PIRLS assessments were based on a sample of all primary schools, on which Ireland can be credited with performing extremely well, but what happens to literacy levels if we isolate those primary schools in disadvantaged areas? The Educational Research Centre (ERC) has published a series of reports on educational disadvantage and the DEIS (Delivering Equality of opportunity In Schools) programme. Some of the key findings are:

- modest increases in both reading and mathematics were observed between 2013 and 2016, smaller than the increases reported in the period 2010 to 2013 (ERC, 2017b).

- DEIS Band 2 schools fared better in literacy and numeracy skills, meeting or exceeding national levels in both, than Band 1 schools which are in areas of greater disadvantage (ERC, 2017b).

- reducing class sizes in disadvantaged areas has proved effective once adequately resourced and supported, with a recommendation that class sizes remain below 20 pupils (ERC, 2017(c).

The *Action Plan for Education 2018* (DES, 2018d) seeks to address the disparity between DEIS bands by increasing literacy and numeracy levels in DEIS Band 1 schools, however the target improvement rates of between 27 and 42 per cent by 2020 do not demonstrate sufficient ambition to really effect change and many young adults will have fallen out of education into low-paid precarious employment before even these targets are met.

The Department of Education and Skills must be commended for introducing designated staffing schedules for DEIS Band 1 schools, giving a PTR of 20:1 in junior schools, and this strategy should be extended to DEIS Band 2 and DEIS Rural schools.[3]

---

[3]   https://www.education.ie/en/Schools-Colleges/Services/DEIS-Delivering-Equality-of-Opportunity-in-Schools-/DEIS-Supporting-Information/Supports-to-DEIS-Schools.html

A recent report (Kavanagh and Weir, 2018) on urban primary schools found that the achievement of pupils in schools with concentrations of pupils from disadvantaged backgrounds is well below that of other schools despite improvements since 2007. The authors conclude that, with family poverty remaining the largest determinant of educational outcomes, the achievement gap between children from poor backgrounds and their more affluent peers will likely continue until economic inequality is addressed.

Education alone cannot solve income inadequacy and inequality. It is vital that Government, through the Department of An Taoiseach, take the lead in implementing and overseeing the new National Action Plan for Social Inclusion to ensure better outcomes for all. Addressing Ireland's stubbornly high levels of poverty and inequality will lead to improved educational outcomes for everyone.

## Second-level Education

Irish second-level students performed relatively well in the 2015 PISA tests in reading, literacy, mathematics and science. The performance of Ireland's fifteen-year-olds shows a trend of significantly improved performance since 2009. However, when compared with 2003 PISA results, the overall performance showed a slower rate of progress. Students from fee paying schools continue to significantly out-perform those from non-fee paying schools, and students who never attended pre-school performed less well than those who attended pre-school (Shiel et al, 2016). The PISA findings suggest that while reading levels among the school-going population are better than the population generally, this difference is much smaller than might be expected. The fact that 10.2 per cent of Irish students have insufficient reading skills to deal with future needs in real life or in further learning (Shiel et al, 2016) should be a cause of considerable concern for policymakers even accounting for the potential impact of changes to the design and scaling of the test. That notwithstanding, A useful tool to inform policy at this level would be a comparative analysis of the learning environment of students in fee-paying and non-fee paying schools to establish if there are practices that could be introduced to non-fee paying schools, in addition to home-based supports and after-school programmes, which could enhance learning outcomes.

Progress on meeting the targets set out in the *National Literacy and Numeracy Strategy* at second-level is slower than that at primary level. However the impact of measures in the strategy to improve literacy and numeracy at second-level (including Project Maths) is reflected in the improvements in the PISA results between 2011 and 2015. The strategy also proposes fundamental changes to teacher education and the curriculum in schools and radical improvements in the assessment and reporting of progress at student, school and national level. Progress on this issue is overdue, and budgetary and economic constraints must not be allowed to impede the implementation of the strategy.

Reform of the education system at second-level is being implemented with the phased replacement of the Junior Certificate examination with the Junior Cycle

Student Award, incorporating a school-based approach to assessment. This award was developed in response to weaknesses in the current model highlighted by the National Council for Curriculum and Assessment and to address the issue of second-level students underperforming in PISA. *Social Justice Ireland* welcomes the new student-centred approach to the Junior Cycle and the emphasis on helping students who are not performing well in Irish schools. In particular we welcome the emphasis on learners thinking for themselves, being creative in solving problems and applying their learning to new challenges and situations. It is important that such reforms be followed through to the Leaving Certificate to ensure policy coherence and a truly student centred approach in the second-level education system. This is especially important in light of the recent findings on the revised marking scheme for leaving certificate from McCoy et al (2019) which found that the gap between DEIS and non-DEIS schools in terms of students taking higher level courses has widened. These findings should inform the review of the senior cycle programme and the narrowing of the gap between DEIS and non-DEIS schools should be a priority for further reforms.

While career-focused programmes are necessary, school should prepare students for life, not just for work. This is a sentiment echoed by Dr. Katriona O'Sullivan in her submission to the Joint Oireachtas Committee on Education and Skills in November 2017 when she said a 'move towards a skilled based curriculum which focused primarily on employability was important but that it should be approached with caution.', that education should be 'the tool we use to develop engaged, enquiring, creative minds empowered to live lives they deem to be valuable'.[4] Her recommendations centred on the viability of vocational courses in all schools, not just some, and the provision of extra resources to DEIS schools to tackle disadvantage. *Social Justice Ireland* supports these recommendations to ensure that all students, but particularly those in disadvantaged areas, have equality of opportunity once they complete their second level education.

The most recent evaluation of DEIS at post-primary level finds that there have been marked positive improvements in attainment and achievement in DEIS post primary schools since 2002. There has been an increase in retention rates in junior and senior cycle in DEIS post primary schools and an increased in the proportion of students in DEIS schools taking Higher Level papers in English and Mathematics. The fact that the achievement and attainment gaps between DEIS and non-DEIS post primary schools is closing is very positive. However significant gaps still exist and this is a cause for concern. One of the key findings of this report echoes that of the evaluation of DEIS at primary level; that many of the achievement gaps that still exist have their basis in income inequality (Weir and Kavanagh, 2019).

---

[4]   https://www.oireachtas.ie/en/debates/debate/joint_committee_on_education_and_
      skills/2017-11-21/3/

**Early School Leaving**

A report published by the Central Statistics Office showed that Ireland ranked second in European Union for the percentage of people aged 20-24 with at least upper-second level education at 94 per cent (CSO, 2018). However, while the gap between retention rates in DEIS and non-DEIS schools has halved since 2001, it still stands at 8.5 per cent. This means that the rate of early school leaving in DEIS schools stands at 15.6 per cent. Ireland's early school leaving rate must also be viewed in light of NEET (Not in Employment, Education of Training) rate of 16.1 per cent.[5] Early school-leaving not only presents problems for the school-leavers themselves, but it also has economic and social consequences for society. A review of the economic costs of early school leaving across Europe confirms that there are major costs to individuals, families, States and societies (European Commission, 2013). That study showed that inadequate education can lead to large public and social costs in the form of lower income and economic growth, reduced tax revenues and higher costs of public services related, for example, to healthcare, criminal justice and social benefit payments.

Ireland's National Reform Programme refers to the DEIS scheme as a key measure in supporting the achievement of the national target in regard to early school leaving (Department of the Taoiseach, 2018). Evaluation suggests that the DEIS programme is having a positive effect on educational disadvantage – including on retention rates (to Leaving Certificate). However, unfortunately the DEIS scheme suffered cut-backs in Budget 2012, which were subsequently only partially rolled-back. More generally, capitation grants for schools have been cut by more than 10 per cent following the economic crisis in 2008 and subsequent Budgets have not restored the value of these cuts (*Social Justice Ireland* 2015; 2016; 2017). Increased and sustained funding and support for the DEIS scheme is required if it is to continue to support improvements in literacy, numeracy and early school leaving.

Clearly, despite making steady progress, Ireland still faces challenges in the area of early school leaving and young people not engaged in employment, education or training (NEETs) in disadvantaged areas. Government must work to ensure that schools in disadvantaged areas are supported to bring the rate of early school leavers to below the EU target of 10 per cent, and onwards to Ireland's country-specific target of 8 per cent under the EU2020 Strategy. This would provide additional support for Ireland to revise its overall target downwards to 4 per cent. Overall, we believe that the situation calls for a long-term policy response, which would encompass alternative approaches aimed at ensuring that people who leave school early have alternative means to acquire the skills required to progress in employment and to participate in society. Approaches in the area of adult literacy and lifelong learning are important in this context, discussed later in this Chapter.

The socio-economic effects of inequality in education are clearly seen in Chart 8.2. The longer a person stays in education the more likely they are to be in employment.

---

[5]  https://ec.europa.eu/eurostat/statistics-explained/index.php/Statistics_on_young_ people_neither_in_employment_nor_in_education_or_training

The risk of unemployment increases considerably the lower the level of education. Participation in high quality education has benefits not only for young people themselves but also for taxpayers and society. These benefits typically last over the course of an individual's lifetime.

**Chart 8.2: Economic Status by Age Education Ceased, 2016**

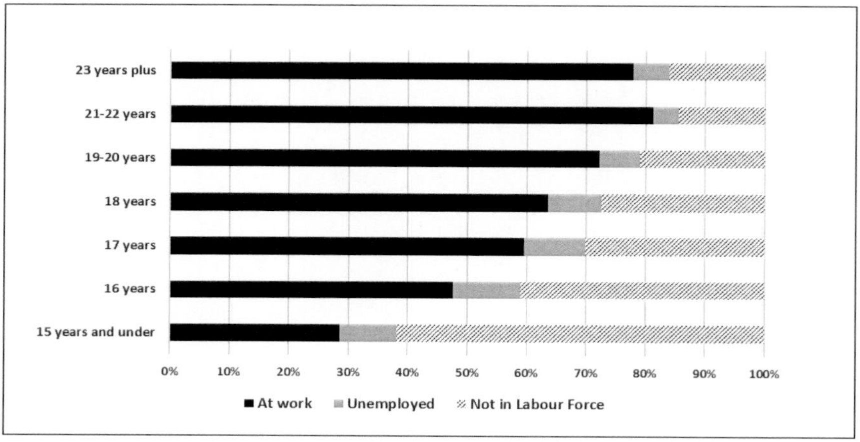

Source: CSO (2016).

The OECD PIAAC (Programme for the International Assessment of Adult Competencies) study found that the children of parents with low levels of education have significantly lower proficiency than those whose parents have higher levels of education, thus continuing the cycle of disadvantage.[6] This is echoed in the 2018 report by the OECD on education in Ireland (OECD, 2018) which found that the educational attainment levels of 25-64 year olds are very similar to that of their parents and that 40 percent of adults whose parents did not attain upper secondary education had also not completed upper secondary education.

The inter-generational transmission of low levels of skills and educational qualification underscores the need for high-quality initial education and second-chance educational pathways, as well as improved access to, and relevance of, lifelong learning and community education opportunities (with both academic and vocational tracks). Clearly ongoing work with parents in disadvantaged areas if of key importance in encouraging support of children in education.

---

[6]  http://www.oecd.org/skills/piaac/Ireland.pdf

## Higher Education

Full-time enrolment in higher education has increased by almost 33 per cent in the last decade to 183,642 students (DES, 2018b). An increasing population of school-leavers demands that considerable investment is required to ensure that the higher education sector in Ireland can continue to cope. However public funding for higher education in Ireland has been decreasing since 2009 despite steadily increasing enrolments both full and part time.

The education sector will require increased public investment and long-term sustainable Government funding to ensure that it can deliver what is expected of it in terms of human capital and engaging with society. *Social Justice Ireland* welcomed the announcement by Government in January 2018 of 'Cornerstone Reform' of higher education, linking funding of higher education with the delivery of 'key national priorities'- including alignment of skills needs of the economy, higher levels of performance and innovation, expansion of research, and better access for students at a disadvantage and improving lifelong and flexible learning opportunities to make Ireland's education and training service 'the best in Europe by 2026'. It is important that the programmes aimed at supporting students in disadvantage and lifelong learning opportunities are one of the priority areas for 2019. In terms of access, the socio-economic background of new enrolments to higher education remains remarkably static over more than a decade. Of new entrants in 2004, 5.7 per cent came from a semi-skilled background and 5 per cent from an unskilled background.[7] In 2016 new entrants to higher education from these backgrounds made up 5.5 per cent and 4.6 per cent respectively. [8]

Another issue impacting on access to higher education is the prohibitive cost of accommodation for students who must study away from home. Lack of adequate student accommodation and a dearth of affordable private rented accommodation makes this a considerable additional cost for many families, which could act as a barrier for students from lower socio-economic backgrounds. The current maximum maintenance grant of €5,915 for families on long term social welfare payments is barely enough to cover housing and utilities, leaving little for other essentials. As already demonstrated earlier in this Chapter, education can be transformative, particularly for those students from lower socio-economic backgrounds, but there is a window of opportunity for this transformation to take place if we are to halt the cycle of disadvantage and unemployment.

An Expert Group was established in 2014 to examine the Future Funding of Higher Education in Ireland. Their Final Report was published in 2018 and recommended three funding options for consideration by Government. These options are (i) a pre-dominantly state-funded system, (ii) increased state funding with continuing upfront student fees and (iii) increased state funding with deferred payment of fees (student loans). The report further points out that funding requirements for higher

---

[7]   http://hea.ie/assets/uploads/2017/06/Who-Went-to-College-in-2004-A-National-Survey-of-New-Entrants-to-Higher-Education.pdf

[8]   http://hea.ie/assets/uploads/2018/01/HEA-Key-Facts-And-Figures-2016-17-.pdf

education should be benchmarked against the funding in those countries we aspire to emulate and compete with. The group noted that the purpose and value of higher education is its ability to add to the understanding of, and hence flourishing of, an integrated social, institutional, cultural and economic life. Higher education contributes to both individual fulfilment and the collective good. Investment in higher education delivers social and economic returns to society in the form of higher tax contributions, reduced welfare dependency, increased contribution to social and economic development from graduates, and greater social mobility.

There are strong arguments for and against the introduction of loans for third-level education, with those in favour pointing to the higher earning capacity of graduates and similar international funding models (OECD, 2016), as well as the equitable argument that 'those who can, should', while those against expressing concerns about the possible costs of administering such a scheme, the risk of escalation in tuition fees, and the prospect of there being no immediate saving to public expenditure as Government's loan guarantee would be recorded as General Government Expenditure (Healy and Delaney, 2014). Fees for part-time higher education courses are a barrier to people who wish to upskill or reskill throughout their lifetime. The policy challenge posed by these arguments is made more difficult by the lack of any alternative funding strategy for higher education. Given the projected increases in student intake it is difficult to see how public spending on higher education can be curtailed. As discussed later in this chapter it would be extremely difficult to fund the sector with a combination of limited public expenditure and student loans

## Further Education and Training

The most recent report from the Expert Group on Future Skills Needs (2018) examines the potential impacts of digitalisation on the workforce in Ireland. The findings indicate significant disruption on job roles and tasks with increased career changes, constant reskilling, and workforce transitions to become a feature for employees. One in three jobs in Ireland has a high risk of being disrupted by digital technologies, although the report points out that this is more likely to mean changes to job roles and tasks rather than job losses. The sectors most at risk are retail, transport, hospitality, agriculture and manufacturing.

The most significant finding is that the jobs at highest risk are elementary, low-skilled occupations and the impact is most likely to be felt by people with lower levels of educational attainment. It is clear that Further Education and Training and Lifelong Learning will play an integral role in the lives of people in the labour force to prepare people for the impact of digitalisation and to enable them to take full advantages of potential opportunities.

## Lifelong Learning

Lifelong learning has an important contribution to make to people's wellbeing, to creating a more inclusive society and to supporting a vibrant and sustainable economy (Department of Education and Skills, 2017). Lifelong learning and community education also bring major social and health benefits to participants outside the labour force and this non-vocational element must also be resourced[9].

Ireland's lifelong learning participation rate is slowly improving, rising to just under 9 per cent in 2017 (see chart 8.3). However, we are still well below our target of 15 per cent by 2025 as set out in the National Skills Strategy.

**Chart 8.3: EU-28 Lifelong Learning Participation Rates, 2017**

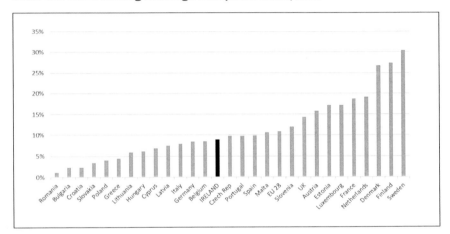

**Source:** Eurostat (2018).

Access to lifelong learning should be an integral part of the education system in order to address the income and labour market challenges that some members of society face. It also must be accessible and flexible to address the challenges of unmet demand and being difficult to access which were identified in the Adult Skills Survey.[10]

Those engaged in lifelong learning are more likely to be professionals than low-skilled operatives and employed in public administration, professional services and finance, sectors that are more likely to provide in-house training, continuous professional development and have policies for subsidising education, than the retail or construction sectors. Employers must be encouraged and incentivised to participate in the development of any lifelong learning strategies. This not only

---

[9]  http://www.aontas.com/pubsandlinks/publications/community-education-more-than-just-a-course-2010/

[10]  https://www.cso.ie/en/releasesandpublications/er/aes/adulteducationsurvey2017/

supports the development of the employee, but contributes to the retention rate and effectiveness of the business, which in turn reduces the costs associated with hiring and developing new staff.

Various agencies (European Commission, Expert Group on Future Skills Needs) identify generic skills and key competences as a core element of the lifelong learning framework. These include basic skills such as literacy, numeracy, digital competence, language skills, people-related and conceptual skills, critical thinking, problem solving, creativity, risk assessment and decision making. The *Action Plan for Education 2018* contains a commitment to rolling out Springboard+ 2018 offering courses to all those in employment for the first time and developing new traineeships and apprenticeships. These actions are to be welcomed, but need to be developed and extended to all employees who wish to partake in further education.

*Social Justice Ireland* welcomed the Department of Education commitment to doubling the number of apprenticeships registered to 9,000 by 2020, with 26 new national apprenticeships approved for further development across a range of sectors including healthcare assistants. In order to meet this target Government must implement the five action areas identified in the review of apprenticeship participation (SOLAS, 2018). Particular focus must be given to increasing diversity of participation and developing and promoting new pathways to apprenticeships.

**Adult Literacy**
Literacy is defined as the capacity to understand, use and reflect critically on written information, the capacity to reason mathematically and use mathematical concepts, procedures and tools to explain and predict situations, and the capacity to think scientifically and to draw evidence-based conclusions (OECD, 2015). The OECD PIAAC study (2013) is the only current measure of adult literacy in Ireland and provides at least a basis for discussion of this important issue.

According to the PIACC study, Ireland is placed 17th out of 24 countries in terms of literacy, with 18 per cent of Irish adults having a literacy level at or below Level 1. People at this level of literacy can understand and follow only basic written instructions and read only very short texts (OECD, 2013). On numeracy, Ireland is placed 19th out of 24 countries with 26 per cent of Irish adults scoring at or below Level 1. In the final category, problem solving in technology rich environments, 42 per cent of Irish adults scored at or below Level 1. In other words, a very significant proportion of Ireland's adult population possesses only very basic literacy, numeracy and information-processing skills, insufficient to compete in a market where the skillsets of even highly-skilled workers are obsolete in a matter of years.

*Social Justice Ireland* welcomed the development of an 'Upskilling Pathways Plan – New Opportunities for Adults' included in the Action Plan for Education 2018 (DES, 2018b) aimed at helping adults attain a basic level of literacy, numeracy and digital skills, and calls on Government to provide ambitious targets incorporating all recommendations made by the Council of the European Union in their Recommendation of the 19th December 2016[11].

Basic literacy skills are required for higher-order skills and 'learning to learn' skills, which are necessary for participating and engaging in the economy. Accurate reporting is critical to determining future education policy. *Social Justice Ireland* calls for continued assessment of literacy and numeracy rates in throughout the education system in order to inform the Government's plans for reform.

### Skills Development

The OECD has called skills 'the new global currency of 21st Century economies' (OECD, 2012a). By providing workers with increased skills, countries can ensure that globalisation translates into job creation and increased productivity, rather than negative economic and social outcomes (OECD, 2017c).

Ireland's performance on digital skills is concerning (see Chart 8.4). Over 50 per cent of the population have low or basic digital skills and almost 20 per cent have no digital skills.

**Chart 8.4: EU-28 Digital Skills Levels, 2017**

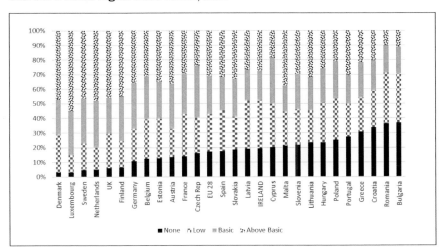

**Source:** Eurostat (2018).

The skills that are easiest to automate or outsource are routine technical skills. Educational success is now about creative and critical approaches to problem

---

[11]  https://eur-lex.europa.eu/legal-content/EN/TXT/PDF/?uri=CELEX:32016H1 224(01)&rid=4

solving, decision making and persuasion, applying the knowledge that we have to different situations. It is about the capacity to live in a multifaceted world as an active and engaged citizen.[12]

According to the World Economic Forum (2018) without investment in our social welfare, training, skills development and education systems we risk facing into an era of technological change accompanied by job losses, mass unemployment, growing inequality and skills shortages. This report also points to the skills that will be in demand by 2022 which include analytical thinking and innovation, technology competencies, active learning creativity, originality and initiative, critical thinking, persuasion and negotiation. Ongoing skills development and lifelong learning for people in employment and people who are not in employment must become an integral part of the education system. The Human Capital Initiative announced in Budget 2019 is a welcome first step in this regard, however significantly more work is required to prepare for the impact of digitalisation.

## 8.2 Key Policies and Reforms

### Addressing educational disadvantage
While advances have been made to address inequality in our education system, and the DEIS programme is proving to have a positive effect, children from lower socio-economic backgrounds continue to underperform in literacy, numeracy and science. Overall performance in DEIS schools remains lower than the national average. Decisions regarding numeracy and literacy policy, investment, and the allocation of resources within the education system must be focussed on reversing this negative trend.

Continued support for DEIS schools must be a policy priority and the positive policy measures which are seeing reductions in the achievement gap must be used as a stepping stone to further improvements. Literacy and numeracy trends in DEIS schools will not be resolved by 2020 so it is important that ambitious targets are set to 2025. It is vital that sufficient ongoing resourcing is available to support the targets in the current DEIS plan.

However, not all children experiencing disadvantage attend DEIS schools and many students who would benefit from the extra supports available in DEIS schools cannot do so. *Social Justice Ireland* recommends that adequate resources are allocated to non-DEIS schools to enable them to fully support disadvantaged pupils.

Government and policy makers must look to those countries with consistent high performance across all levels of education and implement similar policies. The Finnish education system is consistently among the top performers in the OECD

---

[12] http://oecd.org/general/thecasefor21st-centurylearning.htm

and the European Union.[13]   Education policy in Finland is focussed on equity and offers flexible paths between general and vocational education and training options that lead to higher education.  Policymakers must examine what type of resources and strategies could be developed and adapted from the Finnish model to improve outcomes in the Irish education system.

## Funding

Education is widely recognised as crucial to the achievement of our national objectives of economic competitiveness, social inclusion, and active citizenship. However, the levels of public funding for education in Ireland are out of step with these aspirations.  Under-funding is particularly severe in the areas of early childhood education, lifelong learning and second chance and community education – the very areas that are most vital in terms of the promotion of greater equity and fairness.

The projected increased demand outlined earlier in all areas of our education system must be matched by a policy of investment at all levels that is focussed on protecting and promoting quality services for those in the education system.

Government must develop and commit to a long-term sustainable funding strategy for education at all levels recognising the importance of a life-cycle approach to educational support.  This funding strategy should incorporate capital and current expenditure and be coherent with present strategies and funding already allocated as part of Ireland 2040.  The overall priority must be to deliver multiannual funding linked to long-term strategies at all levels.   The Joint Oireachtas Committee on Education and Skills should play a key role in monitoring the implementation of this funding strategy and the outputs in achieving strategic priorities.

## Higher Education

Higher education is facing a significant funding shortfall and future resourcing of this sector is a key challenge currently facing Government.

For Higher Education, the *Final Report of the Independent Expert Panel* (HEA, 2018) points out that funding requirements for higher education should be benchmarked against the funding in those countries we aspire to emulate and compete with. This is critical if we are to maintain our skills base while fostering innovation and upskilling the labour force.  The Report recommends a transparent model of funding providing clarity on where such funding is channelled, with flexibility of allocation depending on student demand and discipline-based weightings in favour of institutions providing courses which are high-cost, such as STEM, in line with the Government's policy to build skills-bases in these areas. *Social Justice*

---

[13]   http://gpseducation.oecd.org/CountryProfile?primaryCountry=FIN&treshold=10&topic=EO

*Ireland* welcomes innovation in funding allocation and a move towards a more demand-based system to support students in their chosen careers.

Increasing demand for places combined with significant cuts in funding between 2010 and 2015 imply that it would be extremely difficult to fund the sector with a combination of limited public expenditure and student loans, meaning one of the recommendations of the HEA Report to supplement funding by way of 'income contingent loans' is no longer feasible.

Investment in higher education will have to increase significantly over the next decade, regardless of which option or funding model Government decides to implement. Government should develop a framework to deliver sustainable funding revenues for higher education over the next five years with a roadmap to 2028. This framework should have clear medium and long-term targets.

**Early Childhood Care and Education**
High quality educational experiences in early childhood contribute significantly to life-long learning success (DES, 2018c). This sector needs to be supported by Government, financially and through policy to ensure that all children have equal access to this success and all of the benefits of quality education.

The Educational Research Centre (ERC, 2017c) found that tackling inequality at pre-school level before a child attends primary school was found to have a significant impact on educational disadvantage if certain conditions are met. These conditions are that the pre-school is of a high quality, are adequately funded, have low adult-child ratios, highly qualified staff with quality continued professional development, positive adult-child interactions, effective collaboration with parents, appropriate curricula, adequate oversight, monitoring and evaluation, and inclusivity and diversity. Government must ensure that all early years settings meet these conditions by 2022.

In addition, the recommendations of the Inter-Departmental Working Group on Future Investment in Early Years and School-Age Care which are: i) incremental investment in fee subsidisation through existing and new programmes (ii) ensuring adequate supply to meet future demand, and (iii) embedding quality in the sector must be implemented. In order to implement these recommendations expenditure on childcare and early education will have to increase to meet the OECD average of 0.8 per cent GDP. Investment should increase by a minimum of 0.1 per cent GDP annually to meet the OECD average.

The Joint Committee on Children and Youth Affairs has recommended that an urgent cost-review of the sector be conducted so as to accurately calculate the necessary finances to ensure the sustainability of the sector. This review should be undertaken in 2019 and the findings presented to the Committee. *Social Justice Ireland* further recommends that this Joint Committee on Children and Youth

Affairs be tasked with monitoring the implementation of the First 5 Early Years Strategy so as to ensure end to end governance of both quality and cost.

**Further Education and Training**

The lifelong opportunities of those who are educationally disadvantaged are in sharp contrast to the opportunities for meaningful participation of those who have completed a second or third-level education.[14] If the Constitutionally-enshrined right to education is to be meaningful, there needs to be recognition of the barriers to learning that some children of school-going age experience, particularly in disadvantaged areas, which result in premature exit from education. In this context, second chance education and continuing education are vitally important and require on-going support and resourcing.

The Human Capital Initiative launched in Budget 2019 is welcome development in lifelong learning and skills development. This initiative must be linked with Further Education, Lifelong Learning and Adult Education and Literacy priorities and strategies.

An education and training strategy focussed on preparing people for the impact of digitalisation and the transitions within the workforce that this transformation will mean should be developed. This strategy must be flexible enough to adapt to regional needs, fully funded and linked to the National Skills Strategy, the Human Capital Initiative and Ireland 2040. People with low skill levels in particular must be a focus of this strategy.

Although the funding available for education increased in Budgets 2016, 2017, 2018 and 2019, the deficits that exist within the system, particularly as a result of the recent austerity budgeting, require significant additional resources. This requires the development of a long-term education policy strategy across the whole educational spectrum to ensure that education and continuous upskilling and development of the workforce is prioritised if Ireland is to remain competitive in an increasingly global marketplace and ensure the availability of sustainable employment.

## 8.3 Key Policy Priorities

*Social Justice Ireland* believes that the following policy positions should be adopted in responding to educational disadvantage:

- Develop and commit to a long-term sustainable education strategy, appropriately funded, that takes a whole-person, life-cycle approach to learning;

- Commit to increasing investment in Early Childhood Care and Education by 0.1 per cent of GDP annually to meet the OECD average by 2025;

---

[14] See Chart 8.2 earlier in this chapter

- Make the improvement of educational outcomes for pupils from disadvantaged backgrounds and disadvantaged communities a policy priority;

- Commit to reach the lifelong learning target set out in the National Skills Strategy and ensure sufficient resources are made available;

- Develop an integrated skills development, vocation training, apprenticeship and reskilling strategy as part of the lifelong learning strategy and the Human Capital Initiative;

- Develop a framework to deliver sustainable funding revenues for higher education over the next five years with a roadmap to 2028.

# REFERENCES

Central Statistics Office (2018) *Educational Attainment Thematic Report 2018*. Dublin: Staionery Office.

Department of An Taoiseach (2018) *National Reform Programme 2018*. Dublin: Stationery Office.

Department of Children and Youth Affairs and Pobal (2018) *Early Years Sector Profile Report 2017/2018*. Dublin: Stationery Office.

Department of Education and Skills (2018a) *Projections of Full-time Enrolment Primary and Seconld Level 2018-2036*. Dublin: Stationery Office.

Department of Education and Skills (2018b) *Projections of Demand for Full-time Third Level Education 2018 to 2040*. Dublin: Stationery Office.

Department of Education and Skills (2018c) *Review of Early-Years Education -Focussed Inspection: April 2016 – June 2017*. Dublin: Stationery Office

Department of Education and Skills (2018 d) *Action Plan for Education 2018*. Dublin: Stationery Office

Education Research Centre (ERC) (2017a): *Reading achievement in PIRLS 2016: Initial report for Ireland,* Dublin: Educational Research Centre.

Education Research Centre (ERC) 2017(b): *The evaluation of DEIS: Monitoring achievement and attitudes among urban primary school pupils from 2007 to 2016,* Dublin: Educational Research Centre.

Education Research Centre (ERC) (2017c): *Addressing Educational Disadvantage, A Review of Evidence from the International Literature and of Strategy in Ireland: An Update since 2015,* Dublin: Educational Research Centre.

Eivers, Eemer and Mary Delaney (2018) *PIRLS and ePIRLS 2016: test content and Irish pupils' performance.* Dublin: Educational Research Centre.

European Commission (2013) *Reducing Early School Leaving: Key Messages and Policy Support - Final Report of Thematic Working Group on Early School Leaving.* Brussels: European Commission.

European Commission (2011) *Early Childhood Education and Care: Providing all our children with the best start for the world of tomorrow.* Brussels: European Commission.

Expert Group on Future Skills Needs (2018) *Digital Transformation: Assessing the Impact for Digitalisation on the Irish Workforce.*

Report of Inter-Departmental Working Group (2015) *Future Investment in Childcare in Ireland – Options and Recommendations for Government.* Dublin Stationery Office.

Government of Ireland (2018) *First 5: A Whole of Government Strategy for Babies, Young Children and their Families 2019-2028*. Dublin: Stationary Office.

Kavanagh, L. and Weir, S. (2018) *The evaluation of DEIS: The lives and learning of urban primary school pupils, 2007-2016.* Dublin: Educational Research Centre.

McCoy, S., Byrne, D., O'Sullivan, J. and Smyth, E. (2019) *The Early Impact of the Revised Leaving Certificate Scheme on Student Perceptions and Behaviour.* Dublin: ESRI

OECD (2018) "Ireland", in *Education at a Glance 2018: OECD Indicators,* Paris: OECD Publishing

OECD (2017a) *Education at a Glance 2017, OECD Indicators.* Paris: OECD Publishing

OECD (2017b): *Education at a Glance 2017, Country Note Ireland.* Paris: OECD Publishing

OECD (2017c): *Skills Outlook 2017.* Paris: OECD Publishing

OECD (2016): *PISA 2015 Results (Volume II), Policies and Practices for Successful Schools.* Paris: OECD Publishing

OECD (2015) *Universal Basic Skills: What Countries Stand to Gain.* Paris: OECD Publishing.

OECD (2013) *OECD Skills Outlook 2013: First Results from the Survey of Adult Skills.* Paris: OECD Publishing.

OECD (2012): *OECD Skills Strategy 212* Paris: OECD Publishing.

Shiel, G., Kelleher, C., McKeown, C. and Denner, S. (2016) *Future Ready? The Performance of 15-years-olds in Ireland on Science, Reading Literacy and Mathematics in PISA 2015.* Dublin: Educational Research Centre.

SOLAS (2018) *Review of Pathways to Participation in Apprenticeship.* Dublin: SOLAS

Weir, S. and Kavanagh, L. (2019) *The evaluation of DEIS at post primary level: Closing the achievement and attainment gaps.* Dublin: Educational Research Centre.

World Economic forum (2018) *The Future of Jobs Report 2018.* Geneva: World Economic Forum

# Chapter 9
## Other Public Services

**Core Policy Objective:**
To ensure the provision of, and access to, a level of public services regarded as acceptable by Irish society generally.

### Key Issues/Evidence/Policies

Public Transport - especially in rural areas is inadequate.

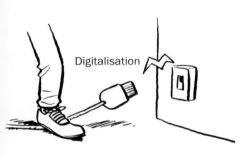

Access to Financial Services – many people are excluded.

Digitalisation

Affordable Childcare

Sports and recreation facilities

Extending library opening hours

Funding for civil legal aid and free legal services

# 9.

# OTHER PUBLIC SERVICES

> **CORE POLICY OBJECTIVE: PUBLIC SERVICES**
>
> To ensure the provision of, and access to, a level of public services regarded as acceptable by Irish society generally

This chapter looks at public services in a range of areas not addressed elsewhere in the Review.

These include public transport, childcare, library services, financial services, information and communications technology, free legal aid, sports and recreational facilities and regulation.

In the context of the objective of providing 'Decent Services and Infrastructure' – a core pillar of *Social Justice Ireland*'s proposed Policy Framework for a Just Society - Government, in addition to proposals contained in earlier chapters, must also:

- Increase the provision of public transport in rural areas and provide greater investment in sustainable transport and biofuels.

- Develop a multiannual investment strategy of €150m per annum in early childhood education and care and after-school care up to 2021

- Track levels of financial exclusion and build and monitor policies and practices aimed at eliminating it in its entirety by 2020.

- Develop programmes to enable all internet users to critically analyse information and to become "savvy, safe surfers" and a grants scheme to support low income and vulnerable households to purchase ICT equipment needed to access public services on implementation of the National Digital Strategy.

- Ensure connectivity to affordable high speed broadband access right across the country.

- Ensure that the Legal Aid Board is adequately funded so that people in the court system are guaranteed equality of access to justice.

- Increase funding to encourage sports participation and active lifestyle programmes.

- Ring-fence revenue gained through the sweetened drinks tax to fund sport and recreational facilities and services.

- Improve transparency and accessibility of lobbying activity by the general public.

### *Context – The Privatisation of Public Services*
The Irish Government has increasingly looked to private enterprise to provide public services and basic needs. The formation of public private partnerships (PPPs) to build schools, roads and houses; the outsourcing of healthcare services to consultancy firms and the privatisation of utilities has gutted public services and created a quality-chasm between the public and private sector, where competition trumps the consumer and 'efficiency' is valued over efficacy.

## Key Evidence

### *Public Transport*
According to the National Travel Survey 2016 (CSO, 2017), 74.3 per cent of all journeys taken in 2016 were by private car (as driver or passenger), whereas public transport accounted for just 5.5 per cent of all journeys. Those in densely populated areas were less likely to use a car than those in thinly populated areas, with private cars accounting for 65 per cent of all journeys in urbanised areas, compared to 75.9 per cent in thinly populated areas and public transport was used over three times as much in densely populated areas. This may be explained by the greater availability of public transport in more densely populated areas, while thinly populated areas are reliant on private car use. This report also showed that the proportion of potential travellers who did not travel due to lack of access to transport doubled in the period 2014 to 2016, from 1.8 per cent to 3.6 per cent.

The Transport Omnibus 2017 (CSO, 2018) showed an overall increase in passengers on public transport between 2010 and 2017, from 198.5 million to 217.6 million. However, while passenger numbers increased in Dublin city and Provincial city and town services, numbers on 'other scheduled services' and school transport schemes have declined (Table 9.1).

In addition to the 139 million bus passengers in Dublin city, over 37.6 million passengers used the two Luas lines in 2017 and a further 32.6 million passengers used the Dublin suburban rail and DART services. Mainline and other services and international journeys accounted for a further 23 million passengers across the rest of the country.

**Table 9.1: Summary of Scheduled Bus Passenger Services 2010 to 2017**

|  | 2010 (,000) | 2017 (,000) | % Change 2010-2017 |
|---|---|---|---|
| Dublin city services | 118,977 | 138,978 | +16.8 |
| Provincial city and town services | 16,620 | 20,178 | +21.4 |
| Other scheduled services | 20,640 | 17,683 | -14.3 |
| School Transport Scheme | 42,327 | 40,766 | -3.7 |

Source: CSO, Transport Omnibus 2017, extracted from Table 8.1

The recently developed bicycle sharing scheme in Dublin saw 4.1 million journeys undertaken in 2017, a reduction of 350,000 on the previous year. Similar schemes in Cork, Galway and Limerick reported journey numbers of 281,266, 23,758, and 32,481 respectively.

In July 2018, the Irish Government Economic and Evaluation Service (IGEES) prepared a report for the Department of Transport, Tourism and Sport on Transport Trends (IGEES, 2018). This report, primarily based on data for 2016/2017, indicated that 16.3 million additional passengers used the four main State operators in 2017 than in 2016, an increase of 7 per cent. It found that travel was a 'major element of consumer spending costing the average Irish household €2,300 a year in 2015', higher than the EU average, but accounting for the same proportion of household expenditure (13 per cent).

Traffic congestion due to our reliance on private cars contributes to our carbon footprint, adds to our commute times and reduces our quality of life. According to the IGEES report, commute times increased between 2011 and 2016 with commuters in the counties bordering Dublin experiencing the longest average commute. Trips inside Dublin tend to be shorter than those outside, but take longer. In Dublin 21 per cent of commuters use public transport, compared to just 2 per cent in rural areas. Walking to work has also declined from a high of 15.2 per cent in 1986 to 3 per cent in 2016. A profile of the emissions share by transport sector showed road transport attributed 76 per cent of all transport emissions in 2015, higher than the EU average of 73 per cent. Government expenditure on public transport as a percentage of total land transport expenditure has fluctuated since 2002, reaching a low of 30 per cent in 2006. In 2018, the proportion attributed to public transport was 44 per cent in 2018, a reduction of 1 percentage point on 2017. Just 0.3 per cent was allocated for sustainable transport (IGEES, 2018).

The lack of reliable public transport in rural areas means that rural households are more reliant on their car to access basic services and community to and from work and school. This reliance is contributing to our carbon footprint, with Transport being one of three main contributing industries. In order to combat the effects of climate change, Government will need to introduce a carbon tax. In terms of transport, this will disproportionately affect rural households and must be mitigated through the development of a transition plan, which should include an ambitious target for sustainable transport and the use of biofuels.

More must be done to promote the use of public transport. Infrastructure must be in place to support thinly populated areas to grow and thrive, while those living in Dublin and surrounds, with access to an extensive public transport network, should be encouraged and incentivised to use it.

### Childcare and After-school Care

*Childcare Reliance*
The provision of quality, affordable, accessible childcare for working parents is essential, particularly for families who have moved away from their home towns and counties, and familial support structures, to take up employment. According to Census 2016, 47.8 per cent of lone parents are 'at work' – 102,934 families who need to use some method of childcare in order to continue in employment. This is compared to two parent households, where 70.2 per cent reported the head of the household was at work (CSO, 2017(b)). A sample used in the QNHS Module on Childcare showed that 66 per cent of lone parents of pre-school aged children who worked full-time relied on non-parental childcare, increasing to 72 per cent for those with children at primary school, while 70 per cent of couples with children of pre-school age who work full-time rely on non-parental childcare, decreasing to 68 per cent when children are in primary school (CSO, 2017(c)). This is a significant proportion of one- and two- parent families relying on childcare outside of the home.

*Childcare Affordability*
Affordable childcare and child-friendly employment arrangements are key requirements for greater labour participation among young mothers (OECD, 2016). High childcare costs present a barrier to employment, particularly among young women with children. In Ireland, the average cost of child care is 35 per cent of a family's income. As a percentage of wages, net childcare costs in Ireland are the highest in the EU (European Commission, 2016). According to the OECD, childcare accounts for 42 per cent of the net income of lone parents. Research by the Vincentian Partnership for Social Justice (2015) shows that the minimum income cost required to afford formal childcare and all the essential elements of a socially acceptable minimum standard of living, is up to 150 per cent of the National Minimum Wage for two parent households, and up to 260 per cent of the National Minimum Wage for one parent families[1].

Research conducted by the Nevin Economic Research Institute (Nugent, 2017) found that affordability of childcare is much more of an issue in Dublin and surrounds, and Cork, than the rest of the country, with the subsidy accounting for

---

[1]   Based on Minimum Essential Budget Standards (MEBS) model and Minimum Essential Standard of Living

just 9 per cent of the cost in the most expensive area[2]. While the cost of childcare may have grown nationally by 4.3 per cent between 2015/2016 and 2016/2017, this hides the geographical disparity where, for example, in Leitrim the average cost of childcare, including the subsidy is €530, or one-third of a full-time minimum wage worker's take-home pay, this increases to 49 per cent of take-home pay in Dublin City Centre. Rates for part-time childcare have dropped in many counties, increasing the disparity, with Carlow cited as seeing a decrease of 30 per cent to €230 and Dun Laoghaire-Rathdown experiencing an 8 per cent increase to €558. This accounts for a cost of between 15 and 31 per cent of the take-home pay of a full-time minimum wage worker.

In addition, there are increasing demands on childcare workers to improve their skills and qualifications, leading to a realistic expectation of better pay. *Social Justice Ireland* believes that childcare staff should earn a decent wage and that Government should cover any such increases in pay, however care must be taken to ensure that any such subsidy aimed at improving conditions of childcare staff are not used to increase costs to parents.

*Early Years Strategy – First 5*
In November 2018, the Department of Children and Youth Affairs published the first Early Years Strategy. *First 5, A Whole of Government Strategy for Babies, Young Children and their Families 2019-2028* (Department of Children and Youth Affairs, 2018) states that 96 per cent of children aged 0-5 years participate in some form of early learning and care provision before starting school. It recognises the importance of family care in the first twelve months of a child's life and outlines the objective to allow a mother or father access to paid parental leave during this time, with a further action point of encouraging greater work-life balance practices in employment, as outlined in the EU Directive on Work-Life Balance. A further objective, set out under Goal C – Positive play-based early learning, is to increase safe, high-quality, developmentally appropriate, integrated childcare, which reflects diversity of need, which will be met through making childcare more affordable, extend the provision of subsidised childcare and the integration of additional supports for children with increased needs.

*Social Justice Ireland* welcomed the publication of the Early Years Strategy, with its child-centred focus and inter-Departmental governance and implementation plan. The successful implementation of this ambitious Strategy will be determined in large part by the resources allocated to fund it. *Social Justice Ireland* has previously proposed that Government develop a multiannual investment strategy of €150m per annum in early childhood education and care and after-school care up to 2021 (Social Justice Ireland, 2018). This level of investment is crucial to ensuring that all children have access to quality childcare and after-school care which supports their development and facilitates parents to participate in the labour market.

---

[2]   Dunlaoghaire-Rathdown

*Library Services*
Libraries provide an important social outlet and educational role in Ireland, with 17.2 million visits recorded in 2016 by 754,748 members across 330 branch libraries and 31 mobile libraries (Department of Rural and Community Development, 2018). Operated by Local Authorities, they play an important role in ensuring access to information, reading and learning material. In recent years, libraries have greatly expanded their offering, with a rollout of digital services including e-books, and access to journals and catalogues online. They also provide affordable internet access and support for people who may not own a computer. Many libraries also offer exhibition and meeting spaces, specific activities such as book clubs, parent and child reading events, local history lectures and act as an information hub within a community. In addition to the fixed venues they offer a mobile service for schools and in rural areas. As part of their commitment towards equity of access, library membership is now free for core services. *Social Justice Ireland* welcomes the broadening of the scope of the library service, the introduction of the Libraries Ireland, the availability of e-learning and electronic resources etc. However, it is important that these developments do not result in a closing or downgrading of smaller branch libraries, which play a significant role in supporting local communities.

A new strategy for the public library service was delivered in 2018. *Our Public Libraries 2022* (Department of Rural and Community Development, 2018) sets out three strategic programmes for the delivery of the library service. The first is Reading and Literacy, which includes rolling out Right to Read programmes for children; the second is Learning and Information, which seeks to establish libraries as a key resource for the promotion of and access to lifelong learning and health and wellbeing; and the third is Community and Culture, which intends to establish libraries as central to communities, providing inclusive spaces for cultural, community and civic events. The plan to enhance the position of libraries as community hubs is a welcome one. It contains 'Strategy Enablers' – specific actions underpinning each strategy, which include enhancing library buildings to meet the needs of the surrounding society, expanding the capital build programme, increasing staffed library open hours and 'My Open Library' (that is, the unstaffed opening hours) to more libraries across the country, introducing universal access to library services and removing fines, and upgrading library ICT systems. *Social Justice Ireland* welcomes, in particular, the dedicated Strategy Enabler for Library Teams, focused on their development and support and enhancing communications across teams. The library strategy will only succeed with the commitment of library teams, particularly in the areas of community engagement and education. Their central role to this success should be supported through resources allocated to their continued professional development and wellbeing.

Achieving the vision within the strategy will require significant investment in our library infrastructure, their collections, their staff, their civic and cultural programming, their technology and their outreach services. We recommend a particular focus on encouraging new and disadvantaged communities to avail of the benefits of the library for broad education and recreation purposes. Libraries have an opportunity to collaborate with local stakeholders to become vibrant information hubs and centres of enterprise, culture and learning fit for the 21st century.

### Financial Services

Gloukoviezoff (2011) defines the process of financial exclusion as "the process whereby people face such financial difficulties of access or use that they cannot lead a normal life in the society to which they belong" (Gloukoviezoff, 2011:12). In their 2011 study, Russell et al (2011) found that Ireland had the highest instance of banking exclusion among the EU15 States and that those who are economically and socially disadvantaged, and those on low incomes, are at most risk of financial exclusion (Russell, 2011:29).

Access to financial services, particularly in today's increasingly cashless society, is key to inclusion in society generally. Kempson and Collard (2012) found that those on low incomes are often restricted from accessing mainstream credit, turning instead to subprime and high-cost credit alternatives. The report found that there was a significantly higher instance of over-indebtedness among households with gross annual incomes of under £10,000 (23 per cent) than among households of more than £35,000 (5 per cent). The result of this financial exclusion (Corr, 2006) is that over-indebted and low-income consumers are excluded from banking services on the basis of charges and conditions attaching; affordable credit on the basis of conditions attaching and difficulty of the application process; and insurance costs, as low-income consumers are more likely to live in disadvantaged areas, incurring a higher premium.

In 2015, 6.3 per cent of households (107,244) did not have a current account, 8.2 per cent of households (139,588) did not have an ATM card and 45.5 per cent of households (774,541) did not have a credit card (CSO, 2015). With financial services becoming increasingly digitised and a move towards online and automated telephone banking, cash has become an outdated method of payment. Many essential services now require consumers to set up direct debits, or offer discounted rates to those who do, amounting to a 'poverty tax' for the financially excluded, paying premium rates and surcharges for use of other payment mechanisms for essential utilities (Stamp et al, 2017).

In 2016, the EU Payment Accounts Directive was transcribed into Irish law, requiring banks to offer a basic payment account to financially excluded consumers who met basic criteria. While, in principle, this has happened and banks are ostensibly offering products in line with the requirements of the directive, in practice, internal lender policies on what constitutes identification documentation has meant that those without 'standard' identification (for example, a passport or driving licence, utility bills, Revenue statement) are unable to access this account contrary to the Guidelines on the Criminal Justice (Money Laundering and Terrorist Financing) Act, 2010 under which those policies are purportedly enacted. These Guidelines state:

People who cannot reasonably be expected to produce conventional evidence should not be unreasonably denied access to Services – where people are not in a position to provide 'standard documentation' banks should refer to the list of documents and information requirements in AML Appendix 2, and not cite the requirements of the Act as an excuse for not providing services without giving proper consideration to the evidence available.[3]

The Payment Accounts Directive was applied to Central Bank regulated banks only, and neither credit unions nor post offices were involved in its implementation. The Report of the Post Office Network Business Development Group (2016) also recommended that a basic payment account be rolled out through the Post Office Network. This resulted in the introduction of the 'Smart Account', an account designed with budgeting features to support money management. *Social Justice Ireland* welcomes this development, but is concerned that the transaction costs associated with this account may exacerbate a consumer's financial difficulty.

Financial exclusion is not just about access to bank accounts, but access to reasonable, affordable credit that takes account of the financial position of the consumer while cognisant of the need for people on low incomes to meet contingency expenditures without resorting to high cost credit or 'pay day loans'. Credit unions have traditionally provided low cost credit to members within their 'common bond' area charged at 1 per cent interest per month, or 12 per cent per annum. These loans were provided as an alternative to high cost credit from legal and illegal moneylenders for families having difficulty saving for life events such as a child's communion, home improvements or the unexpected breakdown of an essential appliance. A Policy Paper on Loan Interest Rate Cap published by the Credit Union Advisory Committee (CUAC) in December 2017 proposed increasing this 1 per cent cap to 2 per cent per month (24 per cent per annum, higher than many credit card providers on the market) to provide credit unions with 'greater flexibility to risk price loans and in so doing may create an opportunity for new product offerings' (CUAC, 2017). This report has received media attention recently, with reports that such an increase could allow credit unions to provide loans to people with bad credit history, as an alternative to moneylenders (Weston, 2019; Reddan and Kelly, 2019). However, the 'It Makes Sense' loan, introduced in 2016 and operated through participating credit unions, is already in existence for borrowers with impaired credit. This allows a member of a participating credit union to access a moderate loan, of between €100 and €2,000, with payments deducted at source from their social welfare payments via the Household Budget Scheme. Not all credit unions provide this loan, with some citing regulatory and macroprudential lending issues and others providing a similar product to existing customers. The It Makes Sense loan is an inter-Departmental initiative and, as such, should be subject to monitoring and review, focused on consumer protection and financial inclusion.

---

[3]    Page 44

There is a dearth of up to date data on the extent of financial exclusion in Ireland. One report published in 2018 looked at the experience of people living with inadequate income and experiencing financial difficulty (Deane, 2018). This report looked at the 'income gap' experienced by families dependent on social welfare payments and those outside of this safety net, such as women dependant on their partner's income and people who fail the Habitual Residency Condition (HRC) in order to access supports. These households have no capacity to provide for contingency savings from a budget that cannot provide for basic necessities. The report found that those experiencing financial exclusion were more likely to have housing problems, experience income inadequacy and suffer with mental health issues.

While there are a number of organisations available to provide support for those in financial difficulties, there is not enough emphasis on prevention and money management education. MABS, the State's Money Advice and Budgeting Service, does provide money management education as part of its community supports, however more needs to be done to develop this skill from an early age, with classes in late-primary and secondary schools. In light of the severity of its impact, *Social Justice Ireland* believes that financial inclusion should be a key part of the anticipated National Action Plan on Social Inclusion. It is incumbent on Government to track levels of financial exclusion and to build and monitor policies and practices aimed at eliminating it in its entirety by 2020.

### Telecommunications and Information Technology
A decade ago, the European Commission recognized that 'Digital literacy is increasingly becoming an essential life competence and the inability to access or use ICT has effectively become a barrier to social integration and personal development. Those without sufficient ICT skills are disadvantaged in the labour market and have less access to information to empower themselves as consumers, or as citizens saving time and money in offline activities and using online public services' (European Commission, 2008:4). In the intervening years since this statement was made, progress in Ireland has been intermittent at best, with some (particularly very rural) areas still without access to good quality broadband sufficient to foster this 'essential life competence'. The CSO Information Society Statistics – Households, 2018 report found that the rate of internet access in areas of higher population density (at 94 per cent in Dublin and 92 per cent in the Mid-East region) continues to outpace more thinly populated areas (at 85 per cent in Border regions and 86 per cent in the Midlands and South-East). The rate of growth in internet access has been fastest in the Border region (rising from 60 per cent in 2010 to 85 per cent in 2018), however this is from a low base.

### Broadband Provision
According to the CSO, 89 per cent of households have internet access representing a 24 per cent increase since 2010, but only two percentage points higher than in 2016 and the same as the previous year (CSO, 2018). Coverage rates have been in the 80s since 2012 (when coverage was 81 per cent) meaning that between 11 and

19 per cent of all households in Ireland have been without internet coverage for the 6 years. With the introduction of fiber-net broadband and cloud computing in this time, the rate of growth might have been expected to be higher. Fixed broadband connection is the most commonly used, accounting for 82 per cent of households). As with many aspects of public services, socio-economic status determines the quality of internet connection, with 90 per cent of the fifth quintile (very affluent) accessing fixed broadband, compared to 76 per cent of the first quintile (very disadvantaged). There is also a notable regional disparity in the quality of internet access, with Dublin and the Mid-East region having higher rates of fixed broadband use (at 90 and 86 per cent respectively) compared to the Midlands and Border regions (at 67 and 69 per cent respectively) (Chart 9.1).

**Chart 9.1: Households with Internet Access classified by Type and Household Characteristic, 2018**

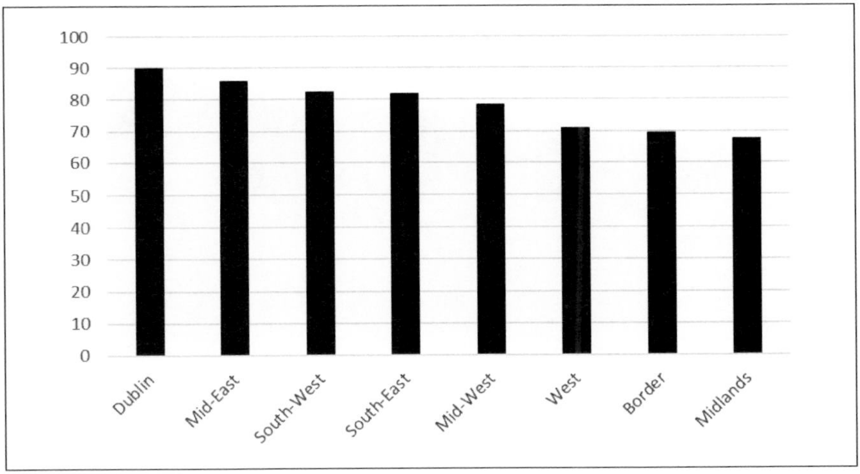

Source: CSO, Information Society Statistics 2018 – Households, Table 1(b)

Only 55 per cent of households in Dublin accessed mobile broadband, compared to 63 per cent in the Mid-West region and 61 per cent in the Mid-East. Narrowband broadband accounted for a very small proportion of broadband use, highest in the West at 3 per cent.

Where households did not have access to the internet, 15 per cent of households in the West region and 10 in the Border reported that this was because of lack of availability of broadband in the area. 50 per cent of households without internet access in the South-West Region stated this was because of a lack of skills, compared to just 4 per cent in the Mid-West.

Socio-economic status was less of a factor on the percentage of households without internet access by virtue of a lack of skills, with 33 per cent of those in the first quintile (very disadvantaged) citing lack of skills, compared to 31 per cent of those in the fifth quintile (very affluent). This data must be taken in light of the higher proportion of households with fixed broadband access in the fifth quintile, however it remains an area of concern that one third of households without internet access do not have it due to lack of skills (Chart 9.2).

**Chart 9.2: Households without Internet Access due to Lack of Skills, by quintile, 2018**

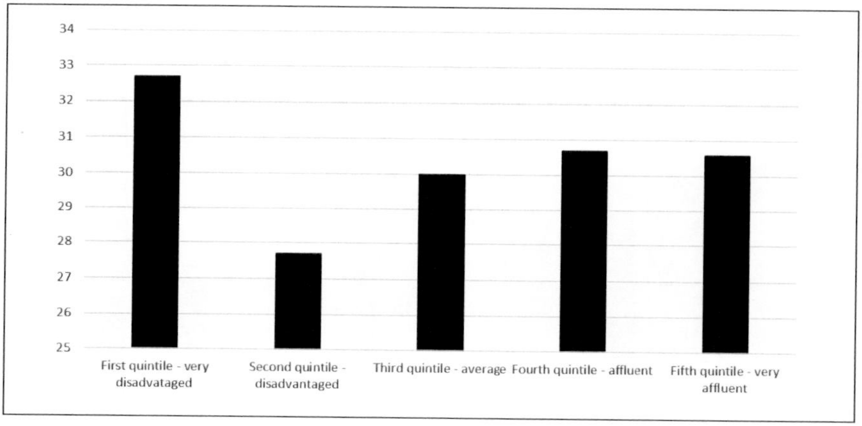

**Source:** CSO, Information Society Statistics 2018 – Households, Table 1(c)

At European level, Ireland ranks 9th in the EU Digital Economy and Society Index (DESI), up three places on the previous year (European Commission, 2018). The report indicates that Ireland excels in areas such as science, technology, engineering and mathematics graduates and the use of online trading by SMEs and Open Data, however we lag behind in basic skills (with over half the adult population lacking basic IT skills) and broadband coverage. Our 'connectivity' ranking has improved from 15th in 2017 to 11th in 2018, as has our 'Human Capital' (from 12th place in 2017 to 9th in 2018) and our 'use of internet' has improved slightly (from 16th to 15th). Ireland's 'integration of digital technology' ranking has fallen from 2nd to 3rd and our 'digital public services' ranking has fallen from 9th to 10th.

Ireland's use of the internet is broadly in line with the European average. We are more likely than our European peers to engage in online banking, social networking and video calls and less likely to use the internet for shopping, news or music, videos or games. Our use of the internet points to a society that is moving away from personal social interaction, towards virtual engagement with others. This can contribute to social isolation and so, while the number of people who have never used the internet is decreasing, we must be cognisant that those who have not are more likely to be aged 60-74 (48 per cent in 2018, an increase of 7 percentage points on 2016), retired (47 per cent in 2018, an increase of 14 percentage points on 2016), or living alone in Border counties (20 per cent in 2018, a decrease of one percentage point on 2016) (CSO, 2018). According to Taylor and Packham (2016) late or non-adoption of ICT tends to be caused by three factors: a lack of skills; a fear of technology and loss of privacy; and a perceived lack of relevance. It is therefore critical that Government adopt ICT strategies aimed at educating the population, particularly those most susceptible to isolation.

In 2018, the Government published its consultation on the National Digital Strategy, seeking submissions on what priorities need to be addressed to ensure that technology was being used in an 'integrated and inclusive' way. This Strategy will see many public services being offered online. As people in low-income households and vulnerable people are disproportionately likely to need access to public services, our submission urged Government to ensure that internet literacy programmes were available, particularly to those who do not currently use the internet, and that grants were made available to low-income and vulnerable households to purchase IT equipment.

*Promoting Internet Use and Security*
Fake news, cyber bullying and cyber fraud are downsides of online activity. 73 per cent of users access reading materials and news online and 73 per cent use social networking sites (CSO, 2018), however only 34 per cent of Irish internet users take basic precautions to protect their personal details on websites (albeit increased from 30 per cent in 2016). In addition to technical skills training for late adopters, *Social Justice Ireland* considers that there is a real need to develop programmes to enable all users to critically analyse information and to become "savvy, safe surfers". Affordable high speed broadband access right across the country is essential for business development, efficient government and participation in society.

*National Broadband Plan*
As part of the Digital Agenda for Europe, the European Commission has set targets of 30mbps broadband for all citizens and 50 per cent of citizens subscribing to 100mbps by 2020. According to ComReg (2017) 70.5 per cent of fixed broadband subscriptions had speeds of 30Mbps or more in Q3 2017, almost 30 per cent behind target. Only 24.8 per cent of connections reached the 100Mbps target.

In December 2008, Government launched its National Broadband Scheme aimed at providing 234,000 properties with broadband speeds of at least 2.3Mbps by 2010. Connections under this Scheme expired in August 2014 with broadband provider Three retaining connection contracts on a commercial basis. In 2012, the Government published its National Broadband Plan, committing to delivering high speed broadband to 1.3 million premises, with minimum download rates of 30Mbps for all, reaching up to 100Mbps for at least half of the premises included, by 2015. This Plan was revised in April 2014 when the then Minister for Communications, Pat Rabbitte, announced that 900,000 premises would receive fiber powered broadband to be delivered in at least three years. In December 2015, Government then published the Broadband Intervention Strategy, detailing just 685,000 properties, all of which would receive download speeds of 30Mbps, and in April 2017 these figures were revised again so that 542,000 premises could expect download speeds of 30Mbps by 2020.

The procurement process for this Plan has been protracted and mired by delays and vested interests. In July 2016, three preferred bidders were announced – Eir, the Enet consortium and SIRO. In September 2017, SIRO announced they were exiting the process, taking 500,000 contracts with them on a commercial basis. The process continued with the remaining two bidders until January 2018 when Eir announced they were also withdrawing, taking their 300,000 commercially viable contracts. This left the Government with one bidder and not a lot of attractive connection contracts.

In late 2018, there was further controversy when the Minister for Communications, Climate Action and the Environment, Denis Naughten, resigned following allegations that the process had been undermined by his private engagements with the sole remaining bidder. A report published shortly after this resignation found that was no undue influence in the process and that Minister Naughten's resignation protected the process as it continued to final stages. *Social Justice Ireland* urges Government to ensure that proper procurement procedures are followed with the remaining tenderer and that public interest is best served when rolling out any contractual terms to end users.

### *Legal Supports and Access to Justice*

Access to justice is a basic human right, however in order to achieve equality of access, there must be a balance of power on both sides. In a legal context, the balance of power almost always rests with those who can afford counsel. Redressing this balance requires the availability of free and low-cost legal services to those who need the advice of a qualified solicitor or barrister but who cannot afford the costs associated with it.

The Legal Aid Board provides advice and representation on criminal and civil matters for those on low income. Criminal legal aid, through the Garda Station Legal Advice Revised Scheme, the Legal Aid – Custody Issues Scheme and the Criminal Assets Bureau Ad-hoc Legal Aid Scheme, is free of charge to the user, subsidised by the State for those dependent on social welfare or having a disposable income of €18,000 per annum or less. Civil legal aid is also subsidised, but it is not free. Applicants are means tested and pay a fee of between €30 and €130 for this service. Their case is also subject to a merits test, to ascertain if the case has a chance of success. Their civil services range from family law matters (including separation, divorce and custody and a free family mediation service), debt, wills, and inheritance. In 2017 there were 14,687 applications for Legal Aid, an increase of 6 per cent on 2016 (Legal Aid Board, 2018).

The regressive nature of most of the changes to the state-funded civil legal aid scheme during the economic downturn disproportionately impacted on vulnerable and marginalised groups (FLAC, 2016). Cuts in both staffing levels and funding for the Legal Aid Board and the decision to raise costs for legal services had the inevitable effect of both to deter and to deny access to justice. Budget 2019 increased the allocation to Criminal Legal Aid by €12 million to €61.3 million, while Civil Legal Aid increased by just €500,000. This is insufficient to allow the Legal Aid Board to deal with its caseload or undertake the necessary review of the eligibility criteria.

Consumers who need legal advice, but do not require legal representation, can access the Free Legal Advice Centres (FLAC) who provide a network of volunteers through clinics held primarily in Citizens Information Centres nationwide. FLAC volunteers provide advice on a range of legal issues, including family law, debt, probate, employment and property. A consultation is twenty minutes long and general advice is usually given, as in many cases the person seeking the advice has little or no paperwork for review. In 2017, 13,813 people attended FLAC clinics and a there were a further 12,003 callers to their telephone information and referral line. The main areas of inquiry to the FLAC information and referral line were family law, employment and housing (FLAC, 2018).

For those who do not qualify for support through the Legal Aid Board, but still require legal representation, the Bar Council of Ireland provides a Voluntary Assistance Scheme (VAS) on referral from NGOs working with vulnerable people. In 2016, the Bar Council spent €17,569 on VAS, increased from €16,801 in 2015 (an increase of 4.5 per cent) (FLAC, 2017).

FLAC, VAS and the Legal Aid Board provide a valuable service, however *Social Justice Ireland* believes that access to justice is such a fundamental human right that it should not be dependent on well-intentioned volunteers dealing with a range of legal topics in twenty minute increments and calls on Government to ensure that people's rights are protected and dignity respected in this most fundamental way, by adequate access to justice through the court system.

### Sports and Recreation Facilities
According to the CSO report *Wellbeing of the Nation* (CSO, 2017) participation in sport declined from 47.2 per cent in 2013 to 45 per cent in 2015, while the average weekly expenditure of a household on sports and leisure increased from €14.40 between 2009-2010 to €17.85 in the period 2015-2016. The report notes that participation in sport has many positive effects on a person's wellbeing, both physical and mental. While higher spending on these activities is reported as a good sign, increased costs may also act as a barrier to participation, particularly in low income households.

*Adult Participation*

The Irish Sports Monitor Annual Report (Sports Ireland, 2018) reported that only 43 per cent of the population had participated in sport in the previous seven days, a decrease of 0.1 percentage points on 2015. The most popular type of sport was 'Exercise' (12.4 per cent), followed by swimming (8.5 per cent) and running (5.1 per cent). Participation by women in every age group from 35-44 and upwards increased between 2015 and 2017. The proportion of men in most age groups from 35-44 and onwards also increased, with the exception of those aged between 45-54, but the rate of increase was less than that of women. Participation rates remain lower for people in lower socio economic groups. Those classified as 'unable to work' had the lowest participation rate, at just 21.2 per cent (although a slight increase from 20 per cent in 2015), while students and employees had the highest participation rates (67.7 per cent and 47.1 per cent respectively). The unemployed and homemakers had participation rates of 36.3 per cent and 34.6 per cent, while those in self-employment had a participation rate of 39 per cent. This is further supported when viewed in the context of the numbers participating in sport by net monthly household income, with those on lower incomes participating less in sport (Chart 9.3). The participation rate has fallen across all incomes between 2015 and 2017, however the pattern remains consistent.

**Chart 9.3: Numbers Participating in Sport by Net Monthly Household Income, 2015 to 2017**

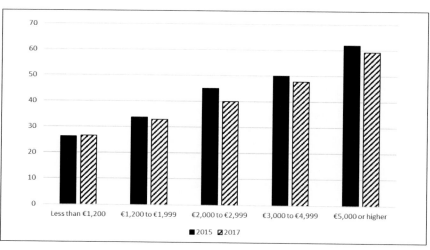

**Source:** Sport Ireland, Annual Report 2017

## Child Participation

*Growing Up in Ireland,* the National Longitudinal Study of Children, reported on the frequency with which participating 13 year olds were participating in hard exercise for at least 20 minutes in a day[4] and found that boys were more likely to exercise than girls, with girls more likely to report exercising for two or fewer days in the previous two weeks and boys more likely to report exercising in nine or more days in that period (Chart 9.4).

**Chart 9.4: Number of Days in past fortnight 13 year old participated in hard exercise**

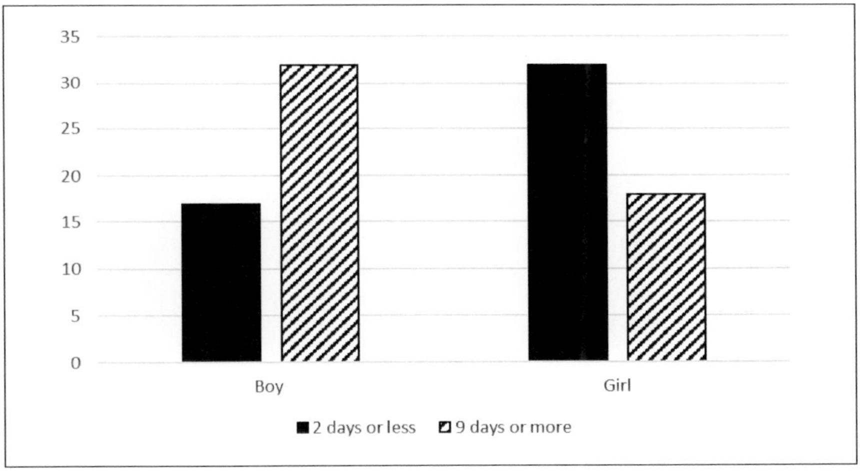

**Source:** Growing Up in Ireland, The Lives of 13 year olds, 2018

Boys were also found to be more likely than girls to spend more than 3 hours watching TV and playing video games, while girls were more likely than boys to spend more then 3 hours reading or using a computer.

## Child Obesity

Child obesity is increasing across many developed countries and is a cause for concern for the future health and wellbeing of the population. The *Growing Up in Ireland* study found that 20 per cent of 13 year olds were overweight and six per cent were classified as obese, with girls more likely to be overweight or obese than boys (Williams et al, 2018). There has been some significant shifts in the weight status of these 13 year olds when compared to the previous report at 9 years old. Of those who were non-overweight at 9 years old, 89 per cent have remained so, with 10 per cent

---

4    Hard exercise was defined on the questionnaire as activity being sufficiently vigorous to make the heart beat faster (football, jogging, fast cycling). Light exercise was defined as exercise that was not hard enough to make the young person breathe heavily and make the heart beat fast (such as walking or slow cycling) (p.78).

becoming overweight and 1 per cent becoming obese in the intervening period. Of those who were overweight at 9 years old, 35 per cent are non-overweight, 54 per cent remained overweight and 11 per cent became obese. Of those who were classified as obese at 9 years old, 9 per cent became non-overweight, 41 per cent became overweight and 50 per cent remained obese (Chart 9.5).

**Chart 9.5: Change in Weight Status of 13 year olds since 9 years of age**

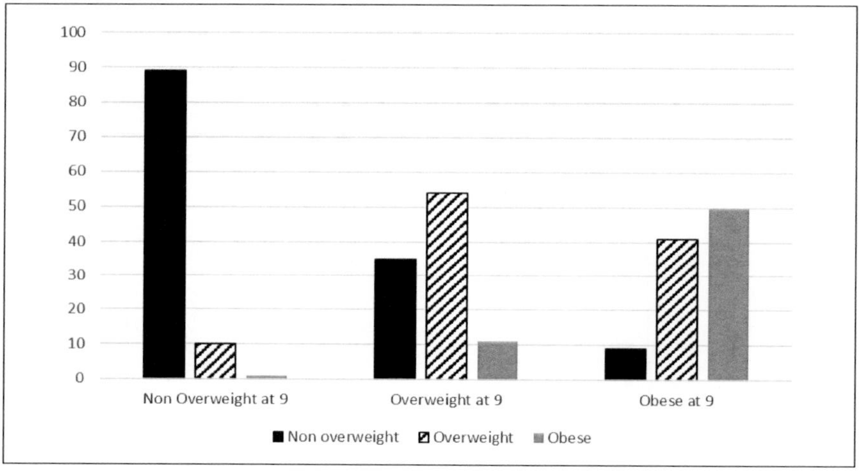

Source: Growing Up in Ireland, The Lives of 13 year olds, 2018

*National Physical Activity Plan*
The low rate of participation in physical activity among Ireland's children and adults, high rates of use of private transport for even short journeys, and the increasing prevalence of online shopping means that Ireland is becoming a more sedentary country. The National Physical Activity Plan, published in 2016 as part of the Healthy Ireland framework, contained ambitious targets for eight key action areas including children and young people, work places, public awareness, and sport and physical activity in the community. *Social Justice Ireland* commends Government on the initiatives undertaken in furtherance of this plan, such as 'Park Runs', 'Operation Transformation', and the site 'getirelandactive.ie' that recommends physical activities for a range of ages and lifestyles and calls on Government to encourage children and adults, particularly those from low socio-economic backgrounds to increase their participation in sports through the further development of playgrounds and subsidised sports centres.

*Sports and Recreation Funding*
Those participating in team sports are more likely than those participating in individual sports to regularly participate in multiple sports (Sports Ireland, 2018).

Just over half (53.4 per cent) of those participating in a team sport have also participated in another sport, compared with 31.4 per cent of those participating in an individual sport.

The largest and most well-known sports organisation in Ireland is the GAA, whose clubs not only provide a physical outlet for those playing the games, but also a social and recreational space for people to volunteer. However, maintaining facilities to a high standard and encouraging wide participation is expensive, and there is a need to offer support-funding to clubs in this regard. This is particularly important for sports which do not have access to large gate receipts. Government must be cognisant of the health, societal and economic benefits of sports and social outlets, and provide sufficient ring-fenced funding to complement this voluntary effort.

Under the Department of Transport, Tourism and Sport, the Sports Capital Programme aims to assist voluntary and community organisations, national governing bodies of sport, local authorities and in some cases schools to:

- develop facilities in appropriate locations
- provide appropriate equipment to help maximise participation in sport and physical recreation,
- prioritise the needs of disadvantaged areas in the provision of sports facilities
- encourage the multi-purpose use of local, regional and national sports facilities by clubs, community organisations and national governing bodies of sport.

Applications under this programme for 2018 closed in October 2018, with a total projects value of €161.9 million (an increase on the €155 million in applications in 2017) applied for from an initial budget of €60 million (double the 2017 budget). Budget 2019 allocated €63 million in capital expenditure for Sports and Recreation Services, less than 40 per cent required to meet the 2018 allocations. Without investment, clubs will continue to need to subsidise these grants by way of significant local fundraising and voluntary activity.

Of course, not every person is attracted by team sports, and the importance of facilities to support individual physical activity right across the lifecycle is very important. The National Physical Activity Plan recognises the importance of facilities for many other activities such as walking, jogging, hiking, biking, swimming, dance and fitness classes. At public level, most of these facilities are provided by Local Authorities, often in conjunction with local community groups and sporting bodies. The expected Local Authority expenditures on Recreation and Amenity for 2018 was €451.5 million, or almost 10 per cent of their combined budgets. This work includes the development and maintenance of a wide range of amenities such as parks, swimming pools, sports complexes, adventure playgrounds, outdoor gyms, parks with cycle and running lanes, Blueways and Greenways, cycling, hill walking, hiking trails and many more. The Healthy Ireland initiative is now being rolled out to a county level, with an emphasis in 2018/19 on physical activity. This funding is welcome and is planned to continue for the coming years.

A source of revenue that could be ring-fenced for sports participation and recreational activities is the Sugar-Sweetened Drinks Tax[5] which was introduced in May 2018. If appropriately allocated, this revenue could move Ireland further towards attaining the targets of the *National Plan for Physical Activity*.

### Regulation
According to the OECD, how accountability is translated into practice can be closely related to the independence of the regulator and its functions and powers (OECD, 2016:17). Regulation in Ireland has been lacking for decades, primarily because of this lack of independence, where 'regulators' were used as an instrument of the State to effect Government policies at the time, rather than to regulate their respective sectors and ensure accountability from participant entities. The area most associated with 'light touch' regulatory policy in Ireland is the financial sector, with thousands of families continuing to feel the effects of the economic crash, but this issue is not confined to that sector alone. Lack of robust regulation of the planning processes have left Ireland with urban sprawl across towns and cities, and inaccessible one-off properties in remote areas, widening the 'urban/rural' divide by making essential services (many discussed earlier in this chapter) inaccessible and ineffective.

### Ireland's Regulatory Position
A lack of vision and direction in the areas of energy, communications and healthcare has created a position whereby regulation is used to protect competitiveness in an increasingly privatised marketplace, rather than as a method of consumer protection. The Register of Lobbying[6] was introduced in 2015 to increase transparency and accountability, making information available to the public on the identity of those lobbying designated public officials and the nature of those lobbying activities. In 2017, 9,828 returns were received by the Commission in Regulating Lobbying, an increase of 18 per cent on the previous year (Commission in Regulating Lobbying 2018). While this increased transparency is to be welcomed the question of what, if any, effect it is having on effecting a cultural shift from vested to public interest remains. Greater attention must be drawn to the information available on the Lobbying Register. *Social Justice Ireland* calls for the inclusion in the Commission's Annual Reports of policy areas with the greatest lobbying activity, the lobbying organisations and the designated public officials engaged so as to highlight to the general public those influencing the political decision-making process.

### Creating Regulatory Policy

---

[5]  For full details on a joint proposal from the Irish Heart Foundation and Social Justice Ireland see http://www.socialjustice.ie/content/publications/reducing-obesity-and-future-health-costs-proposal-health-related-taxation

[6]  https://www.lobbying.ie/

Reactionary regulation, introduced after a crisis, can also serve to further exclude those who it should serve to protect, by placing barriers to goods and services in the way of those without the resources to engage with increasing bureaucracy. *Social Justice Ireland* believes that regulation has a place in protecting the rights of the vulnerable by addressing the balance of power when engaging with corporations and political structures, but not be so involved as to create a barrier rather than a safety net.

The OECD recommends that the governance of regulators follow seven principles to ensure the implementation of proper policy:

1. Role Clarity

2. Preventing Undue Influence and Maintaining Trust

3. Decision Making and Governing Body Structure

4. Accountability and Transparency

5. Engagement

6. Funding

7. Performance Evaluation

These principles work together as a continuum with clarity from the start and performance evaluation informing governance policy, thereby creating greater levels of clarity as learning from the evaluation is utilised. If these principles were ingrained in the process for development of regulation and governance of regulators, consumer protection and independence would naturally follow from regulation developed in line with these central tenets.

*Social Justice Ireland* believes that regulation should have consumer protection at its centre rather than the aim of increasing market participation. Before engaging in any new regulatory processes, the Government should ensure that the rights of its citizens are protected, including the right to a reasonable standard of living with access to basic services at a reasonable cost.

**Key Policy Priorities**
*Social Justice Ireland* believes that the following policy positions should be adopted in addressing Ireland's many public services deficiencies:

- Increase the provision of public transport in rural areas and provide greater investment in sustainable transport and biofuels.

- Develop a multiannual investment strategy of €150m per annum in early childhood education and care and after-school care up to 2021

- Track levels of financial exclusion and build and monitor policies and practices aimed at eliminating it in its entirety by 2020.

- Develop programmes to enable all internet users to critically analyse information and to become "savvy, safe surfers" and a grants scheme to support low income and vulnerable households to purchase ICT equipment needed to access public services on implementation of the National Digital Strategy.

- Ensure connectivity to affordable high-speed broadband access right across the country.

- Ensure that the Legal Aid Board is adequately funded so that people in the court system are guaranteed equality of access to justice.

- Increase funding to encourage sports participation and active lifestyle programmes.

- Ring-fence revenue gained through the sweetened drinks tax to fund sport and recreational facilities and services.

- Improve transparency and accessibility of lobbying activity by the general public.

# REFERENCES

Browne, D., Caulfield, B. and O'Mahony, M (2011) *Barriers to Sustainable Transport in Ireland*. Climate Change Research Programme (CCRP 2007-2013) Report Series no. 7. Dublin:EPA

Central Statistics Office (CSO) (2018(a)): *Transport Omnibus 2017*

Central Statistics Office (CSO) (2018(b)): *National Travel Survey 2017*

Central Statistics Office (CSO) (2018(c)): *Information Society Statistics 2018*

Central Statistics Office (CSO) (2018(d)): *Wellbeing of the Nation 2017*

Central Statistics Office (CSO) (2017(a)): *Census of Population 2016 – Profile 4 Households and Families*

Central Statistics Office (CSO) (2017(b)): *QNHS Childcare Quarter 3 2016, Module on Childcare*

Central Statistics Office (CSO) (2016): *Persons per Household by use of Banking Services and Year*

Corr, C. (2006) *Financial Exclusion in Ireland: An exploratory study and policy review*. Dublin: Combat Poverty Agency

Credit Union Advisory Committee (CUAC) (2017): *Policy Paper, Loan Interest Rates*

Deane, A., (2018): *Money Matters: Addressing the Unmet Need of People with Inadequate Income and Experiencing Financial Exclusion*

Department of Children and Youth Affairs (2018): *First 5: A Whole-of-Government Strategy for Babies, Young Children and their Families*

Department of Communications, Climate Action and Environment (2017) *Report of the Mobile Phone and Broadband Taskforce*

Department of Communications, Energy and Natural Resources (2015) Ireland's Broadband Intervention Strategy Updated December 2015. Dublin: Stationery Office.

Department of Environment, Community and Local Government (2013) *Opportunities for All - The public library as a catalyst for economic, social and cultural development*

Department of Rural and Community Development (2018): *Our Public Libraries 2022, Inspiring, Connecting and Empowering Communities*

European Commission (2018(a)) *Digital Economy and Society Index 2018– Country Profile Ireland*. Brussels: European Commission.

European Commission (2016): *Childcare Costs, Country Profile: Ireland*

European Commission (2008) *Annual Information Society Report 2008 Benchmarking i2010: Progress and Fragmentation in the European Information Society* Brussels: European Commission

Free Legal Advice Centres (2018) *Annual Report 2017*

Free Legal Advice Centres (2016) *Accessing Justice in Hard Times: the impact of the economic downturn on the scheme of civil legal aid in Ireland*. Dublin: Free Legal Advice Centres.

Gloukoviezoff, G, (2011) *Understanding and Combating Financial Exclusion in Ireland: A European Perspective. What could Ireland learn from Belgium, France and the United Kingdom?* Dublin: The Policy Institute, TCD.

Government of Ireland (2018): *Project Ireland 2040: National Development Plan 2018 - 2027*

Irish Government Economic & Evaluation Service (IGEES) (2018): *Transport Trends 2018*

Irish Government Economic & Evaluation Service (IGEES) (2017): *Spending Review 2017, Public Service Obligation (PSO) Funding for Public Transport,* June 2017

Jarret, R., Sullivan, P. and Watkins, N. (2005) '*Developing social capital through participation in organized youth programs: qualitative insights from three programs*'. Journal of Community Psychology, Vol.33, No.1: 41-55

Kempson, E. and Collard, S. (2012) *Developing a vision for financial inclusion.* Bristol: University of Bristol

Legal Aid Board (2018): *Law Centre Waiting Times and Other Statistical Information*

Nugent, Ciaran (2017): *The Affordability of Childcare in Ireland: Measuring Regional Disparities,* NERI Research inBrief, December 2017 (no. 58), Nevin Economic Research Institute

Office of An Taoiseach (2018): *Public Consultation on Ireland's new National Digital Strategy*

OECD (2016): *Society at a Glance 2016: OECD Social Indicators,* OECD Publishing, Paris

Post Office Network Business Development Group (2016) *Final Report of the Post Office Network Business Development Group: Refresh, Renew, Reinvent.* Dublin: DCENR

Reddan, F. and Kelly, F. (2019): *Credit Unions could be allowed to push up the cost of loans,* Irish Times, 07 January 2019

Russell, H., Maître, B. and Donnelly, N. (2011) *Financial Exclusion and Over-indebtedness in Irish Households.* Dublin: ESRI.

Social Justice Ireland (2018): *Budget Choices 2018*

Sports Ireland (2018) *Irish Sports Monitor Annual Report 2017*

Stamp,S., McMahon, A. and McLoughlin C: *Left Behind in the Cold? Fuel Poverty, Money Management & Financial Difficulty Among Dublin 10 & 20 MABS Clients 2013 and 2017*

Standards in Public Office Commission (2018) *Annual Report 2017 in regard to the Regulation of Lobbying Act.*

Taylor, D. and Packham, G. (2016*) Social Inclusion through ICT: Identifying and Overcoming Barriers to ICT Use* Strat. Change 25: 45–60 (2016)

Vincentian Partnership for Social Justice (2015) *Minimum Income Standard and the Cost of Childcare.* Dublin: VPSJ

Weston, C. (2019): *Credit Unions to give out more risky loans, as interest rates may double,* Irish Independent, 17 January 2019

Williams J, Greene S, et al. (2018) *Growing Up in Ireland. National Longitudinal Study of Children. The Lives of 13-year-olds.* Dublin: Department of Children and Youth Affairs.

Woods, C.B., Tannehill D., Quinlan, A., Moyna, N. and Walsh, J. (2010) '*The Children's Sport Participation and Physical Activity Study (CSPPA)*'. Research Report No 1. School of Health and Human Performance, Dublin City University and The Irish Sports Council.

# Chapter 10
## People and Participation

**Core Policy Objective:**
To ensure that all people from different cultures are welcomed in a way that is consistent with our history, our obligations as world citizens and with our economic status.

To ensure that every person has a genuine voice in shaping the decisions that affect them and that every person can contribute to the development of society.

**Key Issues/Evidence**

Centralisation of Government decision making and financing

**Policy Solutions**

Funding for Public
Participation Networks

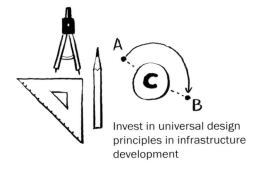

Invest in universal design
principles in infrastructure
development

Address barriers
to social inclusion

Local
Government
reform

# 10.

# PEOPLE AND PARTICIPATION

> ## CORE POLICY OBJECTIVE: PEOPLE AND PARTICIPATION
>
> To ensure that all people from different cultures are welcomed in a way that is consistent with our history, our obligations as world citizens and with our economic status.
>
> To ensure that every person has a genuine voice in shaping the decisions that affect them and that every person can contribute to the development of society.

Decisions made by general and local Government affect every one of us. Policies enacted on healthcare, housing, taxation, planning and so on all have an impact on our day to day lives. Part of the 'Good Governance' pillar in *Social Justice Ireland's* proposed Policy Framework for a Just Society set out in Chapter 2, is the right of all people to meaningfully participate in the decisions and to have their say in shaping their communities and the world around them. These rights are a fundamental part of living in a democracy and, as such, should be experienced by all equally. In this Chapter we explore the changing demographics within Ireland, set out some of the implications of these rights, and how they might be met in Ireland today.

If the objectives set out above are to be achieved *Social Justice Ireland* believes that Government should:

- Focus on combatting racism and discrimination, and promoting interculturalism in Ireland

- Facilitate asylum seekers to take up accessible work and education opportunities.

- Adequately resource the Public Participation Network (PPN) structures for participation at Local Authority level and ensure capacity building is an integral part of the process.

- Promote deliberative democracy and a process of inclusive social dialogue to ensure there is real and effective monitoring and impact assessment of policy development and implementation using an evidence-based approach.

- Resource an initiative to identify how a real participative civil society debate could be developed and maintained.

- Implement the National Framework for Local and Community Development, in a way which supports Community and Voluntary organisations

## Key Evidence

### People

Census 2016 recorded the population of Ireland as 4,757,976 people (CSO, 2017a). This represents an increase of 169,724 or 3.7 per cent in the previous five years. In general, the main urban areas and their hinterlands increased in population, while rural areas declined. Since then the population has continued to grow with an estimated increase of almost 100,000 people between the Census and April 2018, giving a total of 4.86 million. This increase is due to a combination of natural factors (births – deaths) and net migration.

The composition of the population is also changing, with an increase in diversity (almost 22 per cent of estimated net migration in 2018 is attributed to migrants from outside of the EU) and proportions of young people and older people, with 40 per cent of the estimated population of Ireland consisting of people aged 0-14 and 60 and older. These demographic changes create major challenges for public policy, the implications of which are discussed in the other Chapters in this book. This Chapter looks primarily at migration, integration and participation.

### Emigration and Immigration

Net migration into Ireland was positive in April 2018, continuing a pattern which has been in place since 2015. This means that more people have entered the country than are leaving it. Analysing migration trends over the past 30 years, we see a relatively high rate of emigration in 1988 and 1989, at a time of recession, which decreased slowly over the next 10 years. In the 2000s, emigration patterns were a little more erratic prior to the recession in 2008, which saw an increase from 49,200 in 2008 to 72,000 the following year (Chart 10.1). Immigration to Ireland peaked in 2007, where 151,100 people came into the country, 37,600 more than the following year.

Emigration of Irish nationals continues to fall, decreasing from 49,700 in 2012, to 42,500 in 2015 and an estimated 28,300 in 2018 (CSO, 2018). While there was a slight decrease in Irish nationals returning in 2017, 2018 saw a return to 2016 levels of immigration with 28,400 Irish emigrants returning (CSO, 2018). Decreasing emigration and increasing immigration indicates a renewed confidence in Ireland's economic prospects. However, the issues explored elsewhere in this book, particularly in respect of housing, call this fledgling confidence into question.

**Chart 10.1: Immigration, Emigration and Net Migration, ,000 people, 1988-2018**

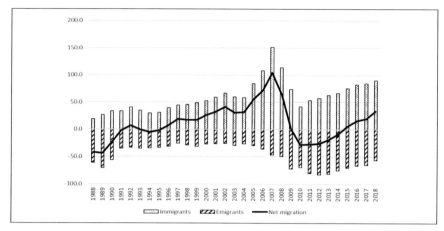

**Source:** CSO, Population and Migration Estimates Table 1, 2018.
**Note:** Figures for 2016 taken from Census 2016; Figures for 2017 and 2018 are preliminary

In terms of origin, 26 per cent of total immigrants to Ireland in 2018 came from the EU (excluding Ireland and the UK), 8 per cent came from the UK and 34 per cent from the rest of the world. When the nationalities of emigrants is considered, 25 per cent were from the EU (excluding Ireland and the UK), 7 per cent were from the UK and 18 per cent were from the rest of the world (CSO, 2018) (Table 10.1).

**Table 10.1: Estimated Migration by Nationality, 2016 – 18, by '000**

| Year | | Irish | UK | Rest of EU 15 | EU 16-28 | Rest of World | Total |
|------|------------|-------|------|------|------|------|------|
| 2016 | Immigration | 28.4 | 5.9 | 11.4 | 13.2 | 23.6 | 82.3 |
|      | Emigration | -37.1 | -5.2 | -5.7 | -6.8 | -11.4 | -66.2 |
|      | Net | -8.8 | 0.7 | 5.6 | 6.4 | 12.3 | 16.2 |
| 2017 | Immigration | 27.4 | 6.1 | 10.8 | 10.9 | 29.4 | 84.6 |
|      | Emigration | -30.8 | -4.0 | -6.7 | -9.6 | -13.7 | -64.8 |
|      | Net | -3.4 | 2.1 | 4.1 | 1.3 | 15.7 | 19.8 |
| 2018 | Immigration | 28.4 | 7.3 | 11.6 | 12.2 | 30.9 | 90.3 |
|      | Emigration | -28.3 | -4.1 | -6.8 | -7.1 | -10.0 | -56.3 |
|      | Net | 0.1 | 3.2 | 4.8 | 5.0 | 20.8 | 34.0 |

**Source:** CSO (2018), *Population and Migration Estimates*.
**Notes:** Data relates to the year to April
  'Rest of EU' refers to Pre 2004 EU members less UK and Ireland.
  'EU 16-28' refers to EU Members that joined after 2004

Social Justice Matters 2019

The numbers of migrants with a third level education continued to rise in 2018. Of those immigrating to Ireland, both the number (from 28,200 in 2012 to 49,200 in 2018) and proportion (56 per cent in 2012 to 62 per cent of all immigrants in 2018) with a third level education has increased. Migrants tend to be younger than the general population with half of both immigrants and emigrants aged between 25 and 44. People aged over 65 were the least likely to migrate.

Although the number of emigrants with a third level education has been in decline since 2012, the proportion of all emigrants with a third level education has increased, from 47 per cent in 2012 to 53 per cent in 2018. Fifty-six per cent of those who left Ireland were employed and a further 19 per cent were students. The proportion of emigrants who are unemployed has also declined since 2012, falling from 22.5 per cent to 13 per cent, reflecting the decrease in unemployment in the country over that period.

In light of the higher educational attainment levels of immigrants into Ireland, and the increasing number of Irish people returning to this country, there is a need for a skills transfer programme for returning migrants in order to ensure the skills that they have acquired whilst working abroad are recognised in Ireland. This is something that *Social Justice Ireland* has advocated for previously. Given the investment made in the education of young graduates, it is essential that steps are taken to retain them and their expertise within Ireland, and to attract back those who have emigrated in recent years. Of course, this is coupled with the need to provide both decent work and infrastructure to support increasing numbers of immigrants who will need to be housed and whose healthcare and childcare needs must be accommodated.

For many migrants immigration is not temporary. They will remain in Ireland and make it their home. In turn, Irish people are experiencing life in different cultural contexts around the world. Ireland is now a multi-racial and multi-cultural country and Government policies should promote and encourage the development of an inclusive and integrated society with respect for and recognition of diverse cultures.

**Ireland as a multicultural society**
The internationalisation of the population presents Ireland with the key challenge of developing a truly integrated society that values cultural and ethnic diversity. Integration is defined in current Irish policy as the 'ability to participate to the extent that a person needs and wishes in all of the major components of society without having to relinquish his or her own cultural identity' (Department of Justice and Equality, 2017).

Census 2016 showed that there was a total of 535,475 non-Irish nationals – representing 200 different nations - living in Ireland (CSO, 2017c). The main nationalities were Polish (23 per cent) and UK (19 per cent). Other nationalities with over 10,000 residents included USA, Brazil, France, Germany, India, Latvia,

Lithuania, Romania and Spain. Non Irish nationals have a very different age profile to the rest of the population with half aged between 25 and 42 compared with a quarter of the Irish population. There are proportionately fewer children under 14 (12.3 per cent versus 22.5 per cent), and older people (4 per cent versus 13 per cent) among non-Irish nationals. The unemployment rate among non-Irish nationals was 15.4 per cent, compared with a rate of 12.6 per cent among the Irish population.

Census 2016 also asked people to identify their ethnicity and cultural background. 681,016 people identify themselves as other than "White Irish", of whom 234,289 identify as Black, Asian or other people of colour (Table 10.2). The period between 2011 and 2016 also showed a 3 per cent reduction in people from traditional Christian religions, an increase of 74 per cent in those with no religion and a growth in other religions with 63,400 Muslims (+29 per cent), 62,200 Orthodox (+37 per cent) and 34,100 Hindus (+34 per cent).

**Table 10.2: Ethnic and cultural background of usual residents of Ireland 2011-2016**

| Category | 2011 | 2016 | % Change |
|---|---|---|---|
| White Irish | 3,821,995 | 3,854,226 | 0.8 |
| Irish Travellers | 29,495 | 30,987 | 5.1 |
| Other White | 412,975 | 446,727 | 8.2 |
| Black Irish or Black African | 58,697 | 57,850 | -1.4 |
| Other Black | 6,381 | 6,789 | 6.4 |
| Chinese | 17,832 | 19,447 | 9.1 |
| Other Asian | 66,858 | 79,273 | 18.6 |
| Other | 40,724 | 70,603 | 73.4 |
| Not Stated | 70,324 | 124,019 | 76.4 |
| Total | 4,525,281 | 4,689,921 | 3.6 |

**Source:** CSO, Census 2016.

In July 2018, the ESRI published a study on barriers to social inclusion (McGuinness, et al., 2018) which found that belonging to an ethnic minority was one of five barriers to social inclusion in Ireland (where 'ethnic minority' included members of the Traveller community, Roma, refugees and asylum seekers). Because of the age profile of immigrants, discussed earlier in this Chapter, there is a strong correlation between the barrier of ethnic minority and those Not in Employment, Education or Training (NEETs). It is also reported as being more heavily associated with lower educational attainment, living in an urban location and being short-term unemployed (McGuinness, et al., 2018, p. 30). However, it is because of this younger age profile that there are greater opportunities to address issues of social inclusion and to develop supports and programmes for greater integration and inclusion, including training and job activation programmes targeted at ethnic minorities.

## Racism in Ireland

The European Network against Racism reported 256 incidents of reported racism (it should be noted that not all incidents will be reported) in the latter half of 2017, with almost half of these (113) concerning online abuse (European Network against Racism (Ireland), 2018). A further 23 incidents involved racial assaults, 35 cases involved ongoing harassment, 11 cases involved threats to kill and 20 cases involved 'other threats'. The number of racist crimes reported is increasing. This is concerning in and of itself, however when considered in the context of reports of racism being made against five politicians and 10 newspapers publishing racist items in just six months of 2017, people and institutions who play a significant role in shaping the national consciousness, we may anticipate a further rise (ibid).

A study on young people from minority ethnic backgrounds identified racism and exclusion as a "normal" feature of their lives (National Youth Council of Ireland, 2017). It also described the extra stresses of developing identity, belonging and integration in a different culture to their parents. The report highlights the key role that appropriately trained youth workers can play in supporting young people from minorities, and in promoting interculturalism to all young people.

The consequences of racism are very a serious, increasing fear and insecurity. The European Network Against Racism (European Network against Racism (Ireland), 2018) noted that "Racism has a demonstrable impact on the lives of those targeted.... there is psychological impact, ... impact on their social connectedness, and economic impacts through for example increased costs or lost income." This is unacceptable in a society that prides itself on its open and accepting character. But racism is not only socially damaging, it is also harmful to the economy. As Ireland seeks to attract FDI and is sourcing workers from all over the world to meet skills shortages, it is imperative that racism in all areas is definitively addressed.

The Migrant Integration Strategy was published in early 2017 (Department of Justice and Equality, 2017a). The strategy proposes a wide range of initiatives across all Government Departments, including language courses, producing documents in multiple languages, promoting integration via sports, culture and community funding programmes and specific supports for labour market integration. It also undertakes to monitor and review current procedures in a wide range of areas. A welcome development is training for frontline staff in State agencies in anti-racism and cultural awareness. The first report under the Strategy, published in November 2018, showed that migrants were more likely to be at work than their Irish peers (the working age employment rate of migrants in 2017 was 69.6 per cent, compared to 66.4 per cent for Irish nationals), they were more likely to have a third level education (the share of 25-34 year old migrants with a tertiary education was 56 per cent, compared to 51 per cent for Irish nationals), but their median annual net income (needs adjusted) was lower at €17,804 compared to €20,890 for Irish people (McGinnity, et al., 2018). Higher education, higher employment and lower disposable income is not an attractive proposition for someone looking to relocate to Ireland. Government needs to address areas of discrimination to provide a supportive environment for our migrant workers.

**Travellers**
There were 30,897 Irish Travellers in 2016, an increase of 5 per cent from 2011 (Census 2016). The long-sought recognition of Travellers as an ethnic minority was achieved in 2016, however, Travellers continue to face discrimination in education, employment and accommodation, with a widening gap in health over the life course (Watson, et al., 2017).

According to the 2016 Census, education levels amongst Travellers remain low, with 62 per cent having primary education or less, 13 per cent having completed second level and only one per cent having a college degree. Eighty per cent of Travellers reported as being unemployed, compared with 13 per cent for non-Travellers. Watson, et al., 2017 suggest that much of this is directly related to low levels of education. Traveller health is also poor with 19 per cent categorised as having a disability compared to 13.5 per cent of the general population. The suicide rate amongst Traveller men is almost seven times higher than in the general population, and this is an indicator of a serious mental health issues in the Traveller Community. Overall life expectancy for Travellers is low with only 7.5 per cent of Travellers aged over 54 years compared with 23 per cent of the overall population. Housing continues to be problematic for Travellers with Census 2016 figures showing that 39 per cent of Traveller accommodation was overcrowded compared with 6 per cent for all households. In contrast to previous trends, the number of caravans being used increased by 10 per cent between 2016 and 2011. 517 Travellers (1.7 per cent) were recorded as homeless on Census night 2016 compared with 0.1 per cent of the overall population.

Incidents of racism against Travellers (European Network against Racism (Ireland), 2018) indicate a more concerted and targeted approach, with reports of pubs collectively closing in an area around the time of a Traveller funeral and Travellers being excluded from events having produced paid tickets (European Network against Racism (Ireland), 2018). The report for 2018 has yet to be published, but in light of comments made at the time of the Presidential election, it is likely that reports of Traveller racism have increased.

The National Traveller and Roma Inclusion Strategy (Department of Justice and Equality, 2017b) was published in 2017. This lists 149 actions across Government under the headings of cultural identity, education, employment, children and youth, health, gender equality, anti-discrimination, accommodation and access to public services. We note that Traveller services were disproportionately hit during the austerity programme, and that reversing the impact of those cuts will require concerted action (Pavee Point, 2013). *Social Justice Ireland* calls for the full implementation of the new Strategy, in particular in the critical areas of education and accommodation. In July 2018, Minister for Justice and Equality, Charlie Flanagan, provided an update on the Strategy in a Written Response to a Parliamentary Question (Flanagan, 2018) that, at that point, work had begun on 130 of the 149 actions and further updates predominantly concerning the working of subcommittees. In light of the levels of discrimination faced by members of the Traveller community, more urgent action is needed to protect and support Traveller people.

## Migrant Workers

After a significant fall between 2006 and 2012 the numbers of non-Irish nationals in employment has begun to increase, and in 2018 surpassed pre-Recession levels (Table 10.3).

**Table 10.3: Estimated number of persons ('000s) aged 15 years and over in employment and classified by nationality Q3 2006- 2018, by '000**

| Year | 2006 | 2008 | 2010 | 2012 | 2014 | 2016 | 2018 |
|---|---|---|---|---|---|---|---|
| Irish | 1,869.5 | 1,864.7 | 1,653.2 | 1,612.3 | 1,725.6 | 1,834.6 | 1,905.2 |
| Non-Irish | 290.1 | 345.1 | 277.4 | 274.8 | 283.4 | 323.4 | 368.0 |
| Including | | | | | | | |
| UK | 58.2 | 56.3 | 50.5 | 47.2 | 46.7 | 53.1 | 55.8 |
| EU15 excluding Irish and UK | 33.4 | 33.7 | 30.0 | 33.5 | 37.2 | 46.4 | 55.2 |
| EU15 to EU28 states | 117.8 | 171.5 | 125.0 | 130.5 | 142.6 | 153.3 | 166.7 |
| Other | 80.8 | 83.6 | 71.9 | 63.5 | 56.9 | 70.6 | 90.3 |
| Total | 2,159.6 | 2,209.8 | 1,930.6 | 1,887.0 | 2,008.9 | 2,158.0 | 2,273.2 |

**Source:** CSO Labour Force Survey Series Statbank 2006-2018, QLF26.
**Note:** All data for Q3 of year

Census 2016 reports that 342,000 people in the work force were non-Irish nationals, with the four leading origins being the UK, Poland, Lithuania and Romania. Forty-two percent of all non-Irish national workers were employed in four main sectors, namely Wholesale and Retail Trade (45,812), Accommodation and Food Services (40,859), Manufacturing Industries (36,387) and Human Health and Social Work (21,779). In terms of socio-economic groupings, nearly half (47 per cent) were classified in non-manual, manual skilled, semi-skilled or unskilled occupations, compared with 39 per cent of Irish nationals. This is at variance with the high educational qualifications of immigrants, indicating that many are employed below their skill level. There is a need to accelerate the appropriate recognition of qualifications gained in other countries, so that migrants can work in their fields of expertise. Non-EEA nationals require a work permit to take up employment in Ireland in sectors where there is a skills shortage. 10,518 such permits were issued in

2018, a decrease of 7 per cent, with the majority in the medical /nursing or services sector including IT (Department of Business, Enterprise and Innovation, 2018).

There has been criticism of Irish immigration policy and legislation specifically due to the lack of support for the integration of immigrants and a lack of adequate recognition of the permanency of immigration. The Migrant Rights Centre of Ireland (MRCI, 2014 and 2015) has highlighted specific areas of concern regarding vulnerable employment especially in live-in hospitality, domestic and care work, where migrants are over-represented. They note that the issuing of work permits primarily to employers, rather than employees, ties the employee to a specific employer, increasing their vulnerability to trafficking, exploitation and reducing their labour market mobility. The new General Employment Permit introduced in 2018, will go some way towards addressing this issue, however its implementation is yet to be tested to any great extent.

There are up to 26,000 undocumented migrants working in Ireland, one in five of whom has been here for over ten years (Migrant Rights Centre of Ireland, 2014). Without credentials they are denied access to basic services and vulnerable to exploitation by employers. In October 2018, Government announced a new scheme to regularise undocumented people who came to Ireland as students between 2005 and 2010. This was welcomed by the Migrant Rights Centre of Ireland as a 'long-awaited, life-changing' scheme, with calls for 'clarity, flexibility and common sense' from policy makers in their implementation of the scheme.

The second report on Ireland's performance on implementing the Council of Europe Convention on Action against Trafficking in Human Beings (GRETA, 2017), confirms that trafficking is on the increase in Ireland, mainly for sexual and labour exploitation. It suggests that there is a mismatch between the demand for workers and legal migration options for those workers which can create the conditions for trafficking. They note a high number of undocumented migrants working in personal care, hospitality, fisheries, agriculture (including illegal activities such as cannabis grow houses). While all these individuals may not have specifically been trafficked into Ireland, their precarious employment conditions put them at a serious disadvantage and restrict their choices. The report notes that the Government's second action plan on the topic has been published but there is no indication of the agencies responsible for the different actions, nor is there an indication of the budget allocation, or a plan for external monitoring and evaluation. In their response (Government of Ireland, 2018) the Government of Ireland outlined their plans to support victims of human trafficking in Ireland, including the enactment of statutory protections, offering a period of recovery and reflection backed by training of front-line officers who may come into contact with victims of trafficking, providing access to legal supports for victims of trafficking, and improving victim supports.

## Asylum Seekers and Direct Provision
*Asylum Seekers*

Asylum seekers are defined as those who come to Ireland seeking permission to live in Ireland because there are substantial grounds for believing that they would face a real risk of suffering serious harm if returned to their country of origin. In contrast to programme refugees, asylum seekers must have their immigration status defined when they arrive. Chart 10.2 shows the number of applications for asylum in Ireland between 2003 and 2018.

**Chart 10.2: Applications for Asylum in Ireland, 2003 to 2018**

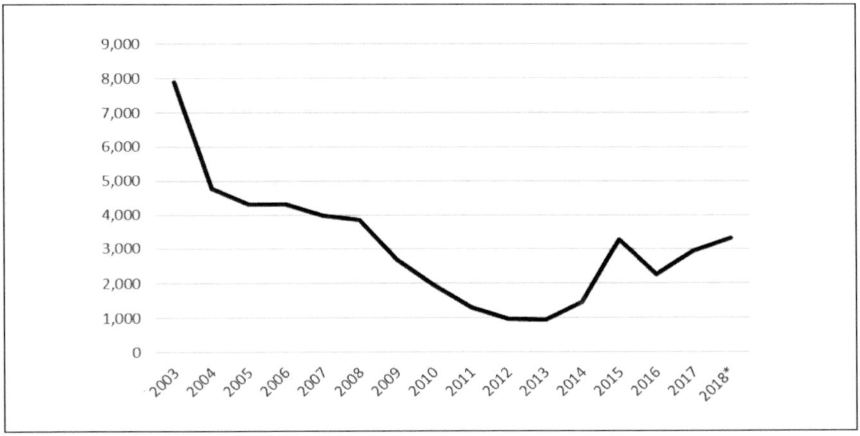

Source: International Protection Office, Monthly Statistical Report, various years
Note: Data for 2018 refers to up to November 2018

Up to November 2018, the number of asylum applications to Ireland increased by 27 per cent on the same time in the previous year, with the majority of applicants coming from Georgia, Albania, Syria, Zimbabwe and Pakistan. In 2016, the most recent year for which data is available, 4,446 people were deported from Ireland. Of these, the vast majority (3,951) were turned back at ports of entry. A further 428 failed asylum seekers or illegal migrants were deported (Department of Justice and Equality, 2017c). Given the introduction in 2017 of the new International Protection Office and some changes to the asylum process, it is disappointing that updated figures are not yet available for 2017 or 2018 in order to monitor trends and policy implications.

*Direct Provision*
At the end of September 2018 there were 37 accommodation centres throughout the country accommodating 5,375 people, with only 66 vacancies in total. Since 2002, occupancy has consistently been over 70 per cent of capacity in Ireland's reception

centres. As at the end of September 2018, it was at 97.1 per cent. The largest centre, at Mosney in County Meath, has capacity for 600 people. In September 2018 it held 672, an over-occupancy rate of 12 per cent (Reception and Integration Agency, 2018). Overcrowding also featured in four other centres, with one centre in Dublin, over-occupied by 25 people, making additional beds available to deal with the demand.

Under Direct Provision as operated in almost all of these centres, asylum-seekers receive accommodation and board, together with a weekly allowance. The Working Group on Direct Provision (Department of Justice and Equality , 2015) reported a combination of issues contributing to stress and poor mental and physical health for people who are already traumatised and vulnerable, making them among the most excluded and marginalised groups in Ireland. These included significant child protection concerns, a lack of privacy, overcrowding, limited autonomy, insufficient homework and play areas for children, a lack of facilities for families to prepare their own meals and meet their own dietary needs, and no access to employment, or formal adult education and training. A total of 2,441 people (41 per cent) have been in direct provision centres for two or more years, and while the numbers who have been there for four or more years have reduced in the past three years, more work is needed. It cannot be acceptable that vulnerable people are sent to live in overcrowded accommodation, with little income or access to amenities, for over a year.

Budget 2019 increased the weekly allowance for those in Direct Provision, to €38.80 per week for an adult and €29.80 for a child. While welcome, this increase still places the allowance below the recommendations set out by the Working Group and does not account for inflation in the intervening period. In December 2018, the Centre for Criminal Justice and Human Rights and NASC, together with the School of Law in UCC published their conference book entitled 'Beyond McMahon – Reflections on the Future of Asylum Reception in Ireland', a collection of papers presented at the conference of the same name (NASC & UCC, 2018). These papers considered improvements since the publication of the McMahon Report, including the development of draft National Standards for accommodation offered to people in the protection process, limited access to the workplace for asylum seekers who have not received a first-instance decision within nine months and the introduction of the EU Reception Directive. However while these are certainly welcome developments, the papers contained in the book each conclude with a call for further improvements to be made to afford those seeking asylum in Ireland their basic human rights.

As is the case in other areas of accommodation, discussed elsewhere in this book, the system of Direct Provision relies heavily on private operators. €67.4 million was spent on Direct Provision centres in 2017, including payments to 27 commercially owned centres. Reports of sick children being denied food and basic care by untrained staff, and of former staff of hotels being used as reception centres being redeployed as reception centre staff is concerning. The State must ensure that the holders of these lucrative contracts employ adequately trained staff who can deliver a high level of service to enable the people in their centres to live life with dignity.

## Participation

Recent international political events, and even the outcome of our own Presidential election last year, points to a public who feel alienated from the political classes and democracy generally. It has been suggested (Antonucci, 2017; Dauderstadt, 2017) that increasing inequality between classes, within and between countries and even continents is a major contributor to this alienation.

In any democracy, voting in elections is a core right. Voter turnout in Irish general elections is close to the European average of 66 per cent. However, there are concerns about the participation of young people and those living in poorer areas.

But real participation goes beyond voting (representative democracy) to a situation where people and government work in partnership to co-create infrastructure and services, solve problems and work towards the well-being of all in this generation and the generations to come (deliberative democracy). By definition, such a deliberative democracy approach requires a leaving aside of power differentials and making a specific effort to ensure that the voices and views of people who are not traditionally influential are heard and taken into account (Coote, 2011; Healy & Reynolds, 2011; Elster, 1998),

In a deliberative process, issues and positions are argued and discussed based on the available evidence rather than based on assertions by those who are powerful and unwilling to consider the facts. It produces evidence-based policy and ensures a high level of accountability among stakeholders. Deliberative participation by all is essential if society is to develop and, in practice, to maintain principles guaranteeing satisfaction of basic needs, respect for others as equals, economic, religious, social, gender and ethnic equality.

Some of the decision-making structures of our society, and of our world, allow people to be represented in the process. However, almost all of these structures fail to provide genuine participation for most people affected by their decisions, resulting in an apathy towards the political system as a whole. The lack of participation is exacerbated by the primacy given to the market by many analysts, commentators, policy-makers, politicians and media. Most people are not involved in the processes that produce plans and decisions which affect their lives. They sense they have little power of these decisions and, more critically, they realise that they and their families will be forced to live with the consequences of the decisions taken. This is particularly relevant in Ireland where, ten years since the bank bailout, people are still living with the consequences of a decade of austerity policies.

Although Government has engaged with members of civil society on specific issues as part of the Constitutional Convention[1], and the Citizens Assembly[2] such initiatives are extremely limited.

People want to be more involved and to participate in debates concerning policies, particularly those that directly affect them. The extensive use of social media as a forum for discussion and debate indicates a capacity to question the best use of State resources to develop a just and fair society. What that society might look like may change depending on the individual and their ideology, but there is certainly appetite for debate. It is crucially important for our democracy that people feel engaged in this process and all voices are heard in a constructive way. There are many ways in which this can be done via both technology and personal engagement. With local elections coming shortly, it is imperative that groups with power, recognise and engage with, and develop partnerships with people to co-create services and policy.

**A forum for dialogue on civil society issues**
The need for a new forum and structure for discussion of issues on which people disagree is becoming more obvious as political and mass communication systems develop. A civil society forum and the formulation of a new social contract against exclusion has the potential to re-engage people with the democratic process. Our highly centralised government, both in terms of decision-making and financially, means that citizens are represented more by professional politicians than by their local constituency representatives. While there have been some structural improvements, such as an enhanced committee structure, the introduction of Public Participation Networks (PPNs) (discussed later in this Chapter), better success rates for Bills led by the opposition and a budgetary oversight process, much remains to be done before Ireland has a genuinely participative decision-making structure.

The democratic process would also benefit from the development of a new social contract against exclusion and in favour of a just society. This contract would include a forum for dialogue on civil society issues. Short-term initiatives such as the Presidents Ethics Initiative,[3] the Constitutional Convention and Citizens Assembly are welcome but need to be mainstreamed and reach all sections of Irish Society. *Social Justice Ireland* welcomed the appointment of a new National Economic and Social Council (NESC), whose role is to advise the Taoiseach on strategic policy issues relating to sustainable economic, social and environmental development. The annual National Economic Dialogue is also a useful model to share the perspectives of civil society, Government and the various sectors of society on key budgetary issues. However, a single event is inadequate. *Social Justice Ireland*

---

[1]  For more information see https://www.constitution.ie/Convention.aspx
[2]  For more information see https://www.citizensassembly.ie/en/
[3]  For further details see  http://www.president.ie/en/the-president/special-initiatives/ethics

recommends that such a National Dialogue takes place more frequently, and that the focus is broadened from the economic to include social and environmental issues.

*Social Justice Ireland* proposes that Government authorises and resources an initiative to identify how a civil society forum[4] could be developed and maintained and to examine how it might connect to the growing debate at European level around civil society issues. There are many issues such a forum could address including the meaning of citizenship in the 21st Century, the shape of the social model Ireland wishes to develop; how to move towards a low carbon sustainable future and so on.

**Participation in Local Government - Public Participation Networks (PPNs)**
In 2014, the Local Government Act was amended to introduce Public Participation Networks (PPNs).   The PPN recognises the contribution of volunteer-led organisations to local economic, social and environmental capital.  It facilitates input by these organisations into local government through a structure that ensures public participation and representation on decision-making committees within local government (Department of Housing, Planning and Local Government, 2017).  These PPNs have been established in every local authority area in Ireland.  By the end of 2018, over 14,000 community and voluntary, social inclusion and environmental organisations were members of a PPN.  Over 880 PPN representatives were elected to over 380 committees on issues such as strategic policy, local community development, joint policing and so on.

Local authorities and PPNs work together collaboratively to support communities and build the capacity of member organisations to engage meaningfully on issues that concern them.  PPNs have a significant role in the development and education of their member groups, sharing information, promoting best practice and facilitating networking.  Local authorities also have a vital role to play in facilitating participation through open consultative processes and active engagement. Building real engagement at local level is a developmental process that requires intensive work and investment.  Following recommendations from the National Advisory Group for PPNs, *Social Justice Ireland* and others, the PPNs received an increase in resources in 2018 to support better engagement in communities and ensure that the PPN can place itself as both an information 'hub' and advocate for policy within their area.

**Supporting the Community & Voluntary Sector**
Community and Voluntary organisations have a long history of providing services and infrastructure at local and national level. They are engaged in most, if not all, areas of Irish society.   They provide huge resources in energy, personnel, finance and commitment that, were it to be sourced on the open market, would come at considerable cost to the State.  They have developed flexible approaches and

---

[4]   For a further discussion of this issue see Healy and Reynolds (2003:191-197).

collaborative practices that are responsive and effective in meeting the needs of diverse target groups. According to a report undertaken on behalf of the Charities Regulator (Indecon, 2018) there are an estimated 189,000 employees in registered charitable organisations in Ireland. The same report indicated that over half of all registered charities had between one and 20 volunteers, with three per cent having 250 or more. Indecon estimate that the value of this volunteering work, using the minimum wage, is €648.8 million per year (this increases to €1.5 billion when using the average income). It is important to note, however, that this report is based on those charities that are required to register with the Charities Regulator, which accounts for approximately 300,536 volunteers. The CSO put the number of volunteers at nearer one million, when sporting, human rights, religious and political organisations are included.

During the recession Government funding for the Community and Voluntary sector reduced dramatically and this has not been restored. It is essential that Government appropriately resource this sector into the future and that it remains committed to the principle of providing multi-annual statutory funding. The introduction of the Charities Regulatory Authority, the Governance Code and the Lobbying Register in recent years is intended to foster transparency and improve public trust. However, it is essential that the regulatory requirements are proportional to the size and scope of organisations, and do not create an unmanageable administrative burden which detracts from the core work and deters volunteers from getting involved.

*Our Communities – A Framework Policy for Local and Community Development in Ireland* articulates Government policy to

> create vibrant, sustainable, self-determining communities that have the social, cultural and economic well-being of all community members at their core, built upon a shared understanding of their needs and aspirations, and where both participative and local democracy provides community members with the opportunity, means, confidence, and skills to influence, shape and participate in decision-making structures and processes that affect them and their communities.
> (Department of Housing, Planning, Community and Local Government, 2015)

*Social Justice Ireland* recommends that implementation of the Framework be resourced in a way that recognises the important local role of the PPNs, and the challenges of community development, and generating real partnerships between communities and agencies.

## National Social Dialogue
Social dialogue is a critically important component of effective decision making in a modern democracy. Government needs to engage all sectors of society to develop policies that will shape the future and to ensure priority is given to well-being and the common good; to address the challenges of markets and their failures; to link

rights and responsibilities. Otherwise policy is likely to produce lop-sided outcomes that will benefit those who with access, while excluding others, most notably the vulnerable. If Government wishes the whole of society to take responsibility for producing a more viable future, then it must involve all of society.

The Community & Voluntary Pillar provides a mechanism for social dialogue that should be engaged with by Government across the range of policy issues in which the Pillar's members are deeply involved. All aspects of governance should be characterised by transparency and accountability. Social dialogue contributes to this. We believe governance along these lines can and should be developed in Ireland.

*Social Justice Ireland* fully endorses the closing comments of the report of the President's Ethics Commission (2016: p 36)

> "What is needed ..... is structured opportunities, occasions and situations that would support and enable conditions in which people can have meaningful conversations and discussions about those questions and decisions that really matter. These structured opportunities would provide the space for dialogue on the values that we share; the ideals we aspire towards; the laws we would want to be beholden to; the rights that we would want to enjoy; the responsibilities and duties that we would want to uphold and refine in the common project of renewing our Republic."

**Key Policy Priorities**
*Social Justice Ireland* believes that the following policy positions should be adopted to improve the lives of all those living in Ireland today:

- Focus on combatting racism and discrimination, and promoting interculturalism in Ireland.

- Facilitate asylum seekers to take up accessible work and education opportunities.

- Adequately resource the Public Participation Network (PPN) structures for participation at Local Authority level and ensure capacity building is an integral part of the process.

- Promote deliberative democracy and a process of inclusive social dialogue to ensure there is real and effective monitoring and impact assessment of policy development and implementation using an evidence-based approach.

- Resource an initiative to identify how a real participative civil society debate could be developed and maintained.

- Implement the National Framework for Local and Community Development, in a way which supports Community and Voluntary organisations

# REFERENCES

Antonucci, L., 2017. Addressing Inequality in a changing world. In: B. Reynolds & S. Healy, eds. *Society Matters: Reconnecting People and the State*. Dublin: Social Justice Ireland.

Barrett, A., McGinnitty, F. & Quinn, E., 2017. *Monitoring report on integration 2016,* Dublin: ESRI.

Bourke, S., 2017. Public Participation Networks in Ireland. In: B. Reynolds & S. Healy, eds. *Society Matters: Reconnecting People and the State*. Dublin: Social Justice Ireland.

Coote, A., 2011. Equal participation: making shared social responsibility work for everyone. *Trends in Social Cohesion ,* Volume 23, pp. 281-311.

CSO, 2015. *Volunteering and Wellbeing,* Dublin: Stationery Office.

CSO, 2017a. *Census 2016: Published Reports.* CSO, 2017c. *Census 2016: Profile 7 Migration and Diversity.*

CSO, 2018. *Population and Migration Estimates.* [Online] Dauderstadt, M., 2017. Europes Fragile Cohesion. In: B. Reynolds & S. Healy, eds. *Society Matters: Reconnecting People and the State*. Dublin: Social Justice Ireland.

Department of Business and Innovation, 2018. *Employment Permit Statistics 2017.* [Online]

Department of Environment, Community and Local Government, 2012. *Putting People First — Action Programme for Effective Local Government.* [Online]

Department of Housing, Planning and Local Government, 2017. *Public Participation Networks: A User Guide.* [Online]

Department of Housing, Planning, Community and Local Government, 2015. *Our Communities: A Framework Policy for Local and Community Development.* [Online]

Department of Justice and Equality , 2015. *Working Group on Improvements to the Protection Process, including Direct Provision and Supports to Asylum Seekers (2015) Report to Government ,* Dublin: Department of Justice and Equality.

Department of Justice and Equality, 2017a. *The Migrant Integration Strategy - A blueprint for the future,* Dublin: DJE.

Department of Justice and Equality, 2017b. *National Traveller and Roma Inclusion Strategy 2017-2021,* Dublin: Stationary Office.

Department of Justice and Equality, 2017c. *Irish Naturalisation and Immigration Service. Immigration in Ireland: Annual review 2016.,* Dublin: Stationary Office.

Department of Justice and Equality, 2017. *The Migrant Integration Strategy, A Blueprint for the Future,* s.l.: s.n.

Department of Rural and Community Affairs, 2017. [Online].

DJE International Protection Office, 2018. *Monthly Statistical Report - December 2017.* [Online]

Elster, J., 1998. *Deliberative Democracy.* Cambridge: Cambridge University Press.

European Network Against Racism (Ireland) , 2016. *iReport.ie Reports of Racism in Ireland January to June 2016 ,* Dublin : ENAR Ireland.

European Network against Racism (Ireland), 2018. *Reports of Racism in Ireland July - December 2017.* [Online]

Flanagan, C., 2018. *Parliamentary Question, Written Answers, 06 November 2018.* s.l.:s.n.

Flanagan, C., 2018. *Parliamentary Questions, Written Response, 05 July 2018*. s.l.:s.n.

Government of Ireland, 2018. *Report submitted by the Irish authorities on measures taken to comply with Committee of the Parties Recommendation CP(2017)29 on the implementation of the Council of Europe Convention on Action against Trafficking in Human Beings*. s.l.:s.n.

GRETA, 2017. *Report concerning the implementation of the Council of Europe Convention on Action against Trafficking in Human Beings by Ireland*. [Online]

Healy, S. & Reynolds, B., 2011. Sharing Responsibility for Shaping the Future - Why and How?. In: B. Reynolds & S. Healy, eds. *Sharing Responsibility in Shaping the Future*. Dublin: Social Justice Ireland..

Indecon, 2018. *Registered Irish Charities Social and Economic Impact Report 2018*. s.l.:s.n.

Irish Human Rights Commission, 2017. *Who experiences Discrimination? Evidence from the QNHS Equality Modules*. [Online]

Joint Oireachtas Committee on Justice and Equality, 2017. *Report on asylum immigration and the refugee crisis*. [Online]

McGinnity, F. et al., 2018. *Monitoring Report on Integration 2018,* s.l.: s.n.

McGuinness, S., Whelan, A., Bergin, A. & and Delaney, J., 2018. *Profiling Barriers to Social Inclusion in Ireland, The Relative Roles of Individual Characteristics and Location,* s.l.: s.n.

Migrant Rights Centre Ireland , 2016. *Justice for the Undocumented*. [Online]

Migrant Rights Centre of Ireland, 2014. *Ireland is Home: An analysis of the current situation of undocumented migrants in Ireland Dublin:MRCI,* Dublin: MRCI.

Migrant Rights Centre of Ireland, 2015. *WORKERS ON THE MOVE Past Lessons and Future Perspectives on Ireland's Labour Migration,* Dublin: MRCI .

NASC & UCC, 2018. *Beyond McMahon - Reflections on the Future of Asylum Reception in Ireland*. s.l.:s.n.

National Youth Council of Ireland, 2017. *Make Minority a Priority*. [Online]

Office of the Ombudsman, 2018. *The Ombudsman & Direct Provision - The story so far*. [Online]

Pavee Point, 2013. *Travelling with Austerity: Impacts of cuts on Travellers, Traveller projects and services*. [Online]

Reception and Integration Agency, 2018. *RIA Monthly Report September 2018*. [Online].

Watson, D., Kenny, O. & McGinnitty, F., 2017. *A Social Portrait of Travellers in Ireland,* Dublin: ESRI.

# Chapter 11
## Sustainability

**Core Policy Objective:**
To ensure that all development is socially, economically and environmentally sustainable.

## Key Issues/Evidence

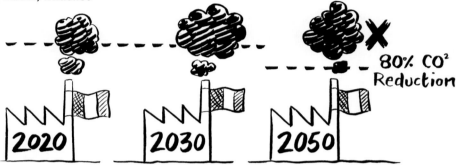

**80% CO$^2$ Reduction**

**2020**

**2030**

**2050**

Ireland is on track to overshoot our 2020 emissions targets and it looks likely that we will not meet our 2030 targets.

Ireland is headed in the wrong direction to meet our national 2050 goal to reduce CO2 emissions by 80 per cent

Ireland's greenhouse gas emissions continue to increase in line with economic and employment growth in the energy industries, agriculture and transport sectors.

Our emissions are dominated by agriculture, transport and energy.

**Lack of policy coherence**

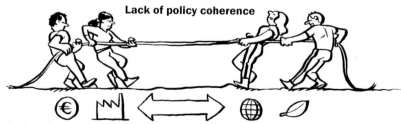

agricultural expansion and economic expansion policies

commitments in the Sustainable Development Goals on climate action and protecting our environment

**Policy Solutions**

Set ambitious emissions
reduction targets for 2030 and
ensure sufficient resources
to support implementation of
these targets

Ensure our
climate mitigation
plans support
implementation of
ambitious emissions
reduction targets

Develop an
environmental
taxation system

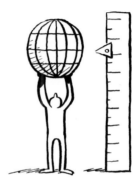

Adopt targets and a reporting
system for each of the Sustainable
Development Goals

Assign natural capital and ecosystems
value in our national accounting systems

Set out a mitigation and transition strategy
to prepare communities and people for
changes that adapting to meet our climate
targets will bring.

# 11.

# SUSTAINABILITY

**CORE POLICY OBJECTIVE: SUSTAINABILITY**

**To ensure that all development is socially, economically and environmentally sustainable**

Sustainable development is defined as 'development which meets the needs of the present, without compromising the ability of future generations to meet their needs' (World Commission on Environment and Development, 1987). It encompasses three pillars; environment, society and economy. A sustainable development framework integrates these three pillars in a balanced manner with consideration for the needs of future generations. Maintaining this balance is crucial to the long-term development of a sustainable resource-efficient future for Ireland. While growth and economic competitiveness are important, they should be considered in the context of sustainability, using a framework for sustainable development which gives equal consideration to the environmental, social and economic pillars.

Ireland has signed up to achieve the Sustainable Development Goals by 2030 (United Nations, 2015) and is committed to legally binding climate commitments in 2020 and 2030 and a national commitment to be carbon neutral by 2050. Ensuring development is sustainable socially, economically and environmentally will be key to achieving our environmental and sustainability targets.

To achieve this sustainable development in the years ahead, *Social Justice Ireland* believes that policy should:

- Set ambitious emissions reduction targets for 2030 and ensure sufficient resources to support implementation of these targets;
- Adopt targets and a reporting system for each of the Sustainable Development Goals;
- Introduce a strategy for Ireland that includes the principles of the circular economy and cradle to cradle development;

- Introduce shadow national accounts, and assign natural capital and ecosystems value in our national accounting systems;
- Develop a comprehensive mitigation and transition programme to support communities and people in the transition to a low carbon society;
- Develop a progressive and equitable environmental taxation system.

## 11.1 Key Evidence

### Climate Change

The international commitments that Ireland has signed up to with COP21[1] mean that clear commitments are required to ensure that Ireland meets its emission reduction targets. However Ireland is the worst performing EU country on climate change according to the most recent Climate Change Performance Index (Burck et al, 2018). The report notes that Ireland has not introduced the essential policy measures necessary to put Ireland on a pathway to meeting our COP21 targets and playing out part in reducing emissions in order to keep global warming below 2 °C, and our national policy performance is rated as very low.

The Climate Change Framework was published in 2012, and with the passing of the Climate Action and Low Carbon Development Act, 2015, Government committed to adopting a national adaptation framework which was published in January 2018 (DCCEA, 2018). The seven Government Departments identified as having a role within the framework will be required to submit their sectoral adaptation plans by August 2019.[2] Sectoral adaptation plans covering the areas of Flood Risk Management, Agriculture and Forestry, Transport, and Electricity and Gas have been published and are viewed as a 'step towards the statutory requirement to develop sectoral plans in accordance with the...Act' (2018:41). First steps are not enough, and Ireland has a significant distance to travel to meet climate change commitments.

The increased incidence of flooding and other severe weather events highlights the impact that climate change and changing weather patterns is having on Ireland, and has exposed how vulnerable many of our services, communities and utilities are to disruption (Climate Change Advisory Council, 2018). In Ireland, six of the ten warmest years on record have occurred since 1990.[3] Among the predicted adverse impacts of climate change are sea level rise, more intense storms, increased likelihood and magnitude of river and coastal flooding, adverse impacts on water quality, decrease in rainfall in spring and summer, an increase in intensity of storms, and changes in distribution of plant and animal species (EPA, 2015). The present

---

[1]  https://www.gouvernement.fr/en/cop21
[2]  https://www.dccae.gov.ie/en-ie/climate-action/topics/adapting-to-climate-change/national-adaptation-framework/Pages/Sectoral.aspx
[3]  http://www.epa.ie/climate/communicatingclimatescience/whatisclimatechange/whatimpactwillclimatechangehaveforireland/

rate of climate change demands a more urgent response if Ireland is to safeguard its resources, society and economy from its impacts.

## Emissions

As a member of the European Union Ireland has committed to legally binding emissions reduction targets in 2020 and 2030. We have committed to a 20 per cent reduction on 2005 emission levels by 2020, and a 30 per cent reduction of emissions compared to 2005 levels by 2030.

Ireland will not meet the 2020 target. At present we are projected to achieve an abysmal 1 per cent reduction on 2005 emission levels (EPA, 2018a). Our greenhouse gas emissions are nearly 3 million tonnes over the pathway required to meet our 2020 targets and we are on track to overshoot these targets significantly (EPA, 2018b). In fact, we are completely off course in terms of achieving our 2030 emissions reduction targets as well (Climate Change Advisory Council, 2018). This has very serious implications for our environment, our society and our economy.

The latest report on our greenhouse gas emissions shows that they decreased very slightly in 2017 due to 'circumstantial' issues, but emissions from agriculture increased by almost 3 per cent (EPA, 2018b). This increase is primarily due to the expansion of the dairy herd and increase in milk production. Emissions from agriculture have increased annually since 2012 as a result of the Foodwise 2025 agriculture policy and the removal of milk quotas in 2015. This increase is entirely at odds with environmental policy since 2012, the Climate Change Framework, the Climate Action and Low Carbon Development Act, and our national and international commitments. Such policy incoherence at national level is unacceptable, particularly when agriculture accounts for one third of Ireland's total greenhouse gas emissions.

The EPA points out that Ireland's greenhouse gas emissions continue to increase in line with economic and employment growth in the energy industries, agriculture and transport sectors and that Ireland is headed in the wrong direction to meet our national climate policy goal to reduce CO2 emissions by 80 per cent by 2050. In 2016, the EPA recommended that Government implement measures to decarbonise the transport and energy sectors and ensure policy coherence between agricultural output targets and environmental ones (EPA, 2016). Government has clearly not taken heed of these recommendations.

While the environmental implications of not meeting our emissions targets are obvious, there are also significant economic implications as a result of not meeting our EU 2020 targets. As outlined earlier Ireland is projected to miss the 2020 targets by a large margin. This means that Ireland will have to make 'statistical transfers' at an estimated cost of between €65 million and €130 million per percentage point below the overall 16 per cent target (DCCAE, 2017:37). A bulletin published in March 2016 assessing Ireland's progress towards achieving emission reduction targets set under EU Effort Sharing Decision No 406/2009/EU for 2013-2020 suggests that Ireland's non-ETS emissions are projected to be 11 per cent below 2005 levels in 2020 (EPA, 2016). The target is 20 per cent.

Table 11.1 shows potential costs if we remain on this course – as well as variations on that scenario – assuming the two extremes noted above (€65m and €130m per percentage shortfall), as well as a mid-point. If Ireland remains on its current course, a best-case scenario looks like a fine in the region of €715m, but this could potentially be closer to €1.4 billion.

**Table 11.1: Projection of Possible Environmental Fines for Ireland in 2020 (€m)**

| Various scenarios | Fine per percentage point shortfall | | |
|---|---|---|---|
| | €65m | €97.5m | €130m |
| EPA's projected scenario is met (11% below 2005 levels) | €715 | €1,072 | €1,430 |
| 20% above EPA projection | €858 | €1,287 | €1,716 |
| 20% below EPA projection | €572 | €858 | €1,144 |
| 40% above EPA projection | €1,001 | €1,501 | €2,002 |
| 40% below EPA projection | €429 | €643 | €858 |

Source:     *Social Justice Ireland* calculation based on EPA projections.

## Global Context

Increased levels of greenhouse gases, such as $CO_2$, increase the amount of energy trapped in the atmosphere which leads to global effects such as increased temperatures, melting of snow and ice, and raised global average sea-level. If these issues are not addressed with urgency the projected effects of climate change present a serious risk of dangerous and irreversible climate impacts at national and global levels (IPCC, 2014). Food production and ecosystems are particularly vulnerable. The latest research from the World Meteorological Organisation has ranked 2016 as the hottest year on record, followed by 2015 and 2017 (WMO, 2017), and finds that sixteen of the seventeen hottest years ever recorded have been in this century. Underlining the long-term trend, 2013-17 was the warmest five-year period on record.

At the Paris climate conference (COP21) in December 2015, 195 countries adopted the first ever legally binding global climate deal. This agreement is due to enter into force by 2020 with the aim to keep global warming below 2°C by 2100. Countries agreed:

• a long-term goal of keeping the increase in global average temperature to well below 2°C above pre-industrial levels;

- to aim to limit the increase to 1.5°C, since this would significantly reduce risks and the impacts of climate change;

- to come together every five years to set more ambitious targets as required by science;

- to provide continued and enhanced international support for adaptation to developing countries.

The recent conference on climate change held in Katowice in Poland (COP24) has been widely reported. Although heralded as a 'global rulebook' for emissions reporting at international level, its conclusions fall far short of what is required if the world is the address the major climate threats to in the decades ahead. Many issues remain outstanding, including the issue of climate finance and agreement on voluntary market mechanisms. The latest Emission Gap Report from the United Nations (UN) (UNEP, 2018) finds that current national commitments for emissions reductions are insufficient to ensure global warming stays below 2°C by 2030. If countries do not commit to more ambitious emission reduction targets then global warming cannot be contained below 1.5°C as recommended by the Intergovernmental Panel on Climate Change (IPCC) in 2018. In 2017 global $CO_2$ emissions increased. Countries need to triple their level of ambition to stay below 2°C warming and increase fivefold to stay below 1.5°C. The most recent IPCC report published to coincide with the COP24 climate conference contained the most stark findings yet that the Earth is well on its way to exceeding the 1.5°C increase in warming. The report states that emissions in 2030 need to be 45 per cent below what they were in 2010 in order to limit global warming to 1.5°C. This requires an enormous and concerted global effort over the next 11 years.

### Renewable Energy
Ireland's fuel mix for electricity generation is dominated by carbon-based fossil fuels, with 90 per cent of all energy used in Ireland coming from fossil fuels in 2017 (SEAI, 2018). The latest SEAI report notes that although Ireland has reduced its dependence on imported energy, the increase in our domestic energy generation is primarily from natural gas which is a fossil fuel. This runs contrary to our targets of reducing emissions, increasing renewable energy and eliminating our dependence on fossil fuels. Overall in 2017 renewables made up 10.6 per cent of final energy consumption, and our 2020 target is 16 per cent. Ireland needs to do significantly more in terms of producing renewable energy in order to meet our 2020 target.

The *White Paper on Energy* (DCENR, 2015) envisages Ireland reducing emissions from energy systems by up to 95 per cent (based on 1990 levels) by 2050 and zero by 2100. Ireland's target is part of the overall headline target pledged by the European Union of at least a 40 per cent reduction in domestic greenhouse gas emissions by 2030 compared to 1990. Ireland's individual country target is set at a headline rate of 30 per cent but this has yet to be agreed. The White Paper states that Ireland will make a technically feasible, cost-effective and equitable contribution to the overall EU target. While overall the White Paper contains some very positive aspirations, it is short on detail as to how we are going to achieve these aspirations. *Social Justice Ireland* believes Ireland should be ambitious in setting our individual 2030 target and think of the longer-term outcomes and benefits rather than the short-term benefit for cost-effectiveness. Chapter 3 of the National Mitigation Plan sets out in more detail the ambition for Ireland in decarbonising electricity generation, with a stated aim of moving from a fossil fuel-based electricity system to a low carbon power system by 2050. However, the actions put forward concentrate again on feasibility studies, further action and research, without any real pathway to how this might be achieved. At present there is a consultation process underway until February 2019 on Ireland's National Energy and Climate Plan 2021-2030. The implementation of ambitious targets and innovative policies are essential if Ireland is to meet our national goals.

**Sustainable Development Goals**

The Global Goals for Sustainable Development were adopted at the UN General Assembly on 25th September 2015 and came into effect on 1st January 2016. These goals make up the 2030 Sustainable Development Agenda which is defined as a 'plan of action for people, planet and prosperity'.[4] This Agenda builds on the Millennium Development Goals and commits to completing what they did not achieve. It recognises the urgency behind the need to shift the world onto a more sustainable path.

World leaders have committed to seventeen Global Goals (also known as SDGs) containing 169 targets to achieve three distinct aims: to end poverty, fight inequality and tackle climate change over the next fifteen years. The seventeen goals are outlined in chart 11.1.

The emphasis is on national ownership of the goals, with each Government setting its own national targets to be supported by national development strategies and financing frameworks (UN, 2015). This will require ambitious national targets matched by adequate resources[5].

---

[4]   https://sustainabledevelopment.un.org/post2015/transformingourworld
[5]   The scale of the implementation challenge for the SDGs is immense with UNCTAD calculating that the annual investment gap for implementing the SDGs is in the region of $2.5 trillion

**Chart 11.1: Sustainable Development Goals**

**Source:** United Nations.

The link between sustainable development and economic, social and environmental policies is highlighted by the UN, as is the need to support the most vulnerable countries that face particular challenges in achieving sustainable development (UN, 2015:35). These countries also face the greatest risk of the consequences of climate change. The SDGs commit countries to achieving sustainable development in its three dimensions – economic, social and environmental – in a balanced and integrated manner. To ensure these three dimensions are valued equally, new measures of progress will be required to ensure that economic progress does not come at the price of social or environmental progress.

### Sustainable Development
Ireland published the Sustainable Development Goals National Implementation Plan 2018-2020 in April 2018. Four strategic priorities have been identified to guide the implementation plan. These are awareness, participation, support and policy alignment. The publication of the plan is welcome, however new and ambitious policy measure are required if Ireland is to achieve the SDG's by 2030. It is important that the CSO Sustainable Development Indicators are aligned with the National Implementation Plan so that Ireland has a comprehensive set of data to measure progress.

## Sustainable Progress Index

*Social Justice Ireland* monitors Ireland's performance towards achieving the SDGs through the Sustainable Progress Index (Clark et al., 2018). Ireland's first *Sustainable Progress Index,* published in 2017, argued against GDP as the main barometer of a country's wellbeing and success and compared Ireland's performance across all 17 SDGs with those of the remaining EU 15 countries. Using this system Ireland ranked 11th out of the EU15 countries in 2017, and we had improved one place to 10th in 2018 (see table 11.2). The Sustainable Progress Index allocates each of the 17 SDGs into three separate indexes; the Economy SDG Index (SDGs 8 and 9), the Society SDG Index (SDGs 1,2,3,4,5,10,16,17) and the Environment SDG Index (SDGs 6,7,11,12,13,14,15). These indexes are then combined to give the overall Sustainable Progress Index for each of the EU 15.

The purpose of the Sustainable Progress Index is to provide a clear and simple picture of how Ireland is performing on the SDGs relative to countries with similar economic development experience. It provides a comprehensive overview on how Ireland is performing on each of the 17 SDGs and a summary of Ireland's strengths and weaknesses. The Index tracks Ireland's performance over time and compared to our EU15 peers to provide an indication of progress, to help raise awareness of the SDGs and to encourage policy action and provides an annual contribution to the strategic priorities outlined in the National Implementation Plan for the SDGs.

### Economy Index – SDG 8 and 9

It is acknowledged that GDP is not an ideal, or even accurate, measure of progress. The problem with using GDP as a measure of progress was particularly evident in the spike in GDP growth in 2015, caused by multinational corporations shifting profits to Ireland to take advantage of our low corporate tax rate. It is, however, an important tool for public policy, as it allows for comparative analysis of market activity. In *Social Justice Ireland's* Sustainable Progress Index, the Economy Index uses household consumption as a more accurate measure of real economic growth.

The Index also looks at unemployment and long-term unemployment. Both have been falling since 2012, having risen significantly since 2008. However the move towards higher employment rates must be viewed alongside the increasing instance of low pay and precarious working practices, as well as wage stagnation.

In looking at 'industry, innovation and infrastructure' (SDG9), the Index considers expenditure on Research & Development (R&D) and internet access and notes a decline in the rate of expenditure on R&D, which may be attributed at least in part to the issues with GDP mentioned earlier.

Overall, the Index ranks Ireland 10th out of the EU15 on Economy in 2018.

*Society Index – SDG 1, 2, 3, 4, 5, 10, 16, 17*
In considering SDG 1, the elimination of poverty, the Index points out that Ireland has a 'structural poverty problem that will not be fixed by economic growth alone' (Clark et al, 2018:27), and again underlines the point made earlier about the inadequacy of GDP as a measure of progress, where even the GDP spike in 2015 did not significantly reduce the poverty level. Ireland does better on the goal of ending hunger, though our obesity rate (4.1 per cent higher than the EU average) remains a concern. Ireland's performance in respect of health and wellbeing is also good, with longer life expectancy and better levels of health perception than previous years.

Ireland has made moderate progress in the areas of education quality, reducing inequalities (within the country, our progress on reducing global inequality is stated as being 'minimal') and improvements to our score on the Social Justice Index[6]. There is more to be done within each area, however, with falling rates of adult literacy, persistent household debt compensating for income inequality, and much ground to be made in respect of Ireland's ranking on the Social Justice Index with comparison to its placement in 2008.

Ireland's performance under SDG 16, peace, justice and strong institutions, is mixed, with fluctuations in homicide rates from 2000 to 2014 and the slight reversal of the upward trend in Ireland's Corruption Perception Index in 2016.

Finally under the Society Index, our progress under SDG 17, partnership for the goals, it is important to acknowledge the increase in official development assistance and financing to developing countries announced as part of Budget 2019.

Overall, the Index ranks Ireland 10th out of the EU15 on Society.

*Environment Index – SDG 6, 7, 11, 12, 13, 14, 15*

Ireland has performed well on some of the indicators under this index, with Irish water and sanitation being among the best in Europe, good air quality relative to other European countries and a reduction, albeit small in the context of the rate of increase between 1960 and 2001, in $CO_2$ emissions. However, Ireland still has work to do to increase the proportion of renewable energy consumed and forestry coverage, reduce the amount of municipal waste generated, and meet the requirements of the EU Habitats Directive to meet the challenges of marine conservation.

Overall, the Index ranks Ireland 13th out of the EU15 on Environment.

---

[6]   The Social Justice Index is designed to measure progress (or decline) on various social justice indicators. It is composed of 28 quantitative and 8 qualitative indicators in six dimensions of social justice.  https://www.bertelsmann-stiftung.de/fileadmin/files/BSt/Publikationen/GrauePublikationen/NW_EU_Social_Justice_Index_2017.pdf

The results of the Sustainable Progress Index strongly suggest that Ireland faces significant challenges in meeting the development objectives enshrined in the SDGs. Focussing exclusively on GDP will divert policy-makers attention from action that must be taken to close the gaps in order to achieve the SDGs.

**Table 11.2: Sustainable Progress Index 2018**

| Country | Index Score | Country Rank |
|---|---|---|
| Sweden | 78.96 | 1 |
| Denmark | 74.81 | 2 |
| Finland | 65.76 | 3 |
| Netherlands | 54.98 | 4 |
| Germany | 54.82 | 5 |
| Austria | 53.67 | 6 |
| United Kingdom | 50.96 | 7 |
| France | 50.71 | 8 |
| Belgium | 49.62 | 9 |
| Ireland | 44.25 | 10 |
| Luxembourg | 43.75 | 11 |
| Spain | 40.53 | 12 |
| Portugal | 39.76 | 13 |
| Italy | 35.74 | 14 |
| Greece | 22.92 | 15 |

**Source:**  *Social Justice Ireland* Sustainable Progress Index 2018.

## 11.2 Key Policies and Reforms

Despite recent announcements on options to meet environmental targets Ireland has made little tangible progress on implementing the policies required to transition Ireland towards a carbon neutral future[7]. There is a small window of opportunity to introduce these policies, which will require significant upfront investment and a strong implementation effort. Ireland has the capacity to develop ambitious policy, as the Fossil Fuel Divestment Bill and the Citizen's Assembly report on climate change attest to. These policies may be difficult politically to 'sell', but if we do not implement them now future generations will pay an enormous cost.

---

[7]  https://www.dccae.gov.ie/en-ie/news-and-media/press-releases/Pages/Minister-Bruton-Announces-Government-will-Lead-the-Way-in-Reducing-Single-Use-Plastics-.aspx

A key starting point to move towards a sustainable model of development which protects the environment and enhances our natural capital is the assessment of Ireland's environment by the Environmental Protection Agency:

> Essentially we have to rethink, and redesign what we mean by social and economic 'prosperity' in order to deliver the resilience essential for us to prevail. We must all learn to live, produce and consume within the physical and biological limits of the planet. To achieve this will require integrated and enduring governance, including brave social and economic measures (EPA, 2016:159).

## Emissions reductions

Ireland must make firm commitments to reduce total emissions outputs from agriculture, transport and energy. These commitments must be underpinned by ambitious and substantive policies which must be implemented fully. These policies will require sufficient resourcing and an all-of-Government approach to ensure that we meet our domestic and international environmental targets. In a paper presented at *Social Justice Ireland's* 2018 Annual Policy Conference, Dr. Cara Augustenborg pointed out that one 'advantage' of Ireland's poor climate performance is the myriad of ways to reduce greenhouse gas emissions when starting from such a low base (Augustenborg, 2018). Dr. Augustenborg also noted that in order to lead in climate smart agriculture Ireland needs to reduce absolute emission from agriculture. This will require a step change in agricultural policy, and an end to incoherence of pursuing strategies that lead to an annual increase in agricultural emissions whilst simultaneously setting emissions reductions targets. Ireland should focus on developing alternative agricultural models and move away from extensive livestock farming.

Support for sustainable agricultural practice is important to ensure the long-term viability of the sector and consideration must also be given to how the projected increase in agricultural emissions can be offset. It is important that the agriculture sector be at the forefront of developing and implementing sustainable farming practices and be innovative in reducing emissions (Curtin and Arnold, 2016). In terms of our national and international climate commitments it must be asked what agricultural policy will be best-placed to ensure Ireland meets its national and international targets: Is it a policy of agricultural expansion and increased emissions to reach additional markets or is it a policy of ensuring Ireland produces the food required to meet our population needs and supports the agricultural sector in the developing world to ensure they can provide the food required to meet their own population needs? Progress towards changing farm practices has been limited and incentives to reduce on-farm greenhouse emissions have not been delivered on a wide scale (Curtin & Hanrahan 2012: 9). The agriculture and food sector must build on its scientific and technical knowledge base to meet the emissions challenge.

Reducing emissions requires the implementation policy decisions being made in the interest of a sustainable future rather than short-term sectoral interests. While this implementation may be difficult in the initial stages, it will lead to reduced emissions and benefits for all. This is where our Government and all members of the Oireachtas must show leadership and act in the national interest. Ireland has a window of opportunity to implement ambitious emission reduction policies that will ensure a sustainable future for us all. This requires immediate policy action.

### Fossil fuels and renewable energies

The Fossil Fuel Divestment Bill 2018, sponsored by Thomas Pringle T.D., was passed by the Houses of the Oireachtas in 2018[8]. This Bill made Ireland the first country in the world to commit to withdrawing public funds that are invested in fossil fuels and makes us world leaders in terms of developing a national divestment strategy. The passing of the Bill and the cross party support it received in the Dáil and the Seanad are to be welcomed. Ireland has set a deadline of five years to divest of all investments in fossil fuels on the passing of the Bill.

The passing of the Fossil Fuel Divestment Bill is an achievement Ireland can be proud of, and it could signal a step change in climate policy. Despite the passing of this bill, and the cross party acknowledgement that fossil fuels are major contributors to emissions (particularly from energy generation), Ireland continues to subsidise climate damaging fossil fuels via the public service obligation (PSO) levy[9]. The policy of subsidising of damaging fossil fuels by the Exchequer is completely at odds with the Fossil Fuel Divestment bill and is another example of policy incoherence when it comes to climate policy.

The PSO levy for peat generation and gas supply and other fossil fuel subsidies which are damaging to the environment should be immediately removed and the subsequent savings invested in renewable energy. By eliminating these harmful subsidies and investing in renewable energy and schemes to address energy poverty Ireland will be in a much better place to meet our energy targets. This is a policy that Government can begin to implement immediately and would be an important component of a national mitigation and transition programme. Peat-fired electricity pollutes the environment and costly to consumers. This is an issue that *Social Justice Ireland* has been consistently highlighting to Government for the past number of years, and so we welcome the retraction of PSO support from electricity generated from fossil fuels in power stations at Edenderry and Lough Ree. If Government is really serious about Ireland transitioning to a low carbon economy all subsidies for fossil fuels should be removed in 2019 and the savings invested in renewable energy.

The national target of converting peat-burning plants to sustainable low-carbon technologies by 2030 is unambitious. Ireland must make immediate changes to reduce our energy emissions. Peat extraction is one of the most polluting forms

8   https://www.oireachtas.ie/en/bills/bill/2016/103/
9   https://www.dccae.gov.ie/en-ie/energy/topics/Electricity/electricity-prices-and-costs/Pages/Pubic-Service-Obligation.aspx

of electricity generation and an area where Ireland can make real progress if the correct policies are pursued. Eliminating peat extraction and developing retraining and employment strategies for the communities that will be affected by this policy should be part of a national mitigation and transition plan designed to support communities and people to move to a low carbon future.

In terms of overall public expenditure systematic reviews should be carried out and published on the sustainability impacts and implications of all public subsidies and other relevant public expenditure and tax differentials. Subsidies which encourage activity that is damaging to natural, environmental and social resources should be abolished.

### Energy efficiency

One of the most cost-effective measures to promote sustainable development is to increase building energy efficiency. Increasing building energy efficiency (through retrofitting, for example), along with reducing food waste are two of the most effective means to increase sustainability and meet international environmental targets (McKinsey Global Institute, 2011). The Sustainable Energy Authority of Ireland (SEAI) are currently supporting a deep retrofitting pilot, at an anticipated spend of €21.2 million to 2019. The SEAI estimate that €35 billion would be needed over the coming 35 years to make Ireland's existing housing stock low carbon by 2050.

*Social Justice Ireland* welcomes the progress made in increasing energy efficiency in modern construction. The SEAI pilot should be closely monitored and if it is successful, Government should reduce the timeframe for the deep retrofit of the entire existing housing stock from 35 years to a more ambitious 10 year timeframe.

### Taxation

Any programme for sustainable development has implications for public spending. In addressing this issue, it needs to be understood that public expenditure programmes and taxes provide a framework which help to shape market prices, reward certain activities and penalise others. A key aspect of this could be to broaden the tax base through environmental taxation. Eco-taxes, which put a price on the full costs of resource extraction and pollution, would help with the transition towards a resource efficient, low carbon green economy. The taxation system should reflect the environmental costs of goods and services. A carbon tax will play a key part in this regard.

The Climate Change Advisory Council recommends that Government ensure that the level of Ireland's carbon tax be sufficiently high to reflect the cost of achieving the 2050 targets, rising to €80 per tonne by 2030. The Council also proposes that Government design a strategy to remove fossil fuel subsidies, including the accelerated removal of price supports for peat generation and the introduction of a carbon price floor. *Social Justice Ireland* has consistently proposed that revenues from carbon taxes are used to support households in energy poverty to improve energy efficiency and in low carbon technologies to improve the energy efficiency of the housing stock. A well-designed carbon policy which can reduce the cost of transition will make the necessary reforms more acceptable. It is vital that any carbon tax is well-designed and accompanied by the necessary measures to assist people and communities to transition to a low carbon economy and society.

When considering environmental taxation measures to support sustainable development and the environment, and to broaden the tax base, the Government should ensure that such taxes are structured in ways that are equitable and effective and do not place a disproportionate burden on rural communities or lower socio-economic groups. The European Commission has recommended the use of economic instruments such as taxation to ensure that product prices better reflect environmental costs. *Social Justice Ireland* believes that there is merit in developing a tax package which places less emphasis on taxing people and organisations on what they earn by their own useful work and enterprise, or on the value they add or on what they contribute to the common good. Rather, the taxes that people and organisations should be required to pay should be based more on the value they subtract by their use of common resources.

Environmental taxation enforcing the polluter pays principle and encouraging waste prevention can help to decouple growth from the use of resources and support the shift towards a low carbon economy. In order to promote sustainable development, it will be necessary to develop the economic system to reward activities that are socially and environmentally benign. This, in turn, would make it easier for people and organisations to make choices that are socially and environmentally responsible. Incorporating social and environmental costs in regulating and pricing both goods and services, combined with promoting those goods and services which are sustainable, should become part of sustainable development policy.


### Transport
Transport emissions have increased in recent years in line with economic growth, and any improvements made during the recessions have been undone. Significant investment is needed to develop a public transport network powered by electricity and renewable energy. To encourage electric car usage the national charging infrastructure should be upgraded and the tax on electric cars should be reduced to make them an affordable option.

In terms of public transport, the initial investment will be substantial, but the long-term social, environmental and economic benefits of such a change outweigh the cost. It is vital that the upgrade to the public transport network also encompasses connectivity to ensure that people travelling from rural or regional areas to urban centres are encouraged to do so by public transport. Government policy must also examine how to discourage private car use, particularly in urban areas in conjunction, with the provision of accessible and quality public transport and a ng network all forming part of a transition to a low-carbon transport

## Circular Economy

A sustainable economy would involve transformative change and policies. The 'circular economy' theory is based on the understanding that it is the reuse of vast amounts of material reclaimed from end of life products, rather than the extraction of new resources, that is the foundation of economic growth (Wijkman and Rockstrom, 2012:166). Furthermore, the shift to a circular economy is labour intensive, focussing on repair, recycling, research and development, regenerating natural capital, and preserving and enhancing land, oceans, forests and wetlands. The business case to move towards a circular economy and decouple economic growth from resource consumption has been outlined by McKinsey in 2014 which shows that such a move could add $1 trillion dollars to the global economy by 2025 and that the EU manufacturing sector could generate savings of up to $360 billion per annum by 2025. A wider benefit of the circular economy is the reduction in carbon dioxide emissions.

In December 2015 the European Commission published an action plan which describes the circular economy as 'where the value of products, materials and resources is maintained in the economy for as long as possible, and the generation of waste minimised' (European Commission, 2015:2). This action plan is essential to the European Union's efforts to develop a sustainable, low carbon, and resource efficient economy. It is explicitly linked to the EU's SDG commitments.

The 2018 Circular Economy Package (European Commission, 2018) includes a Europe-wide Strategy for Plastics in the Circular Economy; a communication on options to address the interface between chemical, product and waste legislation; a Monitoring Framework on progress towards a circular economy; and a Report on Critical Raw Materials and the circular economy. The Monitoring Framework is particularly instructive in that it 'puts forward a set of key, meaningful indicators which capture the main elements of the circular economy'. Changing from a linear economy to a circular one presents a challenge across all sectors, but bears rewards from an economic, environmental and social standpoint. The monitoring framework attempts to deal with this systemic challenge through the development of these key indicators which take a cross-sectoral view of progress, grouping the ten indicators into four aspects of the circular economy: production and consumption, waste management, secondary and raw materials, and competitiveness and innovation. The monitoring framework goes on to provide examples of each of the indicators and the EU levers, where possible (2018:4).

Finland (which ranks 3rd in the Sustainable Progress Index) published their roadmap to a circular economy in 2016 (Sitra, 2016) which aims to achieve a circular economy by 2025, concentrating on economic, environmental and social growth and benefits. They will initially concentrate their circular economic growth on five areas: sustainable food systems; forest-based loops; technical loops; transport and logistics; and common action. Were Ireland to adopt this model, it would need the support of the agricultural sector to engage in more sustainable practices in food production to minimise emissions; a concerted effort to increase forestry (and other natural resources); a commitment to R&D that focuses on longevity and sustainable production; greater incentives to use clean fuels in transport; and recognition of the relationships and interconnectivity between the economy, environment and society. Ireland should be at the forefront of rethinking and redeveloping the use of plastics in the global supply chain. An innovative and sustainable plastics industry, where all elements fully respect the circular economy principles would help to create jobs and reduce greenhouse gas emissions.

Ensuring that product design, development and delivery is based on the principles of reusability, reparability and recyclability, and that materials for these products are sourced using sustainable methods, should be at the forefront of any R&D initiatives supported by Government. An expansion of the principles of the Ecodesign Directive (European Council, 2009), which was transposed into Irish law in December 2015 and provides for design specifications for energy products and products on which energy savings could be made, would greatly aid Ireland's progression of a circular economy.

The concept of 'cradle to cradle development' involves reviewing the processes of production to not only minimise waste but eliminate it altogether. Ireland has often been lauded as a hub of innovation. Our environment, and consequently our economy and society, would benefit greatly from the adoption of 'cradle to cradle' design principles[10].

It is important that Ireland now moves to embrace the circular economy and to implement the monitoring framework provided in 2018 Circular Economy Package. A reduction in waste and consumption will help prevent waste of our finite natural resources and aid Ireland in meeting environmental targets. It will also positively impact our economy by eliminating harmful subsidies and implementing more of the 'polluter pays' principle.

### Mitigation and Transition - supporting communities and people

A comprehensive mitigation and transition strategy is required to ensure there is public support for our domestic and international environmental and sustainable development goals. This strategy must pre-empt some of the challenges we face as we move to a more sustainable form of development. *Social Justice Ireland* proposes that the strategy should contain as a minimum:

- retraining and support for those communities who will be most impacted by the loss of employment related to the move away from fossil fuels;

---

[10]  http://www.mcdonough.com/cradle-to-cradle/

- support and investment in the circular economy with regional strategies and targets;
- investment in the deep retrofitting of homes and community facilities;
- investment in community energy advisors and community energy programmes;
- investment in renewable energy schemes;
- policies to eliminate energy poverty;
- investment in a quality, accessible and well-connected public transport network.

The development of a national mitigation and transition strategy is a matter of priority if there is to be public support for the significant and fundamental changes required in the years ahead.

**Stakeholder engagement**
One of the key indicators of sustainability is how a country runs stakeholder involvement. In order to facilitate a move towards a sustainable future for all, stakeholders from all arenas must be involved in the process.

Sustainable local development should be a key policy issue on the local government agenda, and the Public Participation Networks are a forum where sustainable development issues at a local level can become part of local policy making. Sustainable Development Councils (SDCs) are a model for multi-stakeholder bodies comprising members of all major groups – public, private, community, civil society and academic – engaged in evidence-based discussion. The EU-wide experience has been that SDCs are crucial to maintaining a medium and long-term vision for a sustainable future whilst concurrently working to ensure that sustainable development policies are embedded into socio-economic strategies and budgetary processes. The Local Community Development Committees have the potential to fulfil an SDC role in Ireland at local level, and indeed there is a requirement for local authorities to integrate sustainable development principles in the Local Economic and Community Plan and for such plans to contain a statement which may include objectives for the sustainable development of the area concerned.

The Citizen's Assembly when considering 'How the State can Make Ireland a Leader in Tackling Climate Change' made a series of recommendations on tackling climate change and proposed some innovative solutions for addressing emissions from the Agriculture, Energy and Transport sectors[11]. *Social Justice Ireland* supports the recommendations of the Citizens Assembly which is an example of positive

---

[11] https://www.citizensassembly.ie/en/How-the-State-can-make-Ireland-a-leader-in-tackling-climate-change/Final-Report-on-how-the-State-can-make-Ireland-a-leader-in-tackling-climate-change/Climate-Change-Reference Report-Final.pdf

stakeholder engagement and involvement in addressing a major public policy challenge.

## New measurements of progress

Moving towards an economy and society built on sustainable development principles requires that we develop a new metric to measure what is happening in society, to our natural resources, to the environment and in the economy.

As noted earlier, it is widely acknowledged that GDP is an inadequate metric to gauge wellbeing over time, particularly in its environmental, and social dimensions, some aspects of which are often referred to as sustainability (Stiglitz Commission 2009: 8). The OECD recently held its World Forum on Statistics, Knowledge and Policy to discuss what must be measured beyond GDP to assess a country's social and economic performance and to better reflect what constitutes wellbeing[12].

The forum coincided with the publication of the report of the High Level Expert Group on the Measurement of Economic Performance and Social Progress *'Beyond GDP: Measuring What counts for Economic and Social Performance'*. The report shows how focussing solely on GDP can lead to the implementation of inappropriate policies and points to the need to examine a variety of economic, social and environmental indicators to have a true picture of what constitutes progress and improved wellbeing.

As Stiglitz (2019) recently pointed out:

> *"What we measure affects what we do, and if we measure the wrong thing, we will do the wrong thing. If we focus only on material wellbeing – on, say, the production of goods, rather than on health, education, and the environment – we become distorted in the same way that these measures are distorted."*

This reinforces the assumptions underpinning the Sustainable Progress Index and should inform Government policy on the SDGs.

The United Nations High Level Panel on Global Sustainability recommends that the international community measure development beyond GDP and that national accounts should measure and cost social exclusion, unemployment and social inequality and the environmental costs of growth and market failures. Some governments and international agencies have picked up on these issues, especially in the environmental area and have begun to develop 'satellite' or 'shadow' national accounts that include items not traditionally measured. *Social Justice Ireland's* 2009 publication Beyond GDP: What is prosperity and how should it be measured? explored many of these new developments. It included contributions from the OECD, the New Economics Foundation, and other informed bodies, and

---

[12]  http://www.oecd.org/publications/beyond-gdp-9789264307292-en.htm

proposed a series of policy developments which would assist in achieving similar progress in Ireland.

In December 2017, the Environmental Protection Agency (EPA, 2017(c)) published its report on the state of knowledge of climate change impacts in Ireland. It found that while there was sufficient information available to support the integration of environmental protection principles into economic and social policy making, there remained areas on which a number of 'important knowledge gaps' remain, such as coastal and marine, critical infrastructure, emergency planning and human health (2017:31).

The report indicates that climate change potentially impacts all economic sectors, with adaptation measures made difficult by a lack of certainty of the severity of the risks and the subsequent impact on the insurance sector, and makes a number of key recommendations including advancing the knowledge base; developing sectoral risk and vulnerability assessments; developing and assessing adaptation options which would include cost-benefit analysis; and developing and implementing governance structures. The Irish Government needs to take on board these recommendations to mitigate the costs of climate change on our economy, while having the benefit of providing jobs in implementing these measures. At a practical level the CSO should be fully resourced to implement the System for Environmental-Economic Accounts (SEEA) and the future compilation of natural capital accounts. These datasets will be vital to measure progress on environmental issues and the SDGs.

Climate change also has an impact on biodiversity in Ireland. The 2017 report repeats earlier assertions that the economic value of our ecosystem services is €2.6 billion (EPA, 2017:24) but the rate of habitat degradation and loss of biodiversity is accelerating across Europe, including in Ireland. Ireland needs to improve its data collection methods when it comes to biodiversity and to monitor the impact of climate change in this context to protect both our natural resources and our economy. In a sustainable economy our natural capital and ecosystems would be assigned value in our national accounting systems.

Development of 'satellite' or 'shadow' accounts for Ireland should be a key initiative to adequately reflect the economic value of Ireland and support the development of more robust economic, social and environmental policies. The metrics referred to in the *Social Justice Ireland* Sustainable Progress Index, which are widely available and used internationally, could be a baseline for a more cohesive set of national accounts.

### Policy Coherence
At a national level there appears to be a strong degree of policy incoherence in pursuing policies such as Food Harvest 2020 and Food Wise 2025, and the increase

in emissions that this will yield, whilst simultaneously committing to international targets for sustainable development and emission reduction.

The increased emissions from both agriculture and transport mean that Ireland will be subject to fines for not meeting our European targets. In addition to the immediate financial costs of missing our 2020 targets, the potential social, economic and environmental impacts of climate change are immense, and their cost must also be taken into account.

These include an increase of heavy rainfall events in winter and autumn and an increase in the intensity of storms and the risk of damage from storms. Government's commitment to green budgeting and the publication of all Exchequer climate related expenditure is an important part of the policy coherence process and incorporating climate change and the SDGs into the budget process. This should be fully resourced and expedited in 2019.

In order to improve policy coherence the SDGs should be placed at the centre of policy making in Ireland. Government should, as a matter of priority, outline a five year plan containing the following:

- how the CSO will be supported to develop Ireland's System of Environmental-Economic Accounts (SEEA) and how SEEA will be incorporated into the National Development Plan;
- all proposed environmental taxation changes over the period;
- the energy efficiency and renewable energy projects that this revenue will fund over the period to support our low carbon transition;
- a circular economy strategy for Ireland;
- a mitigation and transition programme.

This plan should be overseen and monitored by an Oireachtas committee.

## 11.3 Key Policy Priorities

A successful transition to sustainability requires a vision of a viable future societal model and the ability to overcome obstacles such as vested economic interests, political power struggles and the lack of open social dialogue (Hämäläinen, 2013). Ireland is at the cusp of this transition and *Social Justice Ireland* believes that the following policy positions should be adopted in responding to sustainability and environmental challenges:

- Set ambitious emissions reduction targets for 2030 and ensure sufficient resources to support implementation of these targets;

- Adopt targets and a reporting system for each of the Sustainable Development Goals;

- Introduce a strategy for Ireland that includes the principles of the circular economy and cradle to cradle development;

- Introduce shadow national accounts, and assign value to natural capital and ecosystems in our national accounting systems;

- Develop a comprehensive mitigation and transition programme to support communities and people in the transition to a low carbon society;

- Develop a progressive and equitable environmental taxation system.

# REFERENCES

Augustenborg, C. (2018) 'With 12 years left to limit climate catastrophe, Ireland needs to govern the clock' in Healy, S. and Reynolds, B. ed. *From Here to Where?* Dublin: Social Justice Ireland, pp 31-38.

Burck, Jan, Ursula Hagen, Franziska Marten, Niklas Hohne, and Christoph Bals (2019) *Climate Change Performance Index Results 2019*. Berlin: Germanwatch.

Clark, C., Kavanagh, C. and Lenihan, N. (2018): *Measuring Progress: Economy, Society and Environment in Ireland, Sustainable Progress Index 2018*. Dublin: Social Justice Ireland.

Climate change Advisory Council (2018) *Annual Review 2018*. Dublin: Climate change Advisory Council.

Curtin, J. and Arnold, T. (2016) *A Climate-Smart Pathway for Irish Agricultural Development: Exploring the Leadership Opportunity*. Dublin: IIEA.

Curtin, J and Hanrahan, G (2012) *Why Legislate? Designing a Climate Law for Ireland.* Dublin: IIEA.

Department of Communications, Climate Action and Environment (2018) *National Adaptation Framework, Planning for a Climate Resilient Ireland*. Dublin: Stationery Office.

Department of Communications, Climate Action and Environment (2015) *Ireland's Transition to a Low Carbon Energy Future 2015 – 2030*. Dublin: Stationery Office.

Environmental Protection Agency (2018a) *Ireland's Provisional Greenhouse Gas Emissions 1990 - 2017* Dublin: EPA.

Environmental Protection Agency (2018b) *Ireland's Provisional Greenhouse Gas Emissions Projections 2017- 2035*. Dublin: EPA.

Environmental Protection Agency (2017) *A Summary on the State of Knowledge on Climate Change Impacts for Ireland*. Dublin: EPA.

Environmental Protection Agency (2016) *Ireland's Environment - An Assessment*. Dublin: EPA.

European Commissions (2018) *A European Strategy for Plastics in a Circular Economy Brussels, 16.1.2018 COM(2018) 28 final*. Brussels: European Commission.

Government of Ireland (2018) *Ireland: Voluntary National Review 2018. Report on the implementation of the 2030 Agenda to the UN High Level Political Forum on Sustainable Development*. Dublin: Stationery Office.

Intergovernmental Panel on climate Change (2018) *An IPCC Special Report on the impacts of global warming of 1.5°C above pre-industrial levels and related global greenhouse gas emission pathways, in the context of strengthening the global response to the threat of climate change, sustainable development, and efforts to eradicate poverty*. Switzerland: IPCC.

McKinsey Global Institute (2011) *Resource revolution: Meeting the world's energy, materials, food, and water needs*. London: McKinsey Global Institute.

UNEP (2018) *The Emissions Gap Report 2018*. Nairobi: United Nations Environment Programme.

Sitra (2016): *Leading the Cycle: Finnish road map to a circular economy 2016-2025*. Helsinki: Sitra

Stiglitz, J., (2019) *Beyond GDP*. Available at: https://www.socialeurope.eu/beyond-gdp

Stiglitz, J., J. Fitoussi and M.Durand (2018), *Beyond GDP: Measuring What Counts for Economic and Social Performance.,* OECD Publishing: Paris.

Sustainable Energy Authority of Ireland (2018) *Energy In Ireland 2018.* Dublin: SEAI.

United Nations (2015) *Sustainable Development Goals.* New York: United Nations. World Meteorological Organisation (2018) *State of Climate in 2017 – Extreme weather and high impacts.* Geneva: WMO.

# Chapter 12
## Rural Development

**Core Policy Objective:**
To achieve balanced regional development, with a particular emphasis on providing the sustainable public services and employment opportunities required.

To secure the existence of substantial numbers of viable communities in all parts of rural Ireland where every person would have access to meaningful work adequate income and to social services, and where infrastructures needed for sustainable development would be in place.

### Key Issues/Evidence

By continuing to locate a disproportionate amount of our best health, education and cultural institutions in Dublin, policy is contribution to regional imbalance.

Rural areas have a higher proportion of older people and a lower proportion of young adults. This poses a significant challenge for the delivery of services.

Supporting rural households to ensure that they have sufficient incomes will be crucial to the future of rural Ireland. This requires both social and economic supports, and broader skills and economic development strategies.

Lack of quality broadband is a considerable barrier to the sustainable development of rural Ireland.

**Policy Solutions**

Rebalance investment in regional and rural areas to ensure they do not fall further behind major urban areas.

Invest in an integrated, accessible and flexible rural transport network

Prioritise rolling out high speed broadband to rural areas.

Invest in human capital through targeted education and training programmes aimed in particular at people in low skilled jobs, people who are unemployed or people whose jobs are at risk from automation.

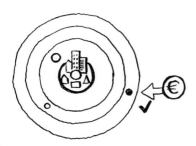

To ensure that development initiatives resource areas which are further from the major urban areas to ensure they do not fall further behind.

Provide integrated supports for rural entrepreneurs, micro-enterprises and SMEs.

Ensure people living in rural areas have access to high quality public services

# 12.

# RURAL AND REGIONAL DEVELOPMENT

> **CORE POLICY OBJECTIVE:**
> **RURAL and REGIONAL DEVELOPMENT**
>
> To achieve balanced regional development, with a particular emphasis on providing the sustainable public services and employment opportunities required.
>
> To secure the existence of substantial numbers of viable communities in all parts of rural Ireland where every person would have access to meaningful work, adequate income and social services, and where infrastructure needed for sustainable development would be in place.

Rural Ireland is a valuable resource with much to contribute to Ireland's future social, environmental and economic development. However, it faces significant challenges in the areas of job creation and service provision for an ageing population; in ensuring the natural capital and biodiversity of rural areas is protected and in encouraging young people who have left to return and settle in rural areas. In order to achieve balanced regional development and viable communities in all parts of Ireland in the years ahead, *Social Justice Ireland* believes that policy should:

- Ensure that investment is balanced between the regions, with due regard to sub-regional areas;

- Ensure rural development policy is underpinned by social, economic and environmental wellbeing;

- Prioritise rolling out high speed broadband to rural areas;

- Invest in an integrated, accessible and flexible rural transport network;

- Ensure that development initiatives resource areas which are far from the major urban areas to ensure they do not fall further behind;

- Invest in human capital through targeted education and training programmes, especially for older workers and those in vulnerable employment;

- Provide integrated supports for rural entrepreneurs, micro-enterprises and SMEs;

- Ensure public service delivery in rural areas according to the equivalence principle.

## 12.1 Key Evidence

### Population and demographics

Ireland remains a predominately rural country. Over 3 million people live in rural Ireland as defined by the Commission for the Economic Development of Rural Areas (CEDRA, 2014) to be outside the administrative boundaries of the 5 main cities of Dublin, Waterford, Galway, Cork and Limerick. The population of different settlement tiers is shown in Figure 12.1. Thirty per cent of people live in open countryside, and a further 20 per cent live in villages and towns of less than 10,000 people (CSO, 2017a). More than 40 per cent of the population live in a rural area (defined by the OECD as within a 60 minute drive of a city) and 28 per cent of the population live in more remote rural regions as classified by the OECD (OECD, 2018).

**Chart 12.1: Proportion of the Irish Population living in different settlement sizes, 2006 and 2016**

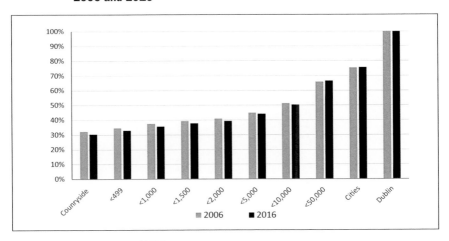

Source: CSO Census 2006 and 2016.

While the overall population of Ireland increased between the censuses in 2011 and 2016, the proportion within the different settlement tiers has remained relatively stable. Spatial analysis shows that the main increases in population occurred in the hinterlands of the larger towns and cities as people moved there for work

(O'Donoghue, et al., 2017). The age profile varies widely between urban and rural areas. Countryside areas and settlements of less than 1,500 people are characterised by a lower proportion of young adults, and a higher proportion of older people compared with areas over 50,000 population. This combination of outmigration of young adults for Third level education and/or work and an ageing population poses a significant challenge for the delivery of services.

## Employment and Unemployment

Census 2016 gives a snapshot of employment and unemployment across the country in April 2016. Table 12.1 shows that the employment rate is correlated with settlement size and that those living in villages of less than 1,500 inhabitants experience the highest rates of unemployment and the lowest participation in the labour market.

In addition, the pool of people of working age who are not in the labour force due to either home duties or disability is at its highest in rural areas. In open countryside, the participation rate is the lowest, but the employment rate is higher reflecting farming, fishing and forestry activity which is 13 per cent of all work in these areas, but much of which is at a subsistence level. It is also likely that a lack of employment opportunities leads to outward migration from very rural areas (O'Donoghue, et al., 2017). Their detailed spatial analysis shows there is a smaller decline in unemployment since the recession in areas furthest from the cities while the largest declines occur in proximity to the cities.

**Table 12.1: Principal Economic Status of People Living in Different Settlement Tiers, 2016**

| | In Labour Force (as % of the Labour Force) | | | Not in Labour Force (as a % of pop 15yrs +) | |
|---|---|---|---|---|---|
| | LFPR | Work | Unemployed | Disability | Home Duties |
| Dublin | 63.7 | 88.1 | 11.9 | 3.6 | 7.0 |
| Other Cities | 58.9 | 85.9 | 14.1 | 5.0 | 7.0 |
| Towns 10-50k | 62.7 | 84.7 | 15.3 | 4.6 | 7.8 |
| Towns 5-10k | 63.6 | 84.8 | 15.2 | 4.7 | 8.3 |
| Towns 1.5k-5k | 61.9 | 83.5 | 16.5 | 5.3 | 8.5 |
| Villages < 1.5k | 59.6 | 83.8 | 16.2 | 5.2 | 9.0 |
| Dispersed | 59.3 | 90.0 | 10.0 | 3.8 | 9.3 |

**Source:** CSO Census 2016.
**Notes:** LFPR = labour force participation rate; others not in the labour force include students and the retired.

*Social Justice Ireland* has consistently argued that employment and enterprise policy should have a rural-specific element designed to support local enterprises, rural-specific jobs, and be cognisant of the need to create full-time, high quality jobs with career progression opportunities. In this regard we welcome the *Realising our Rural Potential Action Plan for Rural Development* (DRCD, 2017) with its strong focus on revitalising rural and regional economies.

The prevalence of low-paid, part-time and seasonal work is a continual feature of rural employment. Whilst there has been a welcome increase in employment nationally in recent years, this was predominantly urban-based initially and has taken longer to spread into the regions/more rural areas.

Significant regional disparities also show up in the employment statistics with different trends relating to education level and age cohort of employed people in the regions emerging[1]. In order to implement appropriate education, training and labour market policies in the regions it is necessary to ensure that they are flexible and can adapt to the differing needs and profile of each region and local area. Initiatives via which Education and Training Boards match their upskilling programmes with local employer skills needs are particularly useful.

Eight Regional Action Plans for Jobs were launched in 2015/16 with a total funding of €250 million over a five-year period. These plans form a core part of the economic strategy of *Realising our Rural Potential* and combined form the job creation target announced as part of the plan. Much of this new employment will be generated in regional cities and larger towns. The third progress report on *Realising our Rural Potential* (DRCD, 2018) outlined progress so far and there has been a welcome increase of 146,000 in the numbers employed in regions outside of Dublin.

There is to be a refocus of these eight action plans to ensure their relevance out to 2020 and to take account of the changing employment and economic environment nationally and internationally. The very slow roll-out of quality rural broadband will continue to pose a challenge for the regional action plans and to the generation of sustainable regional and rural employment. The provision of decent public transport links, and the further expansion of the Local Link service will be vital to the refocus of the eight action plans.

### Rural Economies

Across Europe the secondary and tertiary sectors are now the main drivers of economic growth and job creation in rural regions. The areas include social enterprise and social services (e.g. childcare and elder care), tourism, 'green' products and services, and cultural and creative industries. For rural areas to become sustainable in the long-term these sectors must form an integral part of any future rural development strategy, both in Ireland and in Europe. Rural areas

---

[1]  For further breakdown see https://www.djei.ie/en/Publications/Regional-Labour-Markets-Bulletin-2016.html

with an ageing population can face labour shortages and higher service provision costs. However demand for labour in health and social care is high in rural areas and points to the growth potential of secondary and tertiary economies to boost the employment potential of rural areas (OECD, 2018).

O'Donoghue, et al., (2017) have developed an economic strength model to assess the performance of towns, combining unemployment and migration data. The best performing towns and rural areas and are in general around cities. Conversely, the worst performing towns are more remote, with a band of the weakest towns forming an arc from the South East across the Midlands to the West, North-West and Border regions. Thus access to concentrated labour markets has had a strong impact on the recovery of rural areas and towns. Proximity to major urban centres is a key influence on rural areas, as those communities and villages within a 60 minute drive of an urban centre have better access to services and can retain and attract a younger population due to employment opportunities (OECD, 2018, O'Donoghue et al, 2017).

Furthermore rural areas can compensate for lower wages as a high quality of life is often more important in terms of attracting and retaining workers and their families. This is why high quality and connected public transport links and sustainable regional employment opportunities are vital to the future of rural economies.

The driver of the rural economy in Ireland has moved from the primarily agricultural to a more diverse base involving services, manufacturing, tourism and others. Further development requires support for the provision of public services, investment in micro businesses and small or medium enterprises, innovation, and the sustainable use of natural resources and natural capital in REDZ (Rural Economic Development Zones). REDZ recognise that rural economies are functionally designed around towns and villages of various sizes whose hinterland may cross administrative boundaries. New funding for REDZ is welcome however *Social Justice Ireland* is of the view that resources available need to be increased and success requires a community partnership rather than Local Authority led model to be successful. Initiatives such as SMART villages as promoted by the European Network for Rural Development should also be actively considered.

At county level, the formulation of Local Economic and Community Plans (LECPs) are a positive development, with a six-year timeframe giving an opportunity to take a longer-term view of development. These plans must fit into the National and Regional framework but give counties and communities an opportunity to identify niche areas for development e.g. tourism, food networks, and clusters for specific industries.

Hollowing out is a critical issue affecting rural towns as large retail units on the outskirts attract shoppers, leaving traditional shops and businesses vulnerable. Consultation on the second iteration of LECPs will begin in 2019, led by the Local

Community Development Committees. It is essential that a strong participative process is used for these consultations, and that a real partnership and deliberative approach is taken, involving local authorities, agencies and communities. Rural economic policies must focus on sustaining, developing and diversifying existing small enterprises as much as developing new ones. Local Enterprise Offices (LEOs) have a key role to play here.

In *Ireland 2040* (DHPLG, 2017a) Government accepts that the current challenge is to achieve an appropriate balance between supporting Ireland's agricultural communities and other traditional rural based economic activity whilst simultaneously fostering sustainable economic diversification and development in rural areas. There are various models for diversification of the agricultural economy, the development of on and off farm enterprises and niche added value products and outlets. Of particular interest is the growth of "Agriculture of the Middle" which transitions from food supply chains to value-based supply chains, and a resurgence of small co-operatives (Macken-Walsh, 2017).

As outlined earlier, the social and physical infrastructure must be in place to enable rural economies to diversify. Public policy can play a key role here by ensuring flexible education, training and labour market policies for rural areas; it can also ensure that transport policy is focussed on those areas not already well served by links and on incentivising the use of rail transport, particularly for freight transport. This would decrease traffic congestion on the road network and reduce transport emissions.

The mismatch between a Government policy aimed at attracting Foreign Direct Investment (FDI) and export-led industry, and rural areas which are dominated by micro-businesses and small and medium sized enterprises was acknowledged by the Industrial Development Authority (IDA) and it committed to a greater regional dispersal of FDI in its 2015-2019 strategy (IDA, 2015). This refocus is welcome and there is now a greater regional spread of FDI investment. However, with the on-going challenges facing traditional rural sectors, including agriculture and the potential impact of Brexit, the future success of the rural economy is inextricably linked with the capacity of rural entrepreneurs to innovate and to develop new business opportunities that create jobs and income in rural areas.

Structural shifts in employment and manufacturing and other industries combined with ageing and population loss has left many rural communities struggling. A withdrawal of public services (school, health services) can contribute to a community's decline. Government policy must recognise that low density rural economies are fundamentally different to urban economies and require different polices to meet a different set of opportunities and challenges (OCED, 2018). With over two thirds of the population classified as 'rural' Ireland has the opportunity to be at the forefront of developing renewable energy, sustainable farming, the circular economy, and protecting and enhancing natural resources.

## Income

Supporting rural households to ensure that they have sufficient incomes will be crucial to the future of rural Ireland. This requires both social and economic supports, and broader skills and economic development strategies. About half of farm families require off-farm income to remain sustainable. While recent gains in agriculture-based incomes have had an impact on the most commercial farms, solutions to the wider income problems require a broader approach for all rural families, combining an economic and social dimension (O'Donoghue, et al., 2014).

The amount of money required to achieve the Minimum Essential Standard of Living is over €100 per week higher for rural couples with children than their urban counterparts (Vincentian Partnership for Social Justice, 2018). Higher costs in 2018 related to transport, insurance and fuel. The economies of rural areas have become increasingly dependent on welfare transfers.

A consistent trend over the past decade is the increased at risk of poverty rate in rural areas. The latest figures show the at risk of poverty rate of rural areas is 14 per cent higher in rural areas than in urban areas (CSO, 2018).There is significant regional variation within these figures, and the Northern and Western region has the highest at risk of poverty rate and the lowest median income in the State. Worryingly, this region has also seen one of the greatest reductions of full-time employment since 2008 and has been one of the slowest to see the gains from increased employment growth. The low incomes in the Northern and Western region are also mirrored in farm incomes.

The economic recession and restructuring of agriculture, has led to a narrowing of the economic base in rural areas. Low-paid, part-time and seasonal work and long-term underemployment are significant factors in rural poverty and exclusion (Walsh & Harvey, 2013). This also points to the need to integrate income and labour market supports in regional economic policy.

### Farm Incomes

There are 84,599 farms in Ireland and in 2017 average family farm income was €31,412 (Teagasc, 2018), an increase of 32 per cent on the previous year. This increase was driven almost entirely by increased income on dairy farms. As ever, there was a wide variation in farm incomes, with 35 per cent of farms earning an income of less than 10,000 in 2017 and one in four farms earing between €20,000 and €50,000 in 2017. It is worth noting that the cost of a minimum essential standard of living for a family of 2 adults and 2 children (an average farm family) is €33,176 (Vincentian Partnership for Social Justice, 2018).

Average farm income is highest on dairy farms and in the South East (SE) region. The Northern and Western region is the most disadvantaged region with the lowest farm income and the highest reliance on subsidies. Some key farm statistics (Teagasc, 2018) include:

- Average family farm income was €31,412 in 2017, the highest level ever recorded;

- 35 per cent of farms earned a farm income of less than €10,000 in 2017;

- 21 per cent of farms produce a family farm income of between €10,000 and E20,000 per annum;

- Direct payments made up 56 per cent of average farm income. The average payment in 2017 was €17,659;

- Direct payments accounted for more than 100 per cent of family farm income in the Border region and 87 per cent of family farm income in the West in 2017.

- Just 43 per cent of farms are considered economically viable with 30 per cent considered vulnerable;

- One third of farmers engaged in off-farm employment in 2017. The majority of these were in the Border, Midlands and West region reflecting the low annual farm income and reliance on direct payments.

These statistics mask the huge variation in farm income in Ireland as a whole. Only a minority of farmers are, at present, generating an adequate income from farm activity and even on these farms, income lags behind the national average. Farm incomes are also inconsistent, as the prices of commodities fluctuate and gains are predicated on expanding dairy production which runs contrary to our climate commitments (see Chapter 11).

The abolition of milk quotas in 2015 has resulted in increased supply of milk from the EU. Many Irish farmers borrowed to invest to scale up production with the expectation of demand from Russia, China and other world markets. Whilst dairy farming is the most profitable form of farming in Ireland, it is also the most volatile due to price fluctuations and a high dependency on them is not sustainable to maintain farm incomes.

It is clear that farming itself is not enough to provide an adequate income for many families as evidenced by the over reliance on direct payments and the number of farmers engaged in off farm employment. Of further concern is the age profile of those engaged in farming. In 2016, around a quarter of farm holders in Ireland were aged 65 years and over and just 5 per cent were aged less than 35 years (CSO 2019).

Advances in technology and mechanisation have meant that many farmers can seek alternative ways to generate income. From the mid-1990's, off-farm employment by farmers increased significantly. However, during the recession, many of these jobs were lost. A strong potential has been identified for alternative farm enterprises such as niche tourism and food production. However, these need significant support, and are likely to attract younger and better educated farmers.

Welfare payments also support farmers. In 2017 there were 7,234 families comprising 10,259 adults and 5,641 children receiving the Farm Assist Payment[2]. The Rural Social Scheme (RSS) had 2,850 participants and by extension supported 2,027 children and 1,147 adults in 2017. The extra 250 places in the RSS announced in Budget 2017 and Budget 2018 was a welcome increase in beneficiaries as this scheme facilitates small farmers to develop new skills and do valuable work their local communities.

Agriculture and direct employment from agricultural activities have been declining in Ireland. The *Foodwise 2025* strategy (Department of Agriculture, Food and the Marine, 2015) plans for significant expansion of the Irish Agrifood sector including the creation of 23,000 additional jobs all along the supply chain from producer level to high-end value-added product development.

The third annual report on progress on the strategy (Department of Agriculture, Food and the Marine, 2018) acknowledges the need to break the link between emissions intensity and food production – a reflection that agriculture is the highest contributor to Ireland's GHG emissions. The report also highlights the threat of Brexit and its potential to create instability across the sector. It is important that adequate supports are put in place to facilitate all stakeholders in Agrifood to deal with this potential volatility.

Brexit poses a significant threat to both farm incomes and incomes in rural areas in general and the potential impact on rural communities cannot be underestimated. It is vital that investment in infrastructure in the regions and rural areas is expedited to ensure rural economies and diversify and adapt to support thriving rural communities. A step change in policy is required, focussed on building sustainable and viable rural communities, including farming and other activities. In implementing this policy there needs to be significant investment in sustainable agriculture, as well as rural anti-poverty and social inclusion programmes, in order to protect vulnerable farm households in the transition to a rural development agenda.

**Rural Development**
With over two thirds of Ireland's population classified as 'rural' it is important that our national development policy reflects this (OECD, 2018). To date development has predominantly focussed on Dublin and surrounding region. In order for rural communities to thrive and to improve the wellbeing of communities across all regions in Ireland it is vital that *Ireland 2040the National Planning Framework* (Department of Housing, Planning and Local Government, 2017a) and *Ireland 2040 National Development Plan* (Department of Housing, Planning and Local Government, 2017b) focus on ensuring future development is balanced and not focussed solely on Dublin or the East of the country. Ireland 2040 acknowledged

---

[2]   http://www.welfare.ie/en/downloads/Annual_Statistics_Report_2017.pdf

the present imbalance but significant policy shifts at governance level are required if we are to have a more balanced development.

The OECD (2018) has identified six main drivers influencing the future of rural areas. These are population ageing and migration, urbanisation, global shifts in production, the rise of emerging economies, climate change and environmental pressures and technological advancement. Rural development policy must be cognisant of these drivers of change and the opportunities and the challenges that they present.

*National Planning Framework*
A sustainable society requires balanced regional development. The proportion of the population living in and around the capital city is already very high by international standards, and this is projected to continue growing. Dublin already accounts for half of economic output in Ireland (Morgenroth, 2018), yet we have continued to model our growth path, and design our public services, in a way that encourages, rather than discourages, such concentration. By continuing to locate a disproportionate amount of our best health, education, and cultural institutions in Dublin, we have driven a model of development that precludes the kind of regional balance required for Ireland to thrive. This must change.

Project *Ireland 2040* (DHPLG, 2017a) is the new National Planning Framework (NPF) to cater for the population increases and changing demographic patterns which are projected for Ireland over the next 23 years. The Framework is linked to a new 10-year investment plan, the Project Ireland 2040 National Development Plan 2018-2027 (DHPLG, 2017b).

The Framework recognises that economic activity, infrastructure provision and population growth has been uneven across Ireland's three regions – Northern and Western, Eastern and Midland (including Dublin) and Southern. It advocates for a more balanced approach with parity of future development across the regions. It aims to enhance regional accessibility and strengthen rural economies and communities, promoting sustainable resource management and a transition to a low carbon society. It envisages that 70 per cent of population growth will occur outside Dublin, with Cork, Limerick, Galway and Waterford growing by 50 per cent and becoming cities of scale for their hinterlands. Sligo in the North West and Athlone in the Midlands will develop as regional centres. In the context of Brexit and beyond, there will be a focus on Letterkenny and Drogheda/Dundalk.

Outside the main cities and their hinterlands, the plan is to develop towns of greater than 10,000 population (20-25 per cent growth). It further seeks to limit urban and rural sprawl by concentrating development on underused spaces within current town and village boundaries.

By contrast, growth in small towns and rural areas is targeted to an average of 15 per cent.

Overall this will result in increased urbanisation and suburbanisation, and a reduction in the rural population. This may be a sensible approach from a planning perspective, given the cost of service delivery to areas of low population density. However, from a social perspective, it risks the atrophy of many rural communities, and the further isolation of their inhabitants, unless coherent plans are both put in place and implemented to support rural dwellers.

A fund of €1billion has been allocated to rural regeneration over the next 10 years, to cover areas such as infrastructure deficits, developing the centres of villages and towns, creating enterprise spaces and digital hubs, and promoting tourism, and heritage. However it is apparent that this is not all new funding and the aim is to incorporate many existing funds (e.g. RAPID, CLAR, REDZ) under this umbrella.

Unfortunately, no matter how equally spread future growth may be, unless positive action is taken it will only reinforce the current disparities between the regions, especially between Dublin and its hinterland and the remainder of the country. In addition, these regions are by no means homogenous, and measuring progress at this level may mask further inequalities between predominately urban and mainly rural sub-areas.

The Framework will be underpinned by three Regional Spatial and Economic Strategies (RSES) (currently under consultation). Where relevant Metropolitan Area Strategic Plans (MASP) will be devised for the major cities and their hinterlands. The RSESs and MASPs will be further localised via a hierarchy of sub-regional plans, county development plans, sectoral strategies and finally local area plans. National Policy Objective 70 within Ireland 2040 contains a welcome acknowledgement that MASPs will be prepared where towns and their hinterlands straddle two different local authority areas. All these tiers will have to comply with the overall framework going forward. Thus, the fundamental thrust of Ireland 2040 will have a major impact on the fabric and quality of life across Ireland, and especially in its regions and rural areas.

Overall *Social Justice Ireland* welcomes the Framework as a comprehensive long-term plan, and its coupling with a ten-year investment plan. However, it is essential that an implementation plan is drawn up quickly, and that investment is frontloaded to the areas of greatest disadvantage, and at greatest risk. The implementation plan must ensure that housing, access to employment, and access to health, education and care services are all served by an efficient and comprehensive public transport system. This includes rural communities, and especially those which are distant from the designated centres of growth. Citizens must have an opportunity to participate actively in the development of the regional, county and local implementation plans via the Public Participation Networks (PPNs, c.f. Chapter 10) and other mechanisms.

*Action Plan for Rural Development*
The *Action Plan for Rural Development – Realising our Rural Potential* was published in early 2017 (Department of Arts, Heritage, Rural, Regional and Gaeltacht Affairs, 2017). It is a very welcome development to see a clear focus on rural issues by Government. Drawing much of its basis from the CEDRA report the plan describes 297 actions under the five pillars of

- Supporting Sustainable Communities;

- Supporting Enterprise and Employment;

- Maximising our Rural Tourism and Recreation Potential;

- Fostering Culture and Creativity in rural communities;

- Improving Rural Infrastructure and Connectivity.

Working to a timeframe of 2020 it aims to support 135,000 new jobs, revitalise 600 towns and villages, support community projects and ensure all homes and businesses are connected to broadband. However, implementation requires a whole of Government focus, and dedicated ringfenced resources. To date most of the actions have been previously announced in other action plans e.g. Rebuilding Ireland and Regional Action Plans for Jobs.

While progress is positive, many of these schemes have been rolled out in a hurry and have attracted "shovel ready" projects, supporting communities which are already well organised. In others, the funding available is small, and risks a piecemeal approach to development. In future schemes, more time needs to be given to empower disadvantaged communities and areas to develop projects for funding. This can be facilitated at an interagency level via the Local Community Development Committees (LCDCs).and Local Economic and Community Plans (LECPs).

As will be discussed later in this chapter, little progress has been made on rolling out quality broadband to hard-to-reach areas, or on the significant investment required in rural transport. Without these two key elements of infrastructure, the overall objective of the *Action Plan for Rural Development* cannot be achieved.

**Rural Development Programme**
The Irish Rural Development Programme (RDP) 2014-2020 is still predominantly focussed on agriculture and supporting the agri-sector. Only six per cent of the overall budget is allocated to promoting social inclusion, economic development, and environmental measures in rural areas under the LEADER programme.

LEADER operates from the principle of Community Led Local Development, where project promoters (communities and individuals) identify their needs and potential solutions and then apply for funding. Funding decisions are then made by local action groups (in general the LCDC). The funding for current programmes which runs to 2020 is €250 million. Money began to flow to projects in 2017, and by December 2018 over €50m had been approved for 1,500 projects[3]. Uptake is strongest for "traditional" LEADER projects e.g. focussing on enterprise and infrastructure, including community centres, playgrounds, recreational facilities. Provision of services for people experiencing social exclusion and environmental projects are underrepresented at this stage.

Government has a key role to encourage and stimulate projects which have the capacity to address core issues including rural poverty and a just transition to a low carbon future in rural areas. A reduction in the complexity and bureaucracy of the LEADER programme would also facilitate disadvantaged and less resourced groups to apply for funding.

2018 saw a significant increase in funding programmes which can impact on rural development and regeneration, many of which are likely to be enhanced in 2019. The Department of Rural and Community Development administered more than 10 such schemes (Table 12.2 for examples of schemes and amounts), giving grants from €2m to €500.

While all funding and support is welcomed, and a diversity of schemes is needed to meet a diversity of needs, it is important that there is policy coherence across all the different elements. Application for many programmes is led by the Local Authority and operates to very short (Government imposed) timelines. It is essential that time is given to allow local communities, and especially those traditionally poorly resourced, to develop projects for funding. It is also essential that the administrative requirements are proportional to the grant amount. The LCDC has a key co-ordinating role to play in this in each city/county. This requires the provision of ring-fenced resources and clear independence from the Local Authority.

Arresting rural decline requires urgent action and resources. Government will have to increase investment in the development of rural areas through an increased contribution of national income. Given the scale of the challenge, a far more substantial Government response is required to support communities to create real bottom-up solutions.

---

[3]   https://drcd.gov.ie/about/rural/rural-development/leader/

**Table 12.2: An example of funding streams supporting Rural Development administered by Department of Rural and Community Development 2018**

| Scheme | Funding 2018 | Number of Projects 2018 |
|---|---|---|
| LEADER | €50m | 1500 |
| Town and Village Renewal Scheme | €21m | 224 |
| Community Enhancement Scheme (disadvantaged area including urban) | €12.5m | 3000 |
| Outdoor Recreation Infrastructure | €11m | 78 |
| CLAR | €12.5m | 180 |
| Social Enterprises (re disadvantage and disability supports -also urban) | €2m | 52 |
| Dormant Accounts (Sports, Refugees, Children – Also Urban) | €4.5m | 150 |
| Rural Regeneration and Development Fund | €25m | 18 |

Source: Department of Rural and Community Development Press Releases, various, 2018.

**Infrastructure and services**

The removal of services and associated resources from rural areas makes it increasingly difficult to maintain viable communities. Government must develop policies to deal with the new challenges an ageing population brings to rural areas in relation to health services, social services and accessibility for older and less mobile people. The most effective way of delivering appropriate services is to work in real partnership with local communities. The PPNs are a formal way for Local Authorities to engage with communities and develop such a collaborative approach (c.f. Chapter 10).

The inadequate provision of public services in rural areas in the context of a falling and ageing population is a cause for concern. Following increased levels of emigration in the period 2009-2015 those who are more reliant on public services (the elderly, children and people with disabilities) make up a greater proportion of the rural population than previously.

Decisions need to be made regarding the provision and level of public services in rural areas, including the level of investment needed in areas such as childcare, care for adult dependents and older people, and public transport. Some European countries adopt the equivalence principle for the provision of services in rural areas, which decrees that public services in rural areas should be of an equivalent quality to those in urban areas. Walsh and Harvey (2013) propose that this would be a useful guide for investment in an Irish context.

*Transport*

The lack of an accessible, reliable and integrated rural transport system is one of the key challenges facing people living in rural areas. Car dependency and the reliance of rural dwellers on private car access in order to avail of public services, employment opportunities, healthcare and recreational activities is a key challenge for policy makers. (For a more detailed discussion of public transport see Chapter 9).

A lack of an integrated public transport system connecting more remote areas to major urban centres has a significant impact on quality of life and generating sustainable employment outside of urban centres. It particularly impacts on people on low incomes, those with a disability, or the elderly who may not have access to a car and depend on public transport.

Offering real connectivity to rural dwellers will require innovative and local approaches, some of which are presently hampered by licencing and insurance issues which could be resolved by Government. The reconfiguration of rural transport giving rise to Local Link is welcome, however sustained and increased investment is required and this is not apparent in *Ireland 2040*.

*Broadband*

Lack of quality broadband is a considerable barrier to the sustainable development of rural Ireland. Fast reliable broadband is required for economic and social functions. Whether for farmers to make returns, for businesses to operate and develop, or for people to access information and services, quality broadband is a necessity. The broadband gap between urban and rural areas is an international phenomenon (Salemink & Strijker, 2017). They note that public policy often lags behind fast moving technological developments and that generic policies in this area tend to neglect specific local needs.

Census 2016 shows that only 61 percent of rural households had broadband access as opposed to 76 percent in urban areas. However, this data does not give the connection speed and the major urban areas can access speeds of up to 100mbps compared to 2-10 mbps in rural areas. Access to Information and Communication Technology (ICT) is discussed in more detail in Chapter 9.

The employment commitments in Government's action plan for rural development, *Realising our Rural Potential*, are heavily reliant on the provision of reliable, quality, high-speed broadband. The Public Service Reform strategy includes a commitment to accelerate the digital delivery of services. Retaining the best qualified young people within rural Ireland is also dependent on the availability of high-speed broadband for both quality local employment and social activity. The commitment of Government to roll out the fibre infrastructure to provide broadband to areas which will not be served by commercial operators is welcome. However, the commitment to between 30mbps and 40mbps broadband speed in rural areas contained in the National Broadband Plan for Ireland is insufficient to encourage diversification and economic growth.

The *National Broadband Plan* was launched in 2012, yet we seem to be as far away as ever from seeing its implementation completed. A review of the tendering process, ordered by Government amid concerns that the process may have been compromised, was completed in November 2018. It found that there was no evidence of the tender process being influenced in an inappropriate manner. Government has given approval for the evaluation of the tendering process and this evaluation is continuing. In the intervening period rural dwellers and rural businesses will continue to be disadvantaged. Government must proactively address the issue of universal quality broadband provision in a sustainable way which is not dependent on the commercial priorities of multinational companies.

## 12. 2 Key Policies and Reforms

### Rural development
The Commission for the Economic Development of Rural Areas (2014) adopted a holistic definition of rural areas as those areas being outside the main metropolitan areas and recognises the relational nature of economic and social development and the interconnections between urban and rural areas. *Social Justice Ireland* considers this the most appropriate starting point for rural development policy in Ireland today.

Low density rural economies are fundamentally different to urban economies and as such require different polices to meet a different set of challenges and opportunities (OECD, 2018). Rural areas and small villages are connected and networked to the local regions and these local regional economies are dependent on interaction with the rural areas they connect with for sustainability (Walsh & Harvey, 2013).

Given this interconnection it is important that rural and regional development is integrated to support sustainable local economies and to ensure that local services are utilised most effectively to address the specific needs of a particular region and the rural communities within it. Rural development that is policy appropriate for the challenges faced requires a step change in how we develop policy in Ireland. *Social Justice Ireland* proposes that rural development policy should be place-based, reflect place the strengths, assets and challenges a region faces, and have multi-stakeholder input.

The question we must answer is who is best placed to make and implement policy decisions for rural areas? There is an urgent need to deliver more balanced regional development, and local authorities in conjunction with key local stakeholders can play a major role if they are given the requisite powers and functions.

They must have greater control over funding and the ability to adapt policy to meet regional needs. Local Authorities, civil society, Government Departments, enterprise and industry, PPNs, the community and voluntary sector and others must be involved in delivering place-based rural development policy. Capacity building for all stakeholders at local level is required to ensure that this form of policy development is successful. Investment in capacity building will make rural communities more resilient to external shocks and help to underpin the implementation of rural development policy.

Capacity building will also be vital to implementing appropriate mitigation and transition programmes to support rural communities in the transition to a low carbon society.

The OECD recommends that rural development policy be underpinned by a concept of wellbeing as defined by three multi-dimensional objectives: economic, social and environmental (OECD, 2018). Developing policy via this framework means that household income, access to a broad set of services, and a cohesive community in a pleasant local environment are all key considerations of rural development policy. Support for the Community & Voluntary sector and social enterprise is recognised as an important way to enhance wellbeing in rural communities and should continue to be resourced.

**Investment**
Investment is one of the main instruments for rural development. Public investment policy should prioritise investment in human capital, infrastructure and innovation. Public investment offering a positive return is vital for rural development, not least to mitigate the market failure in the provision of certain goods and services (OECD, 2018). Government must invest to ensure wellbeing in rural areas is improved and address market failure in the delivery of infrastructure and services, especially broadband and transport. Public policy should facilitate connections between remote communities in rural regions to prevent isolation and improve service delivery.

A withdrawal of public services (school, health service, post office) has a negative impact on communities, especially rural communities. The implementation of the action plan for rural development and the *Ireland 2040* project should provide Government and all stakeholders with the opportunity to consider how public services should be provided and delivered in the regions and rural areas. It would also provide an opportunity for the consideration of social, ecological and cultural benefits to, and reasons for investing in, rural areas.

The benefits of such investment must be considered in terms which can encompass more than just economic measurements. The withdrawal of, or lack of provision of, services in rural areas undermines development and compromises the needs of those most reliant on those services (Shucksmith, 2012). The long-term costs of not investing in rural areas and not providing adequate and quality public services to rural and regional communities should be factored into all Government expenditure decisions. The commitment to rural proofing by Government is welcome, however this commitment must be accompanied by front-loaded investment to ensure those living in rural areas have access to an adequate level of services and infrastructure.

### Retraining and skills development
In order to access employment, workers will require the right skills. *Realising our Rural Potential* highlights the coordinated strategies between the Local Enterprise Offices, Education and Training Boards, the Apprenticeship Council, SOLAS, and local businesses as a key policy instrument to ensure that rural workers have the skills required in order to take up or create quality employment in their local area.

Apprenticeships and traineeships have the potential to address unemployment, particularly among older workers and NEETS (young people Not in Education, Employment or Training). Including older workers in traineeships and other active labour market programmes is an important policy tool (OECD, 2014). In this regard it is important that the revised apprenticeship and traineeship programme launched in 2017[4] is promoted as open to all age groups.

Investing in up-skilling lower skilled workers in rural regions has a greater impact on regional economic development than investing in increasing the number of highly skilled workers there (OECD, 2014). Focussed investment in education and training for people in low skilled jobs or those unemployed in rural areas as part of an overall regional employment strategy aimed at generating sustainable jobs should be an integral part of rural development policy.

As with many other aspects of rural development, decent broadband and transport systems are required to enable rural dwellers, and in particular those on low incomes, to access education and skills development opportunities.

## 12.3 Key Policy Priorities
According to the OECD, rural areas will play a central role in meeting the major global opportunities and challenges we face. They can be key leaders in developing new energy sources to meet climate challenge, innovation in food production to meet needs of a growing population, and the provision of natural resources to enable the next production revolution (OECD, 2018).

*Social Justice Ireland* believes that the following policy positions should be adopted to promote balanced rural and regional development:

- Ensure that investment is balanced between the regions, with due regard to sub-regional areas;

---

[4] Further information at https://www.education.ie/en/Press-Events/Press-Releases/2017-Press-Releases/PR17-12-08.html

- Ensure rural development policy is underpinned by social, economic and environmental wellbeing;

- Prioritise rolling out high speed broadband to rural areas;

- Invest in an integrated, accessible and flexible rural transport network;

- Ensure that development initiatives resource areas which are further from the major urban areas to ensure they do not fall further behind;

- Invest in human capital through targeted education and training programmes, especially for older workers and those in vulnerable employment;

- Provide integrated supports for rural entrepreneurs, micro-enterprises and SMEs;

- Ensure public service delivery in rural areas according to the equivalence principle.

# REFERENCES

Central Statistics Office (2019) *Ireland's Facts and Figures 2018*. Dublin: Stationery Office.

Central Statistics Office (2018) *Survey on Income and Living Conditions 2017*. Dublin: Stationery Office.

Central Statistics Office (2017a) *Census 2016: Volume Published Reports*. Dublin: Stationery Office.

Central Statistics Office (2017b) *Labour Force Survey Quarter 3 2017*. Dublin: Stationery Office.

Commission for the Economic Development of Rural Areas (2014) *Energising Ireland's Rural Economy*. Dublin: CEDRA.

Department of Agriculture, Food and the Marine, 2015. *Foodwise 2025: A 10 year vision for the Irish Agrifood industry*. Dublin: Stationery Office.

Department of Agriculture, Food and the Marine (2018) *Steps to Success 2018 Foodwise 2025*. Dublin: Stationery Office.

Department of Arts, Heritage, Rural, Regional and Gaeltacht Affairs, 2017. *Realising our Rural Potential - Action Plan for Rural Ireland*. Dublin: Stationery Office.

Department of Culture, Heritage and the Gaeltacht (2016) *Charter for Rural Ireland*. Dublin: Stationery Office.

Department of Housing, Planning and Local Government (2017a) *Project Ireland 2040 - National Planning Framework*. Dublin: Stationery Office.

Department of Housing, Planning and Local Government (2017b) *Project Ireland 2040: National Development Plan 2018-2027*. Dublin: Stationery Office.

Department of Rural and Community Development (2018) *Action Plan for Rural Development Third Progress Report*. Dublin: Stationery Office.

Department of Rural and Community Development (2017) *Realising our Rural Potential - First Progress Report*. Dublin: Stationery Office.

IDA, (2015) *Winning: Foreign Direct Investment*. Dublin: IDA.

Macken-Walsh, A., 2017. 'Bridging the "Urban-Rural Divide"'. In: B. Reynolds & S. Healy, eds. *Society Matters: Reconnecting People and the State*. Dublin: Social Justice Ireland, pp. 95-128.

Morgenroth, E., 2018. *Prospects for Irish Regions and Counties, Scenarios and Implications*. Dublin: ESRI.

O'Donoghue, C. et al., (2014) *Rural Economic Development in Ireland*. Carlow: Teagasc.

O'Donoghue, C., Kilgarrif, P. & Ryan, M., (2017) *The Local Impact of the Economic Recovery*. Galway: Teagasc.

OECD (2018) *Rural 3.0 A Framework for Policy Development - Policy Note*. Paris: OECD Publishing.

OECD (2014) *Innovating and Modernising the Rural Economy*. Paris: OECD.

Reidy, T. (2018) 'Power Monopoly: Central – local relations in Ireland' in Healy, S. and Reynolds, B. ed. *From Here to Where?* Dublin: Social Justice Ireland, pp. 39-52.

Salemink, K. & Strijker, D. a. B. G., (2017) Rural development in the digital age: A systematic literature review on unequal ICT availability, adoption, and use in rural areas. Journal of Rural Studies, Volume 54, pp. 360-371.

Shucksmith, M., (2012) *Future Directions in Rural Development.* Dunfermline: Carnegie UK Trust.

Teagasc (2018) *Teagasc National Farm Survey 2017*. Athenry: Teagasc.

Vincentian Partnership for Social Justice (2018) *Minimum Essential Standard of Living 2018 –Update report.* Dublin: VPSJ.

Walsh, K. & Harvey, B., (2013*) Employment and Social inclusion in Rural Areas.* Dublin: Pobal.

# Chapter 13
## Global South

**Core Policy Objective:**
To ensure that Ireland plays an active and effective part in promoting sustainable development in the Global South and to ensure that all of Ireland's policies are consistent with such development.

## Key Issues/Evidence

The effects of climate change have increased the vulnerability of many communities leading to enforced migration, internal displacement, poverty, hunger and even death. Food production is a huge challenge for communities constantly forced to move.

€ middle income
o low income

**9 OUT OF 10** countries most at risk of extreme weather are developing countries in the low income or lower-middle income country groups.

Supporting developing countries to develop and implement just taxation systems would give a huge boost to local social and economic activity. Ireland's taxation system should facilitate and not hinder this process.

Renew Government's commitment to meet the United Nations target of contributing 0.7 per cent of GNP to Overseas Development Assistance by 2025.

Ensure Irish and EU policies towards countries in the South are just and that there is coherence between all policies that impact on the Global South either directly or indirectly.

Ensure that Irish businesses operating in developing countries – in particular Irish Aid country partners – are subject to proper scrutiny and engage in sustainable development practices.

Ensure Ireland plays a prominent role in the support and implementation of the Sustainable Development Goals.

# 13.

## THE GLOBAL SOUTH

**CORE POLICY OBJECTIVE: THE GLOBAL SOUTH**
To ensure that Ireland plays an active and effective part in promoting sustainable development in the Global South and to ensure that all of Ireland's policies are consistent with such development.

The *United Nations Human Development Report* (UNHDR) for 2018 noted that, while the overall trend globally is towards continued human development improvements, wide inequalities in people's well-being cast a shadow on this progress. It notes the progress that has been made: People are living longer. More people are rising out of extreme poverty and fewer people are malnourished. People are better educated and have more income.

However, it also notes that 'inequality and conflict are on the rise in many places. Climate change and other environmental concerns are undercutting development now and for future generations. Gender inequality remains one of the greatest barriers to human development. The average Human Development Index (HDI) for women is 6 per cent lower than that of men, with countries in the low development category suffering the widest gaps' (UNHDR, Foreword iii).

If the objective set out above is to be achieved *Social Justice Ireland* believes that policy should:

- See Government renew its commitment to meet the United Nations target of contributing 0.7 per cent of national income to Official Development Assistance (ODA) by 2025;

- Ensure Irish and EU policies towards countries in the South are just and that there is coherence between all policies that impact on the Global South either directly or indirectly;

- Ensure that Irish businesses operating in developing countries – in particular Irish Aid country partners – are subject to proper scrutiny and engage in sustainable development practices;

- Ensure Ireland plays a prominent role in the support and implementation of the Sustainable Development Goals.

2015 was a very important year for global development. In July a new global agenda for financing development was agreed in Addis Ababa. In September the Sustainable Development Goals were adopted in New York. In December the 21$^{st}$ Session of the Conference of the Parties (COP21) took place in Paris. The Paris Agreement advanced the global effort to tackle climate change and there was further progress in COP24 held in Katowice, Poland in December 2018. This global gathering agreed the Katowice Rulebook which spells out some details for the implementation of the Paris Agreement and promises transparency among nations. Each of these agreements can have very positive impacts on human development but action is urgently needed to match the rhetoric of these agreements.

Inequality is a major concern of the United Nations. In its annual report 2018, it notes that out of the 189 countries for which the HDI is calculated, 59 countries are in the very high human development group and 38 countries fall into the low HDI group. In 2010 the figures were 46 and 49 respectively. In its *Global Wealth Report 2018* Credit Suisse (2018) says that the poorest half of the world's population collectively owns less than one per cent of total wealth while the richest 10 per cent of adults own 85 per cent of global wealth and the top one per cent accounts for almost half (47 per cent) of all household wealth.

In a Briefing Paper last January entitled *Reward Work, not Wealth*, Oxfam (2018) calculated that 42 people own the same wealth as the poorest 3.7 billion people. It notes that extreme wealth is not earned; instead it is the 'product of inheritance, monopoly or crony connections to government'. In order to maximise returns to their wealthy shareholders, big corporations are dodging taxes, driving down the wages for their workers and the prices paid to producers, and investing less in their business. Income and wealth have been sucked up to the better off. Oxfam notes that 82 per cent of all growth in global wealth in the previous year went to the top one per cent, while the bottom half of humanity saw no increase at all.

The 2018 UNHDR, while acknowledging improvements, highlights the deprivations, underdevelopment and inequalities that persist despite the progress. Tables 13.1 and Table 13.2 show some of these inequalities.

Tables 13.1 and 13.2 show the sustained differences in the experiences of various regions in the world. These differences go beyond just income and are reflected in each of the indicators reported in both tables. Today, average life expectancy is more than 20 years higher for people in the richest countries compared to those in Sub-Saharan Africa. Similarly, the UN reports that almost one in three adults in Southern Asia and Sub-Saharan Africa are unable to read.

**Table 13.1: United Nations development indicators by region and worldwide**

| Region | GNI per capita (US$ PPP)* | Life Expectancy at Birth (years) | Adult Literacy %** |
|---|---|---|---|
| Least Developed Countries | 2,506 | 64.8 | 59.6 |
| Arab States | 15,837 | 71.5 | 73.4 |
| East Asia and Pacific | 13,688 | 74.7 | 94.4 |
| Europe and Central Asia | 15,331 | 73.4 | 98.2 |
| L. America and Caribbean | 13,671 | 75.7 | 92.8 |
| South Asia | 6,473 | 69.3 | 68.7 |
| Sub-Saharan Africa | 3,399 | 60.7 | 59.9 |
| OECD | 39,595 | 80.6 | n/a |
| **Worldwide total** | **15,295** | **72.2** | **82.1** |

**Source:** UNHDR Statistical Update 2018 (22, 54)
**Notes:**    * Gross National Income (GNI) Data adjusted for differences in purchasing power.
         ** Adult defined as those aged 15yrs and above.
The comparable rates for Ireland are: GNI per capita: $53,754; Life expectancy: 81.6; adult literacy: not available

These inequalities are also reflected in the sizeable differences in income levels (GNI per person) and in the mortality figures in table 13.2. Table 13.2 shows that there are 434 maternal deaths per 100,000 live births in Least Developed Countries as against 15 in the developed OECD countries. There are 77 deaths of children under the age of five per 1,000 live births in Sub-Saharan Africa as against seven in every 1,000 live births in OECD countries.

The UNHD Report in 2017 put a human face on the consequences of these inequality statistics. It notes that one person in nine in the world is hungry, eleven children under the age of five die every minute, on average 24 people are displaced from their home every minute, and more than 21.3 million people in the world are refugees. Water scarcity and climate change have added to international tensions. The report estimates that the economic cost of violence globally is about $1,900 per person.

**Table 13.2: Maternal and Infant Mortality Rates**

| Region | Maternal Mortality Ratio# | Under-5yrs mortality rate* |
|---|---|---|
| Least Developed Countries | 434 | 67.4 |
| Arab States | 149 | 35.9 |
| East Asia and Pacific | 62 | 17.0 |
| Europe and Central Asia | 24 | 17.8 |
| L. America and Caribbean | 67 | 17.4 |
| South Asia | 176 | 46.6 |
| Sub-Saharan Africa | 549 | 77.3 |
| OECD | 15 | 7.0 |
| **Worldwide total**\*\* | **216** | **39.3** |

Source: UNHDR Statistical Update 2018 (38, 50)
Notes:   # ratio of the number of maternal deaths to the number of live births expressed per 100,000 live births
*number of deaths per 1,000 live births.
\*\*The comparable rates for Ireland are: Maternal mortality: 8; Under 5 mortality: 3.6

## Wars

The abuse of power, poor governance, inter-community disputes and the easy availability of arms increase vulnerability and instability for many communities. The plight of refugees, especially children, fleeing from violence and terror in their native countries and trying to access safety in Europe has been graphically displayed on our TV screens and in newspapers in recent years. Much of the commentary and reports from the many 'crisis' meetings of EU leaders is about who should take responsibility for accommodating these people. There is very little focus on the questions of what the causes of these problems are or who is gaining from all this human misery. The UNHDR 2018 notes that the countries with the three steepest declines in human development ranking were in the midst of major conflict: Syria had the largest decline, falling 27 places, followed by Libya (26 places), and Yemen (20 places). If there is to be a peaceful solution to these problems, we need a more comprehensive analysis of the causes and an identification of the beneficiaries. In particular the rewards to the arms industry need to be highlighted and challenged.

On this issue the latest figures from the Stockholm International Peace Research Institute (SIPRI) (2018) give us food for thought. World military expenditure was estimated at $1,739 billion or $230 per person in 2017. Total global expenditure in 2017 was about 1.1 per cent higher in real terms than in 2016. Military expenditure in North America fell by 0.2 per cent compared to 2016 while in Western Europe spending was up by 1.7 per cent on 2016. Spending continued to rise in Asia and Oceania and Eastern Europe. In contrast, military spending fell in Africa, South and Central America and the Caribbean and those countries in the Middle East for which data is available.

In the light of military expenditure SIPRI has noted the number of studies that have considered the cost of achieving the various Sustainable Development Goals (SDGs) which were adopted by the United Nations in 2015. It notes that SDG 4 – quality education for all – could comfortably be achieved for well under 10 per cent of annual global military spending, while eliminating extreme poverty and hunger (SDGs 1 & 2) would cost just over 10 per cent. It concludes that a little less than half the world's annual military spending would be sufficient to meet the majority of those SDGs for which additional economic resources are a central requirement.

The volume of international transfers of major weapons rose by 10 per cent between 2008-12 and 2013-17 to reach its highest level since the Cold War. The five largest arms suppliers in 2013-17 were USA, Russia, France, Germany and China and they accounted for 74 per cent of the total global volume of exports of major weapons. The biggest importers of arms in this period were India, Saudi Arabia, Egypt, UAE and China. Asia and Oceania were the main recipient regions, accounting for 42 per cent of total arms imports, followed by the Middle East, which accounted for 32 per cent. The flow of arms to the Middle East grew by 103 per cent between 2008-12 and 2013-17. By contrast the flow of arms to Europe decreased by 22 per cent, as did those to the Americas, by 29 per cent, and Africa, by 22 per cent (SIPRI, 2018).

On a global basis the overwhelming majority of violent conflicts are intra-state conflicts, and their victims are mostly civilians. These conflicts are fought with small arms. The production and trade of these arms is the least transparent of all weapons systems. Ireland as a neutral country should have a role in researching, challenging and advocating for tight controls in the production and distribution of weapons.

A number of Irish Aid's partner countries neighbour nations currently mired in conflict, such as Ethiopia (which shares a border with South Sudan and Somalia) and Uganda (which shares a border with Democratic Republic of Congo and South Sudan). Ireland should ensure its country offices and overseas programmes engage in mediation efforts where possible and promote positive reconciliation efforts amongst civil society groups. Lessons learned from the Department of Foreign Affairs and Trade's (DFAT) Reconciliation Fund projects - fostering peace and community interaction within Northern Ireland, as well as between communities in Northern Ireland, Republic of Ireland and Britain – would allow the DFAT to offer positive insights on reconciliation and cross-border co-operation in other settings.

## Climate Change

*(Note: climate change is also discussed in Chapter 11. We return to the issue briefly to highlight the particular vulnerabilities of those living in developing countries)*

The Germanwatch Global Climate Risk Index 2018 (Germanwatch, 2018), which ranks countries according to their extreme weather risks, shows that less developed countries are generally more affected than industrialised countries. Of the ten most affected countries between 1997 and 2016, nine were developing countries in the low income or lower-middle income country groups, while only one, Thailand, was classified as an upper-middle income country.

More than 524,000 people died as a direct result of more than 11,000 extreme weather events in the period, and losses between 1997 and 2016 amounted to US$3,160 billion. Small Island Developing States (SIDS) are severely affected by climate events. Five SIDS rank among the 20 countries worldwide most affected by weather related catastrophes in the past 20 years (Germanwatch, 2018, p4).

The effects of climate change have increased the vulnerability of many communities leading to enforced migration, internal displacement, poverty, hunger and even death. Food production is a huge challenge for communities constantly forced to move. The Intergovernmental Panel on Climate Change (IPCC) estimates that such scarcity will lead to increased conflict and regional instability in many of the poorest parts of the world:

> Climate change can indirectly increase risks of violent conflicts in the form of civil war and inter-group violence by amplifying well-documented drivers of these conflicts such as poverty and economic shocks (medium confidence). Multiple lines of evidence relate climate variability to these forms of conflict. (IPCC, 2014, p.20).

A World Bank report in 2009 indicated, 'the major challenge is to identify actions that will support and/or accelerate ongoing development efforts while making them more resilient to climatic risks' (World Bank, 2009, p xvi). The *African Union Common African Position (CAP) on the post-2015 Development Agenda* stressed that African nations 'recognise that adaptation to the phenomenon represents an immediate and urgent global priority' (African Union, 2014, p.13).

However, research by the Overseas Development Institute (ODI) and Climate and Development Knowledge Network (2015) noted a concern that many African countries are not preparing adequately for the effects of climate change. The majority of Irish ODA is focused on African countries and the Irish Government must ensure Irish Aid engages and fosters climate change planning in future planning. It is imperative that the richer nations of the world, including Ireland, take the lead on climate change for the simple reason that 'the richest seven per cent of world's population (equal to half a billion people) are responsible for 50 per cent of global $CO_2$ emissions, whereas the poorest 50 per cent emit only seven per cent of worldwide emissions' (Oxfam, 2014, p.41).

## Migration

Wars, inter-state conflicts and climate change result in the mass movement of peoples. Within the last five years the number of refugees worldwide has risen by 45 per cent. The United Nations High Commission for Refugees (UNHCR, 2018) estimates that 68.5 million individuals were forced to leave their homes due to persecution, conflict, generalised violence, or human rights violations by the end of 2017. This figure included 25.4 million refugees and 40 million internally displaced persons. Millions of people around the world were also stateless. These people have been denied a nationality and access to basic rights such as education, healthcare, employment and freedom of movement. The UNHCR recorded that 667,400 refugees were able to return home in 2017, up from 552,200 the previous year. They submitted 75,200 refugees for resettlement but saw a reduction in the number of places made available.

Major sources of refugees were South Sudan, where more than a third of the country's 12 million citizens were displaced internally and across borders. In the Middle East, the Syrian conflict entered its eight year and the situation in Yemen deteriorated significantly, becoming the world's most acute humanitarian crisis. The exodus of some 1.5 million Venezuelans created significant challenges for neighbouring countries. Low and middle-income countries continue to shoulder the largest burden and responsibility, hosting 85 per cent of refugees globally. 63 per cent of the refugees under the UNHCR's responsibility lived in just 10 countries.

The EU is a destination of choice for many migrants, and it is estimated that 687,000 people have sought asylum in the EU in the 12 months to September 2017 compared with 1.37m the previous year (Eurostat, 2017). Given the number of refugees worldwide, this halving of the number of people seeking asylum in the EU is likely due to the various deterrence programmes which have been implemented by the EU.

The EU and Ireland's response to the crisis overall has been inadequate. *Social Justice Ireland* believes that Ireland must accelerate the arrival of programme refugees, and also facilitate their full family reunification as soon as possible. Irish people have our own experiences of emigration, historically due to hunger and more recently due to a lack of economic opportunities at home. In addition, we have had a long tradition of solidarity with people facing oppression within their own countries. Unfortunately, that tradition is not reflected in our policies towards refugees and asylum seekers.

*Social Justice Ireland* believes that Ireland should use its position in international fora to highlight the causes of displacement of peoples. In particular, Ireland should use these fora to challenge the production, sale and easy access to arms and the implements of torture. Ireland should also take a leadership position within the EU promoting a human rights and humanitarian approach to addressing the refugee crisis and challenge the "closed border" policy of some governments. We should also take a leadership role in assisting the Least Developed Countries in strengthening and implementing the Katowice Rulebook on climate change.

## Sustainable Development Goals (SDGs)

*(Note: The Sustainable Development Goals are also discussed in Chapter 11. We return to the issue briefly to highlight the particular need and urgency for their implementation, to support the people of developing countries)*

The vision of the SDGs is outlined in the Report of a study by the UN Stakeholder Forum (Osborn et al, 2015). The SDGs are intended to be universal in the sense of embodying a universally shared common global vision of progress towards a safe, just and sustainable space for all human beings on the planet to thrive. They reflect the moral principles that no-one and no country should be left behind, and that everyone and every country should be regarded as having a common responsibility for playing their part in delivering the global vision.

In the formulation of these Goals much of the international discussion focused on the pressing development needs of the developing countries and the support they will need from more developed countries and the international community in achieving the goals. Some of the individual goals and targets have been particularly shaped and calibrated to express the needs and aspirations of developing countries; others express the responsibilities of the developed world to assist the development process in the developing world.

Of critical importance where Ireland is concerned in this context are two key issues:

- The need for Ireland to provide funding and support to developing countries to help them achieve the SDGs in their own countries; and

- Ensuring 'policy coherence for development' i.e. not having any policy initiative taken by Ireland that works against the achievement of any SDG in a developing country.

Below we will analyse Ireland's ODA Budget which will give us an opportunity to assess how Ireland is performing on the first of these issues. Here we focus on the second issue i.e. policy coherence. Policy coherence for development was recognised as a major issue long before the SDGs were agreed. It is, in fact, enshrined in the EU's Lisbon Treaty. It recognises that the activities of any country have impacts far beyond that country's borders. These impacts can be negative or positive and often have major implications for the well-being of people in developing countries. We have already highlighted wars and climate change – two impacts with extremely negative consequences for many developing countries. Below we will look at the areas of human rights, governance, trade, tax and debt. All of these are areas where a lack of policy coherence can see better off countries taking initiatives that impact negatively on the realisation of the SDGs in developing countries.

As a contribution to the work that needs to be done to promote policy coherence and implement the commitments made under the SDGs, *Social Justice Ireland* commissioned Professor Charles Clark and Dr Catherine Kavanagh to produce a report (Clark et al, 2018) to measure progress for Ireland. In order to track the achievement of the SDGs in a simple and easy to follow manner, the report aggregated the 17 SDGs into three indexes by broad dimension: economy, society and environment. The indicators were compared to the other 14 countries in the EU-15 to see how the situation had changed over the past decade and to see how Ireland is performing currently.

Under all three headings Ireland's ranking is worse now than it was in 2006. On the economy Ireland has slipped from 6th in 2006 to 10th in 2016, the latest year for which data was available, despite an excellent performance in GDP growth (although GDP is a problematic measurement as has been pointed out previously in this publication).

On the environment, Ireland is ranked 13th of the fifteen countries compared and going in the wrong direction on some indicators. Measuring its progress as a society, Ireland fell from 7th to 10th position. This index will be updated each year. The preparation of this index exposed gaps in data collection and highlighted the need for more relevant indicators to measure progress on the various goals. International cooperation is needed so that comparable data can be produced.

*Social Justice Ireland* urges the Irish Government to give leadership in the various international fora in which it operates to ensure appropriate indicators and reliable statistics are available to monitor and evaluate progress on the SDGs. We also urge Government to prioritise policy coherence for development so that no policy developed by Ireland will be detrimental in any way to work being done in developing countries to move towards achieving the SDGs in full and on schedule.

**Human Rights and Governance.**
*Social Justice Ireland* is a signatory of the *Galway Platform on Human Rights in Irish Foreign Policy.* This document reflects the views of many groups and academics and is a comprehensive contribution to development policy.

Ireland's foreign policy was subject to a significant review which resulted in the 2015 publication of *The Global Island: Ireland's Foreign Policy for a Changing World* (Department of Foreign Affairs & Trade (DFAT), 2015). In our submission to the Review, we noted the importance of articulating a vision that is inspirational, attractive and achievable, and including a guide to how this vision could be promoted at home and abroad. We urged that a major focus of this review be on human rights and governance. The publication set out to offer the latest comprehensive outline of Irish Foreign policy since the 1996 White Paper *Challenges and Opportunities Abroad* (DFAT, 2015, Foreword, p.1).

*Social Justice Ireland* welcomed the emphasis on human rights and governance in this review, reflecting priorities as set out by the Galway Platform for Human Rights in Irish Foreign Policy. The report emphasises that:

> Good governance and accountability are vital for the realisation of human rights, and key to addressing inequality, discrimination and exclusion which lie at the core of poverty. We will continue to focus on building effective institutions and policies as well as encouraging popular participation in the democratic process (DFAT, 2015, p.40).

Governance is the institutional context within which rights are achieved or denied. It is about how power and authority are exercised in the management of the affairs and resources of a country. *Social Justice Ireland* welcomes this emphasis on good governance, both at home and abroad, and urges the Irish Government to ensure such guiding principles are maintained in all its development projects.

The Review was welcome in many respects, offering a revised outlook of Ireland's foreign policy in the years ahead. This is especially important given the decline in ODA contribution as a percentage of national income in recent years. The Review puts forward a vision of Ireland's foreign policy under five interrelated themes: 'Our People', 'Our Values', 'Our Prosperity', 'Our Place in Europe', 'Our Influence'. Whilst *The Global Island* places a great deal of importance on human rights obligations, it is vague on specific incorporation of human rights criteria throughout the DFATs operations. This should be spelled out clearly in all future policy documents and country-specific projects.

In order to ensure good governance, strong independent civil society organisations are necessary to articulate the views of the people, challenge injustices, and highlight social exclusion. In its Statement of Strategy 2017-2020 (DFAT, 2017) the DFAT has committed to the 'promotion of human rights, equality, rule of law and fundamental freedoms through our contributions at the UN, EU, OSCE, Council of Europe, ICC, and in our bilateral engagement.' It also commits to the 'support for civil society freedoms and the work of human rights defenders' (DFAT, 2017, p5). *Social Justice Ireland* urges Government to be more ambitious in implementing this commitment.

The *Irish Aid Annual Report 2014* (Irish Aid, 2015) emphasises the Irish Government's commitment to foster civil society in host countries. We welcome the outcomes of this commitment which has resulted in a focus on civil society organisation in developing countries. The *Irish Aid Annual Report 2016* (Irish Aid, 2017) shows that 23 per cent of Irish ODA was channeled through civil society organisations. However, we regret that the 2017 Report shows that this has been reduced to 13.5 per cent. Ireland should continue to ensure a space and support for a vibrant promotion of human rights and democratic participation across the globe. This is especially important given some of Ireland's key partner countries have a record of stifling democratic opposition and civil society activism.

## Trade, Tax and debt

The fact that the current inequality between rich and poor regions of the world persists is largely attributable to unfair trade practices and to the backlog of unpayable debt owed by the countries of the South to other governments, to the World Bank, the International Monetary Fund (IMF) and to commercial banks.

The effect of trade barriers cannot be overstated; by limiting or eliminating access to potential markets the Western world is denying poor countries substantial income. In 2002 at the UN Conference on Financing and Development Michael Moore, the President of the World Trade Organisation (WTO), stated that the complete abolition of trade barriers could 'boost global income by $2.8 trillion and lift 320 million people out of poverty by 2015'.

Supporting developing countries to develop and implement just taxation systems would give a huge boost to local social and economic activity. *Social Justice Ireland* noted the initiatives outlined in the 2013 Irish Aid Report, to help developing countries to raise their own revenue and the reiteration of this in *The Global Island* (DFAT, 2015, p.41). We urge Government to learn from and expand these programmes.

Oxfam has called for a Global Compact on Taxation. Whilst some critics argue that such a deal may be difficult to achieve the losses that developing countries incur due to tax evasion is sizeable and galling. The Human Development Report 2014 noted that 'for the least developed countries illicit financial flows increased from $9.7 billion in 1990 to $26.3 billion in 2008, with 79 percent of this due to trade mispricing. To put this in context, for every dollar of official development assistance that the least developed countries received, an average of 60 cents left in illicit flows between 1990 and 2008' (HDR, 2014, p.119).

*Social Justice Ireland* supports Oxfam's call for global tax reform. In its December 2016 Briefing Paper *Tax Battles: The Dangerous Global Race to the Bottom on Corporate Tax*, Oxfam outlined its extensive research on corporate tax. It noted that the net profits posted by the world's largest companies more than tripled in real terms from $2 trillion in 1980 to $7.2 trillion by 2013. However, this increase was not matched by a rising trend in corporate tax contributions. This is mainly due to the existence tax havens. The paper goes on to note that

> Developing countries lose around $100bn annually as a result of corporate tax avoidance schemes. This amount is more than enough to provide an education for all of the 124 million children out of school and to pay health interventions that could save the lives of six million children.' (Oxfam, 2016, p3)

The process of corporate tax avoidance is facilitated by a network of tax havens. The Oxfam paper identifies the top 15 corporate tax havens. It is of great concern that Ireland ranks sixth on this table.

A second element in the trend to reduce corporate tax is the tax rate. Globally corporation tax rates have fallen from an average of 27.5 per cent ten years ago to 23.6 percent today and the process shows signs of accelerating.

As the International Monetary Fund has pointed out (IMF, 2014, Fig. 8), when Governments reduce the tax obligations for large corporations, they tend towards two options: to cut back on the essential spending needed to reduce inequality and poverty; or to make up the shortfall by levying higher taxes, such as value-added tax, which falls disproportionately on less wealthy sections of society.

Eurodad (2017) has published a major study on corporate tax which focuses on Europe's role in supporting an unjust global tax system. Entitled *Tax Games: The Race to the Bottom,* the study took its title from a comment by the IMF's Managing Director Christine Lagarde, who said in the context of tax policy that by definition a race to the bottom leaves everyone at the bottom. It notes that if the current trend continues the global average corporate tax rate will hit zero per cent in 2052 (p8). It is critically important that governments work together to halt and reverse the corporate tax race to the bottom.

A third element in the trend towards a reduction in corporation tax is the offer by governments of a variety of tax incentives. A lack of regulation and transparency around tax incentives gives rise to abuse and corruption. One of the examples highlighted by the Oxfam paper shows that Nigeria spends $2.9 billion on tax incentives, twice as much as it does on education, despite six million girls in the country not attending school (Oxfam, 2016, p6).

The Eurodad study quotes a study by the IMF, OECD, World Bank and the UN which says:

> Tax incentives generally rank low in investment climate surveys in low-income countries, and there are many examples in which they are reported to be redundant – that is, investment would have been undertaken even without them. (Eurodad, 2017, p17).

International institutions should require all governments to be transparent around tax incentives. *Social Justice Ireland* also supports the introduction of a Financial Transaction Tax which it sees as progressive since it is designed to target primarily those engaged in speculation.

The high levels of debt experienced by Third World countries have disastrous consequences for the populations of these indebted countries. Governments that are obliged to dedicate large percentages of their country's GDP to debt repayments cannot afford to pay for health and educational programmes for their people. Ellmers & Hulova (2013) estimated that the external debt of countries of the global South had doubled in the decade preceding their report to reach $4.5 trillion. It is not possible for these countries to develop the kind of healthy economies that would facilitate debt repayment when millions of their people are being denied basic healthcare and education and are either unemployed or earn wages so low that they can barely survive.

The debt relief initiatives of the past 10 years have been very welcome. These initiatives need to be further developed as there is growing concern that the debts of the poorest countries are beginning to rise again. It is now important that Ireland campaign on the international stage to reduce the debt burden on poor countries. Given Ireland's recent experience of debt burdens, the Irish population now has a greater appreciation of the implications of these debts and the merit in having them reduced.

**Ireland's commitment to Official Development Assistance (ODA)**

DFAT's report *One World, One Future,* published in 2013 reiterated the Programme for Government's commitment to achieve the target of 0.7 per cent of national income being allocated to international development cooperation. It went on to state that: 'Recognising the present economic difficulties, the Government will endeavour to maintain aid expenditure at current levels, while moving towards the 0.7 per cent target' (DFAT, 2013, p3). *Social Justice Ireland* welcomed this commitment but is disappointed that a date by which this target would be met has not been set.

As table 13.3 shows, over time Ireland had achieved sizeable increases in our ODA allocation. In 2006 a total of €814m (0.53 per cent of GNP) was allocated to ODA, reaching the interim target set by the Government. Budget 2008 further increased the ODA budget to reach €920.7m (0.59 per cent of GNP) (DFAT, 2018). However, since then the ODA budget has been a focus of government cuts and has fallen by more €103.m or more than 11 per cent.

While this fall is disappointing, *Social Justice Ireland* strongly welcomes the move in Budget 2019 to increase the ODA budget by approximately €110m – a significant increase in nominal monetary terms and firm step in the right direction. However, Ireland still lacks a strategy for reaching the UN-agreed 0.7 per cent target and we call on the Government to develop such a strategy with a view to reaching this target by 2025. Ireland's improving economic situation should be seen as an opportunity to recover lost ground in relation to our ODA commitments.

In table 13.4 below *Social Justice Ireland* proposes a possible pathway to reaching the UN target. This pathway sees Ireland achieve the interim target of 0.59 per cent (reached in 2008) by 2022 and the UN target of 0.7 per cent by 2025. Here, we use GNI* as a more realistic measurement of Ireland's national income. This makes the target all the more achievable.

**Table 13.3: Ireland's net overseas development assistance, 2006-2019**

| Year | €m's | % of GNP |
|---|---|---|
| 2006 | 814.0 | 0.53 |
| 2007 | 870.9 | 0.53 |
| 2008 | 920.7 | 0.59 |
| 2009 | 722.2 | 0.55 |
| 2010 | 675.8 | 0.53 |
| 2011 | 657.0 | 0.46 |
| 2012 | 628.9 | 0.46 |
| 2013 | 637.1 | 0.46 |
| 2014 | 614.9 | 0.39 |
| 2015 | 647.5 | 0.32 |
| 2016 | 725.8 | 0.33 |
| 2017 | 743.4 | 0.32 |
| 2018 | 707** | 0.36* |
| 2019 | 817** | 0.39* |

**Source:** Irish Aid (2017:60) and various Budget Documents.
* Estimate based on GNI*, which *Social Justice Ireland* considers to be a better measurement of Ireland's national income.
** Projections from Budget documentation and Estimates.

**Table 13.4 Possible pathways to ODA targets 2017-2025**

| Year | ODA €m | % of GNI* | Year | ODA €m | % of GNI* |
|---|---|---|---|---|---|
| 2018 | 707 | 0.36% | 2022 | 1,401 | 0.59% |
| 2019 | 817 | 0.39% | 2023 | 1,561 | 0.63% |
| 2020 | 983 | 0.45% | 2024 | 1,698 | 0.66% |
| 2021 | 1,184 | 0.52% | 2025 | 1,815 | 0.70% |

Calculations: *Social Justice Ireland*
*Note: GNI* figures based on Department of Finance projections and assumption that GNI* growth rates eventually converge with those of GNP.

Rebuilding our commitment to ODA and honouring the UN target should be important policy paths for Ireland to pursue in the coming years. Not only would its achievement be a major success for government and an important element in the delivery of promises made but it would also be of significance internationally. Ireland's success would not only provide additional assistance to needy countries but would also provide leadership to those other European countries who do not meet the target.

DFAT and the Irish Government regularly cite the positive assessments of Irish ODA given by international bodies. The OECD's most recent Development Assistance Committee (DAC) Peer Review of Ireland noted how Ireland's 'institutional structures enable it to deliver co-ordinated, quality development co-operation and to be a pragmatic and flexible partner' (OECD 2014: 17). We can be justifiably proud of our record of providing high quality, untied, grant-based aid. We can be especially proud that we allocate aid to Least Developed Countries in a greater proportion than do the vast majority of other OECD countries.

*Social Justice Ireland* supports the Joint Oireachtas Committee on Foreign Affairs and Trade, and Defence (2018, p31) when it says;

> The Committee is of the view that a firm commitment to achieving ODA expenditure of 0.7 per cent of GNI by 2030 is critical to the future of international development and calls on the Government to set out the way it proposes to reach this target. In this regard, the Committee unanimously and unequivocally supports calls for a multiannual plan to increase the aid budget on an incremental, phased basis.

Given Ireland's current and projected economic growth, *Social Justice Ireland* believes this recommendation should be implemented with urgency, replacing this 2030 target with an earlier target of 2025.

## HIV/AIDS

The HIV/AIDS epidemic of the past 30 years has presented governments and development workers with major challenges. Despite these challenges there are reasons for hope. Speaking to the UN General Assembly AIDS review in June 2018 the UN Secretary General Antonio Guterres said, 'The world is making good progress towards ending the AIDS epidemic by 2030, but progress is uneven and fragile'.

The past year has seen a slight decline in new HIV infections. Over 21 million people were receiving antiretroviral therapy. This progress reflects the work being done by many NGOs, agencies and Governments. However, the resources allocated to the fight against HIV/AIDS have been stagnant for the past few years. The recent reduction in US aid to this cause casts a dark shadow over this work. Despite the encouraging progress we cannot be complacent.

On World Aids Day 2018 – December 1st – a UNAIDS publication (UNAIDS, 2018) highlighted the scale of the problem in numbers. Their report notes the facts:

- The number of people living with HIV in 2017 was 36.9 million; of these 35.1 million were adults and 1.8 million were children under 15 years;
- About 1.8 million people were newly infected with HIV in 2017;

- 21.7 million people were receiving antiretroviral therapy globally in 2017;

- In 2017, 59 per cent of all people living with HIV were accessing antiretroviral therapy;

- In 2017 about 940,000 people died of AIDS-related illnesses.

The incidence of HIV throws a spotlight on the inequalities in our world.

- Of the 1.8 million people newly infected with HIV in 2017, 800,000 were in Eastern and Southern Africa; 370,000 were in Western and Central Africa; 280,000 were in Asia and the Pacific region, and 70,000 were in Western and Central Europe and North America.

- Young women and adolescent girls are disproportionately vulnerable and at high risk of infection. Every week, around 7,000 young women aged 15-24 years become infected with HIV.

- In sub-Saharan Africa, three in four new infections among adolescents aged 15-19 years are in girls.

Among the current challenges identified by the UNAIDS Report in the battle against HIV/AIDS are the need to reach the 15.8 million people who still have no access to treatment; the need to protect young women and girls, and the need to focus on the regions lagging behind, especially Eastern Europe and Central Asia.

## Key Policy Priorities

*Social Justice Ireland* believes that the following policy positions should be adopted in responding to the current challenges being experienced by the Global South:

- The Irish Government should renew its commitment to meet the United Nations target of contributing 0.7 per cent of national income to ODA by 2025 and set a clear pathway to achieve this;

- Take a far more proactive stance at government level on ensuring that Irish and EU policies towards countries in the Global South are just. Ensure that Irish businesses operating in developing countries- in particular Irish Aid country partners – are subject to proper scrutiny and engage in sustainable development practices.

- Ireland should play a prominent role in the support and implementation of the Sustainable Development Goals. In particular it should work with other governments to end the race to the bottom on corporate tax rates. This would help all countries deliver on their commitments on Sustainable Development Goals;

- Continue to support the international campaign for the liberation of the poorest nations from the burden of the backlog of unpayable debt and take steps to ensure that further progress is made on this issue;

- Work for changes in the existing international trading regimes to encourage fairer and sustainable forms of trade. In particular, resource the development of Ireland's policies in the WTO to ensure that this goal is pursued;

- Ensure that the government takes a leadership position within the European and international arenas to encourage other states to fund programmes and research aimed at mitigating and eventually resolving the AIDS/HIV crisis.

# REFERENCES

The African Union (2014) *Common African Position (Cap) On The Post- 2015 Development Agenda*. Addis Ababa, Ethopia.

Climate and Development Knowledge Network and Future Climate for Africa (2015) *Promoting the use of climate information to achieve long-term development objectives in sub-Saharan Africa*.

Clark, CMA., Kavanagh, C., and Lenihan, N. (2018) *Measuring Progress: Economy, Society and Environment in Ireland*. Social Justice Ireland: Dublin,

Credit Suisse (2018) *Global Wealth Databook*. Credit Suisse: Zurich

Department of Foreign Affairs & Trade (2018) *Irish Aid Annual Report 2017*

Department of Foreign Affairs and Trade (2017) *Statement of Strategy 2017-2020*.

Department of Foreign Affairs & Trade (2015) *The Global Island: Ireland's Foreign Policy for a Changing World*.

Department of Foreign Affairs and Trade (2013) *One World, One Future*.

Ellmers, Bodo & Diane Hulova, (2013) *The New Debt Vulnerabilities, Why the Debt Crisis is Not Over*. Eurodad: Brussels.

Eurodad, (2017) *Tax Games: The Race to the Bottom: Europe's Role in supporting an Unjust Global Tax System*. Eurodad: Brussels

Eurostat (2017) *Asylum Quarterly Report: Third Quarter 2017*

Germanwatch (2018) *Global Climate Risk Index 2018*. Bonn.

IMF (2014) *Fiscal Policy and Income Inequality*. IMF Policy Paper. IMF, Figure 8,

Intergovernmental Panel on Climate Change (IPCC) (2014) *Impacts, Adaption and Vulnerability*. Cambridge University Press, UK.

Irish Aid (2017) *Irish Aid Annual Report 2014*.

Irish Aid (2015) *Irish Aid Annual Report 2014*.

Joint Oireachtas Committee on Foreign Affairs and Trade, and Defence (2018) *Report on Irish Aid Programme*.

OECD (2014) OECD's Development Assistance Committee (DAC) *Development Co-operation Peer Reviews: Ireland* OECD Publishing

Osborn, D. et al (2015) *Universal Sustainable Development Goals*, UN Stakeholders Forum.

Oxfam (2018) *Reward Work, not Wealth*.

Oxfam (2016) *Tax Battles: The Dangerous Global Race to the Bottom on Corporate Tax*.

Oxfam (2014) *Even it up: Time to End Extreme Inequality*.

Stockholm International Peace Research Institute (SIPRI) (2018) *2018 SIPRI Yearbook*. Oxford University Press.

United Nations (2015) *Sustainable Development Goals*.

UN Development Programme (2018) *Human Development Report*. UN: New York

UNAIDS (2018) *Global Report 2018, Fact Sheet*.

UNHCR (2018) *UN Secretary General's Report to the General Assembly* (A/73/12 Part 1)

World Bank (2009) *Making Development Climate Resilient: A World Bank Strategy for Sub-Saharan Africa*. Washington, DC: World Bank

# 14.

# VALUES

The society we have today is the result of decisions taken over the past decades. It can be changed. If we desire change, it will only come as a result of different decisions being made by a variety of policy-makers and institutions. The proposals made in this Socio-Economic Review could be implemented if those with the competent authority took the decisions required. All decisions are based on values. Everyone can contribute to societal change by raising questions and encouraging debate around vision, values and ethics.

> While there were many factors that contributed to the financial meltdown of 2008, they start with the exclusion of ethics from economic and business decision-making. The designers of the new financial order had complete faith that the 'invisible hand' of market competition would ensure that the self-interested decisions of market participants would promote the common good. (Clark and Alford, 2010).

We need to reclaim and promote ethics in business. Pope Francis reminds us that:

> Politics must not be subject to the economy, nor should the economy be subject to the dictates of an efficiency-driven paradigm of technocracy. Today, in view of the common good, there is urgent need for politics and economics to enter into a frank dialogue in the service of life, especially human life. Saving banks at any cost, making the public pay the price, foregoing a firm commitment to reviewing and reforming the entire system, only reaffirms the absolute power of a financial system, a power which has no future and will only give rise to new crises after a slow, costly and only apparent recovery. The financial crisis of 2007-8 provided an opportunity to develop a new economy, more attentive to ethical principles, and new ways of regulating speculative financial practices and virtual wealth. But the response to the crisis did not include rethinking the outdated criteria which continue to rule the world. (Pope Francis, 2015)

The people who are bearing the cost of the economic crash are obvious, the unemployed; emigrants who were forced to leave Ireland and cannot afford to return; poor, sick and vulnerable people who have had their income and social services cut. We are conscious of much fear, anxiety and anger in our communities. There is a pervasive distrust of many institutions. The critical question now is how do we prevent a recurrence of this type of economic crash? While some people advocate good regulation as the solution, others are sceptical and search for more radical approaches.

Now ten years after the economic crash many commentators are urging us to look at the significant signs of economic recovery. We are being encouraged to embrace the current reality and 'move on'. We are discouraged from taking a critical look at what has happened to sections of our society especially people on middle and lower incomes who have been left behind, and the socio-economic gap that has widened between them and the better off.

These observations, reflections and questions bring to the fore the issue of values. Our fears are easier to admit than our values. Do we as a people accept a two-tier society in fact, while deriding it in principle? The chapters of this review document many aspects of this divided society. It is obvious that we are becoming an even more unequal world. Scarce resources have been taken from poorer people to offset the debts of bankers and speculators. This shift of resources is made possible by the support of our national value system. This dualism in our values allows us to continue with the status quo, which, in reality, means that it is okay to exclude almost one sixth of the population from the mainstream of life of the society, while substantial resources and opportunities are channelled towards other groups in society. This dualism operates at the levels of individual people, communities and sectors.

To change this reality requires a fundamental change of values. We need a rational debate on the kind of society in which we want to live. If it is to be realistic, this debate should challenge our values and support us in articulating our goals and formulating the way forward.

### Human dignity, human rights and the common good
*Social Justice Ireland* wishes to contribute to this debate and believes that the focus for this debate should be human dignity, human rights and the common good. Discussion and reflection on human dignity can be traced back to the writings of ancient philosophers and religious traditions. The history of this discourse is long and complex. However, it was not until 1948 that it was clearly articulated in the Universal Declaration of Human Rights. *Social Justice Ireland* believes that every person should have seven basic socio-economic and cultural rights, that is, the right to:

- sufficient income to live life with dignity,
- meaningful work,
- appropriate accommodation.
- participate in shaping the decisions that affect their lives.

- appropriate education
- essential healthcare
- an environment which respects their culture.

These rights can only be vindicated when society structures itself to provide the resources necessary in the interest of the common good. Hollenbach (1989) reminds us that rights are not simply claims to pursue private interests or to be left alone. Rather, they are claims to share in the common good of civil society.

Related to the discourse on human dignity is the discourse on the common good. This discourse can be traced to Plato, Aristotle and Cicero. More recently, the philosopher John Rawls defined the common good as 'certain general conditions that are...equally to everyone's advantage' (Rawls, 1971 p.246). François Flahault notes 'that the human state of nature is the social state, that there has never been a human being who was not embedded, as it were, in a multiplicity. This necessarily means that relational well-being is the primary form of the common good. Just as air is the vital element for the survival of our bodies, coexistence is the element necessary for our existence as persons. The common good is the sum of all that which supports coexistence, and consequently the very existence of individuals.' (p68)

This understanding was also reflected at an international gathering of Catholic leaders. They saw the common good as 'the sum of those conditions of social life by which individuals, families and groups can achieve their own fulfilment in a relatively thorough and ready way' (Gaudium et Spes no.74). This understanding recognises the fact that the person develops their potential in the context of society where the needs and rights of all members and groups are respected. The common good, then, consists primarily of having the social systems, institutions and environments on which we all depend work in a manner that benefits all people simultaneously and in solidarity. A similar view is expressed in a NESC study (2009) which states that 'at a societal level, a belief in a "common good" has been shown to contribute to the overall well-being of society. This requires a level of recognition of rights and responsibilities, empathy with others and values of citizenship'.

Human rights are the rights of all persons so that each person is not only a right-holder but also has duties to all other persons to respect and promote their rights. Thus there is a sharing of the benefits of rights and the burden of duties. Alan Gewirth (1993) notes that human rights have important implications for social policy. On the one hand the State must protect equally the freedom and basic well-being of all persons and on the other hand it must give assistance to persons who cannot maintain their well-being by their own efforts.

## Understanding of Justice

Christianity subscribes to the values of both human dignity and the centrality of the community. The person is seen as growing and developing in a context that includes other people and the environment. Justice is understood in terms of relationships. The Christian scriptures understand justice as a harmony that comes from fidelity to right relationships with God, people and the environment. A just society is one that is structured in such a way as to promote these right relationships so that human rights are respected, human dignity is protected, human development is facilitated, and the environment is respected and protected (Healy and Reynolds, 2003:188).

## Appropriate structures

As our societies have grown in sophistication, the need for appropriate structures has become more urgent. The aspiration that everyone should enjoy the good life, and the goodwill to make it available to all, are essential ingredients in a just society. But this good life will not happen without the deliberate establishment of structures to facilitate its development. In the past charity, in the sense of alms-giving by some individuals, organisations and Churches on an arbitrary and ad hoc basis, was seen as sufficient to ensure that everyone could cross the threshold of human dignity. Calling on the work of social historians it could be argued that charity in this sense was never an appropriate method for dealing with poverty. Certainly, it is not a suitable methodology for dealing with the problems of today. As recent world disasters have graphically shown, charity and the heroic efforts of voluntary agencies cannot solve these problems on a long-term basis. Appropriate structures should be established to ensure that every person has access to the resources needed to live life with dignity.

## Future Generations

Few people would disagree that the resources of the planet are for the use of the people - not just the present generation, but also the generations still to come. In Old Testament times these resources were closely tied to land and water. A complex system of laws about the Sabbatical and Jubilee years (Lev 25: 1-22, Deut 15: 1-18) was devised to ensure, on the one hand, that no person could be disinherited, and, on the other, that land and debts could not be accumulated. This system also ensured that the land was protected and allowed to renew itself. Today, modern society needs to espouse this principle to ensure the protection and security of existing resources for the use of future generations.

## Ownership and property

These reflections raise questions about ownership. Obviously, there was an acceptance of private property, but it was not an exclusive ownership. It carried social responsibilities. We find similar thinking among the leaders of the early Christian community. St John Chrysostom, (4th century) speaking to those who could manipulate the law so as to accumulate wealth to the detriment of others, taught that 'the rich are in the possession of the goods of the poor even if they have acquired them honestly or inherited them legally' (Homily on Lazarus). These early leaders also established that a person in extreme necessity has the right to take from the riches of others what s/he needs, since private property has a social quality deriving from the law of the communal purpose of earthly goods (Gaudium et Spes 69-71).

In more recent times, Pope Paul VI (1967) said

> private property does not constitute for anyone an absolute and unconditional right. No one is justified in keeping for his/her exclusive use what is not needed when others lack necessities.... The right to property must never be exercised to the detriment of the common good. (Populorum Progressio No. 23).

Pope John Paul II has further developed the understanding of ownership, especially in regard to the ownership of the means of production. Recently this position has been reiterated by Pope Francis (2015): "the Church does indeed defend the legitimate right to private property, but she also teaches no less clearly that there is always a social mortgage on all private property, in order that goods may serve the general purpose that God gave them." (No 93)

## Technology

One of the major contributors to the generation of wealth is technology. The technology we have today is the product of the work of many people through many generations. Through the laws of patenting and exploration a very small group of people has claimed legal rights to a large portion of the world's wealth. Pope John Paul II questioned the morality of these structures. He said 'if it is true that capital as the whole of the means of production is at the same time the product of the work of generations, it is equally true that capital is being unceasingly created through the work done with the help of all these means of production'. Therefore, no one can claim exclusive rights over the means of production. Rather, that right 'is subordinated to the right to common use, to the fact that goods are meant for everyone'. (Laborem Exercens No.14). Since everyone has a right to a proportion of the goods of the country, society is faced with two responsibilities regarding economic resources: firstly, each person should have sufficient resources to access the good life; and secondly, since the earth's resources are finite, and since "more" is not necessarily "better", it is time that society faced the question of putting a limit on the wealth that any person or corporation can accumulate. Espousing the value of environmental sustainability requires a commitment to establish systems that ensure the protection of our planet.

In his exhortation, *The Joy of the Gospel,* (Evangelii Gaudium) Pope Francis (2013) named the trends that are detrimental to the common good, equality and the future of the planet. He says:

While the earnings of the minority are growing exponentially, so too is the gap separating the majority from the prosperity enjoyed by those happy few. This imbalance is the result of ideologies which defend the absolute autonomy of the marketplace and financial speculation. Consequently, they reject the right of states, charged with vigilance for the common good, to exercise any form of control. A new tyranny is thus born, invisible and often virtual, which unilaterally and relentlessly imposes its own laws and rules. Debt and the accumulation of interest also make it difficult for countries to realise the potential of their economies and keep citizens from enjoying their real purchasing power. To all this we can add widespread corruption and self-serving tax evasion, which have taken on worldwide dimensions. The thirst for power and possessions knows no limits. In this system, which tends to devour everything which stands in the way of increased profits, whatever is fragile, like the environment, is defenceless before the interests of a deified market, which becomes the only rule. (par 56)

The concern of Pope Francis to build right relationships extends from the interpersonal to the inter-state to the global.

Interdependence, mutuality, solidarity and connectedness are words that are used loosely today to express a consciousness which resonates with Christian values. All of creation is seen as a unit that is dynamic - each part is related to every other part, depends on it in some way, and can also affect it. When we focus on the human family, this means that each person depends on others initially for life itself, and subsequently for the resources and relationships needed to grow and develop. To ensure that the connectedness of the web of life is maintained, each person depending on their age and ability is expected to reach out to support others in ways that are appropriate for their growth and in harmony with the rest of creation. This thinking respects the integrity of the person, while recognising that the person can achieve his or her potential only in right relationships with others and with the environment.

As a democratic society we elect our leaders regularly. We expect them to lead the way in developing the society we want for ourselves and our children. Election and budget times give an opportunity to scrutinise the vision politicians have for our society. Because this vision is based on values, it is worth evaluating the values being articulated. It is important that we check if the plans proposed are compatible with the values articulated and likely to deliver the society we desire.

Most people in Irish society would subscribe to the values articulated here. However, these values will only be operative in our society when appropriate structures and infrastructures are put in place. These are the values that *Social Justice Ireland* wishes to promote. We wish to work with others to develop and support appropriate systems, structures and infrastructures which will give practical expression to these values in Irish society.

# REFERENCES

Clark C.M.A. and Alford, H. (2010) *Rich and Poor: Rebalancing the economy.* London: Catholic Truth Society.

Flahault François , (2011) *Conceiving the social bond and the common good through a refinement of human rights,* in *Rethinking progress and ensuring a secure future for all: what we can learn from the crises.* Trends in social cohesion No 22. Council of Europe, Strasbourg.

Gewirth, Alan (1993), *Common Morality and the Community of Rights,* published in 'Prospects For a Common Morality, Gene Outka and John P. Reeder, Jr., Editors. Princeton University Press, New Jersey, USA.

Healy, S and Reynolds, B. (2003) "Christian Critique of Economic Policy and Practice" in Mackay, J.P. and McDonagh, E. eds. *Religion and Politics in Ireland at the turn of the millennium,* Dublin: Columba Press.

Hollenbach, David, (1989) *The Common Good Revisited,* Theological Studies 50.

NESC, (2009) *Well-Being Matters: A Social Report for Ireland, Vols1 and ",* Report No. 119, Dublin.

Pope Francis (2013) *Evangelii Gaudium, Exhortation on the Joy of the Gospel.* Vatican City.

Pope Francis (2015) *Laudato Si on Care of our Common Home.* Veritas, Dublin

Pope John Paul II. (1981) *Laborum Exercens, Encyclical Letter on Human Work.* London Catholic Truth Society.

Pope Paul VI. (1967) *Populorem Progressio.* Vatican City, Rome.

Rawls, J. (1971) *A Theory of Justice,* Harvard Press, Cambridge, Massachusetts.

Vatican Council (1965) *Gaudium et Spes,* Dominican publications, Dublin.